OUTSOURCING ECONOMICS

Outsourcing Economics has a double meaning. First, it is a book about the economics of outsourcing. Second, it examines the way that economists have understood globalization as a pure market phenomenon, and as a result have "outsourced" the explanation of world economic forces to other disciplines. Markets are embedded in a set of institutions – labor, government, corporate, civil society, and household – that mold the power asymmetries that influence the distribution of the gains from globalization. In this book, William Milberg and Deborah Winkler propose an institutional theory of trade and development starting with the growth of global value chains – international networks of production that have restructured the global economy and its governance over the past twenty-five years. They find that expanded offshoring leads to a lower labor share of income in the United States and to greater economic insecurity in industrialized countries that lack institutions supporting workers. They also find that offshoring allows firms to reduce domestic investment and focus on finance and short-run stock movements. Economic development has become synonymous with "upgrading" in global value chains, but this is not sufficient for improved wages or labor standards, raising obstacles to sustained economic development for many emerging economies.

William Milberg is Professor of Economics at the New School for Social Research in New York. He has served as a consultant to the ILO, the World Bank, and the UN Conference on Trade and Development (UNCTAD). He is the author (with Robert Heilbroner) of *The Making of Economic Society* and *The Crisis of Vision in Modern Economic Thought*, the editor of *Labor and the Globalization of Production* as well as the author of numerous articles on the labor market effects of international trade and on the methodology of economics. Professor Milberg received his PhD in economics from Rutgers University.

Deborah Winkler is a Research Associate with the Schwartz Center for Economic Policy Analysis at the New School for Social Research. She also serves as a consultant to the World Bank's International Trade Department. She is the author of the book *Services Offshoring and Its Impact on the Labor Market*. Her recent articles have appeared in *World Development*, the *Journal of Economic Geography*, and *World Economy* as well as in edited volumes of the World Bank, the ILO-WTO, and the Oxford Handbook Series. Dr.Winkler received her PhD in economics from Hohenheim University, Germany.

Outsourcing Economics

Global Value Chains in Capitalist Development

WILLIAM MILBERG

New School for Social Research, New York

DEBORAH WINKLER

Schwartz Center for Economic Policy Analysis, New York

CAMBRIDGE
UNIVERSITY PRESS

32 Avenue of the Americas, New York, NY 10013-2473, USA

Cambridge University Press is part of the University of Cambridge.

It furthers the University's mission by disseminating knowledge in the pursuit of education, learning, and research at the highest international levels of excellence.

www.cambridge.org
Information on this title: www.cambridge.org/9781107609624

First published 2013
Reprinted 2014

A catalog record for this publication is available from the British Library.

Library of Congress Cataloging in Publication data
Milberg,William S., 1957–
Outsourcing economics : global value chains in capitalist development /William Milberg, DeborahWinkler.
    p.   cm.
Includes bibliographical references and index.
ISBN 978-1-107-02699-5 (hardback) – ISBN 978-1-107-60962-4 (pbk.)
1. Offshore outsourcing – United States.   2. Labor market – United States.   3. Foreign trade and employment – United States.   4. Globalization – Economic aspects.   5. Free trade – United States.   I.Winkler, Deborah.   II. Title.
HD2368.U6M55   2013
338.6–dc23   2012035199

ISBN 978-1-107-02699-5 Hardback
ISBN 978-1-107-60962-4 Paperback

For Sylvie, Eva, and Natalie – WM

For my parents – DW

Contents

List of Figures

List of Tables

List of Appendices

List of Variables

A	Sector, good A
a	Labor coefficient
AC	Autonomous capitalists' consumption
AS	Asset specificity
B	Sector, good B
C	Costs
c	Country dimension
C_Π	Marginal propensity to consume out of profit income
D	Demand
DEV	Developing countries
D_i	Unobserved time-constant fixed sector effect
D_t	Unobserved cross-sector fixed year effect
E	Exchange rate
EPL	Employment protection legislation
EX	Exports
FIN	Financialization
G	Government spending
H	Hierarchy
HHI	Herfindahl-Hirschman Index
I	Private investment
i	Sector dimension, product type
IM	Imports
j/J	Non-energy input
K	Capital
k	Capital intensity = capital divided by output or value added
k^{equip}	Capital intensity of equipment and software
k^{struc}	Capital intensity of structures
L	Labor

L^D	Demand for labor
LBP	Labor bargaining power
LMP	Spending on labor market programs / gross domestic product
LP	Labor productivity = value added / employment
LS	Labor share = compensation of employees / value added
M	Market
m	Markup
MP	Import prices
OSE	Energy offshoring intensity = imported energy inputs / total inputs
OSG	Goods offshoring intensity = manufacturing imports from low- and middle-income countries / total manufacturing imports
OSJ	Offshoring intensity of input j = imported inputs j / total non-energy inputs
OSM	Materials offshoring intensity = imported material inputs / total non-energy inputs
OSS	Services offshoring intensity = imported service inputs / total non-energy inputs
P	Output price, good price
P^{inp}	Intermediate input price
$\overline{P}$	Average price
PS	Profit share = $1 - LS$
q	Consumption
R	Interest rate
r	Rental rate on capital
ROE	Return on equity
RULC	Relative unit labor costs
S_w	Savings out of wage income
T	Technology shifter, technological progress
t	Time dimension
T^K	Capital-augmenting technological progress
T^L	Labor-augmenting technological progress
TR	Tax revenue
U	Utility
u	Average prime costs
UND	Union density = number of union members / number of workers
URB_LT	Unemployment replacement benefit (long-term)
URB_ST	Unemployment replacement benefit (short-term)
v	Share of inputs produced abroad

VA	Value added
W	World
w	Wage rate
WI	Wage income
X	Hybrid
Y	Output, income
Y^D	Demand for output
z	"Upgrading ratio" = growth in value added / growth in exports
ε	Random error term
Π	Total profits
σ	Elasticity of substitution

List of Abbreviations

B.	Billion
BEA	Bureau of Economic Analysis
BEC	Broad economic categories
CAGR	Compound annual growth rate
CEO	Chief executive officer
CEPR	Centre for Economic Policy Research
DESA	Department of Economic and Social Affairs
EOI	Export-oriented industrialization
EPI	Economic Policy Institute
EPL	Employment protection legislation
EPZ	Export processing zone
EU	European Union
FDI	Foreign direct investment
GB	Gigabyte
GDP	Gross domestic product
GPN	Global production network
GVA	Gross value added
GVC	Global value chain
HHI	Herfindahl-Hirschman index
H-O	Heckscher-Ohlin
H-O-W	Heckscher-Ohlin-Wood
ICC	International Chamber of Commerce
ICT	Information and communication technology
ILO	International Labour Office
IMF	International Monetary Fund
ISI	Import substitution industrialization
ISIC	International Standard Industrial Classification
IT	Information technology

LMICs	Low- and middle-income countries
NBER	National Bureau of Economic Research
n.e.s.	Not elsewhere specified
NIE	New International Economics
M.	Million
M&A	Merger and acquisition
MNC	Multinational corporation
OECD	Organisation of Economic Co-operation and Development
OLS	Ordinary Least Squares
OPEC	Organization of the Petroleum Exporting Countries
PhD	Doctor of Philosophy
R&D	Research and development
ROE	Return on equity
ROFA	Return on foreign assets
SEZ	Special economic zone
SITC	Standard International Trade Classification
U.K.	United Kingdom
UN	United Nations
UNCTAD	United Nations Conference on Trade and Development
UNIDO	United Nations Industrial Development Organization
U.S.	United States
VSI	Vertically specialized industrialization
WTO	World Trade Organization
$	U.S. Dollar

Acknowledgments

This book is the result of research and conversation over a number of years, and it gives us great pleasure to have a chance to thank the many people who have generously provided criticism, support, and inspiration to us over that time. There is no way to cite everyone who helped as we tested our ideas at university seminars, academic conferences, before the U.S. International Trade Commission, the AFL-CIO, the Peterson Institute for International Economics, panels at the ILO, OECD, World Bank, and WTO, and in postings on deliberatelyconsidered.com. The great variety of venues where we have put out our ideas has led to a useful diversity of responses in return.

An invaluable source of intellectual input for the book came from the research group based at the University of Manchester called "Capturing the Gains from Globalization: Economic and Social Upgrading in Global Value Chains," where Will serves on the Research Coordinating Committee. We have benefited from the diverse, interdisciplinary, and deep knowledge from colleagues in that group, including Stephanie Barrientos, Barbara Evers, Gary Gereffi, Shayne Godfrey, Fritz Mayer, Dev Nathan, John Pickles, and Anne Posthuma.

Our work has also been supported, both intellectually and financially, by a number of divisions of the United Nations, the U.K. Department for International Development and the Ev. Studienwerk e.V. We are deeply grateful to Richard Kozul-Wright (UN DESA and UNCTAD), Joerg Mayer (UNCTAD), Marion Jensen (then ILO), Marc Bacchetta (WTO), Hubert Escaith (WTO), Olivier Cattaneo (then World Bank), and Cornelia Staritz (then World Bank). The U.S. Bureau of Economic Analysis was very responsive to various inquiries regarding the data we used.

Friends and colleagues have helped in ways that they probably don't even realize. We are grateful to Eileen Appelbaum, Gunseli Berick, Robert

Blecker, Ha-Joon Chang, Keith Cowling, James Crotty, Cedric Durand, Thomas Farole, Stephen Gelb, Peter Gibbon, Jeff Goldfarb, Susan Houseman, Raphael Kaplinsky, David Kotz, Bill Lazonick, Mark Levinson, Barry Lynn, Michael Mandel, Sebastien Miroudot, Khalid Nadvi, Susan Newman, Florence Palpacuer, Pascal Petit, Bill Powers, Jill Rubery, David Ruccio, Malcolm Sawyer, Andrew Schrank, Stephanie Seguino, Nina Shapiro, Ben Shepherd, Peter Spiegler, Guy Standing, Tim Sturgeon, Daria Taglioni, and Hans-Michael Trautwein.

The New School for Social Research has been an ideal incubator for our construction of a critical and alternative perspective on globalization. We have both benefited from the steady support and input from the New School's Schwartz Center for Economic Policy Analysis and especially from Teresa Ghilarducci and David Howell. Thomas Bernhardt, Mary Borrowman, Xiao Jiang, Jan Keil, Lauren Schmitz, and Sheba Tejani served as research assistants at various stages of the project and were often invaluable sounding boards for the ideas as they developed.

At Cambridge University Press, Scott Parris's enthusiasm, grace, and guidance were essential. Kristin Purdy helped in many small but important ways. A number of the chapters of this book were revised and expanded versions of papers that have been published elsewhere. Therefore, we are grateful to the following for permission to use material from our previously published work: Oxford University Press, Taylor and Francis Books, Springer Science + Business Media, and The World Bank.

Our mentors Alfred Eichner (Will) and Harald Hagemann (Deborah) have informed our thinking over many years, and we hope this book reflects their influence.

We have dedicated the book to our families, for their support and their inspiration as the project moved forward. Deborah thanks Stephan Winkler for his steady support and continued inspiration. SDG. Will thanks Hedy Kalikoff for her unbending support and her unending wisdom and good judgment. She patiently and carefully read long sections of the manuscript, always insisting that clarity and style are especially essential elements of a book on economics.

ONE

Introduction

1.1 The Public Debate versus the Economics Profession

1.1.1 "Ricardo Is Still Right..."

In his bestselling account of globalization, *The World is Flat*, Thomas Friedman (2005) describes standing in Bangalore one morning in front of the gates of the Infosys Corporation – a major Indian provider of software and office services to U.S. corporations – and watching as young employees stream in to work. "Oh my God," he thinks to himself,

There are so many of them, and they all look so serious, so eager for work... How in the world can it possibly be good for my daughters and millions of other young Americans that these Indians can do the same jobs as they can for a fraction of the wages? I struggled over what to make of this scene. I don't want to see any American lose his or her job to foreign competition (Friedman 2005, 226).

Yes, Friedman is concerned about the future of the American workforce, but he is also grappling with his faith in Ricardo's principle of comparative advantage, a harmonious view of globalization in which all countries can gain from trade liberalization. The sight of so many energetic young Indians, "all looking as if they had scored 1,600 on their SATs," is alarming because it would seem that the success of Infosys can only mean fewer jobs for their American counterparts, including Friedman's daughters (Friedman 2005, 225). But if Friedman is a true Ricardian, he can calmly consider the bustling activity of Infosys without worrying that it bodes ill for American enterprise. He writes:

No book about the flat world would be honest if it did not acknowledge such concerns, or acknowledge that there is some debate among economists about whether Ricardo is still right. Having listened to the arguments on both sides, though, I

1

come down where the great majority of economists come down – that Ricardo is still right (Friedman 2005, 264).

This belief in the positive welfare effects of trade liberalization makes Friedman a rarity among journalists who write about globalization and offshoring. We define offshoring as all purchases of intermediate inputs from abroad, whether done through arm's-length contract – offshore outsourcing – or within the confines of a single multinational corporation (MNC) – intra-firm trade.

More typical of popular views of offshoring are those of Lou Dobbs. Dobbs is a populist who distinguishes the national interest of the United States from the profitability of American corporations – the stakeholders not just the stockholders, as Dobbs puts it in his 2004 book, *Exporting America: Why Corporate Greed is Shipping American Jobs Overseas*. Dobbs identifies himself as a lifelong Republican and a capitalist. However, when it comes to U.S. trade policy, Dobbs takes the side of American workers rather than corporations. "Incredibly," he writes,

> The proponents of outsourcing and free trade will tell you that it's all a win-win proposition. It's been my experience that you should reach for your wallet when anyone says "win-win" (Dobbs 2004, 64).

Dobbs asserts that offshoring hurts American workers and should thus be seen as against American interests. For Dobbs, the growth of offshoring reflects how corporate interests have taken control of the political process.

In his musings over the effects of the Indian information technology (IT) sector boom on U.S. industry and employment, Friedman comes down on the side of traditional economists who endorse the primacy of comparative advantage and the ease of adjustment to payments balance and full employment. But his angst – his head tells him one thing and his heart another – more than Dobbs' populist resistance, is an indication of the gap between academic and public discourse on the issue of offshoring.

Why is there such a gap? Why do economists have such little credibility in the popular discourse about offshoring? The problem is not a lack of awareness by economists of popular views. Economists are keenly cognizant of public sentiment on offshoring and, in fact, much academic writing on the issue of offshoring is motivated by a stated goal of quelling "fear" or dispelling "myth."[1] The motivation for this extensive body of scholarly research is to explain that public fears are unjustified. The public does

---

[1] Examples are Amiti and Wei (2005) "Fear of Services Offshoring," Harrison and McMillan (2006) "Dispelling Some Myths about Outsourcing," Blinder (2007a) "Offshoring: Big Deal, or Business as Usual," and Jensen (2011) "Global Trade in Services: Fear, Facts, and Offshoring".

not grasp the theory of the optimality of free trade. Despite their efforts, economists have gained very little traction in public discussion.

Is it simply that the American public doesn't get it? Our glance at the writings of Thomas Friedman and Lou Dobbs shows this is not the case. The U.S. presidential campaign of 2012 gives additional evidence that public debate over offshoring can go beyond the question of its direct effect on employment and consider also the longer-run investment issues that are at stake when companies are under the control of a private equity firm like Bain Capital. Nonetheless, the economics profession has largely viewed the popular skepticism about offshoring as a continuation of the anti-free trade sentiment rooted in special interests that economists have fought against for decades, if not centuries (Irwin 1996, 2005).

At a press conference, Harvard's Gregory Mankiw, then George W. Bush's chief economic advisor, was asked about the economic effect of corporate offshoring of services. His now famous response is excerpted here:

I think outsourcing is a growing phenomenon for white-collar workers, but it's something that we should realize is probably a plus for the economy in the long run. We're very used to goods being produced abroad and being shipped here on ships or planes. What we are not used to is services being produced abroad and being sent here over the Internet or telephone wires. But does it matter from an economic standpoint whether values of items produced abroad come on planes and ships or over fiber-optic cables? Well, no, the economics is basically the same (Andrews 2004, 93–94).

Mankiw's matter-of-fact optimism outraged the public – leading to considerable effort at pre-election damage control by the White House – but was widely supported by economists. Once again, the economics profession found itself stunned by the public's concern over the labor market effects of growing international trade in intermediates.[2] According to one economist, "free traders are trapped in a public policy version of [the movie] 'Groundhog Day,' forced to refute the same fallacious arguments over and over again, decade after decade" (Sanchez 2003, cited in Irwin 2005, 5).[3]

An alternative view is expressed by Alan Blinder, who writes:

If we economists stubbornly insist on chanting "free trade is good for you" to people who know it is not, we will quickly become irrelevant to the public debate. Compared with that, a little apostasy should be welcome (Blinder 2007b).

---

[2] For a blow-by-blow account of how Mankiw saw the events, in which he thought his words were taken out of context and subject to inaccurate press reports, see Mankiw and Swagel (2005).

[3] This amusing Hollywood reference is perhaps more revealing than the author intended, because the point of the movie was that the day would repeat itself until the protagonist (played by Bill Murray) gets it "right"!

Ruccio and Amariglio (2003) argue that academic condescension toward popular views on the economy reflects an underlying insecurity about the alternative views of economic life expressed in popular culture, that is, "the differences in content between academic and everyday economics" (Ruccio and Amariglio 2003, 276). The field of international economics exemplified this in the 1990s and again in the 2000s. In the 1990s, economists sought to ridicule popular calls for trade protection and industrial policy. At the same time, traditional free trade theories were being overturned by the New International Economics that found conditions under which state intervention in international trade and technology development could raise national (and in some cases global) welfare. In a heated debate in the pages of the journal *Foreign Affairs* in 1994, Paul Krugman accused those supporting government intervention in the form of trade protection or industrial policy as suffering from a "dangerous obsession."

In the 2000s, as the offshoring issue heated up in public debate, economists attacked other economists for not defending the traditional free trade line – when the welfare gains from offshoring were questionable even by their own standards. Dissent by Paul Samuelson and Alan Blinder over the importance of offshoring and its beneficence for U.S. economic welfare was met by outrage from colleagues who perceived them as traitors against economic faith. Samuelson reported back to the editors of the *Journal of Economic Perspectives* on the response to his article. His essay expressed considerable skepticism about the beneficial welfare effects of offshoring, and strong doubts about the potential Pareto welfare criterion that often underpins the assertion of such benefits. Responding to the many criticisms he received following the publication of this article, Samuelson writes that

none of my chastening pals expressed concern about globalization's effects on greater inequality in a modern age when transfers from winners to losers do trend politically downward in present-day democracies (Samuelson 2005, 243).

Gregory Mankiw criticized two very prominent economists for not defending him publicly after he was attacked for minimizing the effects of job losses occurring from offshoring. Mankiw writes that,

Notable in his initial silence was Paul Krugman... Notable as well for his silence was then-Harvard President Larry Summers... Summers declined when journalists asked him for an on-the-record comment on the outsourcing controversy, even though as Harvard President he had shown considerably less reluctance to engage in the public debate on other issues (Mankiw and Swagel 2005, 12–13).

At the core of the conflict between academic and public sentiment is not simply ignorance on the part of non-economists. What we propose in this book is that there are considerable limits to the economists' own models. In particular, the economists' views on offshoring are closely tied to an outmoded theory of comparative advantage and to an implausible criterion for assessing social welfare. The models of comparative advantage on which the economists' views are based have conceptual, historical, and ethical limitations that generally fail to capture the broader institutional context – including corporate strategies, labor market segmentation, buyer-supplier asymmetries, and government regulations – which are key to understanding the social welfare and economic development consequences of globalized production. Profits, their sources and their uses, have largely disappeared from the analysis, despite their centrality in determining the international division of labor and in driving the dynamic gains from offshoring. As a result of these shortcomings, economists have ceded the academic voice in the debate over offshoring – to sociologists and geographers, experts in management, development studies, labor relations and, yes, to journalists and popular writers. Economics, it would appear, has been outsourced to the non-economists.

Therefore, this book has – among others – the following two purposes: First, to provide an alternative, and institutionally grounded, theory of offshoring and, second, to offer a critique of the role that the economics profession has played in the course of decades of public debate over the economic and social consequences of globalization.

1.1.2 Perceived and Actual Effects of Globalization

Americans have become increasingly skeptical of the effects of offshoring on employment and wages in the United States. A recent *New York Times* poll of 951 Americans showed their view that,

Outsourcing is . . . clearly a cause of fewer jobs domestically. And two-thirds of the public wants American companies to shoulder a lot of responsibility to keep manufacturing jobs in the United States (Conelly 2012).

International comparisons of sentiment toward globalization also shows strong American pessimism about its labor market consequences. Surveys show that about half of Americans and Europeans think that "freer trade"

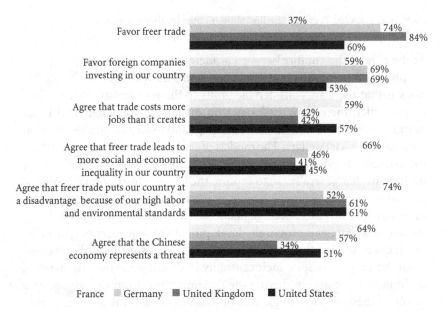

Figure 1.1. Concerns about Free Trade (% of Respondents). *Source*: Own illustration. Based on Milberg and Winkler (2011a, 182). Data: German Marshall Fund (2007), Trade and Poverty Reduction Survey, Topline Data October 2007.

results in more job loss than job creation, although between 2005 and 2007 American sentiment turned against freer trade while European sentiment became less skeptical of the employment benefits of trade liberalization. Half of Americans and a higher percentage of French and Germans "agree that the Chinese economy represents a threat" (see Figure 1.1). Of all countries surveyed, France and the United States showed the highest percentage of those who "did not favor foreign companies investing in our country," with 40 percent of Americans and 38 percent of French (not shown in Figure 1.1). This contrasted with 69 percent of English and German respondents who were favorable to foreign direct investment (FDI).[4]

In the United States, 40 percent of Americans expect that the next generation will have a lower standard of living, 62 percent said job security had declined, and 59 percent said they have to work harder to earn a decent living. Most striking is that 75 percent of Americans said that "outsourcing work overseas hurts American workers" (Anderson and Gascon 2007, 1). Although this expression of economic insecurity was greatest among those

---

[4] Scheve and Slaughter (2003) find that in the United Kingdom between 1991 and 1999, perceived economic insecurity was higher in those sectors with greater outward FDI.

with less education, expressions of a rise in economic insecurity as a result of offshoring were found for all educational categories.[5]

Do the perceptions of the effect of globalization on economic security bear any relation to the actual impact of trade and FDI on industrialized countries? In Chapter 5, we estimate the impact of offshoring on the labor share of income for fifteen countries in the Organisation of Economic Co-operation and Development (OECD), and we compare these results to the survey evidence of the perception of the impact of globalization. We find that concerns over globalization are heightened in those countries where the negative effects on the labor market are greatest. The negative correlations support the notion that perceptions and reality are, in this case, linked. This conclusion is consistent with the findings for the United States by Scheve and Slaughter (2003), in which low-skill workers were found to be more skeptical of globalization and trade liberalization than workers with higher skills.

Our estimates in Chapter 5 for the United States suggest that offshoring – measured in over thirty manufacturing and service sectors from 1998 to 2006 – led to a drop in employment of approximately 3.5 million full-time equivalent jobs. A 10 percent increase in services and materials offshoring is associated with a 2.6 percent reduction in the share of value added going to workers, one indicator of the level of inequality in America.

Economists who express great surprise at these conclusions either don't believe that their theories could possibly be falsified by data or they believe that people have misperceived reality. Our evidence indicates that these economists are wrong on both counts: Popular perceptions of globalization are not rooted in fantasy, but in the actual experience of heightened economic insecurity.

1.1.3 The "Kletzer Effect"

To further complicate the matter, there is an epistemological challenge to economists coming from the empirical studies of job loss from trade. One of the strengths of many of the theoretical models of offshoring is the indeterminacy of their results (Bhagwati et al. 2004; Grossman and Rossi-Hansberg 2008). In these cases, the ultimate assessment of the gains from offshoring hinges on results of empirical research. This is all well and good, except for

---

[5] Even on the issue of perception of insecurity, there is conflicting evidence. Kierkegaard (2007) shows that among European countries there is not a statistically significant relation between "public anxiety" over offshoring (as measured by the Eurobarometer 63 of 2005) and the intensity of offshoring.

the fact that empirical evidence rarely resolves a debate among academic economists, especially when there are deep-seated differences of vision on an issue. The problem is partly due to the inherent nature of empirical analysis, limited as it necessarily is in terms of sample size and variable choice. For example, we have seen that much analysis of offshoring focuses on the impact on "high-skill" and "low-skill" workers. Yet even the standard way of operationalizing "high skill" and "low skill" – associating high-skill with non-production workers and low-skill with production workers – is highly contentious (Howell 2005).

The classic problems of induction, that is, of the impossibility of drawing general conclusions from observation, already well understood in the nineteenth century, is exacerbated in the era of econometrics where results are also contingent on model specification and estimation technique.[6] In their econometric study of offshoring and employment, for example, Amiti and Wei (2006) report that the employment effects of services offshoring in the U.S. manufacturing sector are negative when they use a disaggregated industry breakdown but show no negative effect when the aggregated industry classification is used. In contrast, we find a negative relation using more recent data at the aggregated level, as we report in Chapter 5. This is a standard empirical debate, where results can change with the choice of unit of observation and time period.

The offshoring debate, however, raises empirical argumentation to a new level of complication: Different sides in the debate *give very different interpretations of the same exact empirical study.* Those who support the expansion of offshoring and who think that its effect on U.S. labor markets is not important cite Kletzer's (2001) study to bolster their view. Those who find the detrimental labor market effects of offshoring to be unacceptably high cite the very same study. We call this phenomenon "the Kletzer effect," because it revolves around the research of Lori Kletzer, professor of economics at Colby College and author of the study in question, *Job Loss from Imports: Measuring the Costs,* published through the Peterson Institute for International Economics.

Bhagwati et al. (2004) introduce the Kletzer study by calling it "one of the most influential studies of the costs of trade displacement" (Bhagwati et al. 2004, 111). They see the study as justifying their claim that displacement from trade is like any other job displacement, and all displacement is rooted in technological change:

---

[6] Mirowski and Sklivas (1991) calculated the variation across estimates ("birge ratios") for some of the supposed "constants" in economics and found very large ranges, especially in comparison with the ranges typically found in the natural sciences and even psychology.

Kletzer (2001) divides manufacturing industries into low, medium and high import competing, based on the change in import share during 1979–1994... Across all three groups of industries, about two-thirds of those displaced are reemployed within two years, with about half of that group ending up with a job that paid roughly as much or more than their previous job and the other half experiencing a wage cut of 15 percent or more... Thus, the rate of reemployment and wage changes for workers that Kletzer characterizes as trade displaced are quite similar to those for other workers. In other words, a common factor, most likely technological change, is behind the displacement in all categories (Bhagwati et al. 2004, 111–112).

Farrell and Agrawal (2005) also cite the Kletzer report in support of their view that the labor market effects of services offshoring are minimal.

David Levy (2005) has a different interpretation:

The notion that trade enables industrialized countries to specialize in highly skilled well-paying jobs is widespread. The data, however, are mixed at best. In an extensive study of workers displaced by imports, Kletzer (2001) concluded that (p. 2) 'the earnings losses of job dislocation are large and persistent over time.' She found that 63.4 per cent of workers displaced between 1979 and 1999 were reemployed with an average earnings *loss* of 13 per cent. Workers displaced from non-manufacturing sectors did a little better: 69 per cent found reemployment, with average earnings losses of only 4 per cent, though 55 per cent took lower paid jobs, and around 25 per cent suffered pay cuts of 30 per cent or more. In other words, 86 per cent were worse off after displacement, 56 per cent were greatly so (Levy 2005, 687).

Somewhere in between the views of Bhagwati and Levy are those of Amiti and Wei (2005), who are slightly more tempered in their view of the implications of the Kletzer study for the offshoring debate. They write:

The McKinsey report [which relies on Kletzer's study] indicated that more than 69% of workers who lost jobs due to imports in the United States between 1979 and 1999 were re-employed... Of course, this means that 31% were not re-employed, highlighting that there may be some rigidities in the labor market (Amiti and Wei 2005, 317).

In this view, it is "labor market rigidities" (presumably meaning institutions which make firing workers costly) rather than offshoring *per se* that are keeping labor markets from clearing more quickly. In fact, in Chapter 5, our estimations show that a country's level of labor market flexibility and labor support matter for the labor market effects from offshoring.

Economists all present themselves as objective; to do otherwise would jeopardize the claim for scientificity. But all empirical assessment requires norms or standards which allow for a serious conversation among experts. With the use of econometrics for hypothesis testing this becomes even more important. The lack of such norms is one of the reasons that econometric analysis alone has rarely clinched an argument, even among economists themselves. Without accepted conventions for what constitutes "big," "important," or "significant," it is inevitable that economists will make competing claims about a single estimate.

Underpinning the Kletzer effect is the importance of economists' prior beliefs that they bring into even the most scientific-seeming analysis. Schumpeter (1994[1954]) referred to this as "vision," which he described as the "pre-analytic cognitive act." Schumpeter writes:

Analytic work begins with material provided by our vision of things, and this vision is ideological almost by definition. It embodies the definition of things as we see them, and wherever there is any possible motive for wishing to see them in a given rather than another light, the way in which we see things can hardly be distinguished from the way we wish to see them (Schumpeter 1994[1954], 42).

Vision is an inevitable aspect of science, but especially in social sciences, where the "observer" is also a clear "participant." Whereas the adoption of norms and conventions of assessment in themselves reflect vision, in the absence of such norms and conventions the interpretation of analytical results becomes even more prone to the whimsy of vision.

1.2 A Global Value Chain Approach to Offshoring

By globalization we mean not simply a quantitative increase in international economic activity: it is also characterized by a qualitative shift. Production has become increasingly organized within global value chains (GVCs), led by large firms based typically in the industrialized countries, and relying often on complex networks of suppliers around the world. GVCs, sometimes called global supply chains or global production networks (GPNs), are defined by Sturgeon (2001) as "the sequence of productive (that is, value added) activities leading to and supporting end use" (Sturgeon 2001, 2). While sourcing in GVCs goes back centuries, it has increased since the 1970s to become the dominant mode of international trade.[7] From the Chevy Cobalt to the Mattel Barbie Doll, from the Boeing 777 to the JP Morgan Chase Bank Visa credit card, and now to the IBM "smart grid" computer network, the production process has been broken up into parts, with different parts performed in different countries.

Low-wage countries are now able to produce high-quality manufactured goods and U.S. companies have taken advantage of this process by offshoring

---

[7] Hamilton (2006) discusses U.S. retail firm offshoring beginning in the 1960s. Lazonick (2009) documents that U.S. firms began sourcing the production of semiconductors overseas in the 1960s. Clarence-Smith and Topik (2003) discuss the coffee supply chain dating back to the 1800s.

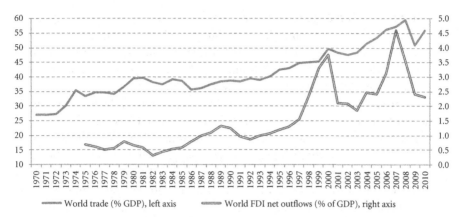

Figure 1.2. World Trade and FDI Net Outflows (% of GDP), 1970–2010. *Source:* Own illustration. Data: World Development Indicators, World Bank.

production overseas. It is this shift in the degree and nature of global production that is the focus of this book. Our purpose is to provide a new view of the economics of globalized production by analyzing it from the perspective of the international supply chain and thus focusing on the forces that govern that chain and, in particular, on the business strategies of the lead firms in those chains. We show in this book that this view has implications for the theories of international trade and foreign investment, price determination, industrial organization, economic development, and for key policy debates in industrialized and developing countries related to deindustrialization, labor market regulation, and export processing zones (EPZs).

1.2.1 Globalization and the Economic Crisis of 2008–2009

Our current wave of economic globalization, typically dated to the early 1980s, can be understood as having two prongs: production and finance. The globalization of finance involves the massive expansion of international portfolio capital flows. The large holdings of risky mortgage-backed securities by European banks are a recent sign of how globalized financial markets have become. Daily foreign exchange transactions rose to $40 trillion in 2008, from an average of $4 trillion in 1990 (Kozul-Wright and Rayment 2008). The globalization of production itself has two dimensions: trade and FDI. These too have increased to historic levels over the past twenty years, not only in absolute terms, but also relative to world output, as seen in Figure 1.2.

Technological change and economic liberalization were no doubt important factors in the increasing globalization of production. The internet has raised the speed and lowered the cost of global commerce and of managing a fragmented and international supply chain. Trade liberalization occurred both bilaterally and multilaterally, with most of the developing world brought into the process of trade liberalization with the founding of the World Trade Organization (WTO) in 1994. Capital account liberalization became an important goal of the International Monetary Fund (IMF) in the 1980s and has been broadly adopted since then. But perhaps most important in the political realm is the emergence of non-capitalist countries – Communist Russia, China, and Eastern Europe, and a previously protectionist India – as large and active players in world capitalism.[8] Critics of globalization often see the politics of neoliberalism as the main driver of globalization. Although this view may be exaggerated, it is certainly correct in one sense, which is that globalization is a social choice rather than determined by some inevitable and exogenous trend in technology.

Our own account adds another factor to the explanation of globalization: A shift in corporate strategy, involving a search for lower costs and greater flexibility to implement a process of 'mass customization,' and a desire to focus on 'core' activities and allocate more resources to financial activity and short-run shareholder value while reducing commitments to long-term employment and job security. Offshoring – a key component of the globalization of production – is part of the larger corporate strategic shift over the past twenty-five years which attempted to realign the interests of shareholders and managers, reduce the scope of the firm and long-term employment relations while pursuing production strategies that better serve market demand for brand quality and variety. Globalization should be seen in the context of this broader corporate strategy shift, as offshoring has given firms the chance to raise profits while keeping price increases low by reducing costs, raising flexibility, offloading risks, and occasionally bypassing labor and environmental regulation, all the while retaining rents from design, marketing, and financial activity.

Evidence of this shift in the globalization of production is the increase in the level of offshoring intensity. In Chapter 2, we look at input-output based measures and more general measures of offshoring intensity, and find that in the 2000s it increased to unprecedented levels. The cumulative picture that emerges from this offshoring trend is a "new wave" of globalization,

---

[8] Freeman (2007) has described this as the "great doubling" of the capitalist economy's labor force.

in which production and the realization of value are more de-linked geographically than ever before.[9] The new wave of globalization has altered the magnitude, structure, and role of international trade. It has changed the nature of economic growth in the developing world and it has heightened economic insecurity in many industrialized countries where it has created new relations between shareholders and management, between management and domestic employees, and between managers in lead firms and their counterparts in supplier companies.

The change in the structure of international trade (rather than just in its magnitude) has also altered the politics of trade and exchange rates. Historically, management and labor both came to Washington to lobby for import protection. Today, imports are crucial to firm profitability, and thus lobbying for trade protection in the United States is largely left to (shrinking) labor unions. Whereas in earlier times a weak U.S. dollar was good for corporate profitability because it boosted exports, today a strong dollar can just as well boost profitability by reducing the dollar price of foreign-produced inputs. This may explain Washington's limited diplomatic effort to alter China's undervaluation policy, despite a lot of public noise.

Our analysis in this book focuses mainly on the United States in the 1990s and 2000s. Over this period, the globalization of production contributed to stable consumer prices and encouraged the introduction of new products, allowed for the production of seemingly infinite varieties of existing products, cheap and fashionable clothing and electronics, and instant communication around the world. The new production of these goods and services – in China, Brazil, India, Mexico, Vietnam, and elsewhere – has created millions of new jobs, brought many people out of poverty, and expanded the middle classes. It also helped to raise corporate profitability and – despite an intervening financial crisis – stock prices.

But there has been a downside as well. The globalization of production is increasing the pace of U.S. deindustrialization, contributing to a reduction in the labor share of national income in many industrialized countries (as shown in Chapter 5), dampening wages and employment among low-skill workers, and more recently among workers at all skill levels. In the low-income countries, many of the jobs created in the service of GVCs are temporary and have unacceptable work conditions and wages. China's electronics factories are notorious for violation of international labor standards. The Vietnamese boom in apparel exports has been underpinned by a labor force without rights to organize unions. Mexico's entry into the

---

[9] On this point, see Levy (2005).

North American Free Trade Agreement and the resulting improved access to North American markets resulted in annual manufacturing export growth of 6.3 percent from the period 1995 to 2008. At the same time, average real compensation per worker in Mexican manufacturing was effectively stagnant, with growth of 0.6 percent per year and, as we analyze in Chapter 7, with real wage declines in a number of important sectors.

To add to the problems, China's export market share gains have come at the expense of Latin American and African exports of manufactures, as recent studies show (Wood and Mayer 2011). Finally, despite the name "globalization," much of the world has been left out of the process, with parts of South Asia, South America, and Africa destitute, and with little prospect for sustained economic growth and development in the foreseeable future. While China experienced a reduction in the number of people in poverty by 400 million between 1990 and 2005, the percentage of the population living on less than $2 per day in sub-Saharan Africa fell only from 76 to 73 percent (Chen and Ravallion 2008, World Development Indicators online).

The rise in importance of GVC-based trade has altered some of the basic relations of international trade. First, imports and exports are now often closely tied to each other, as supplier firms must often import parts, components, and services in order to process goods for export, but also capital goods such as machinery. Such "vertical specialization" – that is, the degree to which exports rely on imports – has increased enormously and in fact accounts for much of the increase in world trade over the past few decades (Hummels et al. 1998, 2001). Koopman et al. (2010) find that China's vertical specialization in manufacturing is 63 percent, implying a heavy reliance on East Asian GVCs. As WTO Director-General Pascal Lamy (2011) writes,

What we call "made in China" is indeed assembled in China, but its commercial value comes from those numerous countries that precede its assembly. It no longer makes sense to think of trade in terms of "us" versus "them" (Lamy 2011).

The new wave of globalization, rooted in the extension of GVCs, has changed the relation between trade flows and gross domestic product (GDP). This has been observed starkly over the recent period of crisis and recovery, as trade flows were more volatile relative to GDP than ever in history. The importance of offshoring as a firm strategy has altered the relation between imports and profits. We show that this has had economy-wide implications for income distribution in the United States and elsewhere, where increased offshoring has been associated with a higher share of income going to profits. Traditionally it is held that, *ceteris paribus*, export growth raises firm profitability, whereas imports compete with domestic producers, lowering profitability.

One of the causes of the large and persistent trade imbalances in the era of globalization is greater capital flow, both portfolio capital and FDI. The traditional accounts of international trade, despite their general equilibrium approach, usually leave capital out of the model on the grounds that international mobility of capital implies that it is equally accessible and earns the same return globally. But capital investment, knowledge flows, and the search for economic rents are distinguishing features of globalization, and among the key determinants of offshoring.[10] Moreover, financial activity by firms is categorically ruled out for discussion when capital is absent. The presumption is that cost saving from offshoring constitutes an efficiency gain by reallocating resources into more productive uses, which generates a shift out of the country's production possibilities. Houseman et al. (2010) show that these productivity gains are overstated in the standard calculations because they undercount spending on foreign capital and labor. As we find in our empirical analysis in Chapter 6, profit gains have to a significant degree been put toward the purchase of financial assets rather than productive investment.

Finally, while the skills-based, full employment general equilibrium models of trade predict that there are "winners" and "losers" from trade liberalization, they also conclude that free trade is optimal, since losers can potentially be compensated. The policy message is typically that individuals need to get more skills, meaning that the state has a minimal role in managing the welfare effects of offshoring and the burden lies largely with the individual to invest optimally in his own human capital. The most recent theoretical models in fact assume no need even for a policy response of this type since they find that workers of *all* skill levels should benefit from offshoring (Grossman and Rossi-Hansberg 2006a, 2006b, 2008; Baldwin and Robert-Nicoud 2007).

The slump that began in 2008 is the first major economic crisis among industrialized countries in the contemporary era of globalization, and analysts will draw lessons from it for a long time. There are a number of connections between the new wave of globalized production and the recent economic downturn. The first is through its effect on incomes. In Chapter 5, we find that U.S. offshoring has reduced the demand for U.S. labor, put downward pressure on average real wages, and generally contributed to the decline in the labor share of value added. This finding is contrary to the

---

[10] See Wood (2001). An exception is Bhagwati et al. (2004).

theoretical model of Grossman and Rossi-Hansberg (2008) that is often cited in support of expanded offshoring. One implication of our findings is that offshoring appears to have been one of the reasons behind the expansion of household borrowing that was, in retrospect, unsustainable, but which allowed household consumption to continue amidst the rising cost of healthcare, education, and housing.

Second, the era of globalization has also been a time of historically large and persistent trade imbalances, and some have argued that these are a cause of the recent crisis (Dooley and Garber 2009). There are competing views of the causes of the imbalances. Some argue that there has been a "savings glut," whereby China and other East Asians, in response to the crisis of the 1990s, wanted to accumulate reserves for safety and therefore kept wages and exchange rates weak in order to run current account surpluses. The other view is of a "money glut," according to which the Federal Reserve ran such loose policy that interest rates were too low and consumers borrowed and spent too much. In Chapter 8, our analysis points to the possibility of a third explanation whereby the growth of corporate profits was built, in part, on weak wage growth and growing imports. This promoted both the growth of household debt and a worsening of the trade deficit. We call this the "profits glut" explanation of the United States–China imbalance, again emphasizing the role of firms and their governance of GVCs.

Third, the globalization of production has been a factor in the crisis to the extent that it has supported a "financialization" of the U.S. economy. The focus in much analysis of the crisis and slow recovery is the financial sector and its out-of-control and failed speculative activity. But non-financial firms also moved more into finance over the past decade, dedicating large sums of their income to the purchase of financial assets, especially their own stock, which is share buybacks. In Chapter 6, we find that the financialization of non-financial corporations was stronger in those firms and sectors where offshoring was more intense.

Finally, the globalization of production has flourished in part as a result of trade liberalization, the deregulation of finance, tax cuts, lax antitrust enforcement, and a retrenchment of the welfare state. Whether it was a lack of regulation along these lines that led to the crisis will be debated by historians, but it is clear that this was indeed the policy environment in which the economic crisis of 2008 to 2009 took place.

1.2.2 The Governance of Value Chains

The concept of the GVC comprises the column vector of an input-output table. But whereas input-output tables show the value of inputs required for each unit of output, the study of GVCs emphasizes the ownership, governance, and power structures within each link and across links in the production process; for example, between lead firms and supplier firms, or between supplier firms and smaller – even home-based – subcontractors. Whereas input-output analysis focuses on technology, GVC analysis considers also the ownership and social arrangements (politics and cultural norms) that underpin the distribution of value added across the chain and their changes over time.

The main focus of the GVC framework is the governance of the supply chain, including the nature of contracting with suppliers, the degree of sharing of technology, the extent of entry barriers along the supply chain, and the ability of firms to "upgrade" within the supply chain by moving into aspects of production generating higher value added per worker. The relations between the lead firms and their suppliers may take a variety of forms, often intermediate forms between the extremes of hierarchy and market, involving some sort of knowledge sharing and regular extra-contractual relations between buyer and supplier firms.[11]

The coordination of this globalized production and its implications for work and economic development have been most fully described in the study of GVCs. The governance structure in any GVC affects the composition, volume, and nature of international trade. Such trade is the result of lead firm concern with costs, flexibility, and risk, with the productive capacity of suppliers and the degree of reliability of supplier contracting. These strategic decisions are influenced by the institutional context in which they occur, including labor market conditions, regulations, trade policies, financial and tax regulations, and corporate codes of conduct.

Thus, whereas traditional trade theory sees "natural" endowments of labor and capital, and given preferences and technologies as determining comparative advantage and the pattern of trade, the GVC approach tends to focus on the power relations between producers, between management and labor within firms, and among governments, firms, and households as determinants of the direction and volume of trade. The centrality of upgrading to the value chain approach indicates its concern for dynamic and qualitative aspects of international trade and the gains from trade. Upgrading is the result of government policies and firm strategies aimed precisely at overcoming the specialization pattern dictated by comparative advantage, an effort to avoid the static equilibrium of trade theory, what has been termed by Reinert (2008) as a "low-level equilibrium trap" (Reinert 2007, 142).

---

[11] Gereffi et al. (2005) propose a taxonomy of five forms these relations may take.

The lead firm is by definition the firm that controls the GVC, and typically this is the firm responsible for the final sale of the product (although we will see cases where suppliers or even distributors are in positions of considerable power). Gereffi (1994) distinguishes between "buyer-driven" and "producer-driven" value chains, the distinction depending on the nature of the lead firm in the chain. Buyer-driven value chains occur mainly in consumer products such as apparel, footwear and toys. In this case, the GVC is driven by large retailers (such as Wal-Mart, Target, and Sears). Such firms do no manufacturing themselves but focus instead on design and marketing while subcontracting the actual production of the good. Wal-Mart, which alone accounted for approximately 9.3 percent of U.S. imports from China between 2001 and 2006, is the premier example of a lead firm in a consumer-led chain. But major retailers in all industrialized countries actively control their global supply chains.[12]

A producer-driven chain is typical in industries requiring medium-to high-technology production that are characterized by significant scale economies, and driven by multinational producing firms who may subcontract some aspects of production but who keep research and development (R&D) and final good production within the firm. Automobiles and aircraft are examples of this. Generally speaking, consumer-led chains are more likely to trade with foreign supplier firms at arm's length. Producer-led chains are more likely to expand through FDI, resulting in intra-firm trade. However, there are plenty of exceptions to this profile, as the massive expansion of auto parts supplier firms in the developing world attests. With increasing digitization of services in finance, accounting, medicine, software design, payroll management, and marketing, producer-driven chains have rapidly expanded with arm's-length supplier relations in many of these areas and this form of vertical disintegration, what Grossman and Rossi-Hansberg (2006a, 2006b, 2008) call "task trade," is predicted to greatly expand in the future.

The GVC approach focuses on lead firm governance strategy and power, supplier firms' upgrading possibilities, and the distribution of value added in the value chain. This contrasts with the transactions cost approach to international production that has been adopted in most economic models of the make-or-buy decision in outsourcing. The transactions cost approach provides a straightforward objective function that can be subject to standard optimization techniques (minimizing transactions costs subject to

---

[12] On Wal-Mart, see Scott (2007). For a discussion of European retailers' supply chain management strategies, see Palpacuer et al. (2005) and Gibbon (2002).

constraints). The value chain approach – pursued mainly by sociologists and geographers – eschews optimization as a useful characterization of lead firm behavior, and emphasizes instead how power is wielded and technology and markets managed, as well as how this affects lead firms' performance and supplier firms' upgrading.

Despite its conceptual emphasis on lead firms as buyers or producers, most value chain research has focused on developing countries. The GVC has proven to be a powerful device for the study of industrial upgrading because it is within the confines of the GVC that supplier firms have raised their productive capabilities, especially through learning from relations with buyers as these supplier firms seek to attain internationally competitive production standards. A report from the United Nations Industrial Development Organization, for example, notes that

the main cause of the large upward leaps [developing country firms' industrial performance in the 1990s] appears to be participation in integrated global production networks, which sharply raises the share of complex products in exports (UNIDO 2002, 42).

Thus, industrial upgrading is seen as occurring mainly within GVCs, which may or may not involve FDI and international labor migration, but for which international trade is their lifeblood.

There is a rich literature analyzing GVCs, but for our purposes we focus on how this form of industrial organization is captured in the analysis of trade and investment. From the perspective of international trade statistics, the network form is most like a market, because international trade within such a network is considered an arm's-length exchange. In addition to arm's-length offshoring of intermediate goods, there has been a rise in trade in final goods at the wholesale level, that is, goods whose production is complete except for marketing and retailing. These goods are imported by large retailers (Wal-Mart and the Gap, for example) or by so-called "manufacturers without factories" or "fab-less" firms, such as Nike, Calvin Klein, or Fisher-Price, who import goods fully assembled – but containing the lead firm label or package – from a foreign producer or middle man. In all these cases, the value added by the lead firm comes from its design, marketing, retailing, or financial activity.

In other respects, the relation among firms in networks or quasi-hierarchies is closer to that of a single firm and its majority-owned affiliate. Information may be shared between lead and supplier firms that traditionally would be kept within the firm. The lead firm might provide technical and communications support in order to smooth the delivery of supplies.

Production blueprints may even be provided to developing country supplier firms (Tybout 2000). Japanese subcontractors, for example, use "long-term close relations with suppliers" including "rich information sharing" (Holmstrom and Roberts 1998, 80–82, cited in Williamson 2002, 190). Nolan et al. (2002) describe such suppliers as "the external firm" of the large global corporations (Nolan et al. 2002, 101), an ambiguous term that reflects precisely this organizational arrangement that is between a market and a hierarchy. This means that whereas there may be no measured FDI between lead and supplier firms in a network, there is possibly significant capital flow, if only of the intangible kind.

Thus, as supply chains developed and supplier firms gained in technological sophistication and scale of operations, the dichotomy between in-house or arm's-length international supply relations has given way to a multiplicity of lead firm-supplier firm relations involving various degrees of investment, technical support, long-term contracting, and monitoring. In some cases, large supplier firms – especially in autos, apparel, footwear, electronics, and business services – have captured scale economies and developed modular production systems, enabling them to produce a range of related products, and allowing them to supply inputs and finished goods to many companies within a given sector and sometimes across sectors.[13] In many cases, continual entry of new supplier firms has added to global excess capacity, leading to a decline in the terms of trade for developing countries' manufacturers, and enhancing the scope for lead firms to induce competition among supplier firms, further lowering lead firm input costs.

The international trade that occurs as a result of the formation and growth of GVCs may be intra-firm trade – which presumes prior FDI – or arm's-length trade when suppliers are independently owned. The distinction is shown in Figure 1.3, which breaks down international trade according to how it is governed and whether it involves intermediate or final goods and services. Quadrants 1 and 2 represent trade in intermediate goods and services, with quadrant 1 representing trade within the MNC, such as when Ford Motors imports radios from Mexico for its assembly operations in Detroit, and quadrant 2 the trade at arm's-length with a subcontractor, such as Boeing's imports from Japan of parts for assembly in Seattle of 777s.

Quadrant 3 is the traditional final goods or services trade at arm's-length, such as the sale of a Sony Walkman by a wholesaler. Quadrant 4 is final goods or services produced and exchanged within the MNC, such as when a fully-assembled car is imported from Japan by Toyota's U.S.

---

[13] On the variety of forms of lead firm-supplier firm relations, see Gereffi et al. (2005). For a discussion of "modularity" in global supply chains, see Sturgeon (2002). For a study of scale economies in first-tier suppliers, see Appelbaum (2008) and Gereffi (2006).

| | Governance of global value chain | |
	Arm's-length	Intra-firm
Intermediate	2	1
Final	3	4

Figure 1.3. The Governance of Trade. *Source:* Own illustration. Based on Bardhan and Jaffee (2004), Figure 1.

subsidiary. Trade within the MNC fits into quadrants 1 and 4, and is intra-firm trade. Offshoring in popular parlance and much economic research is associated with transactions that fit in quadrants 1 and 2, which involves intermediate goods. But GVCs also govern some trade in final goods, and these should be included in any discussion of offshoring. To the extent that parent or affiliate firms add value (in marketing or after-sales services, for example) these too are imports of intermediates. The traditional theory of international trade is concerned mainly with arm's-length trade in final goods and services, that is, transactions that fall into quadrant 3.

The economics of offshoring has largely been built on the principle of comparative advantage. In this view, the purchase of components and services from abroad is a refinement of the international division of labor and thus provides the same gains from trade that free trade was said to have traditionally brought in the nineteenth and twentieth centuries. In the 1990s, international trade economists revived the Heckscher-Ohlin (H-O) trade model to show how trade liberalization had shifted labor demand in a biased fashion – in favor of "high-skill" workers and against "low-skill" workers – in countries relatively abundant in skilled labor.

While there is evidence that wages of skilled workers have risen relatively in most industrialized countries, the focus on wages by skill level has limited the analysis of globalization in a number of ways. For one, almost all these models assume full employment, and thus the only way labor markets can be affected by trade in the models is through wages, and only relative wages at that. Offshoring, in this view, cannot create unemployment. Thurow (2004) thus describes the labor market assumptions of the H-O model as "counterfactual."[14] Perhaps even more to the point is Joan Robinson's comment that the assumption of full employment that underpins the neoclassical theory of international trade "consists merely in assuming what it hopes to prove" (Robinson 1973, 16). As a result of these theoretical limitations, the engagement of trade economists in the debate over the benefits of offshoring has been problematic from the start. A monograph by the International Labour Office and WTO (2007) on "Trade and Employment," for example, barely mentions employment, focusing instead on wages of high- and low-skill workers.

We use the GVC as the organizing principle for the analysis of international trade because it permits us to focus on global business strategy – including mass customization, core competence, branding, and other barriers to entry, financialization, and inducing competition among suppliers – that are crucial for corporate profitability. Moreover, the value chain approach is particularly relevant for developing country firms and countries that seek to capture dynamic gains from trade that come with industrial upgrading within and across value chains. Therefore, we also build on the work of Chang (2002, 2007) and others for whom industrial upgrading requires comparative advantage "defiance" (Reinert 2007; Kozul-Wright and Rayment 2008).

Firms and governments have sought precisely to defy comparative advantage and move into higher value added production and export. Hamilton and Feenstra (2006), for example, show that Taiwan's specialization in microwave oven production in the 1970s had little to do with natural endowments and comparative advantage, and all to do with industrial targeting and picking a niche market in the hope of its export potential. Lee (1995) identifies South Korea's movement into the production of higher value added production between the 1960s and 1980s, and attributes it to the emergence of "noncomparative advantage"-based trade. Amsden (1989) details the careful policies of the Korean government to subsidize

---

[14] We should note that the skills-based factor endowments trade model basically reaffirms the importance of skills-biased technological change. But that hypothesis has come under considerable criticism on empirical grounds of late, both because the timing in the story is at odds with the evidence (inequality began to rise before the IT revolution began) and because it has been found that a more important factor in the low-skill wage decline is the collapse of institutions, including unions and labor market regulations, that historically supported wage growth and protected employment. See Temin and Levy (2007) on the United States. Howell (2005) provides similar evidence for a set of industrialized countries. Paul Krugman (2008), an important participant in the trade versus technology debate over rising income inequality, has shifted his view to claim the primacy of politics as a cause of the distributional shift.

and target exports in return for export and productivity growth by Korean manufacturers. The key, Amsden argues, is "getting prices wrong" (Amsden 1989, 139), by which she means providing incentives that defy market-driven price signals in order to spur production, exports, upgrading, and employment.

Mexico's entry into hardware production was not triggered by any change in comparative advantage, but by a decision by American computer companies to invest in low-wage operations (Gallagher and Zarsky 2007). China's move into high-tech and green-tech manufactures and R&D has relied on careful government regulation of foreign capital, control of the exchange rate, and a wealth of subsidies and support for state-owned and private enterprises. These are just a few examples of comparative advantage defiance, especially important in the recent era when economic growth has been closely tied to export performance.

The importance of successful governance of GVCs by lead firms has been widely studied by sociologists, geographers, political scientists, and anthropologists interested in economic development. Whereas Gereffi (1994) distinguished GVCs by the nature of the lead firm, the research in most of these disciplines has focused on supplier firms in developing countries. With the shift by many developing countries from an import substitution to an export-led growth strategy and with the enormous expansion in the scope of value chains in international trade and global production, "upgrading" in such value chains has become synonymous with economic development. This has offered enormous opportunity for some countries to expand exports and move into the production of higher value added goods and services. China's manufacturing success and India's IT services boom are among the most visible examples. But the governance of many GVCs can result in an asymmetry of market structures through the chain, which can also pose obstacles for economic development. Whereas lead firms may campaign to be perceived as "socially responsible," GVCs are not governed for the purpose of generating economic development, but to expand lead firm shareholder value.

There are many studies of successful industrial upgrading. We suspect that the case study literature may suffer from a selection bias whereby researchers take up success stories rather than a random sample of value chains. Still the rapid growth of manufacturing exports from developing countries is an important feature of today's world economy. In Chapter 7, we propose a simple, operational framework for measuring upgrading in GVCs as captured by the relation between the growth in export market share and in export unit value. We find that successful industrial upgrading is not as common as the case study literature might lead us to believe. Moreover, we find that such industrial upgrading is not a guarantee of proportional "social upgrading," which we define by a growth in employment and wages.

1.2.3 Re-Embedding the Market

In this book, we propose an alternative account of globalization and inequality, which does not deny the importance of firm profitability and shareholder value, but which proposes corporate strategy and its institutional context as the driver in distinct contrast to approaches that take as their starting point the natural endowment of factors of production. We adopt a classical view of the social benefits of offshoring by focusing on profits and their use. The classicals viewed trade liberalization as beneficial because it allowed firms to lower input costs, raise profits, and thus to increase investment and economic growth. As Maneschi (1998) has shown with reference to famous writings on international trade by David Ricardo, the emphasis of the classical theory of international trade is not the efficiency gains that result from the playing out of the forces of comparative advantage, but the rise in profitability – and especially the subsequent investment, employment, and productivity growth – that expanded international trade can bring.

We thus resist modeling the corporate decision to offshore aspects of the production process as short-run profit maximization or even as transactions cost minimization, as is characteristic of much of theoretical research on offshoring. Instead, we locate the logic of offshoring in the broader context of corporate strategies and their evolution since the 1980s. Faced with continued product market competition and a growing sense of the need for immediate gains in stock price, managers of large lead firms have increasingly looked to cost control as a means to maintain cost markups. Firms pursued a strategy of "mass customization" of their product lines, while focusing effort on their "core competence" – typically related to design, marketing, and finance. They retreated from post–World War II human resource management practices of long-term, full-time employment with the provision of health insurance and pension benefits, and focused on reducing costs by hiring younger workers, with less tenure and fewer benefits. Executive compensation rose at the same time that average compensation levels of American workers stagnated relative to productivity growth. Offshoring has been an important part of the cost control strategy, raising cost markups and thus profit, and allowing firms to maintain flexibility and to keep product prices down. As Gomory (2009) writes,

> If you are the CEO of a major firm and can increase your profits by offshoring, why not do it? If you don't relocate some of your operations offshore and your competitors do – and increase their own profits in the process – you are unlikely to last (Gomory 2009, 1).

Lazonick and O'Sullivan (2000) describe this general shift in corporate strategy since the early 1980s as a shift from an emphasis on the retention of earnings and reinvestment of profits, to a focus on downsizing and distributing profits to shareholders. Aspects of this shift have long been recognized in the fields of finance, management, design, and industrial relations.[15]

An important feature of offshoring is that it both reduces costs and reduces the need to reinvest profits at home, leaving a greater share of profits for distribution to shareholders. The most important channel in the 2000s has been firms buying back their own stock – share buybacks – although the rise in dividend payments and cash-based mergers and acquisitions has also played a role. This is referred to as financialization. Offshoring provides one clue to solving the "puzzle" of the declining share of investment out of profits experienced in many industrialized countries and the delinking of stock prices movements from real, productive investment in firms' expansion and innovation.[16]

The success of offshoring as a business strategy is partly because of the ability of lead firms to govern the value chain. Lead firms in GVCs have succeeded in building international networks of production, using direct investment, joint ventures, and especially subcontracting. They have successfully stoked competition among suppliers so as to minimize input costs and raise flexibility in their supplier base. They have maintained oligopoly-type markups in product markets by sustaining their oligopsony position in the value chain. This asymmetry in market structure observed in many GVCs is endogenous to the competitive process in a world in which lead firms have governance power in global networks of firms. Firms diversify supplier relations because it gives flexibility and leverage.

---

[15] On the link to shareholder pressures, see Lazonick (2009) and Davis (2009). On mass customization, see Pine (1993). On core competence, see Prahalad and Hamel (1990). On shareholder value, see Jensen and Meckling (1976).

[16] On the "puzzle," see Van Treek (2008). On innovation and firm strategy in the recent crisis, see Shapiro and Milberg (2012).

One implication of an endogenous asymmetry of market structures in GVCs is a tendency toward more externalization of aspects of production rather than internalization through expansion of MNCs. In this view, the expansion of arm's-length or externalized supplier relations is less the result of declining transactions costs and more due to power asymmetries in GVCs. Transactions cost theorists have made the correct prediction in recent years – more externalization of buyer-supplier relations due to the increased efficiency of markets compared to hierarchies – but not necessarily for the correct reason.[17]

The analysis in this book supports the alternative account. We find that offshoring by U.S. firms has contributed to higher cost markups, higher profits, and a rise in the corporate profit share of income. We interpret this boost to the profit share (equivalent by definition to a fall in the labor share) as an indicator of higher economic insecurity that has been experienced in the United States and some other industrialized countries. In Chapter 5, our econometric analysis shows that between 1998 and 2006, offshoring in U.S. manufacturing and service sectors is associated with lower employment and labor share. By raising the profit share and at the same time reducing the domestic demand for investment, offshoring supported other aspects of corporate strategy, including a focus on core competence and a surge in the purchase of financial assets.

In this sense, the global macro imbalances that are often cited as a factor in the world economic crisis have their microfoundations in a rational corporate strategy that emphasizes offshoring and the development of global supply chains. U.S. imports are increasingly non-competitive – that is they do not compete with domestic producers but are integral to the business strategy of domestic firms. The imports have served to raise U.S. firms' profits and the profit share in the U.S. economy. Given our unconventional and interdisciplinary approach to globalization, we are careful throughout this book to use traditional methods and functional forms.

Is this newfound role of imports necessarily a bad thing for the U.S. economy? Our answer is no, based on the possibility of what we call "dynamic gains from trade." The gains from trade liberalization are traditionally understood to be the result of the combined gains from specialization and from exchange at world prices. Gains from task trade are distributed differently. When there are fewer competitive imports, and more "competitive

---

[17] For the transactions cost view of externalization trends, see Langlois (2003). This view has dominated recent efforts to model outsourcing, for example in Grossman and Helpman (2002, 2005) and Antràs (2005).

tasks," imports reduce firm costs, raising profit margins, while some labor and capital within the firm may be rendered obsolete. Thus, the static efficiency gains from trade liberalization accrue to profits and to those tasks not facing low-cost competition. Losses are incurred most by those performing mobile (including digitizable) tasks. Consumers gain from lower prices of goods and services. Another source of improved social welfare from offshoring is the capture of "dynamic gains," that are the result of extra demand for output and, therefore, for domestically-produced inputs and labor, due to lower-priced imported inputs. Dynamic gains accrue not for traditional efficiency reasons, but because of the extra business spending on domestic goods and services that the cost saving from offshoring spurs.

In sum, the gains from offshoring should not just be viewed in terms of their direct effect on real wages or employment but also on gains over a period of time, during which higher profits resulting from lower costs lead to private investment and growth in output, productivity, and employment. In this vein, we analyze the reinvestment of profits from offshoring, and find that financial investment represents a significant leakage from the potential dynamic gains from U.S. offshoring from the period 1998 to 2006. The collapse and then slow recovery of share prices since 2007 have in retrospect made the share buybacks the ultimate unproductive investment out of profits. If we measure the efficiency gains from trade in this way, then expanded international trade has been remarkably inefficient. Offshoring has supported the financialization process that has been part of the overall economic crisis, and this has reduced the dynamic gains from offshoring.

The financialization of the non-financial corporate sector has been a somewhat hidden dimension of the economic crisis of today, because so much of the focus has been on the financial sector itself. Studies of financialization tend to leave as implicit the link to production and investment. In addition, analysis of GVCs often leaves aside the financial implications. In Chapters 4 and 6 we argue that the globalization of production and financialization are fundamentally connected. Financialization has encouraged a restructuring of production, with firms narrowing their scope of operations strictly to an area of "core competence." The practice cuts across sectors of the economy. Cisco Systems adopted this strategy almost from its inception, relying almost exclusively on arm's-length contracts with foreign manufacturers. The Gap has found its niche in brand and fashion design and retail, and uses offshoring to perform all production and even most logistics activity. The rising ability of firms to disintegrate production vertically and internationally has allowed these firms to maintain cost markups – and thus profits and shareholder value – even in a context of slower economic growth. The point is not that globalized production triggered financialization, but that global production strategies have helped to sustain financialization.

The interdependence between the two processes will continue to grow in scale and scope, as services offshoring continues to expand very rapidly and as more countries participate in GVCs. In sum, corporate governance and GVC governance are linked. We conclude that the gains from offshoring would be much greater if the profits from offshoring were reinvested in productive activity rather than being used for the purchase of financial assets and the payment of dividends.

But this is not the end of the story. In analyzing the welfare implications of offshoring it is important to go beyond corporate strategy and to consider also the institutional context in which corporations function. We draw on the rich literature on "varieties of capitalism" to identify different regimes of labor market regulation among industrialized countries. In Chapter 5, we find that offshoring has a different effect on the labor market under different arrangements. In the developing world, our focus is on trade policies, especially the regulatory environment of EPZs and labor market practices with respect to gender segmentation. Both of these have had a great impact on GVCs and on international trade in general.

There is a broader issue at play here, which is the role of the firm in innovation. Similar to our critique of the traditional theory of trade, we propose that the traditional theory of the firm, which sees the firm as choosing inputs and production levels with given technology and factor prices in order to maximize profits, generally fails to capture the role of the firm in capitalist development. The firm is absolutely the place where profits and investment are made, but the firm is also the locus of product and process innovation. The firm does not take constraints as given, but typically makes great efforts and takes considerable risk in order to alter its cost structure. Such behavior is part of process innovation, but can also help overcome instability through product innovation and the development of the market.

Contrary to the textbook rendering, we argue that it is not some set of natural "market forces" that determines the allocation of capital across the economy, but the decisions by firms and the strategic and power dynamic in their production network (Lazonick 2009). International trade must be seen from this same perspective on the firm. The point is not just that competitive advantages are produced by firms in a particular environment of macroeconomics, regulation, culture, and nature. Firms allocate capital in markets that are embedded in this social context. Another implication is that factors of production themselves are in part the outcome of this embedded process.

1.2.4 An Interdisciplinary Account of Offshoring

One of the goals of this book is to connect the accounts from these different academic disciplines, combining the strengths of the economic and the sociological treatments of offshoring. Economics – in particular the classical and Post Keynesian traditions on which we draw – has a strong theory of market power, linking markup pricing to investment and financialization in a global context. Sociology, geography, and development studies research has brought the issues of corporate power, technology management, labor relations, and development policy to the center of the analysis. Political scientists have explored how varieties in the regulation of capitalist economies can affect trade patterns and the sharing of the gains from trade. We draw on each of these contributions. The advantage of this interdisciplinary approach is to place the economic analysis in a richer institutional context of corporate strategy and politics, and to infuse the sociological discourse on power and globalization with insights from the economic theory on trade, pricing, investment, and growth. The specific goal is to add some precision to the analysis of the sources and uses of lead firm profits and of the asymmetries in input markets that have important consequences for the inter- and intra-national distribution of value added.

This alternative, interdisciplinary account of offshoring leads to a different set of policy proposals than those found either in the traditional economics approach or in the GVC case study literature. The first policy goal is to raise the dynamic gains from offshoring in the lead firm home countries by promoting investment and discouraging financialization. This is a great challenge, and especially important as the U.S. economy recovers from the Great Recession of 2008 by leaning heavily on public spending instead of private investment. Firms are again profitable and building cash holdings rather than undertaking investment. The second proposal related to industrialized countries, especially the United States, has the goal of reducing the cost of job loss from offshoring and increasing corporate flexibility while minimizing the cost to households. This would require making health insurance and pensions fully portable across jobs and even to those without jobs.

The third policy proposal is the need to promote higher labor standards globally, by tying trade agreements to the enforcement of labor standards and by creating greater accountability for labor standards by lead firms in GVCs. The current governance structure of GVCs is something of an obstacle to this. Buyers sometimes even use arm's-length supplier relations to have plausible deniability about the labor conditions among suppliers. However, there are exceptions to this pattern, including the United States–Cambodia trade agreement, which has been somewhat successful in raising labor standards in the Cambodian apparel sector as exports have duty-free access to the world market.

What type of economic globalization do we want as we emerge from the "Great Recession" of the twenty-first century? The analysis in this book provides some basic principles. The first is the need to maximize dynamic gains from offshoring, by encouraging reinvestment of profits in both expansion and innovation. Financialization can be made less profitable, for example through regulation of share repurchases, especially when executive compensation is in stock options. The second principle is to promote firm flexibility by reducing workers' economic insecurity. Basic needs associated with economic security, such as health insurance, education, and retirement pensions, should be provided universally across all jobs and even to those without jobs. Contrary to popular belief, in the industrialized countries international competitiveness has generally not been adversely affected by more active social provision of economic protection.[18] Germany and Denmark, for example, have both retained high levels of public intervention in labor markets and at the same time have become export juggernauts. The third policy principle that emerges is to reduce asymmetries in power across the GVC. One way to begin to get at this issue is to include labor and environmental standards in trade agreements, to discourage a competitive race to the bottom in such standards and to encourage accountability for lead firms in GVCs.

For the most part economic research on globalization has been motivated by the desire to show that the social tensions created by the new wave of globalization are more imagined than real. Economists often aim to prove that offshoring generates efficiencies that lead to greater output globally, and that this offsets the relative wage declines for low-skill workers and any loss of jobs that results from substituting foreign for domestic labor in any one country. Thus, the economic analysis of offshoring typically begins with an assertion of the principle of comparative advantage and the mutual benefits of the resulting pattern of specialization. Offshoring is seen as a refinement of the international division of labor and thus as the source of

---

[18] See Milberg and Houston (2005). A similar finding, looking at a different set of variables related to labor rights and standards, has been made for the case of developing countries. See Kucera and Sarna (2004).

a welfare improvement for each nation and the world as a whole, in which the gains by high-skill workers are greater than the losses suffered by those with low-skill attainment.

By assuming away problems of unemployment, persistent trade imbalances, financialization, and economic development through upgrading in global networks of production, international trade economists have had difficulty explaining the key issues of globalization to non-economists and especially to the general public. Thomas Friedman, in the excerpt cited at the beginning of this chapter, describes himself as struggling to reconcile his experience in Bangalore with his understanding of the theory of international trade. The conflict is between his head, which supports a theory with which "the great majority of economists" agree (Friedman 2005, 227), and his heart, which tells him that the future for his children's generation is uncertain. Much economic analysis of offshoring has been done under the banner of "quelling public fears," but the reigning economic theory of offshoring has had little influence on public attitudes. Therefore, the skepticism of commentators such as Lou Dobbs holds sway.

The public debate has been most informed by non-economists – including sociologists, geographers, and industrial relations experts – who have emphasized the shift in corporate strategy and industrial relations that are associated with the new wave of globalization, and by journalists who have actively debated the role of public policy in reducing economic insecurity that arises from globalized production. Because economists have generally not matched their rigorous models with an equally rigorous appeal for a redistribution of the gains from offshoring, their credibility in public debate has been further compromised.

Thus, the title of this book has a double meaning, referring both to our presentation of an alternative and institutionally-grounded economics of offshoring, and at the same time to the fact that the task of analyzing offshoring and debating its policy implications has been "outsourced" from the economics profession and put into the hands of sociologists, geographers, historians, journalists, and others who better articulate this institutional context and its welfare implications. The failure of this branch of economics is but one example of the general weakness of the profession to explain the causes of the Great Recession of the twenty-first century.

Macroeconomists touted the efficiency and beneficence of financial deregulation and the insistence on the stability and existence of a (dynamic and stochastic) general equilibrium indicated that economic downturn could only occur as a result of some exogenous shock, not from endogenous tendencies. Microeconomics continued to teach that perfect competition was the benchmark form of market organization, despite the evidence of a deep connection between states and markets in all successful moments of capitalism.

The field of economics risks losing its relevance when it is unable to depict globalization as people live and experience it. New explanations of globalization open up the range of policy responses to move debate beyond questions of free trade versus protectionism. Rather than seek to quell public fears by promoting hermetically sealed models of pure and efficient market systems, economists should seek to describe the economic world in which the public lives.

TWO

The New Wave of Globalization

The international trade and investment environment has changed since the mid-1980s, reflecting political, economic, and technological shifts. These shifts have encouraged more international trade and foreign direct investment (FDI), altered the structure of trade, and changed the relation between trade and FDI, the effect of trade on income distribution, and the role of foreign demand in economic development. Trade has occurred increasingly through sophisticated global value chains (GVCs), as more and more companies in industrialized countries have looked offshore to perform both manufacturing and services, and to focus at home on core competencies related to marketing, finance, research and development (R&D), and design. These companies now rely more on imported inputs of goods and services, and increasingly on low-income countries.

These changes in the globalization of production have come gradually over the past twenty-five years. Global networks of production have a cumulative and herd-like character: As firms have success in expanding their networks globally, they expand them even more. This is accelerated by the development of networking capacity globally. As one firm in an industry has success, others have tended to follow, with modular production facility in developing countries allowing contract supply simultaneously to many firms in an industry and even to firms in different industries.

GVCs – also referred to as global supply chains, global commodity chains, and global production networks (GPNs) – may be as simple as the relation between a U.S. firm such as Ford Motors and its wholly-owned subsidiary producing engines in Mexico. These international production networks may also be highly complex in terms of geography, technology, and the variety of types of firms involved – from large retailers to highly mechanized large-scale manufacturers to small, even home-based, production. Apple's iPod, for example, involves 451 parts produced in multiple countries, which are then

33

assembled in another country and shipped for sale worldwide. The GVC may involve such a variety of intra-firm and interfirm linkages that it is impossible even to identify all the countries that are involved or the extent of their involvement.

The complexity of slicing up the value chain can make the measurement of the size and scope of these chains with traditional economic data difficult. But it should not veil the extent of offshoring. At the extreme are "fabless" manufacturers, companies that sell manufactured goods but do no manufacturing themselves. This is the case of retailers, of course, and they have become an important force in GVCs. Wal-Mart alone accounted for 9.3 percent of U.S. imports from China between 2001 and 2006, some $26 billion of imports in 2006 alone (Scott 2007).

Many firms that previously were involved in manufacturing are now purchasing finished goods for sale as their own brand. These firms, ranging across sectors from clothing (The Gap) to toys (Mattel), electronics and computers (Apple, Dell, or Japan's Toshiba) to servers (Cisco Systems), even to semiconductors (Xilinx), have chosen to focus on their core competence, which generally includes design, marketing, and finance (Perrow 2008). In these cases, almost all manufacturing is done abroad and mostly through arm's-length contracts.

Consider more closely the case of the Apple iPod. A 2007 study (Linden et al. 2007) finds that the 30 GB video iPod made by Apple Computer contained hundreds of components, the most expensive of which are the following:

- A hard drive made by the Japanese company Toshiba ($73.39). Toshiba (which no longer does any manufacturing of its own) offshores its hard drive production to companies in the Philippines and China.
- A display module ($20.39) by Toshiba-Matsushita produced in Japan.
- A multimedia processor chip ($8.36) made by the U.S. company Broadcom, which offshores most of its production to Taiwan.
- A central processing unit ($4.94) produced by the U.S. company PortalPlayer.
- Final insertion, test, and assembly, done in China by Taiwanese-owned company Inventec, valued at $3.70.

Apple earns a profit of $80 per unit, after overseeing distribution and retail costs of $75. About $21 of the $299, which is the retail price of a new iPod, could not be accounted for even in this highly detailed study.

The iPod example shows not only the complexity of GVCs, but also that it is the design and branding of a product that often bring the lion's share of the value added. Apple had only about 60,000 employees in the United States in 2012, whereas its subcontractors abroad employed approximately 700,000 workers. Foxconn, the Taiwanese-owned, China-based contract manufacturer that does the iPhone assembly employs around 1.2 million Chinese workers (not all of its contracts are with Apple), more than 230,000 at the iPhone assembly plant Foxconn City alone. Apple employees in the United States have an average annual profit per employee of about $400,000, whereas many workers at Foxconn earned less than $400 per month in 2012 (Duhigg and Bradsher 2012; Barboza and Duhigg 2012).

The Apple example is extreme in the complexity of the technology, the organization of the supply chain, and in terms of the level of value added per employee in the United States relative to China. Globalized production – both of goods and services – is common to many sectors of today's economy, but in many sectors this is not a new development. In some areas, globalized production has existed for centuries and been recognized for decades by social scientists and historians.[1] Traditionally they involved the purchase of commodity inputs by manufacturing firms in industrialized (or industrializing) countries.

Offshoring has for years been part of U.S. business strategy in manufacturing, aimed at lowering costs by controlling commodity supply conditions. Even in the retail sector, offshoring has a long tradition, dating back to the purchase in the early 1960s of electronics products from Japan, South Korea, and Taiwan (see Hamilton 2006 on U.S. retail offshoring in the 1960s). But there has been a leap in the past twenty-five years in the degree of internationalization of production and the scope of offshore transactions. We call this period the "new wave" of globalization.

The new wave of globalization is hard to capture precisely with standard trade statistics. Therefore, in the next section, we present a variety of ways to measure offshoring and the international "disintegration" of production. The picture that emerges is of a growing phenomenon that has reached large proportions, shows no signs of reversing itself, and thus must be taken into consideration in any analysis of the world economy. Feenstra (1998) and Krugman (1995) noted that the global disintegration of production was occurring while a massive global integration of markets (trade liberalization) was taking place, but not until the essays by Grossman and Rossi-Hansberg (2006a, 2006b, 2008) on the welfare effects of offshoring was there broad acknowledgment by economists of the extraordinary nature

---

[1] See Wallerstein (2011[1974]) and Hopkins and Wallerstein (1977) on the notion of global production from a world systems perspective. From economics, Hawtrey (1913) discusses the importance of a global network of production for U.K. companies.

Table 2.1. *Elasticity of Trade to World Income, 1960–2000s*

1960s	1970s	1980s	1990s	2000s
1.77	1.94	2.75	3.36	3.69

Source: Own illustration. Data: Freund (2009).

of trade within GVCs – what the authors call "trade in tasks" rather than traditional trade in final goods. Similarly, Baldwin (2006, 2012) describes a new phase of international trade corresponding to the "unbundling" of production and its coordination globally.

The new wave of globalization is attributed with raising both world trade volumes and the income elasticities of imports and exports over the past few decades. The income elasticity of trade has risen steadily each decade since the 1960s (see Table 2.1), although these estimates do not capture the extreme swings in trade volume – both down and up – that occurred in the crisis and slow recovery since 2008. The rise in the income elasticities of trade are not the result of a rise in trade openness *per se*, but from the rising sensitivity of trade to changes in gross domestic product (GDP).[2]

Perhaps more important than the problem of error when measuring the magnitude of globalization is that the standard trade statistics can be misleading, especially when the focus is on bilateral trade relations such as between the United States and China. The Chinese surplus with the United States also includes value imported by China from elsewhere. Another Apple case study, this time of the iPhone, makes the point clearly (Xing and Detert 2010). Apple imports the iPhone from Foxconn in China for $179 and sells it for $600 in the U.S. retail market. In 2007, China ran a $1.9 billion trade surplus with the United States in iPhones. The cost of assembly in China of all iPhones shipped to the United States was $73.5 million. U.S.-made parts that were included in the Chinese assembly process were valued at $121.5 million. Thus, in value terms, the Chinese actually ran a trade *deficit* with the United States in iPhones ($73.5 − $121.5 = −$48 million), despite the official statistics showing China's $1.9 billion surplus in iPhone trade with the United States.

Standard trade statistics can be misleading, not only quantitatively, but also qualitatively. The implication of the Chinese iPhone surplus is that China specializes in and exports high-tech products. Closer analysis of China's reliance on a regional network of production shows that in fact China's involvement is largely in low-skill intensive assembly

[2] We show this in detail in Milberg and Winkler (2010a).

operations. China *imports* the higher-tech components. Note also that Apple's profit margin on iPhones was 55 percent, and thus an enormous share of the total value added in iPhones comes from design and brand marketing.

In the following section, we provide a number of offshoring measures to give a sense of the magnitude and the changes in the degree of offshoring over the past twenty years. We define offshoring as all purchases of intermediate inputs from abroad, whether done through arm's-length contract (offshore outsourcing) or within the confines of a single multinational corporation (intra-firm trade). We provide an update of the traditional measure of offshoring intensity and, given the limitations of this measure, we also propose some alternative indicators.

We then turn to an analysis of the drivers of this trend, emphasizing the role of governance strategies of lead firms. We conclude this chapter by assessing the effect of the global crisis on a world trading system organized in GVCs. We discuss the dramatic decline and recovery of world trade in the recent economic crisis. Just as the formation of GVCs brought a rapid increase in world trade since the 1980s, so was the decline and subsequent recovery in world trade disproportionately large in relation to GDP declines. This sets the stage for the discussion of international trade theory and the GVC-based alternative in Chapters 3 and 4.

2.1 Measures of Offshoring

2.1.1 The Changing Nature of Trade in Intermediates

The simplest measure of the extent of offshoring is the share of intermediate goods in total trade. Using a simulation model, Yi (2003) calculates that expansion of "the sequential, vertical trading chain stretching across many countries, with each country specializing in particular stages of a good's production sequence" (Yi 2003, 53), accounted for more than 50 percent in the growth of U.S. trade in the period from 1962 to 1997.

The United Nations (UN) Comtrade data break out trade according to consumption goods, capital goods, and intermediates (see Appendix 2.1 for a definition of broad economic categories [BEC]). Imports of intermediate goods have accounted for around 50 percent of world trade since the early 1990s (see Figure 2.1). Although the level is high and indicative of a highly globalized world production system, the constant share is surprising in light of the attention on MNCs and their offshoring activity. Miroudot et al. (2009) conclude from these data that globalization has resulted in similar growth in both final and intermediate goods, and

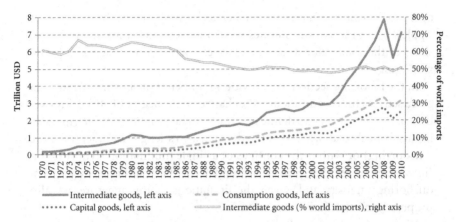

Figure 2.1. World Imports by Broad Economic Categories, 1970–2010. *Source*: Own illustration. Data: UN Comtrade.

they see a plateau of the share of intermediates trade as a result of limits to the extent that firms can benefit from remote and disintegrated production. Sturgeon and Memedovic (2011) attribute the constancy of the intermediates share as a measurement problem, noting that "the BEC categories are too highly aggregated to provide clear evidence of trends in GVCs" (Sturgeon and Memedovic 2011, 10). We agree that the constancy of intermediates in world trade veils some important details. We briefly discuss four.

First, the share of generic (commodity-type products) in intermediates has fallen as more specialized intermediates goods trade has risen. The rise of regional and global supply chains in electronics products, especially computers and mobile phones, is important in this respect, but so too is the increase in international trade in auto parts, aircraft parts, business and professional services, apparel and footwear, vegetables, fruits and flowers, and so on. In fact, there are very few products and services for which production has not become international.

Second, the share of intermediates trade in manufacturing and services from developing countries as a share of total trade in manufactured intermediates has increased significantly during the past twenty-five years to 35 percent in 2006, up from 26 percent in 1992, while the industrialized countries' share fell from 72 percent to 63 percent over the same period (Sturgeon and Memedovic 2011). Today, China is the third largest exporter globally of manufactured intermediates, accounting for 8.5 percent of the world total in 2006. Taiwan and Hong Kong account for 3.9 and 2.6 percent each, with other developing countries contributing significantly, including

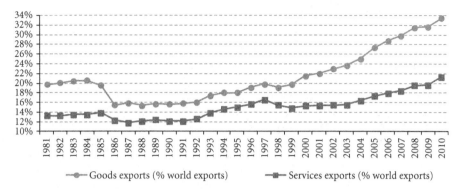

Figure 2.2. Low- and Middle-Income Country Exports (% World Exports), 1981–2010. *Source*: Own illustration. Data: World Development Indicators, World Bank.

Mexico (2.4 percent), Malaysia (1.7 percent), Thailand (1.3 percent), India (1.2 percent), Brazil (1.0 percent), and Turkey (0.9 percent).

Developing country export success over the past thirty years in both goods and services has created a greater reliance on export revenue in aggregate demand. Their dramatic export success is evident in Figure 2.2, which shows that since the early 1980s, the share of low- and middle-income countries (LMICs) in world exports of goods and services rose almost steadily. The goods export share rose from 16 percent in 1986 to 33 percent in 2010, whereas the services export share grew from 13 to 21 percent in 2010. This shift in world trade patterns also means that developing countries are much more reliant on export revenues for final demand. On average, LMICs became steadily more export-oriented, with exports of goods and services as a share of GDP growing to 28 percent in 2010, compared to less than 10 percent in 1970.

China's enormous success is well known; its export reliance went from around 3 percent of GDP in 1970 to almost 43 percent in 2007, falling back to 30 percent in 2010. China accounts for 12 percent of imports by Organisation of Economic Co-operation and Development (OECD) countries, but the increased export orientation was also dramatic in Argentina, India, Mexico, and South Korea, among others (Figure 2.3).

Developing country export success has been driven by the simultaneous expansion of GVCs and the enhanced production capability of many countries. Chapter 7 takes this up in detail, yet here we note simply that it hinged in part on the expansion of export processing zones (EPZs) where MNCs and their management of process trade have played a significant role, the entry

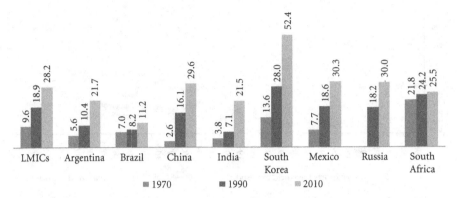

Figure 2.3. Exports of Goods and Services (% of GDP), Selected Countries and Years. *Source:* Own illustration. Data: World Development Indicators, World Bank.

of women into the labor force and the ability to keep wages low, a broad-based increase in education and training, R&D that raised product standards to international levels in many instances, and effective exchange rate management.

Third, the Comtrade data by BEC do not show the increased reliance on imports by exporting firms, a clear indication of the globalization of production and the expansion of global networks of production. Economists have defined this as "vertical specialization," known as the import content of exports.[3] The international networks of production that grew so rapidly in the 1990s and 2000s often brought about considerable growth in imports in the same countries and industries that saw a growing reliance on exports. Hummels et al. (1998) were the first to define this import content of exports as vertical specialization, and they find that a large share of world trade in recent decades was the result of increased vertical specialization. Koopman et al. (2010) calculate the degree of vertical specialization in manufactures exports by country for 2000 and 2009. They find that industrialized countries have vertical specialization levels of around 80 percent, with the United States at 75 percent. By comparison, the level of vertical specialization in China in 2004 was 63 percent, Mexico was 51 percent, and Singapore was 36 percent (Koopman et al. 2010). Meng et al. (2011) find that between 1995 and 2005 vertical specialization increased in forty-two of the forty-five countries they studied. This picture is confirmed by the firm-level trade data for the United States, which shows that the most successful exporting

[3] See Jiang and Milberg (2012) for the input-output algorithm and an analysis of economic development in relation to changes in the import content of exports.

firms are also the same firms that do the most importing (Bernard et al. 2007). High levels of vertical specialization, that is, a higher import content of exports, imply that increased export value generates proportionally less domestic value added. The flip side of this, of course, is that export growth is increasingly a function of success within GVCs.

When there is no trade in intermediate goods, the value of a country's exports reflects only domestic value added. When exports rely on previously imported inputs, then a given dollar of exports contains less domestic value added. Therefore, with high levels of vertical specialization in a sector, a label indicating a single country of origin can be very deceptive. Bilateral and sector-specific trade balances can also be deceptive, because trade statistics assign the full value of the good or service to the country that exports the final product. It is clearly misleading, for example, to ascribe comparative advantage to a country based on the composition of its final goods and services trade, because its intermediates trade may account for much of the value added or use of a particular factor of production (Baldone et al. 2007; Xing and Detert 2010). The case studies of China's exports of Apple consumer electronics products previously discussed give a dramatic picture of the phenomenon. Of the Chinese unit value of iPod exports to the United States of $150, China's value added (in the final assembly) was about $5. In the case of the iPhone, China's exports to the United States in 2009 were $2 billion, and China's value added was $73.5 million or 3.6 percent.[4] The issue has become a focus of concern for the agencies responsible for trade data, including the OECD and the World Trade Organization (WTO), who fear that policy is misguided if it fails to consider value added in trade. Using value added trade would reduce the U.S.–China bilateral trade balance by almost half.[5]

Finally, despite the globalization of production and thus the growth in importance of MNCs, the share of intermediates trade that occurs in the form of arm's-length transactions (as opposed to intra-firm trade that occurs within divisions of a MNC) has not declined and may have increased. The United States collects the most comprehensive data on intra-firm trade between the United States and its trading partners. Because of the visibility of MNCs, we tend to assume that most trade in intermediates takes place on an intra-firm basis. In fact, as a share of U.S. goods imports, related party

---

[4] On the iPod, see Linden et al. (2007); on the iPhone, see Xing and Detert (2010); and on the iPad, see Linden et al. (2011).

[5] For an overview of the literature on vertical specialization and the measurement methodology, see OECD (2013). On the WTO's "Made in the World" initiative, see http://www.wto.org/english/res_e/statis_e/miwi_e/miwi_e.htm.

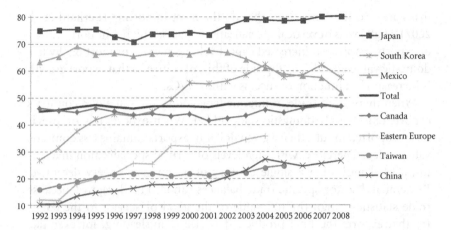

Figure 2.4. Related Party Goods Imports (% of Total Bilateral Goods Imports), United States, 1992–2008. *Source*: Own illustration. Data: U.S. Department of Commerce, Related Party Trade, several issues, 2004–2008.

goods imports (defined as imports between firms where one has at least 5 percent ownership interest in the other) are relatively constant, which implies that arm's-length goods imports are also constant as a share of the (growing) total of U.S. goods imports, as shown in Figure 2.4. Related party goods imports from China have grown steadily as a share of U.S. goods imports from China, but still remain well below the U.S. average.

The United Nations Conference on Trade and Development (UNCTAD) (2011) points to the increased use of external supplier relations due to the rise of "non-equity modes" of internationalized production. This development is further reason to analyze the governance structure of GVCs and its implications for the distribution of the value added across firms and workers within the chain. It is also a reason to question whether the trend is being driven entirely by falling transactions costs and, by implication if we need an explicit theory of the externalization rather than viewing it as simply the outcome that occurs when a firm does *not* internalize production.

2.1.2 Trade and Broader Measures of Offshoring

To get a broader sense of the extent and growth of offshoring by industrialized countries, we compare the United States, United Kingdom, Japan, Germany, France, and Denmark. Although offshoring began to pick up in the 1980s, we begin our analysis in 1991 in order to have comprehensive data for Germany. All six countries increased their trade openness over the

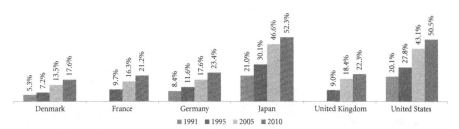

Figure 2.5. Goods Offshoring Intensity, Selected Countries and Years. *Source*: Own illustration. Data: UN Comtrade. Measure: manufacturing imports from low- and middle-income countries as percentage of total manufacturing imports.

period, defined as exports plus imports as share of GDP, although the level of trade openness in the United States and Japan is much lower than among the Europeans, due in part to high levels of intra-European trade. Nonetheless, we show that the United States and Japan have the highest offshoring intensities of the group.

Before looking at the standard input-output measure of sectoral offshoring intensity, which captures only intermediate materials and services, we first consider a broader measure of goods offshoring that also includes final goods shipments, but looks only at imports from LMICs. The definition of LMICs is based on the classification according to the World Bank.[6] Figure 2.5 shows manufacturing imports from LMICs as a share of total manufacturing imports for six countries.[7] All countries have seen more than a doubling of the share of their imported manufacturing goods coming from LMICs since 1991. Japan and the United States now rely heavily on manufacturing imports from LMICs (52 and 50 percent, respectively), whereas the European countries are at much lower levels, ranging from 21 to 23 percent in the United Kingdom, France, and Germany, and reaching only 18 percent in Denmark.

Because comparable services import data by source country are not available for this time period, we cannot derive a measure of services offshoring such as the one for goods offshoring. Instead, we look at each country's import share of tradable business services, namely 'computer and information services,' 'communication services,' 'financial services,' and 'other

---

[6] The World Bank income classification is based on 2008 gross national income per capita. LMICs include low-income = $975 or less; lower-middle-income = $976 to $3,855; and upper-middle-income = $3,856 to $11,905 countries. Appendix 7.1 shows the classification of a sample of thirty developing countries.

[7] Manufacturing imports comprise imports to sectors 15 to 36 at the two-digit International Standard Industrial Classification Rev. 3 level.

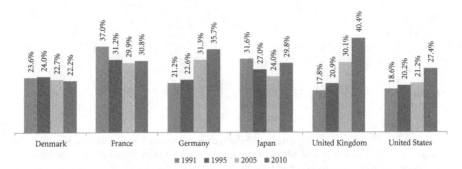

Figure 2.6. Services Offshoring Intensity, Selected Countries and Years. *Source:* Own illustration. Data: UNCTAD Handbook of Statistics. Measure: imports of tradable business services ('computer and information services,' 'communication services,' 'financial services,' and 'other business services') as percentage of total services imports.

business services' in total services imports. Only one and a half decades ago, many of these services categories were considered non-tradable, but the emergence and development of new information and communication technologies has made them internationally tradable.

In Figure 2.6, we see that Denmark saw a small decline in services offshoring intensities between 1991 and 2010 to around 22 percent. France and Japan saw their shares fall between 1991 and 2005, but show higher services offshoring intensities in 2010 of around 30 percent. In 2010, the other countries experienced increases in their services offshoring intensities, reaching 40 percent in the United Kingdom, 36 percent in Germany, and 27 percent in the United States. Milberg and Winkler (2010b) confirm the mixed results for a broader sample of twenty-two OECD countries. Between 1991 and 2006, services offshoring intensities increased in roughly two-thirds of countries, but declined in the others.

2.1.3 U.S. Aggregate Offshoring Intensities

The conventional economics measure of offshoring intensity is based on input-output tables. U.S. input-output tables do not differentiate between domestically produced inputs and imported inputs, so we apply the methodology of Feenstra and Hanson (1996) to calculate the proportion of imported inputs in total non-energy inputs as follows:

$$OSJ_{ijt} = \left[\frac{J_{ijt}}{J_{it}}\right] \left[\frac{IM_{jt}}{Y_{jt} + IM_{jt} - EX_{jt}}\right] \tag{2.1}$$

where J_{ijt} denotes purchases of intermediate non-energy input j by sector i, J_{it} total non-energy inputs used by sector i, IM_{jt} imports of j, EX_{jt} exports of j, Y_{jt} production, and t the time dimension.

The first bracket on the right-hand side of equation (2.1) is the share of the purchased input j in total non-energy inputs for sector i at time t. The data are based on symmetric input-output data and cover thirty-five sectors, including twenty-one manufacturing sectors and fourteen service sectors (see Figures 2.10 and 2.11 for the sector coverage).[8]

Because the first ratio in equation (2.1) does not distinguish between domestically and foreign purchased inputs, it is multiplied by the share of imports of that input in total domestic consumption (the second bracket). Due to a lack of U.S. data on each sector's imported inputs, this import penetration ratio is assumed to be the same across all sectors i using input j. In other words, the economy-wide use of an input relative to total domestic consumption of that input is assumed to be the ratio of import use of that input in all sectors that use that input.[9]

We calculated import shares based on import, export, and output data from the input-output tables, which were available for 30 inputs. We computed import shares for the five remaining inputs (construction; broadcasting and telecommunications; securities, commodity contracts, and investments; funds, trusts, and other financial vehicles; and management of companies and enterprises) based on trade data from UNCTAD and output data from the OECD.

The offshoring intensity for sector i at time t is calculated by taking the sum of all the imported inputs j:

$$OSJ_{it} = \sum_j OSJ_{ijt} \qquad (2.2)$$

---

[8] The data are obtained from the U.S. Bureau of Economic Analysis (Annual I/O Accounts, The Use of Commodities by Industries after Redefinitions). We combined available data for 1998–2006 (downloaded on October 14, 2008) with data for 2007–2010 (downloaded on August 30, 2012).

[9] This "proportionality assumption," as it has been called by the OECD, may introduce a bias in the measurement of offshoring. Because the German Federal Statistical Office publishes a full matrix of imported inputs, we used the German data to test if there is a significant difference in using the direct measure versus the measure based on the proportionality assumption. We calculated both measures for Germany over the period from 1995 to 2006 and estimated the impact on labor demand in German manufacturing with each measure. We found that the proxy measure based on the proportionality assumption is not or in some cases even positively related with labor demand whereas the measure that uses sectoral import data is negatively related with labor demand. See Winkler and Milberg (2012a) for a full discussion.

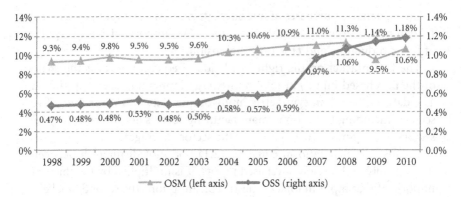

Figure 2.7. Average Offshoring Intensities in the Manufacturing and Service Sector, United States, 1998–2010. *Source*: Own illustration. Data: U.S. Bureau of Economic Analysis. Measure: imported material (OSM) and service (OSS) inputs as percentage of total non-energy inputs as defined in equations (2.1) and (2.3).

The average offshoring intensity at time t across all sectors and inputs is obtained by aggregating the respective OSJ_{it}, weighted by total non-energy inputs:

$$OSJ_t = \sum_i OSJ_{it} * (J_{it}/J_t) \qquad (2.3)$$

where $J_t = \sum_i J_{it}$ is the sum total of non-energy inputs.[10]

We can also sum just the imports of materials or services. Figure 2.7 shows the average materials and services offshoring intensities across all thirty-five manufacturing and service sectors for the United States. Average materials offshoring intensities (OSM) in the United States grew from 9.3 percent in 1998 to 11.3 percent in 2008, dropped to 9.5 percent in 2009, but reached 10.6 percent again in 2010. The compound annual growth rate was 2 percent between 1998 and 2008. The average services offshoring intensities (OSS) in the manufacturing and service sectors grew at an average annual growth rate of 2.8 percent between 1998 and 2006 from 0.47 to 0.59 percent. According to the new input-output tables, services offshoring grew at an annualized growth rate of 6.8 percent between 2007 and 2010, from 0.97 to 1.18 percent.

---

[10] This is the definition first used by Feenstra and Hanson (1996). Amiti and Wei (2005, 2006, 2009) use sectoral outputs as weights. Using total non-energy inputs instead of output results in a more accurate overall offshoring intensity, as it directly refers to the denominator of the offshoring measure.

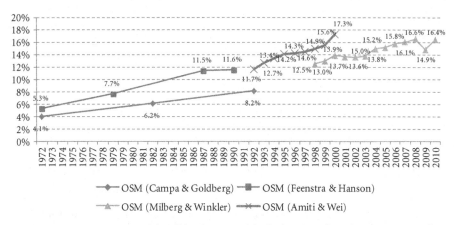

—◆— OSM (Campa & Goldberg)   —■— OSM (Feenstra & Hanson)

—▲— OSM (Milberg & Winkler)   —✕— OSM (Amiti & Wei)

Figure 2.8. Average Materials Offshoring Intensities in the Manufacturing Sector, United States, 1972–2010. *Source*: Own illustration. Data: Based on Feenstra and Hanson (1996), Campa and Goldberg (1997), Amiti and Wei (2009), and own calculations using U.S. Bureau of Economic Analysis data. Measure: imported material inputs as percentage of total non-energy inputs as defined in equations (2.1) and (2.3).

Average materials offshoring intensity in manufacturing alone reached 16.4 percent in 2010, up from 12.5 percent in 1998, 6.2 percent in 1984, and 4.1 percent in 1974[11] (see Figure 2.8). Average services offshoring intensity in manufacturing alone increased strongly between 1998 and 2010 with an intensity of 0.43 percent in 1998, 0.48 percent in 2006 and 0.78 in 2010 (see Figure 2.9). In the service sector alone, the services offshoring intensity increased from 0.56 percent in 1998 to 0.75 in 2006 to 1.69 percent in 2010.

2.1.4 U.S. Sectoral Offshoring Intensities

Figures 2.10 and 2.11 show materials and services offshoring intensities for each of the thirty-five sectors for the United States in 1998, 2006, and 2010. Sectoral materials offshoring intensities grew in all twenty-one manufacturing sectors and in ten out of fourteen service sectors, reaching levels of more than 25 percent in some sectors, including apparel and motor vehicles. Services offshoring intensities showed positive growth rates in twenty manufacturing and in thirteen service sectors.

---

[11] The 1974 and 1984 figures are from Campa and Goldberg (1997). The data in Figure 2.8 indicate that the rate of growth of offshoring has slowed slightly since the 1990s. Amiti and Wei (2009) report materials offshoring growth of 4.4 percent per annum and services offshoring growth of 6.3 percent per annum from 1992 to 2000. Burke et al. (2004) show higher levels of offshoring intensity (not shown in Figure 2.8) because they use total material inputs in the denominator while we use total non-energy inputs (which also includes service inputs).

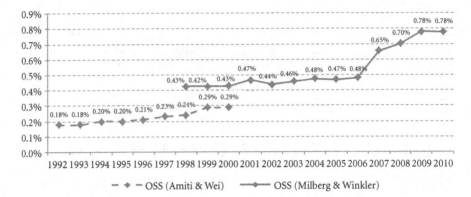

Figure 2.9. Average Services Offshoring Intensities in the Manufacturing Sector, United States, 1992–2010. *Source:* Own illustration. Data: Based on Amiti and Wei (2009) and own calculations using U.S. Bureau of Economic Analysis data. Measure: imported service inputs as percentage of total non-energy inputs as defined in equations (2.1) and (2.3).

2.2 Drivers of the New Wave of Globalization

The new wave of globalized production has involved not just a quantitative change but also a qualitative shift in the nature of international trade, from a world of trade in commodities and finished goods to one in which international exchange increasingly involves what Grossman and Rossi-Hansberg (2006a, 60) describe as "trading in specific tasks," made possible by technological progress in transportation and communication which has "weakened the link between specialization and geographic concentration" (Grossman and Rossi-Hansberg 2006a, 64). Levy (2005) writes that offshoring "decouples the linkages between economic value creation and geographic location" (Levy 2005, 685). Blinder (2006) refers to the likely future expansion of services offshoring as ushering in a "Third Industrial Revolution." In sum, offshoring has altered the traditional link between international trade and value added and between production and profit.[12] Because of the growing import share of exports, there is less domestic value added per unit of exports than previously. And because offshoring has become such an integral part of business strategy, imports (of intermediates) now play an important role in firm profitability.

---

[12] See also Serfati (2008) for a "new paradigm" in international economics to account for the importance of GPNs.

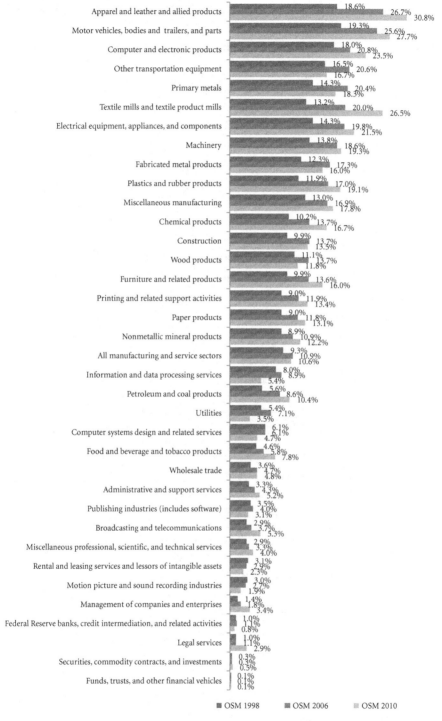

Figure 2.10. Sectoral Materials Offshoring Intensities, United States, 1998, 2006, and 2010, Ranked by 2006 Intensity. *Source*: Own illustration. Data: U.S. Bureau of Economic Analysis. Measure: imported material inputs as percentage of total non-energy inputs as defined in equations (2.1) and (2.2).

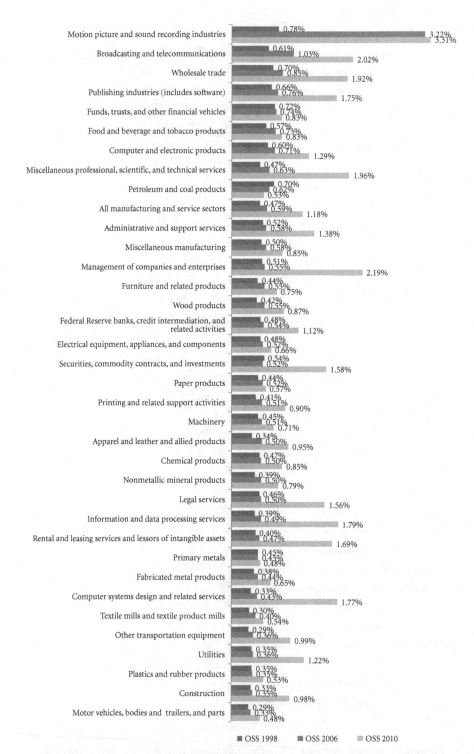

Figure 2.11. Sectoral Services Offshoring Intensities, United States, 1998, 2006, and 2010, Ranked by 2006 Intensity. *Source:* Own illustration. Data: U.S. Bureau of Economic Analysis. Measure: imported service inputs as percentage of total non-energy inputs as defined in equations (2.1) and (2.2).

What is behind the new wave of globalization? The explosion of lead firms investing abroad or subcontracting with foreign producers in search of cost reductions, more flexibility, or to better serve local markets, has no doubt been given an important boost by advances in communication, in particular with the integration of computers into mass production, including product design, management of supply chain logistics, monitoring of inventory, sales, and distribution, as well as payroll, finance, and accounting. These innovations have reduced the cost of coordinating operations internationally, and have allowed an increasingly sophisticated slicing up of the value chain, with very specific tasks performed in one location (such as marketing phone calls) whereas other aspects of production are performed elsewhere. Digitization of design, communications, logistics, and data management is just one aspect of the technological impetus for offshoring.

Politics and business strategy also have played important roles. Politically, perhaps the most significant development of this period was the entry into the capitalist world economy by former-Communist and other largely closed economies. The collapse of the Soviet Union and of communist governments throughout Eastern Europe and East Asia, the capitalist turn of communist China's economic plan, and even the opening and liberalization of India's economy have all served to expand global productive capacity, international trade, foreign investment, and international subcontracting.

Freeman (2007) has characterized these developments as "the great doubling" of the world capitalist system's labor force, as it had added 1.3 billion people to the existing pool of labor globally of about the same size, all seeking work under market-based systems. Freeman argues that by itself such a labor supply expansion is enough to radically alter trade relations and to dampen wage growth in the rest of the world, including the industrialized countries. When such a labor supply "shock" occurs in a period of slower demand growth compared, say, to the "Golden Age" period of relatively rapid global economic growth between 1950 and 1973 (see Chapter 5 for some indicators in both periods), the effect on labor markets around the world is likely to be significant. Moreover, as tax revenues generally rise with growth in national income, the macro environment in a period of more rapid growth also provides the fiscal space for greater government support for unemployment insurance and retraining.

Another dimension of the "great doubling" phenomenon is the extraordinary increase in the supply of skilled labor in the developing countries. The total number of knowledge professionals in the Indian information technology (IT) sector grew from around 56,000 in 1990 to 1991 to almost

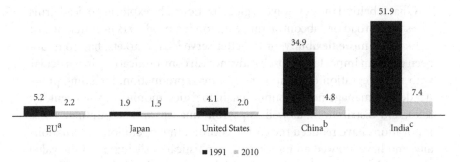

Figure 2.12. Import Tariff Rates on Non-Agricultural and Non-Fuel Products, 1991 versus 2010 (Weighted Average of Effectively Applied Rates). *Source*: Own illustration, Data: UNCTAD GlobStat Database. [a]Tariffs refer to all EU members during respective year. [b]Data for China available for 1992. [c]Data for India available for 1992 and 2009.

1.3 million in 2005 to 2008 (NASSCOM). Gereffi et al. (2008) estimate that the annual number of graduates with an engineering, computer science, or IT bachelor in India was nearly 220,000 in 2005 to 2006, compared to 129,000 in the United States. In China, the number of engineering and technology bachelors awarded reached 575,000 in 2005 to 2006 compared to roughly 150,000 in 1995 to 1996. In 2005 to 2006, the number of masters in these subjects was 82,000 in China, 60,000 in India (this combines the Master's of Computer Applications and technical engineering master degrees), and 50,000 in the United States. China is also leading in terms of the number of technical Doctors of Philosophy (PhDs) with 12,000 PhD degrees in 2005 to 2006, compared to 8,900 PhD degrees in the United States, but less than 1,000 degrees in India (India figure based on 2003 to 2004).

A second, and related, political development affecting the volume and direction of international trade and investment is the reorientation of the developing world to export-based growth strategies in the 1980s, following the debt crisis and the end of import substitution industrialization (ISI) strategies. The shift is embodied in the subsequent wave of trade agreements, covering more countries than ever in history, which have reduced tariff and non-tariff barriers and have provided protection for foreign investors. The WTO has quintupled its membership over the original General Agreement on Tariffs and Trade, hundreds of bilateral investment treaties have been signed, and numerous regional trade agreements have gone into effect. Figure 2.12 gives a general picture of tariff reductions outside agriculture since 1991. Industrialized countries had already largely liberalized. During this period, developing countries aggressively seeking export expansion – India and China in Figure 2.12 – shifted from highly protectionist to essentially liberal trading regimes.

As part of this broad liberalization process, the developing world embraced policies promoting export growth in the context of a growing network of international production. The expanded use of EPZs reflects countries' efforts to integrate into these supply chains. EPZs have expanded in scope and number (and continue to expand today), offering foreign firms long tax holidays on corporate profits, considerable subsidy of infrastructure needs, and unrestricted profit repatriation. According to Milberg (2007), the number of countries using EPZs increased to 130 in 2006, up from 116 in 2002 and 25 in 1975.[13]

The combination of technology and politics which made possible the new wave of globalization would not have been adequate without the business impetus. Offshoring is first and foremost a business strategy, and it is not a new business practice. Raw materials imports – from iron ore to cotton – spurred the industrialization in England in the eighteenth and nineteenth centuries. In fact, even the present-day version of retail firm offshoring of consumer goods production dates back at least fifty years.[14] But in the last twenty-five years offshoring has become an integral part of a broad business strategy shift from the large-scale multidivisional firm to one with increasing flexibility in terms of products and markets, an increasing focus on "core competence," and a growing concern for shareholder value in the short-run.

Export-oriented industrialization (EOI) strategies first implemented in the 1980s and 1990s were compatible with the logic of expanding buyer-led and producer-led GVCs. An important reason for lead firms to establish GPNs in the first place is the flexibility they provide. GVCs allow adjustment to changes in market demand to occur quickly and enable the risk of demand declines and inventory adjustment to be borne to a greater extent by supplier firms. Innovations in lean retailing, fast fashion, just-in-time inventory management control, and full-package offshoring have all been the product of lead firm value chain governance strategies. Suppliers too

---

[13] See Chapter 7 for a discussion of the expansion of EPZs in the 2000s and its implication for upgrading in GVCs.

[14] See Hamilton (2006) on East Asian sales of light consumer goods to U.S. retailers in the 1960s.

have developed in a way that seeks to manage the environment of flexibility-seeking lead firms. Modular production processes give supplier firms the capacity to simultaneously serve different product lines and even different GVCs (Sturgeon 2002).

This transition has been described by experts in a variety of fields, from management (the shift to "core competence") to product development (the move to "mass customization") to finance (the "shareholder value revolution") to industrial relations ("flexible specialization") to labor markets (the rise of part-time and temporary jobs with fewer health and pension benefits).[15] Each of these captures a different aspect of the phenomenon that Lazonick (2009) describes as a transition from the "old economy business model" to the "new economy business model." The shift has been different in the apparel sector than in the IT sector, and different in finance and insurance than in motor vehicles, for example, but offshoring has played an important role in corporate strategy across almost all sectors of the economy as the combination of technological change, political change, and global capacities has placed offshoring at the heart of business strategy.

2.3 Trade Crisis and Recovery

The prominence of GVCs has also been connected to the large swings in international trade volumes that occurred as part of the economic downturn that began in 2008. A trade collapse has potentially devastating effects on export-oriented developing countries. The decline in U.S. goods imports in the fourth quarter of 2008 and the first two quarters of 2009 was greater than the decline in U.S. GDP, and the drop in the ratio of imports to GDP over that period represented by far the greatest three quarter decline in imports, both absolutely and relative to GDP, since 1980 at least. The European Union has undergone a similar, if less dramatic, import decline. A similar pattern was observed on a global scale as well. Ominously, the drop in trade in the 2008 to 2009 crisis was found to be even more rapid than the decline in world trade at the beginning of the Great Depression in 1929 (Eichengreen and O'Rourke 2009).

GVCs may be key to understanding this historic swing in world trade. There is no doubt that the globalization of production has raised the ratio

---

[15] On core competence, see Prahalad and Hamel (1990); on mass customization, see Pine (1993) and Blecker and Friedrich (2010); on shareholder value, see Jensen and Meckling (1976); and on flexible specialization see Piore and Sabel (1984).

of global imports and exports per unit of output over time. For example, Freund (2009) writes that

an increase in GDP may lead to more outsourcing and much more measured trade, as an increasing number of parts travel around the globe to be assembled, and again to their final consumer (Freund 2009, 6).

Greater vertical specialization means that the import content of exports has risen, and thus as final goods and services exports and imports grow, so do exports and imports of intermediates. The process works in both directions: With vertical specialization, a decline in final demand reduces trade in both final and intermediate goods and services. Ferrantino and Larsen (2009) note the connection between U.S. imports and exports, writing that, "the drop in U.S. imports for computers and cell phones leads indirectly to a drop in U.S. exports of semiconductors and components" (Ferrantino and Larsen 2009, 177).

In a study of the recent export decline in Japan, Fukao and Yuan (2009) find that adding to the decline in U.S. demand for Japanese final goods is the decline in demand for intermediate goods intended for assembly in East Asia for shipment to the United States. Note that this does not mean there is more value added in international trade, but simply that there is more trade per unit of output and likelihood of a greater change in the volume of trade for a given change in real output. There is also some double counting of value added in GVC-based trade, as the value of imported inputs is included in the value of exports. Chen et al. (2005) find that double counting of value in trade figures occurs more in manufactures than in services. For the United States in 2000, adjusted exports would be $198 billion, or 9 percentage points less than reported in the 2000 trade figures.

The rise in the income elasticities of trade are not the result of a rise in trade openness *per se* but from the rising sensitivity of trade to changes in GDP. GVCs may be key here: Adding to the speed of adjustment in trade in a downturn is the fact that firms might make use of accumulated inventories first (Freund 2009; Baldwin 2009). In a world of disintegrated production and lean retailing, the 2008 to 2009 GDP downturn resulted not only in larger declines in trade than had occurred previously but also declines that were more rapid. The trade collapse was "synchronized" across countries, which Baldwin (2009) also attributes to the internationalization of the supply chain. GVCs are a channel for the rapid transmission of both real and financial shocks. Shifts in demand for final goods can immediately affect flows of intermediates, especially when supplier contracts are short-term.

Credit market problems can also cascade throughout the chain. For example, a denial of credit to importers in one country can reduce access to credit for sellers in others, thus affecting their ability to import (Escaith and Gonguet 2009). This is a vicious cycle between the real and the financial sides of the economy (see also analyses by Amiti and Weinstein 2009; Mora and Powers 2009). In fact, one factor driving the volatility of trade in the recent downturn was the freezing up of lines of credit for undertaking international trade transactions, also known as trade finance. Moreover, a bottleneck resulting from lack of credit in one part of the chain can reduce trade for the entire chain. As described by the International Chamber of Commerce (ICC):

Supply chains have produced undesirable side effects. Exporters in international supply chains are better shielded from financial turmoil because they have access to credit from buyers. However, with their own access to finance drying up, global buyers will become more restrictive in providing finance along their supply chains (ICC 2009, 4).

There are offsetting factors in this scenario of volatile trade: Lead firms with declining profits will seek drastic means to cut costs and thus may substitute cheaper foreign inputs for domestic inputs (substitution effect). This substitution from domestic to foreign production will have a positive effect on trade flows of intermediates. For example, there are reports, that with the burst of the dot-com bubble in 2001, IT firms faced a profit squeeze and turned increasingly to offshore sourcing for both hardware and software (reported in Friedman 2005). Scott (2009) notes that an important part of U.S. auto companies' adjustment to their current unprofitable position is likely to be a significant increase in offshoring, especially from Mexico. Sturgeon and Van Biesebroeck (2010) identify the likelihood of such a substitution effect by lead firms in the automobile sector in the United States and Western Europe (sourcing in Mexico and Eastern and Central Europe, respectively) if market shares continue to decline. The large declines in the volume of trade seen in the recent crisis indicate clearly that the effect of the high income elasticity of demand was not particularly altered by the substitution effect.

We have described the magnitude and main drivers of the long-term pattern of globalized production over the past twenty-five years. But we have said little about how the theory of international trade can be used to analyze these trends and their implications for social welfare. This is the task of Chapters 3 and 4. Many of the long-term patterns related to the globalization of production broke down during the crisis of 2008 to 2009. But as the world economy slowly began to recover, so did the volume of trade, the GPNs and the business practices that have been associated with that. With the slow growth in the United States and the European Union and uninterrupted high growth in China, India and Brazil, new trends also emerged, including a greater reliance on domestic and emerging market demand, an intensification of the regionalization of value chains, expansion in the size and scope of some first-tier suppliers and logistics firms, and a turn to a new version of industrial policy in which GVC presence is an accepted part of the landscape of economic development. In Chapter 8 we refer to this as the era of "vertically-specialized industrialization," in contrast to both ISI and EOI. The industrial policies emerging in this post-Washington Consensus era are not a return to the import substitution policies of the 1960s and 1970s, but are a new form that recognizes the new elements in play, including new end markets, new products (consumer electronics, internet services and other business services, engineering services) with new skills requirements and knowledge bases, and new sources of credit and aid. This configuration of old and new facets of globalization is further reason to rethink the theoretical foundations of our understanding of global production and international trade.

APPENDIX 2.1 CLASSIFICATION OF SECTORS BY BROAD ECONOMIC CATEGORIES

The broad economic categories classification, as defined by the UN, comprises nineteen basic categories that are assigned to the final use of the good, namely capital good, consumption good, and intermediate good (see Table 2.2). Two categories (motor spirit, passenger motor cars, and goods n.e.s. [not elsewhere specified]) are not assigned to these categories. The authors suggest classifying motor spirit as intermediate goods and passenger motor cars as consumption goods, whereas the assignment of goods that are not specified elsewhere cannot be done.

Table 2.2. *Classification of Sectors by Broad Economic Categories*

Broad economic category		Final use
1	Food and beverages	
11	Primary	
111	Mainly for industry	Intermediate goods
112	Mainly for household consumption	Consumption goods
12	Processed	
121	Mainly for industry	Intermediate goods
122	Mainly for household consumption	Consumption goods
2	Industrial supplies (n.e.s)	
21	Primary	Intermediate goods
22	Processed	Intermediate goods
3	Fuels and lubricants	
31	Primary	Intermediate goods
32	Processed	
321	Motor spirit	Intermediate and consumption goods
322	Other	Intermediate goods
4	Capital goods (exc. transp. equip.)	
41	Capital goods (exc. transp. equip.)	Capital goods
42	Parts and accessories	Intermediate goods
5	Transport equipment	
51	Passenger motor cars	Intermediate and consumption goods
52	Other	
521	Industrial	Capital goods
522	Non-industrial	Consumption goods
53	Parts and accessories	Intermediate goods
6	Consumer goods (n.e.s.)	
61	Durable	Consumption goods
62	Semi-durable	Consumption goods
63	Non-durable	Consumption goods
7	Goods not elsewhere specified	Intermediate, consumption, and capital goods

Source: Own illustration. Based on UN "Classification by Broad Economic Categories," 2002.

THREE

What Role for Comparative Advantage?

3.1 Introduction

The relatively recent recognition of the importance of global value chains (GVCs) for the organization of production and international trade means that they are only now being integrated into the theory of international trade. Grossman and Rossi-Hansberg (2006a, 2006b, 2008) assert that the new wave of globalization requires a new theory of trade, because trade in intermediate goods and services – what the authors refer to as "trade in tasks" – is of a different nature than trade in final goods. Referring to Ricardo's famous example, Grossman and Rossi-Hansberg write that "it's not wine for cloth anymore." In this chapter, we show that the structure and governance of GVCs call for quite a different account of international trade – with a change in the traditional thinking on the determinants of trade as well as a different connection between trade and growth and between trade and economic development – than that offered in the traditional theory.

The economics of GVCs has not been fully developed within the theory of international trade. Economists analyzing offshoring, with a few exceptions, have emphasized the traditional gains from trade, focusing on static efficiency effects of offshoring and assuming full employment and balanced trade in a trade model driven by relative factor endowments or different technologies. The welfare analysis based on Pareto optimality has presumed that adjustment costs for factors displaced by offshoring are insignificant and that potential compensation of losers by the winners is adequate to establish the economic case for offshoring. Regarding lead firm behavior in GVCs, transactions costs theory has placed great emphasis on the costs of contracting with suppliers as the determinant of the decision to "make" or "buy" inputs.

In this chapter and Chapter 4, we argue that both the GVC governance strategies and the outcomes they produce are much more varied than the static factor endowments theory and transactions cost approach would imply. The outcomes are tied more broadly to institutional arrangements and power structures than to a single objective function that can be solved via optimization theory. The institutions that are the focus of our analysis are: (i) the firms and their strategies for allocating resources, innovating and actively seeking to alter their cost structures through arrangements with their domestic and foreign suppliers and workforce; (ii) the structure and regulatory framework of labor and capital markets, including the strictness of hiring and firing regulation, active labor market policies, the segmentation of labor markets and the regulation of finance; and, (iii) government policies related to trade and investment, ranging from quotas and tariffs, to the tax treatment of corporate profits, to exchange rate management, to the support of export processing zones (EPZs) to the developmental policies of governments seeking to promote upgrading within GVCs. All of these, and other, institutions have molded the form and effects of the globalization of production.

For purposes of understanding the welfare implications of offshoring, we argue for a shift in focus from static efficiency gains (resulting from specialization and from exchange) to the question of the sources and uses of profits for firm investment, employment demand, and innovation. This focus on *dynamic gains* from offshoring follows the classical economists more than the neoclassicals in seeing higher profits and profitability from offshoring as key to the expansion of investment and the rate of economic growth.[1] Regarding developing country supplier firm behavior in GVCs, trade theory is largely silent on the movement away from specialization rooted in relative factor endowments and technological differences. In practice, we observe enormous effort, and some success, by firms and governments to upgrade operations within and across GVCs, in defiance of the natural endowment driven comparative advantage pattern of specialization. We also observe the great difficulty of upgrading given problems of a fallacy of composition in globalized production and an asymmetry of power relations within GVCs.

The important issues in both of these lacunae of traditional trade theory – gains from profit reinvestment and upgrading within GVCs – are captured

---

[1] From the perspective of structuralist macroeconomics, the approach assumes a profit-led rather than a wage-led growth regime (Taylor 2004). If investment is driven by an accelerator effect and by the rate of capacity utilization, then growth will presumably be wage-led. The U.S. economy is traditionally viewed as profit-led, but structures are of course subject to change. Nastepaad and Storm (2006/2007) find that the United States and a number of European countries are now wage-led. For a recent review of the evidence, see Stockhammer and Onaran (2012).

in the dynamic effects of trade. For lead firms, offshoring can raise markups and profit margins, leading to higher retained earnings, and an increase in expenditure on productive and financial assets. For supplier firms, the goal of industrial upgrading in GVCs is now practically synonymous with economic development itself. Although international trade is at the heart of the process of industrial upgrading, the theory of international trade gives few insights into the process and provides only a mechanical view of how industrial upgrading translates into broader social outcomes. The silence of the traditional theories of trade on these dynamic aspects of firm behavior means that economics has had little to say about the relation between trade and investment, or even between trade and economic development.

The return to comparative advantage models of trade has reinforced the static analysis of international economics, and its criterion of welfare assessment has led to numerous conceptual difficulties, historical conundrums, and ethical dilemmas regarding the role of international trade and trade policy in capitalist development. As a result, both the analysis and the policy debate of these crucial economic issues has been "outsourced" to economic sociology, geography, political science, management, and development studies. A broader, institutionally-richer perspective has been offered by many from outside the discipline of economics. In this chapter and the next, our goal is to bring some of these insights to bear on the economics of offshoring. At the same time, we bring the more sociological aspects of GVC analysis in contact with economic theory. Our hope is that the combination will move the discussion of globalization forward in a useful way.

A number of economists have recently pointed in the direction of the thinking presented here. Chang (2002, 2007) and Lin and Chang (2009) show how the "defiance" of comparative advantage pursued by developing country firms and governments have historically been a necessity for economic development. According to Reinert (2007), mainstream trade theory neglects the possibility that specialization according to relative efficiency leaves many countries producing low value added goods or those with slow-growing markets. He argues that the static gains from trade are small in comparison to the possible dynamic gains from scale and learning.

Ricardo's theory is often interpreted as "proving" the optimality of free trade. Reinert argues that this ignores that such an optimal specialization pattern of global trade will leave some countries specializing in dynamic sectors that have a high growth potential and are eligible for value enhancing technological improvement. Others would be left with goods that do not have these properties, condemning these countries to poverty and stagnation, because the sectors in which they specialize are not prone to productivity growth and do not provide the basis for spillovers to other, new, high-productivity and high-growth sectors. As Reinert puts it, Ricardian trade theory "creates the possibility for a nation to achieve a 'comparative advantage' in being poor and ignorant" (Reinert 2007, 26). Those able to capture scale economies and to benefit from learning and "synergy effects," such as cumulative forces that are greater than the sum of their parts and that can produce structural change, will see great productivity and market gains.

Even Joseph Stiglitz, in his more recent writings, avoids the terminology of static factor endowments theory and refers to "long-run dynamic competitiveness" (Stiglitz and Charlton 2010). Some interpretation may be useful here: "Long-run" refers to the goal of specializing in sectors that are not necessarily associated with today's pattern of comparative advantage. "Dynamic" refers to the transition this requires into higher value added and higher growth lines of production. "Competitiveness" is an alternative to "comparative advantage" and its use points to the limitations of the concept of comparative advantage as an outcome from both a positive and normative perspective.

Two distinct issues are at play. One is the questioning of the principle of comparative advantage, and in particular the role of relative factor endowments, as the determinant of the direction of trade and of the welfare effects of trade liberalization. The second issue is the relegation of static efficiency considerations to subsidiary importance compared to the dynamic aspects of international trade that play a role in firm expansion, capital accumulation, and economic growth. In Section 3.2, we focus on the issue of comparative advantage and its application to the issue of offshoring. We characterize the limitations of the model in three ways: conceptual, historical, and ethical. In the process, we present a variety of alternative trade models that provide the basis for an institutionally-grounded analysis of offshoring that we develop in Chapter 4, which shifts the focus to the dynamic gains from international trade.

3.2 The Fall and Revival of Comparative Advantage

Despite the popular view that comparative advantage is the great constant in the knowledge of economists, for the past thirty years there has been considerable debate over the role that comparative advantage plays in determining the direction of international trade and its effect on welfare. There has even been a Nobel Prize in economics awarded – to Paul Krugman in 2008 – for the development of non-comparative advantage models of international trade.

But the principle of comparative advantage made a comeback in the 1990s. Pushed to the side in the 1980s by the New International Economics (NIE) pioneered by Krugman, which rooted trade in increasing returns to scale, imperfect competition, and strategic behavior by firms and states, the principle of comparative advantage returned to the center of some key debates in economic policy. In this section, we review the "fall and revival" of the principle of comparative advantage in economic thought and its application to the issue of offshoring.

3.2.1 The Fall of Comparative Advantage

The NIE emerged in part out of a concern for the lack of realism of the Heckscher-Ohlin (H-O) model of trade. The H-O model had been criticized from early on with Leontief's famous "paradoxical" finding that U.S. imports were relatively capital-intensive and U.S. exports were relatively labor-intensive, contrary to the most basic prediction of the H-O model. The assumptions of perfect competition and constant returns to scale were considered unrealistic.[2] But the NIE also arose as an effort to explain the large volume of intra-industry trade and the apparent success of a number of government policies aimed at export promotion, especially in Japan and South Korea but also the other Asian "Tigers" such as Taiwan and Singapore, that subsidized and protected domestic industry.[3]

Krugman's (1979) two-country, one factor model of intra-industry trade, for example, allows for imperfect competition with increasing returns to scale in the production of each variety of a particular good. He assumes a very particular utility function in which utility rises with more variety and which gives a demand pattern whereby consumers in each country spend half their income on each country's varieties. The model generates some very unorthodox results, most importantly that countries with similar factor endowments engage in international trade and that this trade is of the intra-industry sort, as profit-maximizing firms in an industry located in different countries specialize in different varieties of the same product

---

[2] It is not easy to explain the staying power of the H-O model in light of these empirical studies. The best attempt is by De Marchi (1976), who used Lakatosian criteria to argue that the H-O model, despite its empirical refutation, remained theoretically "progressive" in the sense that it continued to lead to new hypotheses.

[3] The NIE was part of a broader shift across fields in economics. See Milberg (2009a).

category. Because consumer utility rises with more choice of variety, import demand arises from the demand for variety. The presence of scale economies along with the possibility of producing a new variety at no additional fixed cost gives the intra-industry trade result. No rational firm would produce a full range of varieties of a product if that would lead to fewer scale economies.

Krugman's (1979) model is just one of the many varieties of models that emerged as part of the abandonment of the H-O lens. The NIE constitutes a fundamental break from the H-O tradition, in particular from the latter's emphasis on comparative advantage as a determinant of the direction of trade and the unambiguous welfare effects of trade liberalization. Writing about the early development of the NIE, Krugman (1983) notes that,

> the alternatives include the "product cycle" view... the arguments of many observers that much trade among industrial countries is based on scale economies rather than comparative advantage; and the common argument that a protected home market can promote exports... The situation of significant scale economies combined with weak comparative advantage is precisely that of trade in manufactured goods among industrialized countries (Krugman 1983, 43, 45).

The NIE models have a lot of attractive features, because they seem more realistic than the H-O model. Increasing returns to scale, product differentiation, strategic trade policy, including research and development (R&D) subsidies, are all arguably important features of world trade conditions today. Some of the NIE models allow for the possibility of zero-sum outcomes from trade policy changes, which is a recognition that trade policy intervention can benefit some countries while hurting others. These interventions (and those that generate a positive sum of welfare gains) indicate that an activist state can raise national welfare.

3.2.2 The New International Economics Backlash

This last point – the welfare-enhancing role of government intervention in the international trade of advanced capitalist countries – is perhaps the most radical aspect of the NIE, and certainly plays a role in its demise and the reemergence of the H-O model of comparative advantage in academic research. Simply put, the policy implications of the NIE were unacceptable to most economists, who have a long tradition of consensus on the issue of free trade. The NIE gave predictions that violated economists' longstanding support for free trade and that were thus considered by many in the profession with much skepticism. Grossman (1986) warned of the limited applicability of the NIE models. Baldwin (1992) wondered if the new trade theory really required a new trade policy position.

The NIE theorists themselves struggled with their own discovery. Economists found their models predicting one thing – the possibility of welfare-enhancing state intervention – and their vision dictating something else – the optimality of free trade. The conflict created some irreconcilable differences for some trade economists, in particular by two of its leading lights, Elhanan Helpman and Paul Krugman. In a review of their 1989 book that encapsulated the NIE research to that point, Robert Lucas (1990) writes:

> Throughout *Trade Policy and Market Structure*, Helpman and Krugman exhibit what strikes a reader as extreme discomfort with the policy implications of the new trade theory. At one point they even protest that "this book is about theory and methods, and not about policy," (p. 8) as though someone else had chosen the title of the book! The clearest statement of the source of the discomfort comes in the concluding chapter. "Is the case for free trade, so long a central tenet, now invalidated? Despite what we have said about the effects of trade policy we do not think so," (p. 185) . . . Helpman and Krugman seem not so much to be defending the validity of what they are calling the "central economic tenet" of free trade as trying to avoid the blame for being the first to expose its emptiness (Lucas 1990, 666)!

A second problem with the NIE models was the new set of assumptions, in distinct contrast to the H-O tradition that the NIE models replaced, leading to a lack of robustness. Consider the utility function that dominated theory in the NIE, the so-called Dixit-Stiglitz utility function:

$$U = \left(\sum_{i=0}^{N} q_i^{\sigma} \right)^{1/\sigma} , \quad 0 < \sigma < 1$$

where U is utility, q_i is consumption of variety i and σ is a parameter reflecting the elasticity of substitution, that is, the consumer's willingness to substitute one good for another.

The standard general equilibrium utility function is a general relation between utility and commodity consumption, whereas the new function assumes imperfect competition and multiple varieties of a good with equal cross-price elasticities for all varieties of goods. Krugman acknowledges that the functional forms were selected because they generated the desired result, not because of their "realism." The NIE constitutes an internally generated crack in the grand metanarrative in economics, that the general equilibrium (with all agents' preferences satisfied at market clearing and given prices) exists, is unique, stable, and Pareto optimal. Even the concern with Pareto optimality is often abandoned – too difficult to prove under the new assumptions – in favor of a "representative agent," whose utility became the focus of welfare assessment. The results are certainly more varied, contingent, explosive, and path dependent than those produced in the era of competitive general equilibrium. The NIE shifts the focus away from competitive general equilibrium and toward the provision of a rational choice foundation to otherwise *ad hoc* hypotheses. Heilbroner and Milberg (1996) describe the changes in this period as an "inward turn." The goal appeared to be to explain in rational choice terms a variety of casually observed phenomena. Such an explanation is important mainly to render these phenomena logical in the eyes of other economists.[4]

While these new sets of assumptions are typically identified as the chief characteristics of the NIE, methodologically speaking the important shift is the move away from the strict hypothetico-deductivism of general equilibrium analysis and toward a vaguely construed inductivism. The NIE does not involve an abandonment of rational choice mathematical modeling, but nonetheless constitutes the beginning of a reversal of causality between observation and hypothesis, which is to say a shift in the accepted conventions for producing economic knowledge. In the NIE, theories are often derived in a way so as to give a particular result or they are constructed in a way that leads to instability or path dependence. Results are not only not unique – multiple equilibria are now the norm rather than the exception – they are not robust; that is, the results are highly sensitive to the choice of assumptions, parameter values, and functional forms.[5]

A little-notice but significant aspect of the move from H-O to NIE is the abandonment of the criterion for assessing the progress of knowledge. In the era of competitive general equilibrium analysis, as previously noted, an economic model is understood to generate new knowledge if it provides a proof of a known result, but requires weaker, that is more general, assumptions than do existing proofs of that same result. The great strength of this methodology is the clarity of its criterion for establishing the progress of knowledge – increased mathematical generality, or robustness, of its proofs.

---

[4] In a telling anecdote, Warsh (2006) reports that when Krugman discussed his New Economics insights related to economic geography with a "noneconomist friend" the reply was "Isn't that all kind of obvious?" (Warsh 2006, 318).

[5] The lack of robustness was identified early on in the development of this paradigm, and was used to downplay the significance of its policy implications. See, for example, Grossman (1986).

In the era of NIE, robustness is inadvertently abandoned as a methodological principle.[6]

Most importantly, the result of this unstable theoretical position of the NIE is an appeal among international economists to move back to the basics of comparative advantage. Krugman writes that "the essential things to teach students are still the insights of Hume and Ricardo" (Krugman 1993, 26), that is the basic notions that comparative advantage determines the direction of trade and that trade imbalances will generate price or exchange rate changes that will lead automatically to balanced trade.[7]

Before describing the revival of comparative advantage, we have to point out that the NIE has been experiencing a revival itself, since Melitz (2003) introduced the "New New Trade Theory" with the interesting innovation of heterogeneous firms, who have different levels of (marginal labor) productivity and thus different degrees of export competitiveness including firms that do not export at all. Like the NIE models, Melitz also assumes increasing returns to scale. Firms also face potentially significant barriers to entry ("fixed market entry costs") and thus can only establish themselves in the market if they are sufficiently productive (in autarky).

Firms only become exporters if they are sufficiently productive (and profitable) to overcome "fixed entry costs to exporting" (which are different from market entry costs) and some variable costs – two additional assumptions of the Melitz model. In this context, trade liberalization makes it more difficult for less-productive firms to survive, as the productivity threshold for domestic firms increases due to additional competition with foreign exporters. Because these entry costs are fixed (by assumption), firms who lose market share because of trade-induced competition at home can still be compensated by gaining market shares abroad. With the prospect of higher profits, new firms enter the market, putting further pressure on less-productive firms. Moreover, real wages may increase as both exporters and new firms require more workers, further damaging the least productive firms. Trade thus leads to a reallocation of overall market shares, where the most productive firms gain and the least productive firms lose, increasing aggregate productivity. Unlike in most NIE models with product

---

[6] This issue is discussed more fully in Milberg (2004a, 2009b).

[7] The central debate between Paul Krugman and those using Krugman's and other trade models to justify trade protection took place in the journal *Foreign Affairs*. See Krugman (1994).

differentiation, in Melitz (2003) welfare increases also when the variety of products remains constant or declines.

3.2.3 The Revival of Comparative Advantage

The demise of the NIE and the revival of comparative advantage thus resulted from a variety of factors. The discomfort with policy conclusions that ran up against traditional free trade views certainly played a role. However, so did the models' lack of robustness, which gave a sense that with the new methodology any results could be shown with "rigorous" micro-foundations. A third factor also loomed large, which is that the old trade model seemed, once again, directly relevant to some broad-based developments in the world economy. In particular, the model was consistent with the apparent correlation between rising exports from low-wage countries to industrialized countries and the increase in income inequality in these industrialized countries, and especially in the United States.

Adrian Wood (1994, 1995) and others revived the factor endowments model and put the Stolper-Samuelson theorem front and center in the lively debate among economists over the importance of technological change versus globalization in accounting for the rising wage inequality between high-skill and low-skill workers observed in many developed countries, most notably the United States. Wood argues that the H-O model fails empirical testing because it is misspecified. Because capital is internationally mobile (and thus should tend to earn a similar rate of return globally), capital cannot be the basis for comparative advantage. It is skills, or knowledge – embodied in humans – that determines the pattern of international trade.[8]

In his book, *North-South Trade, Employment and Inequality: Changing Fortunes in a Skill-Driven World*, Wood (1994) uses factor content analysis to show that shifts in world trade patterns increasingly involved high-skill labor-intensive exports from the industrialized countries and low-skill labor-intensive goods and services from the developing countries. In Wood (1995), he explicitly respecifies the H-O model to reflect the North-South situation. Instead of considering the two-factor model to be about capital and labor, Wood defines the two factors as "skilled labor" and "unskilled labor," and reinterprets all the classic postulates of the theory accordingly.

---

[8] Wood (1995) argues that capital intensity is a positive function of the wage and that countries with more high-skill labor and thus higher wages will also be those with relatively greater capital intensity.

Under the new interpretation, the Stolper-Samuelson theorem predicts that trade liberalization would lead to a rise in the wage of high-skill workers relative to that of the low-skill workers in skill-abundant industrialized countries – precisely what was being observed.

Wood's (1994) book triggered a major debate among economists as to whether trade liberalization or technological change accounted for the observed rise in U.S. wage inequality. Although prominent economists could be found on both sides of the debate, the important thing for the future of the theory of international trade is that the terrain for the debate is essentially the old two-good, two-country, two-factor H-O model and not one of the models from the NIE. As income inequality worsened in the industrialized countries in the 1980s and into the 1990s, the traditional theory of comparative advantage – what should now be referred to as the Heckscher-Ohlin-Wood (H-O-W) model – appears to provide a clear and simple explanation.

Labor economists had identified the heightened inequality as a function of skills attainment: wages of high-skill workers were rising relative to those of the low-skill. They typically attributed this phenomenon to the skill-bias of technological change, in particular the introduction of computers. Although it was difficult to measure skills attainment, and it was hard to precisely identify the dates when new computer technologies were introduced, the skills-biased labor demand explanation for rising wage inequality gained appeal among economists.

By reinterpreting the H-O trade model, international trade economists were able to also attribute some of the rising wage inequality to trade liberalization, because the Stolper-Samuelson theorem implies that trade liberalization will improve the relative position of the abundant factor. In an H-O world of two factors (high-skill and low-skill labor) trade liberalization would benefit high-skill workers in countries abundant in high-skill labor. Thus, a debate ensued over the relative contributions of trade and technological change to the observed rise in income inequality in the United States and elsewhere.

Wood finds that "trade is the main cause of the problems of unskilled workers" (Wood 1995, 57). He identifies the main force as the increasing specialization of the industrialized countries in capital-intensive manufactures, whereas the developing countries increasingly specialize in the production of labor-intensive goods. Wood estimates that 75 percent of the increased wage inequality in the United States between 1980 and 1994 was due to trade. Others argue that because the relative appreciation of human capital is observed more strongly within than between industries, skills-biased technological progress is the main driver. As the research on trade versus technology advanced, it became more difficult to assess the relative effects of the two. For one, there is disagreement over the timing of the techno-logical change story (Gordon and Dew-Becker 2006). By some accounts, inequality began to rise well before much new technology was integrated in production. During the late 1990s, inequality actually fell when the infor-mation technology boom was strongest. For another thing, it also became clear that trade and technological change are connected, and increasingly so as global supply chains developed. Already in 1995, Adrian Wood would write:

the pace and direction of technical change may be influenced by trade . . . So, how-ever one looks at it, trade and new technology are intertwined: no story that excludes one or the other of them is likely to be the whole story (Wood 1995, 62).

Recognition of the importance of offshoring led again to a focus on international trade. Feenstra and Hanson (1996, 1999, 2001) followed this up with a series of studies applying the H-O-W model to the case of off-shoring. In their summary paper on the issue, Feenstra and Hanson (2001) find that offshoring accounts for 15 to 24 percent of the rise in the "non-production wage share" (that is, the share of wages going to higher-skilled workers), whereas computer services and other high-tech capital accounts for between 8 and 31 percent of the shift to nonproduction labor. The range was a function of different specifications of the model estimated. The authors write:

The argument against trade is based, in part, on a misreading of the data. Stable trade to GDP [gross domestic product] ratios, an apparent increase in the relative price of skill-intensive goods, and employment shifts towards skilled workers that occur mainly within, rather than between, industries are all cited as evidence that trade cannot have contributed to rising . . . inequality. This line of reasoning emphasizes trade in final goods and ignores the globalization of production and recent dramatic increases in trade in intermediate inputs (Feenstra and Hanson 2001, 46).

More recently, Krugman (2008) develops a model and a numerical exam-ple showing that when developing countries can take over the low-skill labor-intensive portions of vertically-specialized industries, this can result in a significant increase in wage inequality. However, Krugman (2008) is more skeptical now about estimating the precise contribution of trade to wage inequality because of the increasingly complex pattern of international specialization:

How can the actual effect of rising trade on wages be quantified? The answer, given the current state of the data, is that it can't. As I have said, it is likely that the rapid growth of trade since the early 1990s has had significant distributional effects. Putting numbers on these effects, however, will require a much better understanding of the increasingly fine-grained nature of international specialization and trade (Krugman 2008, 135).

3.2.4 Models of Offshoring in a Comparative Advantage Framework

The recognition of the importance of trade in intermediates in the late 1990s occurred at the same time that the H-O model was being rehabilitated in the eyes of economists, in particular as an explanation of the contribution of international trade to the rise in wage inequality between high-skill and low-skill workers. As a result, the early models of offshoring drew on the comparative advantage framework. From this perspective, offshoring is the outcome of a more refined international pattern of specialization as dictated by relative factor endowments and made possible by a reduction of barriers to trade (tariffs, transportation, and communication). Trade liberalization in a world where fragmentation is possible is thus expected to have the usual Stolper-Samuelson effect on relative factor prices (that is, an increase in the relative wage of high-skill workers in countries relatively abundant in high-skill labor) and an overall beneficial effect on social welfare.[9]

Offshoring as Fragmented Production
Economic theories of offshoring identify two types of welfare gains: static and dynamic. In the static version, offshoring results from new possibilities for a more refined division of labor, the result of technological changes (in particular, the internet) that lower the cost and raise the efficiency of managing a global supply chain. Fragmentation is modeled as isolated in one sector, in which the final good is produced using the inputs from the (fragmented) supply base. In these models, fragmentation is modeled like technological progress, with the outcome dependent on factor endowments, the factor intensity in the fragmented sector, and the factor intensity of the fragment being offshored.[10] From this perspective, the fragmentation of production, including the offshoring of intermediate services, enhances the gains from trade beyond those achieved when trade is limited to final goods and services. According to Arndt and Kierzkowski (2001):

[9] The numerous studies of the effect of offshoring on wage inequality by skill level are reviewed in Chapter 5.

[10] Such models include Jones and Marjit (1992), Arndt (1997, 1999), Findlay and Jones (2000, 2001), Jones and Kierzkowski (2001), and Jones et al. (2002).

Spatial dispersion of production allows the factor intensity of each component, rather than the average factor intensity of the end product, to determine the location of its production. The international division of labor now matches factor intensities of components with factor abundance of locations... [E]xtending specialization to the level of components is generally welfare-enhancing (Arndt and Kierzkowski 2001, 2, 6).

Extensions along the lines of the insight of Arndt and Kierzkowski are general equilibrium models typically exploring the effect of fragmentation in one sector for a small economy.[11] The models do not assume factor price equalization (because this eliminates the basis for cost-saving offshoring), but the results of these models are ambiguous. As Baldwin and Robert-Nicoud (2007) write, these models "present a gallery of special cases that firmly establish the ambiguous sign of the general equilibrium price, production, trade and factor price effects" (Baldwin and Robert–Nicoud 2007, 3). As in the standard trade theory regarding *final* goods, the expansion of offshoring resulting from liberalized trade will bring winners and losers within each country (the Stolper-Samuelson effect) and the overall gain to the country (a potential Pareto improvement) depends on the possibility of compensation of losers by the winners. The apparent bias against low-skill labor in much of the trade expansion of the past decade has led to a host of empirical studies of the impact of offshoring of goods and services on the wages of high-skill workers relative to low-skill workers.

Arndt (2001) shows the efficiency gain by analyzing a shift from integrated to fragmented production in a small, open economy using the H-O model with two goods, A and B, and two factors, capital K and labor L (see Figure 3.1). Suppose the country is capital abundant and thus under free trade will export the capital-intensive good B and import good A. A_0 and B_0 are the unit value isoquants for the two goods. Factor prices (w/r) where w is the price of labor and r the price of capital, are given by world goods prices.

If the importable good can be broken into two components, a_1 and a_2, where a_1 is more capital-intensive, then the country will now produce component a_1 and import component a_2. This is equivalent to an increase in productivity in sector A, represented by an inward shift in the A isoquant (to $A1$). Factor prices change to $(w/r)'$, and the capital intensity rises in both sectors A and B (A to A' and B to B'). The result (not shown in the figure) is an outward shift of the production possibility frontier and, under

---

[11] These studies include Deardorff (2001a, b), Venables (1999), Kohler (2004), and Markusen (2005).

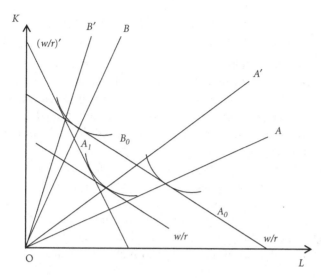

Figure 3.1. Integrated versus Fragmented Production. *Source:* Modified from Arndt (2001: 77), by permission of Oxford University Press.

the usual assumption of full employment, implies an unambiguous increase in national welfare.

Deardorff (2001a, b) uses a H-O framework with two countries, two factors, many goods, and Cobb-Douglas technology and preferences. Cost-saving offshoring is modeled by assuming that the countries' endowments lie in different diversification cones. Deardorff (2001a, b) shows that the capital-to-labor-ratios and the domestic weighted average of the goods' factor intensities determine the wage ratio in both countries. Fragmentation changes the factor intensity of the produced goods and can cause converging or diverging relative factor prices. The outcome is determined by the factor intensities of the fragments and of the original technology.

However, fragmentation models face some problems, as discussed by Grossman and Rossi-Hansberg (2006b):

This research poses apt questions and generates some interesting examples and insights. But, results depend on details about which production process can be dis-integrated, whether factor price equalization holds initially, and what are the absolute and relative factor endowments in each country in relation to world demands for the various goods. It is not easy to glean general principles from the cases that have been considered. Nor do the models lend themselves readily to analysis of new issues, because firms in the model make no marginal decisions about how to organize production and there are many different configurations that could characterize an equilibrium. Moreover, the modeling of fragmentation as a discrete choice makes it difficult to study the evolution of task trade over time (Grossman and Rossi-Hansberg 2006b, 4).

Partly in response to these concerns, models have been more focused on trade in a continuum of inputs. It is assumed that the production of the inputs can happen in different locations and its organization can vary continuously. Some inputs can be produced offshore and traded, for example for cost reasons, but the offshorability varies and depends on the nature of the input. Ultimately, the cost of the marginal input is equalized across the different locations (Grossman and Rossi-Hansberg 2006a, b). Feenstra and Hanson (1997) use a traditional factor endowments approach to the determination of the set of inputs that will be produced offshore. This leads to the interesting result that foreign direct investment (FDI) can raise the average skill intensity of production in both a high-skill abundant and a low-skill abundant country, leading to higher wage inequality in both countries.

Offshoring as Trade in Factor Services

Rather than focus on offshoring directly, Bhagwati et al. (2004) model the factor market in the offshoring process in order to directly address the contentious issue of how offshoring affects income distribution. In the simplest model with only one good and two factors of production, capital and labor, offshoring is treated as the purchase of cheap labor, which raises national income because there is now more domestic production, but with wages lowered (due to the assumption of a diminishing marginal productivity of labor), there is a redistribution of national income from labor to capital.

In a more complex specific factors model of two goods and three factors, each good requires a specific factor for its production: the exportable uses capital as its specific factor, the import-competing good uses low-skill labor as a specific factor and high-skill labor is a common factor in the production of all goods. Offshoring – the "purchase" of high-skill labor at a lower wage than the current wage for high-skill labor – leads again to an increase in national output due to an increase in the supply of high-skill labor.[12] Because the wage of high-skill labor falls, the income of the other two factors (low-skill labor and capital) must rise. If the country is small and thus its terms of trade given, then its welfare unambiguously rises. If the country is large, then it is possible for the terms of trade to deteriorate if it is the output of

---

[12] This approach, also called "shadow migration," has been used by Baldwin and Robert-Nicoud (2007) to prove the standard results of the H-O model within a model with offshoring.

the exportable good that expands. The country can then be worse off if the decline in the terms of trade offsets the increase in national income from offshoring.

In a third model, Bhagwati et al. (2004) introduce a service sector, whose output is assumed initially not to be traded internationally. With innovation there is now trade in this service and it is imported from abroad, wiping out domestic production. The authors assume that full employment continues to hold so that the other two sectors fully absorb the resources initially used in services production. Since the offshoring of the service implies a lower price, then, *ceteris paribus*, the real income of all other factors rises. All workers thus gain because they remain employed, but at a higher real wage. The strength of Bhagwati et al.'s approach is the inclusion of capital as a factor of production. The weakness of the models is that the authors assume full employment, and thus that adjustment costs for those who lose jobs from offshoring will be low and short-lived.

Bhagwati et al. claimed to have cleared up the conceptual "muddle" over offshoring created by Samuelson's (2004) intervention showing that off-shoring could lead to a reversal of the entire basis for comparative advantage-based trade and that without compensation of losers in the process, the gains from specialization and international exchange would be offset by social losses. In the following section, we return below to Samuelson's welfare analysis and its reception in the economics profession. For now we continue to trace out the theory of offshoring. With increased recognition of the growth in the volume of offshoring, as intermediates trade grew and the range of products and services being offshored expanded, economists began to recognize that a qualitatively new form of international exchange was emerging.

Offshoring as "Trade in Tasks"

Grossman and Rossi-Hansberg (2006a 2006b, 2008), in a widely cited set of papers, assert that globalization is no longer characterized by the traditional image of an exchange of "wine for cloth," Ricardo's example that captured the notion of final goods specialization and exchange. Today's world is characterized by what Grossman and Rossi-Hansberg call "trade in tasks." They attribute the rise of this new phase of offshoring primarily to technological improvements in transportation and communication.

In their neoclassical model of offshoring, the production process includes a set of intermediate tasks that can be produced by low-skill or high-skill labor. In the first scenario only low-skill tasks can be offshored. A drop in the cost of offshoring – presumably due to technological improvements in transportation and communication – can affect low-skill labor through three channels: (i) the productivity effect; (ii) the labor supply effect; and, (iii) the relative price effect. The productivity effect is the result of the fact that low-skill tasks in the home country are being performed with less home labor than before the increase in offshoring. This increase in productivity implies a higher marginal product of domestic low-skill labor and thus a higher wage. The labor supply effect occurs when the reduced demand for low-skill domestic workers effectively raises the number of available low-skill workers. The relative price effect is the impact on wages from a decline in the price of the low-skill intensive tasks and thus an improvement in the terms of trade, as the price of imports falls with increased offshoring, resulting in a decline in wages of low-skill workers following the Stolper-Samuelson effect.

The authors distinguish between offshoring in a small economy, which is unable to influence world prices, and in a large economy. Because the model assumes full employment, changing factor supplies have no influence on factor prices, and thus in the small economy case only the productivity effect remains. Low-skill workers reap all the benefits from increased offshoring possibilities in the form of wage increases, whereas high-skill wages are unaffected.

The productivity effect and relative price effect are operative in the case of a large economy like the United States. The expansion of production of labor-intensive goods at initial prices raises world relative prices of skill-intensive goods and increases the developed country's terms of trade. This change in relative prices leads to wage increases of high-skill labor and to wage reductions for low-skill workers in both countries. There is still no labor supply effect due to the assumption of incomplete specialization in both economies. The net effect on the wages of low-skill workers in the developed country is ambiguous due to the two opposing effects.

The labor supply effect can be studied in a small open economy, characterized by a simple H-O world with two factors that produce only one good. Besides the positive productivity effect, the authors derive a negative labor supply effect. The net effect is more likely to be positive if the share of low-skill labor in total costs is large, if the elasticity of substitution between low- and high-skill labor is high, and if there is a sufficiently large decline in costs of offshoring. Finally, the authors consider a second scenario, namely offshoring skill-intensive tasks and also address the possibility that offshoring is not linked to skill-levels.

The key finding of Grossman and Rossi-Hansberg (2006a, 2006b, 2008) is that the productivity effect of offshoring low-skill-intensive tasks was so large in the United States in the period from 1997 to 2004 that it offset the negative effect on wages from the relative price effect and the labor supply effect, resulting in the surprising result that increased offshoring during this period led to an increase in the wages of low-skill domestic workers. The premise is that when the cost of offshoring declines, leading to an increase in trade in tasks, this is equivalent to an increase in productivity of low-skill workers that generates an increase in their real wage.

The Grossman and Rossi-Hansberg model is very flexible, because it goes beyond the standard $2 \times 2 \times 2$ H-O approach to allow for tasks that are produced by other factors of production, such as capital or other categories of labor. Skill-intensive tasks are offshorable, a growing feature of the world economy today. And even "low-skill tasks" vary in their offshorability in the model, another important issue in contemporary discussion of offshorability (e.g., Blinder 2007a). But the Grossman and Rossi-Hansberg model, perhaps the most sophisticated and flexible of the neoclassical models, still suffers from the same limitations as most contemporary models of offshoring, which are discussed in the next section.

Limitations of Contemporary Models of Offshoring
Most models of offshoring assume full employment so that adjustment to imbalances or shocks of any sort occur through changes in wages or the exchange rate. In other words, they are not able to consider the effect of offshoring on employment, because the full employment assumption wipes out any possible negative employment effects from the increased excess supply of low-skill workers. If we were to include unemployed workers in the wage calculations of the Grossman and Rossi-Hansberg model, for example as a zero wage, then surely the positive productivity effect identified in these models would be reduced. Even in the context of a neoclassical model, in which unemployment is due only to search problems, trade liberalization results in a higher rate of unemployment for low-skill workers and an increase in the duration of unemployment for existing unemployed low-skill workers (Davidson et al. 1999).

This immediately separates the academic from the popular discourse because the focus of the latter is precisely on the employment effects of trade.[13] Thurow (2004) describes the labor market assumptions of the comparative advantage model as "counterfactual," arguing that if we consider how the U.S. labor market performed in the 2000s, it is likely that income

---

[13] For example, the joint ILO-WTO (2007) study, titled *Trade and Employment*, is almost entirely about wage inequality between high- and low-skill workers.

losses from trade exceed gains.[14] Davidson et al. (1999), who model trade
in the presence of search unemployment, give a similar conclusion:

> Extending standard trade models to allow for equilibrium unemployment is impor-
> tant for at least two reasons. First, there is the issue of whether trade creates net
> job opportunities... we view this as largely an empirical question... we... show
> that the traditional list of determinants of comparative advantage must be broad-
> ened to include features of the labor market... Our main finding is that when
> a relatively capital-abundant large country begins to trade with a small, relatively
> labor-abundant country, unemployed workers in the large economy unambiguously
> suffer welfare losses. In addition, we find that such trade increases the aggregate
> unemployment in the large country (Davidson et al. 1999, 273).

Grossman and Rossi-Hansberg's "productivity effect" is thus questionable
even independent of the assumption of full employment. If the decline in
domestic labor demand as a result of offshoring is matched by an equivalent
rise in foreign labor demand, then the productivity of operations would be
unchanged. Houseman et al. (2010) criticize the exclusion of foreign labor
from the calculation of productivity gains. Shifting to less productive labor
may lower costs, they argue, but it is likely also to lower labor productivity.
They estimate an adjusted labor content to include outsourced labor and
conclude that the omission of this labor component led to an overstatement
of U.S. manufacturing productivity gains from offshoring by approximately
0.1 to 0.2 percentage points in the period from 1997 to 2007. Outside of
the computer and electronics sectors of manufacturing, the adjustment
indicates that 20 to 50 percent of value added growth is due to this mismea-
surement. Another implication of this analysis is that U.S. gross domestic
product (GDP) is also overstated, because it is based on an inflated measure of productivity. Alterman (2010) discusses the widely-acknowledged
downward bias in U.S. import price changes, the presence of which implies
an upward bias in the measure of U.S. GDP growth.

Lastly, most trade models adopted since the mid-1990s ignore capital. It
is a model of two factors, high-skill and low-skill labor. This has a number
of important implications. The first is the effective disappearance of the
firm and its profits from the discussion of offshoring. We argued in Chapter
2 that the new wave of globalization is different because of the larger role
played by firms in organizing production. It is precisely as part of firms'
efforts to reduce production costs and serve their larger strategic goals
that offshoring has played such an important role. The second implication

---

[14] Thurow (2004) continues: "Why these caveats [the lack of realism of the assumptions of
the theory] are never mentioned when economists jump into public debates about free
trade is an interesting sociological and political question (Thurow 2004, 271)."

is to deny the potential importance of the dynamic effects of offshoring whereby higher profits from offshoring are reinvested in part in domestic operations, leading to further employment, output, and productivity gains. In the Grossman and Rossi-Hansberg model, there is some pass-through to wages (the productivity effect), but this is a very limited view of potential gains from offshoring. The question is not only whether some of the rents from offshoring are shared with the remaining employed workforce, but why more of the gains aren't shared, directly and indirectly through the reinvestment of profits. We address this question in more detail in Chapter 4 when we discuss dynamic gains from offshoring.

Finally, the new generation of H-O models of offshoring with high-skill and low-skill labor give a very simplistic policy conclusion: workers in industrialized countries need to attain more skills! Besides placing the blame for globalization's effects on the victims of the process, the skills bias approach to globalization seems to be less compelling as new technologies, capital mobility, and new capabilities around the world increasingly render all workers vulnerable. The deeper problem is the static, comparative advantage framework which, as we describe in the next section, has conceptual, historical, and ethical shortcomings.

3.3 Limits of Comparative Advantage

With the Panglossian view of Grossman and Rossi-Hansberg, trade theory has come full circle. After a relatively long period of questioning the theoretical foundations of the traditional view of positive welfare implications of trade liberalization, trade theorists have rediscovered the old comparative advantage model and its associated case for the beneficial welfare effects of trade. With the contributions of Grossman and Rossi-Hansberg, even the nagging problem of compensation of the losers from international trade is overcome, because a productivity effect is found that might compensate for the negative labor supply and terms of trade effects.

The policy of free trade is supported by more economists than any other single policy in economics. In one survey, admittedly dated, Frey et al. (1984) found that 95 percent of American-based economists and 88 percent of economists across the United States and Europe support or will support with qualification the view that "tariffs and import quotas reduce general economic welfare." But the reemergence of the comparative advantage-based model on which this policy view is based is problematic in the era of the new wave of globalization. The limitations of the principle of comparative advantage are conceptual, historical, and ethical. We consider each in turn.

3.3.1 Conceptual Limits

The globalization of production and finance has rendered irrelevant some of the key assumptions of the Ricardo-Hume model of trade. One is the assumption of no international movement of capital or input production. The second is the Humean adjustment process that converts comparative advantage into money cost differences that make international trade actually happen. The third is the highly uneven distribution of knowledge-based assets across firms and countries. The principle of comparative advantage is relevant in a world with no capital mobility, no unemployment, little trade in intermediate goods and in which the international payments system brings an automatic reversal of trade imbalances. It is of much less relevance in the world we find ourselves in today, characterized by rapid international capital mobility, footloose input production, intense technological competition, persistent trade imbalances, and stagnant wages in many countries.

Persistent Trade Imbalances
The principle of comparative advantage is as much a description of a process of economic change as it is an algorithm for explaining the conversion of a constellation of comparative costs into a set of absolute cost differences that bring about balanced trade. That is, free trade will be beneficial and balanced for all countries, even for those who have higher costs in all sectors. Paul Krugman (1991) sums up this view nicely:

International competition does not put countries out of business. There are strong equilibrating forces that normally ensure that any country remains able to sell a range of goods in world markets, and to balance its trade on average over the long run, even if its productivity, technology, and product quality are inferior to those of other nations... Both in theory and in practice, countries with lagging productivity are still able to balance their international trade, because what drives trade is comparative rather than absolute advantage (Krugman 1991, 811, 814).

The "equilibrating forces" to which Krugman refers are the price adjustments or exchange rate that should occur in the event that trade is not balanced – Hume's (1985[1777]) "price-specie-flow mechanism." This lowering of prices improves the competitiveness of the nation's goods, and the price or exchange rate movements end when trade is balanced.

What if, contrary to Hume, a trade deficit leads not to a change in the price level (nor to an automatic adjustment of wages or exchange rates) but to a potential liquidity problem for the deficit country? That is, a change in the trade balance may result in a change in the monetary base, leading to a change in the rate of interest. In this view, an improvement to surplus on current account does not bring a rise in wages, but a lowering of interest rates. The country with the improving trade balance thus accrues liquid assets, but there is no reason to assume these will be converted to non-liquid assets, much less into foreign-produced non-liquid assets. Saving thus creates the possibility of both underemployment equilibrium and of persistently unbalanced trade, despite the assumption of price flexibility. From this Keynesian perspective, the law of comparative advantage is the international analogue of Say's Law. Just as wage flexibility is insufficient to bring about full employment in the closed economy Keynesian model, wage flexibility *per se* will not bring about balanced trade in the open economy context.

The logic of comparative advantage implies balanced trade over the long-run. This amounts to the assertion that over time imports and exports are causally related – that is, a decrease in imports should lead to an equivalent decline in exports. If instead an import reduction allows the central bank to lower interest rates, the result could be a higher, lower, or unchanged level of exports. The comparative advantage view that trade automatically tends to an equality of imports and exports ignores this possibility. A further complication arises when the supply of and demand for foreign exchange is dominated by capital market transactions as opposed to the supply and demand for goods and services alone.

In addition to the problem of exchange rate "misalignment," the growing role of non-price competition (that is, over technological change) and "pricing to market" (limited exchange rate pass-through) has further reduced the effectiveness of the Hume mechanism in balancing trade. Exchange rate imbalances can have cumulative effects, especially for firms in industries in which innovation is important and cash flow constrains innovative effort.

Even without issues of credit and money, the issue of unbalanced trade can pose a challenge to the theory of comparative advantage. Deardorff (1994) finds that when trade is not balanced at the outset then comparative advantage operates only under the special conditions where consumer preferences are homothetic, that is, when income changes do not lead to any change in the composition of consumer demand. Similarly, Markusen and MacDonald (1985) argue that the existence of certain non-convexities in preferences and technology can render comparative advantage inoperable, leaving competitiveness and resource allocation as determined by absolute advantage.

International Capital Mobility

Trade imbalances are only possible of course when capital is also mobile internationally. The presence of international capital mobility has been a concern for trade theorists since the origins of the principle of comparative advantage. Ricardo (1981[1817]) himself recognized the reason for assuming no international capital mobility in the discussion of international trade. If capital were fully mobile, all factors of production would move to where labor productivity is higher in all sectors. In his example, that meant from England to Portugal:

It would undoubtedly be advantageous to the capitalists of England, and the consumers in both countries, that under such circumstances, the wine and cloth should both be made in Portugal, and therefore the capital and labour of England employed in making cloth, should be removed to Portugal for that purpose (Ricardo 1981 [1817], 136).

Ricardo then asserts why the assumption of no international capital mobility is a reasonable one:

Experience, however, shows, that the fancied or real insecurity of capital, when not under the immediate control of its owner, together with the natural disinclination which every man has to quit the country of his birth and connexions, and intrust himself with all his habits fixed, to a strange government and new laws, check the emigration of capital. These feelings, which I should be sorry to see weakened, induce most men of property to be satisfied with a low rate of profits in their own country, rather than seek a more advantageous employment for their wealth in foreign nations (Ricardo 1981[1817], 136–137).

Twentieth century trade theorists were able to largely avoid the issue of international capital mobility because of Samuelson's (1948) development of the factor price equalization theorem, which implied that even in the absence of international movements of factors of production, free trade in goods brings about equalization in the remuneration of productive factors. Thus all the welfare benefits of international exchange could be achieved without any international capital (or labor) mobility.[15]

The introduction of an internationally mobile factor of production can have very significant implications for the determination of trade patterns. With free capital mobility, a good will be produced only where it is most profitable, that is, where unit labor costs are lowest. Thus, in a two-country, two-good, two-factor model, if the home country has an absolute advantage in both goods, that is, if unit costs are lower in the production of both goods, the home country will attract foreign capital, reducing foreign production

---

[15] See references on capital mobility in Jones (2000), including classic papers by Mundell (1957) and Purvis (1972).

and employment – potentially to zero in equilibrium. According to Caves (1982):

In general, the more mobile are factors of production, the less does comparative advantage have to do with patterns of production. If all factors are more productive in the United States than in Iceland and nothing impeded their international mobility, all economic activity would be located in the United States (Caves 1982, 55).

Jones (1980) makes a similar point:

Although each nation can, by the law of comparative advantage, find something to produce, it may end up empty-handed in its pursuit of industries requiring footloose factors. Once trade theorists pay proper attention to the significance of these internationally mobile productive factors, the doctrine of comparative advantage must find room as well for the doctrine of "relative attractiveness" where it is not necessarily the technical requirements of one industry versus another that loom important, it is the overall appraisal of one country versus another as a safe, comfortable, and rewarding location for residence of footloose factors (Jones 1980, 258).

Constant Real Wages

When relative productivities or costs do not play a determining role for the direction of trade, absolute advantage is the operative principle, not comparative advantage. Consider the case where real wages are constant. For the classical economists, this was because workers were assumed to earn a subsistence wage. From a neoclassical perspective, this could be viewed as a result of labor market rigidities. Both interpretations have been shown to provide a basis for a diminished role for comparative advantage in the determination of the direction of trade.

In the case of constant real wages, allowing for international capital mobility can result in absolute advantage determining the trade pattern, not comparative advantage. Brewer (1985) shows this in a model of two countries (1 and 2) and two goods (*A* and *B*). Production, which requires capital *K* and labor *L*, takes time. Technology is assumed to exhibit constant returns to scale. There are no trade distortions, implying a single world price for each good. Both labor and capital are measured in real terms, that is, in terms of the bundles of goods they can buy. Labor is assumed to be immobile, which means that wages can be persistently different between the two countries. Wages are assumed constant in both countries, presumably the result of a persistent excess supply of labor. Capital can move internationally, which is captured in the model as a transfer of a certain number of standard consumption baskets and matched by an equivalent change in the value of the capital stock.

Let L_A^1 be the labor required to produce one unit of good A in country 1, w^1 be the real wage, and K^1 be the capital stock of country 1. Prices are then given by labor costs and a profit markup. Generally, $P_A = w^1 L_A^1 (1 + r_A^1)$, where P_A is the price of good A and r_A^1 is the profit rate on good A in country 1. By definition, country 1 has a comparative advantage in good A if its relative productivity advantage in the production of good A is higher than the relative productivity of good A in country 2, that is, if $L_A^1/L_B^1 < L_A^2/L_B^2$. Country 1 has an absolute advantage in good A if the wage costs of producing good A are lower than in country 2, that is, if $w^1 L_A^1 < w^2 L_A^2$.

Suppose that country 1 has both a comparative and absolute advantage in good A. Brewer considers four scenarios, depending on whether wages are fixed or flexible and whether capital is internationally mobile or not. Here we take up only the case of fixed real wages and internationally mobile capital. Capital will flow to where its return is the highest, and each good will be produced only where it is most profitable. That is, good A will be produced in country 1 if and only if $w^1 L_A^1 < w^2 L_A^2$, that is, according to absolute advantage. If each country has an absolute advantage in one good, then both countries specialize completely according to absolute advantage, which gives the same prediction as comparative advantage. If country 1 has an absolute advantage in both goods, then all capital will flow into country 1 and country 2 will have zero output and employment in equilibrium. This is the case where, as Robinson (1973) puts it, country 2 is "undersold all round" (Robinson 1973, 16). Cost reductions in one location, through technological progress or a decline in wages, can cause a reversal in the direction of trade for a given good or, as Brewer (1985) puts it, "the emigration of industries with no mechanisms to ensure their replacement" (Brewer 1985, 180). Similarly, shifts in demand can lead to permanent unemployment.

Footloose Input Production
The rise in trade in intermediate goods in manufacturing constitutes a fundamental shift in the structure of international trade and poses a challenge to economists' understanding of how countries fit into the international division of labor. As we noted in Chapter 2, the assessment of comparative advantage based on the composition of final goods trade is misleading when vertical specialization is significant. But the problems are deeper than this.

The prominence of GVCs – high levels of vertical specialization – indicate that there are no longer clearly indigenous technological capabilities or even endowed factors. Autarky conditions become difficult to conceptualize, because in autarky some of the intermediate goods would not be produced at all. Thus the conditions needed to explain comparative advantage do not exist. More fundamentally, with intermediates goods trade, the basis for trade is no longer entirely driven by comparative advantage, but also by *absolute* advantage, because as Baldone et al. (2007) write:

Traded goods will embody 'advantages' specific to different countries, so it will be impossible to say that the goods exported by a country are the ones where a country has a comparative advantage . . . [T]herefore we do not have the conditions to verify the existence of such comparative advantage. It is at least likely that what gives rise to an advantage in world markets and originates a trade flow is the existence of an absolute cost advantage and a specific combination of phases of production taking place in different countries (Baldone et al. 2007, 1729).

Jones (2000) gives a more formalized explanation of how the introduction of trade in intermediate goods (trade in inputs in Jones's model) alters the determination of the composition of trade in his Ohlin Lectures, entitled *Globalization and the Theory of Input Trade.* Jones writes,

Once international mobility in an input is allowed, absolute advantage becomes a concept that takes its rightful place alongside comparative advantage in explaining the direction of international commerce (Jones 2000, 7).

Jones's model is what he calls an "augmented Ricardian" trade model with two small (such as price-taking) countries and two goods, and in which capital is a physical input for one of the goods and is located in different countries, but which can move from one country to another in response to changes in its rate of return in different countries. Assuming perfect competition implies that no positive economic profit can be made producing either good. Thus for country 1, the cost (and thus price) of goods A and B are given as follows:

$$w^1 L_A^1 = P_A \text{ and } w^1 L_B^1 + r^1 K_B^1 = P_B$$

Jones considers two possibilities. In the first, country 2 is assumed to have lower labor and capital productivity. In this case, specialization and trade follow Ricardian comparative advantage, that is, according to the pattern of relative labor productivities.

In the second scenario, country 2's lower labor productivity is offset in the B sector by its high capital productivity. In this case, capital will move to earn the higher return in country 2 and that country will specialize in and export good *B* irrespective of the comparative advantage. According to Jones,

The augmented Ricardian model usefully illustrates how the doctrine of comparative advantage, so dominant in trade models in which inputs are trapped behind national boundaries, must make room for the doctrine of absolute advantage for any input that enjoys an international market (Jones 2000, 20).

The idea of comparative advantage is linked to the notion that inputs are trapped by national boundaries, so that the only decision that needs to be made concerns the allocation within the country of these inputs... [A] world in which some inputs are internationally mobile or tradable is a world in which... the doctrine of comparative advantage, with its emphasis on the question of what a factor does within the country, needs to share pride of place with the doctrine of absolute advantage guiding the question of where an internationally mobile factor goes (Jones 2000, 136).

Jones takes the discussion one step further than Brewer, considering the role of government policy and other institutional factors in the determination of the composition of trade. In a world of comparative advantage, any government policy that affects all sectors proportionally will have no effect on the trade pattern because it will not alter the relative cost ratios. In such a model, different countries could adopt very different policies, say with respect to taxation or the exchange rate, and there would be no effect on the composition of trade. However, once we allow for the possibility of a mobile factor and a role for absolute advantage in the determination of the trade pattern, then international differences in policy such as tax rates, "take on first-order importance in affecting patterns of production and trade" (Jones 2000, 20).

Belloc (2004) finds in particular that labor market policies affect the pattern of trade in industrialized countries. It is a short step from this analytical point to a recognition of the importance of institutional structure generally for international competitiveness, and we return to this point at the end of this section when we consider issues of social protection policies, the governance of GVCs, and the gender segmentation of labor markets as institutional formations that significantly affect patterns of trade and growth.

Many Goods and Many Countries

Ricardo's theory of comparative advantage is taught to undergraduates in the context of a world of two countries and two goods, and reveals that free trade leads to increased production (and thus consumption) possibilities globally. These results are easily extended to the case of two countries and many commodities as well as that of two commodities and many countries.[16] Going beyond this to a world of many countries and many commodities has proven to be more difficult. The problem is that simple rankings of cost ratios are no longer sufficient (Ethier 1984). The major step forward was made by Graham (1948) who used Mill's examples to show that in a world of three goods and three countries, simple bilateral comparisons do not lead to a consistent algorithm for welfare enhancing specialization and trade.

Jones (1961) went farthest in developing the multi-country, multi-commodity comparative advantage specialization algorithm. Jones defines an "assignment" as a particular pattern of specialization in trade. A "class of assignments" is a set of assignments which are all similar in that they "assign" each country to completely specialize in the same number of commodities. In the Jones solution, an efficient specialization and trade pattern is such that the product of labor requirements in the efficient assignment of commodities to countries must be less than the corresponding product in any other possible assignments in the same class. Jones (1961) considers the special case in higher dimensions, where there are many goods and countries, but the same number of each. Even within this special case of many countries and commodities, Jones considers only the class of assignments in which each country is assigned a different commodity. In words, the Jones algorithm is the following.

In a world of many goods and countries (with the number of goods equal to the number of countries), with the class of assignments where each commodity is produced by one (and only one) country, country c has a "multilateral comparative advantage" in commodity i relative to commodity j compared with "the rest of the world" if and only if the sacrifice of one unit of commodity j in country c yields a greater increase in the production of commodity i than (with reference to the optimal assignment) would a sacrifice of one unit of commodity j in the rest of the world. According to the Jones algorithm, a country should specialize in the production of a commodity if the opportunity cost of producing that commodity (in terms of *any* other commodity) is less than the opportunity cost of producing that good through any possible combination of resource reallocation in all countries in the rest of the world.[17]

---

[16] See any undergraduate textbook in international economics, for example Salvatore (2007).

[17] Paradoxically, the Jones algorithm applied to even the 3 × 3 case is not consistent with all bilateral comparisons from the same group of countries (Jones 1961).

The Jones algorithm gives the optimal assignment for a given class of assignments. But for a given number of countries and commodities there are many classes. The question is, can we determine the optimal assignment for all possible classes for n countries and m commodities? This Jones does not do, and it is impossible with the use of substitution circuits. Thus Jones's result is of a different nature than Ricardo's. Ricardo shows how specialization according to comparative advantage raises global output in a 2×2 case by lowering the real wage facing business. Jones shows that there is an optimal assignment in each of the $n \times m$ classes of assignments, which are feasible in a world of n countries and m commodities. There is no unique optimal specialization pattern in a world of n countries and m commodities (much less with q factors of production).[18]

Deardorff (1979) overcomes a limitation of the Jones result – its determinateness – by placing the issue in a stochastic framework. He summarizes the result of his proof of "The General Validity of the Law of Comparative Advantage," as follows:

There must exist a negative correlation between any country's relative autarky prices and its pattern of net exports. Thus, on average, high autarky prices are associated with imports and low autarky prices are associated with exports (Deardorff 1979, 942).

But Deardorff's result is modest, and he does not solve the problem of the restricted validity of the Jones algorithm. For one, the stochastic nature of the solution puts the whole issue in a different framework.[19] Deardorff's prediction is so general that it is hard to imagine that it is not consistent with most theories of international trade, including the institutionalist absolute advantage approach presented in the chapters that follow. Moreover, Deardorff's result – despite the title of his article – relies on a number of special assumptions, including balanced trade and full employment.

Technology Gap
A further implication of the revival of the factor endowments model of international trade is the presumption of identical technologies globally or,

---

[18] Milberg (1994a) presents a test of the Jones algorithm for five Organisation of Economic Co-operation and Development countries and finds very little relation between the predicted specialization pattern according to the algorithm and the actual pattern observed in the data.

[19] Mirowski (1989) notes that often in the history of economics, the translation of a deterministic theory to a stochastic version has been important for salvaging the scientific status of the theory.

its theoretical equivalent, the instantaneous global diffusion of innovation. Despite the increase in international capital mobility, there is considerable evidence of persistent differences across countries in technology. In fact, the poor prediction of the factor endowments model is often attributed to the presence of significant differences in technology across countries (see, for example, Bowen et al. 1987; Trefler 1995). International gaps in productivity have blocked many developing countries in their pursuit of economic growth through exporting. With persistent differences in technology or knowledge across firms and countries, Amsden (2001) writes:

Because a poor country's lower wages may prove inadequate against a rich country's higher productivity, the model of "comparative advantage" no longer behaves predictably: latecomers cannot necessarily industrialize simply by specializing in a low-technology industry. Even in such an industry, demand may favor skilled incumbents (Amsden 2001, 5–6).[20]

In this case, she writes,

The price of land, labor and capital no longer uniquely determines competitiveness. The market mechanism loses status as its sole arbiter, deferring instead to institutions that nurture productivity (Amsden 2001, 5).

The work of the neo-Schumpeterian trade theorists focuses precisely on the cases where persistent technology gaps lead to persistent trade imbalances because low wages are not adequate to bring about adjustment. A technology gap is the difference between the technology and innovativeness of a given sector (or country) and that used in the lead technology sector (or country). The gap is reflected in a different level of productivity, of mechanization, and of innovation, as captured by innovative effort (that is, R&D expenditures, number of engineers employed) or innovative output (that is, productivity, patents, and scholarly engineering journal articles). Firms seek profits and growth by creating and protecting a knowledge advantage over rivals, be it through innovation, FDI, offshoring, interfirm cooperation, or state subsidies.[21] Technology gaps are observed to be persistent, largely because of scale economies or learning effects. A number of studies

---

[20] For a survey of empirical studies of price versus non-price competition, see Fagerberg (1996).

[21] Schumpeter (1942, 84). Posner and Steer (1979) write that "Historically there is no doubt that non-price influences have dominated. The proportion of total change they 'explain' is on an order of magnitude greater than the explanatory power of price competitiveness (Posner and Steer 1979, 159)."

have shown that productivity differences across sectors within countries are smaller than productivity differences across countries within sectors.[22]

Although there have been neoclassical and neo-Schumpeterian technology gap models,[23] almost all are based on Posner's (1961) simple insight that international differences in process technology, product design, or innovation in a given sector can be the source of international trade, even when they are not reflected in prices. Technological innovation is the central focus, leaving cost and price adjustments as secondary. Amendola et al. (1993) write that the objective is to formalize the intuition behind the notion that, "Country X is losing trade competitiveness because its costs are too high and its innovative performance is sluggish (Amendola et al. 1993, 2)."

In technology gap models, cost-based adjustments are subordinate to the adjustments from persistent technology gaps. Technological change affects export market share. Market share adjustments lead to income changes, which dominate any cost-based changes – such as exchange rate adjustments. The income adjustments affect economic growth more directly than they do the trade balance.[24] By subordinating the role of price competition, technology gap models leave open the possibility that countries can run persistent trade imbalances over the long-run, an impossibility in a world of comparative advantage. According to Dosi et al. (1990):

Our hypothesis is thus that absolute advantages dominate over comparative advantages as determinants of trade flows. Their dominance means that they account for most of the composition of trade flows by country and by commodity at each point in time and explain the evolution of such trade flows over time. This dominance takes two forms. First, absolute advantages/disadvantages are the fundamental factors, which explain sectoral and average competitiveness, and, thus, market shares. Second, they also define the boundaries of the universe within which cost-related adjustments take place (Dosi et al. 1990, 151).

This perspective suggests that sectoral exports depend mainly on three factors, technological advantage/disadvantage, industrial organization and the degree of mechanization, and cost advantage/disadvantage.

Amendola et al. (1993) adopt Silverberg et al.'s (1988) "evolutionary" dynamic formulation, in which changes in exports result from deviations

---

[22] See also Brailovsky et al. (1982), Dollar et al. (1988), Dosi et al. (1990). See Milberg (1994b) for an overview of the concept of technology gaps.

[23] For a comprehensive review of the technology gap literature, see Elmslie (2004).

[24] Thus the close link of this literature to Thirlwall's (1979) balance of payments constrained growth rate based on the income elasticities of demand for imports and exports.

in competitiveness conditions in a given sector relative to rival sectors abroad. This moves the focus away from equilibrium dynamics, as presumed for example in any dynamic model of comparative advantage. According to Amendola et al. (1993), "it implies changes in trade and technology unpegged to some underlying equilibrium and imperfect adjustments in macroeconomic variables to continuously changing technological 'fundamentals'" (Amendola et al. 1993, 456).

The technology gap approach has generated a vast empirical literature, much of which confirms a positive relation between innovative effort and export performance in a large number of industries in industrialized countries, and where technology gap variables are more often significant than traditional price indicators. This implies that there are non-price dimensions to competition, especially important in trade among industrialized countries.

From a Technology Gap to a "Social Gap" Model of Trade

The technology gap approach can be extended to broader institutional considerations. R&D spending alone is of little importance if production is not organized in a way that allows for the efficient introduction of resulting product and process innovations. Further, the nature of the innovations themselves depends on workplace organization, worker motivation, and the incentives for innovation. The degree of flexibility of the production process influences the nature, extent, and impact of innovations. What is needed is an extension of the technology gap approach to include these institutions, what we have elsewhere called a "social gap" model of trade (Milberg and Houston 2005).

Firms seek profits and growth by creating and protecting a knowledge advantage over rivals, be it through innovation, FDI, offshoring, interfirm cooperation, or state subsidies. International differences in social institutions – from systems of innovation and finance to tax treatment of corporate profits, to labor market regulations, the scope of the welfare state and even household relations – can affect both productivity and non-price dimensions of traded goods, in turn affecting the competitiveness of particular sectors and of the overall trading position of a national economy. In his discussion of the institutional foundations of international trade, Piore (1998) notes that,

Productive activity is embedded in a social structure, and economic growth and development, to the extent that they depend on productive relations, are actually dependent on social forces as well . . . Thus society is not something to be taken into account after the economy has done its work, through, for example, a redistributive system of taxes and transfers. A complete economic theory must understand the society and the economy as of a piece (Piore 1998, 259–260).

Following the absolute advantage models previously reviewed, we would expect that a firm's export market share would depend on the overall pattern of these advantages. The Humean adjustment mechanism may be operative to some degree, but as the technology gap models emphasize, it is likely to be dominated by the absolute advantages resulting from knowledge-based differences in productivity. The diminished role for price competition (Fagerberg 1996) because of the dominance of knowledge-based differences further raises the likelihood that trade imbalances will be persistent.

The absence of a consideration of institutional determinants of productivity, innovation, product quality, and production flexibility in the technology gap approach is surprising given the literature on "varieties of capitalism" and on corporatism, which explicitly links labor relations and economic performance.[25] In corporatist systems – the Scandinavian countries often cited as the main examples – economic performance is typically related positively with the degree of centralization of the wage bargain, higher union density and more participatory work environments, and a macroeconomic and policy environment of more job security. Non-corporatist systems – and here the Anglo-Saxon countries are usually seen as the prime examples – are characterized by a negative relation between economic performance and such indicators as labor union strength and government spending on social protection has been found (Gordon 1996 and recent studies).

The incentives for productivity improvement are different in the two systems. Social-corporatist systems rely on a high degree of job security to encourage workers to be open to the introduction of new innovations, techniques, products, and designs. According to Gordon (1996):

In cooperative [corporatist] systems, productivity-enhancing automation is presumably suspected and resisted less by workers, and perhaps even jointly planned by them, because their employment security tends to reduce their fear of technological layoffs (Gordon 1996, 149).

Non-corporatist systems presumably rely more on the "stick" than the "carrot" in the achievement of productivity gains. Thus, for example, higher unemployment rates that raise the expected "cost" of job loss would be expected to increase work intensity in a deregulated system, whereas in a

---

[25] In Chapter 5, we focus on the differential impact of offshoring on the labor share under "varieties of capitalism" in the context of labor support and labor market flexibility.

cooperative system the same increase in the unemployment rate would be expected to lower work intensity as job security falls. Weisskopf (1987), for example, finds that unemployment is most significant [as a determinant of productivity] where industrial conflict is greatest.[26]

Building on the early corporatist literature, Calmfors and Driffill (1988) propose that better macroeconomic performance (more wage restraint, lower unemployment, and inflation) would come from either highly decentralized or highly centralized wage bargaining systems. In highly centralized bargaining arrangements, unions are expected to internalize the negative effects of large wage increases and show wage restraint. In highly decentralized systems, unions are understood to be simply too weak to achieve gains that might raise unemployment or lower international competitiveness. Bargaining systems located in the middle of this spectrum would presumably lack the positive features of either of these extreme cases, and be likely to have the worst economic performance (Calmfors 1993).

These various perspectives on the relation between the degree of cooperation and economic performance are summarized in Figure 3.2. The high-road view shows a positive relation and the low-road view a negative relation. The Calmfors-Driffill "hump-shape" (here inverted) is a combination of the two views, with the high-road hypothesis effective in one range and the low-road one in another, as depicted by the solid lines in Figure 3.2. This hybrid version captures the Calmfors-Driffill view on extreme versus intermediate arrangements, as well as the more important property that the effect of an increase in the degree of cooperativeness depends on whether the system is already in the more or less cooperative range. Thus, for example, moves to more cooperation may be successful in Norway but not England. According to Paloheimo (1990):

Mainly it is countries with medium levels of labor relations that should think about either a decentralization of their labor relations on the one hand, and either a liberalization or a corporatisation of their economic policies on the other (Paloheimo 1990, 135).

Whereas the labor relations dichotomy between corporatism and non-corporatism is seldom applied to the question of international competition, its relevance is clear in a world where absolute advantages are driven by international differences in innovative effort and other institutions. When we turn to a concern with absolute advantage alongside the harmonious

---

[26] See also Green and Weisskopf (1990) and Buchele and Christiansen (1992).

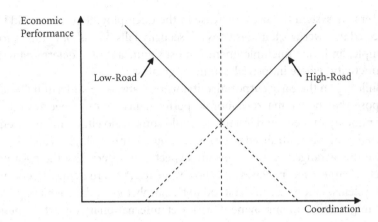

Figure 3.2. Degree of Coordination and Economic Performance. *Source*: Own illustration. Based on Milberg and Houston (2005, 146).

world of comparative advantage, then a variety of institutional arrangements, including corporate strategies, government arrangements for managing trade and labor markets, especially labor market institutions relating to differential treatment of male and female workers, all play an important role in the determination of trade flows and their welfare consequences. Differences in systems of labor relations may be particularly relevant in an environment in which innovativeness and flexibility are crucial elements of international competition, that is, when non-price competition has become so important. The state plays a key role, both in molding the regulatory environment and providing tax incentives for certain types of firm behavior, and by providing a social safety net that complements the private system of labor relations.

3.3.2 Historical Limits

We have emphasized up to this point the theoretical limits of the principle of comparative advantage. But many of the conceptual problems with the principle are reflected in recent economic history. For example, we have seen that when relative costs – such as real wages – do not play a determining role for the direction of trade, absolute advantage is the operative principle, not comparative advantage. The assumption of constant real wages is not far from describing real wages of some major industrialized countries over the past twenty years. In Germany, Japan, and the United States real wage growth was stagnant for long stretches (see Figure 4.2 for data on median hourly compensation for the United States between 1973 and 2009). With constant real wages, the presence of international capital mobility can result in absolute advantage determining the trade pattern, not comparative advantage. We have defined the era of economic globalization by heightened international mobility of capital, shown in the expansion of offshoring, the rising share of FDI in world GDP, and the explosion of international portfolio capital flows. In sum, today's world is not far from the theoretical conditions required to explain the diminished role for comparative advantage in the determination of the direction of trade.

In this section, we look at the limits of comparative advantage in helping us to understand economic history. We focus on two specific issues. The first is the persistence of payments imbalances despite the theoretical prediction that adjustment to trade imbalances is automatic and rapid. The second is the issue of upgrading, that is when firms and countries move into specialization in a new set of goods or processes, which bring higher value added. Such upgrading, we have argued, is the contemporary version of economic development, and it increasingly occurs within GVCs and is thus related to corporate strategies and to international trade. The theory of comparative advantage has no explanation for this process, a process that some have described even as requiring a "defiance" of the specialization pattern indicated by comparative advantage.

Persistent Trade Imbalances

As financial markets, including foreign exchange markets, have been liberalized, exchange rates have increasingly been driven by financial market fluctuations, and certainly have not responded simply to "fundamentals" like the balance of trade. The delinking of exchange rates from the trade balance has led to persistent trade imbalances and the unlikelihood that comparative cost differences will be transformed into a situation of absolute money cost and price differences across countries. In the era of flexible exchange rates, Organisation of Economic Co-operation and Development (OECD) countries have generally experienced larger and more persistent trade imbalances than in the Bretton Woods era.

Table 3.1 shows the cumulative current account balance for major OECD countries and the number of consecutive years the current account remained in surplus or deficit. These are the countries with the most highly developed and liberal financial markets, and thus where current account adjustment would be expected to be most efficient. The persistence of current account imbalances in terms of number of consecutive years of imbalance with the same sign (surplus or deficit) is in almost all cases greater in the 1990s

Table 3.1. *Cumulative Current Account Balances, 1971–2010 (M. $)*

	Cumulative current account balance				Consecutive years with same sign			
	1971–80	1981–90	1991–2000	2001–10	1971–80	1981–90	1991–2000	2001–10
Denmark	n.a.	−19,950	20,069	82,840	n.a.	9	7	10
France	n.a.	−22,969	192,738	−30,684	n.a.	5	9	6
Germany	33,738	281,567	−212,584	139,352	8	9	10	10
Japan	n.a.	475,319	1,069,333	154,989	n.a.	10	10	10
United Kingdom	−14,705	−131,159	−174,621	−49,581	4	5	10	10
United States	31,000	−886,829	−1,567,223	−578,276	4	9	9	10
China	n.a.	11,944[a]	125,838	186,704	n.a.	3[a]	7	10

Source: Own illustration, Data: World Development Indicators, World Bank and OECD Balance of Payments. Note: The cumulative current account balance is the sum of consecutive years of imbalances with the same sign (surplus or deficit).
[a] Based on 1982–1990.

and 2000s than it was in the 1970s and 1980s. By the 2000s, almost all the countries in our sample were running persistent imbalances over the entire period. The magnitude of persistent current account imbalances, that is, the sum over consecutive years of imbalances with the same sign, was mostly greater in the 1990s compared to the 1970s and 1980s, but fell during the 2000s because of the economic crisis beginning in 2008. Adjustment in the U.S. current account deficit that occurred during the crisis has been largely due to changes in income, not prices. As the U.S. economy has slowly recovered, the deficit has again grown.

Krugman (1994) has characterized the concern with "international competitiveness" as a "dangerous obsession." Seventy five years ago, J. M. Keynes warned economists about their dismissal of policy makers' concern with trade imbalances. Keynes (1964[1936]) writes:

The weight of my criticism is directed against the inadequacy of the theoretical foundations of the laissez-faire doctrine upon which I was brought up and which for many years I taught; – against the notion that the rate of interest and the level of investment are self-adjusting at the optimum level, so that preoccupation with the balance of trade is a waste of time. For we, the faculty of economists, prove to have been guilty of presumptuous error in treating as a puerile obsession what for centuries has been a prime object of practical statecraft (Keynes 1964[1936], 339).

In today's globalized economy, international economists would benefit from a serious consideration of Keynes's words. At a minimum, international economists should be more modest in their insistence on the primacy of a theory – comparative advantage – whose applicability is increasingly questionable because of historical and institutional change.[27] Governments have at times been forced to pay attention to the implications of persistent payments imbalance despite the Panglossian views of the international trade economists.

Economic Development and Comparative Advantage "Defiance"

We have argued that it is the strategic behavior of lead firms that has structured and driven the dynamics of GVCs. But governments see the globalization of production as a path to economic development. The notion of industrial upgrading is premised on a rejection of optimality of the given international division of labor based on comparative advantage.

The resistance to a given specialization pattern is not a recent political view, and is often associated with the eighteenth century writings of Liszt and Hamilton. Indeed, the first wave of industrializing countries typically embraced various forms of trade protectionism to promote industrialization. Countries that have successfully developed have consciously resisted specialization according to comparative advantage. This is a testament to the importance of dynamic gains from trade, and it is arguable that selective protection has been a driver of industrialization.

The East Asian miracle was very much the result of careful industrial targeting, import protection, export promotion and other subsidies, and exchange rate manipulation. It has been heavily documented (and debated) that South Korea's stunning growth beginning in the 1960s was the result of protectionism, industrial policy, and what Amsden (1989) terms "reciprocal control," according to which large firms received such government support contingent on meeting specific output, productivity, and export targets.

Amidst the amazement and consternation about China's powerful new role in the global economy, we tend to forget that China's export success has relied very heavily on selective protection, careful controls on inward foreign investment and astute currency management. China's success is not a replica of the strategies of South Korea, Taiwan, and other East Asian countries, in particular because of a greater reliance on state-owned enterprises, extensive use of foreign capital, including within special export zones, and a decentralized process of resource allocation (Bardhan 2010). Nonetheless, the state-led and interventionist nature of China's rapid

---

[27] Deardorff (1994) shows that in the presence of unbalanced trade (that is, exports are not equal to imports), the principle of comparative advantage is operative only when demand is homothetic.

growth falls squarely in the East Asian development tradition. In the 1980s and 1990s, the dismal performance of many economies that heavily liberalized has added further questions to the purported benefits of trade liberalization and specialization according to naturally endowed comparative advantage.

Chang (2002, 2007) shows when the now-developed countries were at the level of development of many of today's developing countries, they were in fact much less open and liberal than today's developing countries are being pressured to be. He argues that economic development, even in its first wave in Europe and North America, was driven not by liberalization but by varied forms of state intervention that nurtured and sometimes squelched market activity.[28] In Chang's version of events, Britain and the United States used trade protection, activist industrial policy, and lax intellectual property rights regimes to develop. Only when they had reached a certain threshold of industrialization did these countries find it in their interest to liberalize.

Global integration, Chang shows, was largely driven by imperialism, not open markets. Britain was one of the most protectionist countries in the world until the mid-nineteenth century. The United States did not permit foreign banks on American soil until well into the twentieth century. Germany had a clear policy of non-enforcement of its patent laws. In most countries, voting rights were originally based on property ownership. These were the true institutional conditions of European and North American industrialization. Successful development, whether the case of Britain, the United States, South Korea, or China results from a "defiance" of the principle of comparative advantage in pursuit of international competitiveness in higher value added processes.

3.3.3 Ethical Limits

When Paul Samuelson, Nobel Prize economist and founder of the modern neoclassical theory of free trade, came out publicly and forcefully with doubts about the benefits of services offshoring for U.S. workers, the profession seemed to be opening up to new perspectives. Samuelson (2004) argued that the traditional case for the mutual beneficence of free trade was of more limited relevance in a world of services offshoring than most economists typically acknowledge. Samuelson made two basic points against

---

[28] Chang (2002, 2007). Also see Kozul-Wright and Rayment (2007) and Reinert (2007). On comparative advantage defiance, see Lin and Chang (2009).

"Mainstream Economists Supporting Globalization" (Samuelson 2004, 135).

First, while it is a standard result in trade theory that trade liberalization will bring winners and losers in all countries it has become commonplace among international economists to adopt a weaker criterion according to which the *potential* for winners to adequately compensate losers is adequate proof of the gains from trade liberalization. This criterion for welfare improvement – the potential Pareto criterion – has been criticized on two accounts. The first is that it ignores the distribution of income and wealth. An initial distribution of wealth could be extremely unequal and nonetheless be Pareto optimal. Moreover, even if an economic change further enriches the rich while leaving the poor unaffected, then according to the Pareto criterion the change is an improvement.

Second, the potential Pareto criterion assumes a welfare improvement even if no compensation of losers by winners takes place in practice. Samuelson (2004) writes:

Should noneconomists accept this as cogent rebuttal [of opposition to trade liberalization] if there is not evidence that compensating fiscal transfers have been made or will be made? Marie Antoinette said, "Let them eat cake." But history records not transfer of sugar and flour to her peasant subjects. Even the sage Dr. Greenspan sometimes sounds Antoinette-ish. The economists' literature of the 1930s – Hicks, Lerner, Kaldor, Scitovsky and others, to say nothing of earlier writings by J.S. Mill, Edgeworth, Pareto and Viner – perpetrates something of a shell game in ethical debates about the conflict between efficiency and greater inequality (Samuelson 2004, 144).

It is this shell game of an ethical argument that is partly responsible for economists having outsourced economics to non-economists on the issue of international trade. As we noted in Chapter 1, Samuelson's dissent from the mainstream view drew attention from the press and a rebuke from fellow economists.

Alan Blinder has also been attacked for his research on the potential employment-displacing effects of offshoring of "impersonally delivered services." Blinder's (2009) breath-taking estimate that around 30 to 40 million jobs are likely in the future to involve impersonally-delivered services and thus be potentially subject to offshoring (equivalent to 22 to 29 percent of the current American workforce), flies in the face of the claim by most economists that services offshoring will be easily absorbed by the U.S. economy (Bhagwati et al. 2004). Blinder's view is not just that the labor market displacement is large, but that because it cuts across all skill levels of the U.S. labor force, it requires a more creative policy response than the usual plea by academic economists for more educational attainment and more training. Without such policies, Blinder asserts, the job displacement and income losses in the United States could be devastating, even if eventually new jobs are created in the United States to replace those lost. He writes:

The job losses [from offshoring] experienced to date are probably just the tip of a much larger iceberg whose contours will only be revealed in time... [T]he likely net job loss is zero. But the gross job losses will be huge, leading to a great deal of churning, much displacement (and re-employment) of labor and many difficult adjustments – occupational, geographical, and in other respects (Blinder 2007, 10, 19).

To be consistent, economists would have to insist on adequate compensation of losers by winners. Blinder, who has been exceptional among economists for his focus on losers and potential losers from services offshoring, has also become insistent on this point:

The basic gains-from-trade "theorem" is that the gains to winners exceed the losses to the losers, leaving the nation as a whole ahead. That's nice to know, and it is the main reason why almost all economists support free trade. But trade liberalization is not, repeat *not*, a Pareto improvement unless the losers are actually, not theoretically, compensated – which they never are (Blinder 2007a, 24, emphasis in the original).

Economists have simply not taken seriously the issue of compensating losers, and in fact have shown hostility to this. There are considerable costs of adjustment and thus the need for adequate compensation of losers. We address several policy ideas in more detail in Chapter 8.

3.4 Conclusion

We have seen that a large and increasing share of international trade is today the result of lead firm activities in GVCs. Should this alter the way we think about the driving forces and welfare implications of international trade? Most economists have answered this question in the negative: Offshoring is just like any other kind of trade, and thus requires no alteration in the theory of trade. From this perspective, the rise to prominence of GVCs in international trade should in fact expand the welfare gains from trade since now comparative advantage applies in a more refined way, that is, at the level of parts of the production process rather than simply to the production of the final good. The implication is that a more refined international division of labor should lead to the capture of more gains from trade.

But the increased international movement of portfolio and direct capital, the increasing vertical disintegration of production, the high levels of global excess capacity, and the importance of technological (as opposed to price) competition have combined to greatly diminish the relevance of the principle of comparative advantage in the determination of trade flows. In this context, absolute advantage matters along with comparative advantage in determining the direction of trade. These conditions reveal many of the conceptual limits of the principle of comparative advantage, but we have also pointed to the theory's historical and ethical limitations.

Historically, countries have intentionally "defied" the dictates of the principle of comparative advantage that risks trapping them at a low-level equilibrium output and trade profile, both in terms of value added per capita and in terms of economic growth. The ethical issue relates to the unequal emphasis that economists have placed on the two policy implications of the principle. One is the free trade principle that is supported by the age-old notion of specialization according to comparative advantage. The other is the Pareto welfare criterion that demands that those who suffer from trade liberalization be compensated. Almost all economists support the first policy implication, despite the fact that it is not a historically accurate view of the role of trade policy in capitalist development. Very few economists defend the second principle with equal fervor or specificity.

In a world with excess capacity, capital mobility, and trade in intermediates, the study of offshoring must allow a role for absolute as well as comparative advantage. In this context, institutions emerge as more important than in a world driven entirely by comparative advantage. Institutions can be seen as important determinants of competitiveness and welfare. In the chapters that follow, we focus on the institutional context in which such supply chains are managed, including corporate strategy and the constellation of bargaining power in global supply chains. We argue that the firm must be understood in a much broader way than that provided by transactions cost economics, in which the given cost structure gives off to a particular strategy of internalization or externalization in order to minimize transactions costs. Firm strategies are what drive structure, and the analysis of the GVC structure should consider firm objectives and strategies beyond the narrow confines of profit maximization or transactions cost minimization.

There is a connection between the methodological issue of institutionalism and the ethical limits of comparative advantage. Thus, we insist that a compelling account of offshoring must also consider the institutional and historical context of corporate strategy, state intervention, and labor market segmentation. While this is a grand claim, it is rooted in a theory of international trade and welfare in which these institutional factors are brought in at the outset. This also allows consideration of institutions to enter when we discuss policy response. Piore, writing in the wake of the North American Free Trade Agreement political battles in the United States, notes that the institutional context in which trade is imagined influences the possibilities for imagining other aspects of globalization policy. He writes:

The problem at root is that the proponents of trade expansion have made their argument as part of a broader argument about the virtues of an unregulated market economy. Trade expansion in this way is tied to a series of other policy proposal (anti-union, deregulation etc.) . . . [T]he formulation of trade policy in terms that disparage governmental policy and public action creates an intellectual climate in which such policies are difficult even to think of. This discourages strategies predicated on supporting public institutions (Piore 1998, 283).

In sum, the context in which trade policy is traditionally imagined generally leaves aside the possibility of active policy. Policies are viewed as distortions and thus as necessarily detrimental. In the chapters that follow, and especially in Chapter 8, we propose that just as the theory of offshoring must account for the embeddedness of markets in a broad institutional structure, so must the policy response to offshoring go beyond the simple dichotomy of free trade versus protection. We argue for a larger discussion of economic institutions of capitalism and the regulation of firms and markets generally that compensate losers, maximize dynamic gains, and promote a high-road rather than a low-road growth trajectory.

FOUR

Lead Firm Strategy and Global Value Chain Structure

In Chapter 3, we saw that a reconsideration of the forces of international capital mobility, technological change and social institutions requires a change in traditional thinking on the determinants of trade. In this chapter, we use the global value chain (GVC) as the unit of analysis of international trade. The gains from offshoring are based on the increase in profits and wages and the creation of jobs. Key is the distribution of value added across producers within the value chain and the resulting potential for "dynamic gains." These gains come especially from the reinvestment of the profits that emerge from successful GVC management. Lead firms in GVCs raise cost markups and profitability by focusing on core competence and otherwise reducing operations, especially in the domestic market.

GVC management has been an important part of corporate strategy to retain oligopoly power and the rents that go with it. The cost and ease of international communication has fallen, the supply of available labor and productive capacity globally has greatly expanded, and the quality of production and logistical capability of developing country firms has grown. The globalization of production along these lines creates an asymmetry of market structures within the GVC with oligopoly lead firms and competition among suppliers. Expansion of offshoring can also support a financialization of the non-financial corporate sector.

The lens of the GVC puts into focus the dynamic aspects of globalized production, rather than just the static efficiency gains that are the focus of economic theory, even the transactions cost version, in which transactions costs are minimized. The competitive struggle by firms to increase value added within GVCs – so-called industrial upgrading – is a function not simply of factor costs, but of an array of institutional features, including the power of firms within the value chain, the structure of households and the labor supply conditions this underpins, and the efforts by governments to support innovation and provide the social protection that are so important in determining competitiveness.

The more important source of gains from offshoring comes from the reinvestment of the profits that result from globalization. In the econometric analysis presented in Chapters 5 and 6, we analyze offshoring in GVCs using sectoral data. In this chapter, we look at the relation from the perspective of firms. There is a direct link between these: the firm's pricing and profits are driven by its growth and investment strategy. This investment behavior has immediate consequences for aggregate demand and growth at the sectoral level. We focus on two sources of power. One is that of lead firms as oligopsony buyers in the market for inputs. The other is that of shareholders and executives in seeking to raise shareholder value in the short-run.

The next section describes the asymmetry of market structures within the GVC with oligopoly lead firms and competition among suppliers. Section 4.2 takes a closer look at this endogenous asymmetry of market structure including its different forms, its sustainability, and how it is coordinated. In Section 4.3, we then turn to the determinants of value chain structure and focus on the transaction costs-based theory, resource-based theory, and the strategic approach. Section 4.4 takes up the dynamic gains from trade and offshoring and concludes.

4.1 Trade, Profits, and Investment

The motives for offshoring for the strategic firm range from the pursuit of greater flexibility to diversification of location in order to reduce risk to the lowering of production costs. All of these goals can support company profitability, especially lower production costs. In fact, the last decade of heightened globalization of production has coincided with an increase in profits as a share of national income in all the major industrialized countries. Figure 4.1 shows the U.S. corporate profit share, measured by corporate profits as a percentage of gross value added by corporations for the period from 1970 to 2010. After stagnating in the 1980s, the profit share recovered beginning in the mid-1990s. It has been higher during the peaks of the last two business cycles than at any time since the 1970s. Despite the recent economic crisis, the profit share was back at pre-crisis levels in 2010.

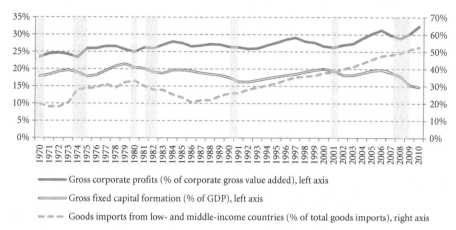

Figure 4.1. Import, Profit, and Investment Shares, United States, 1970–2010. *Source:* Own illustration. Data: U.S. Bureau of Economic Analysis, National Income and Product Accounts; United Nations (UN) Comtrade. Gray bars correspond to U.S. business cycles recessions according to the definition of the National Bureau of Economic Research.

Figure 4.1 also shows the broad measure of goods offshoring, as defined in Chapter 2, which increased constantly from 20 percent in the mid-1980s to over 50 percent in 2009 and 2010. Note that goods offshoring here covers all goods imports rather than only manufacturing imports. In the next section, we show that firms can increase their markup and profit share through increased offshoring. Firms have different options for how to spend their additional savings from offshoring, one of which is investment, which we refer to as the dynamic gains from offshoring and is the focus of the last section of this chapter and also of Chapter 6. Figure 4.1 shows that the U.S. share of gross fixed capital formation as percentage of gross domestic product (GDP) declined slightly since the end of the 1970s and strongly since 2000. This happened despite the simultaneous increase in offshoring and the profit share, providing a first indicator that firms have alternative options to spend their savings from offshoring.

4.1.1 Cost Markups, the Profit Share, and Offshoring

Price Competition, Markups, and the Profit Share
In this section, we consider the firms' markups over costs and their relationship to the profit share from the perspective of the lead firms in GVCs. In Chapters 5 and 6, we look at the profit share in terms of its implications for economic security and for financialization. Economic theories of

markup pricing emphasize the role of product price setting power rather than cost setting power. But substituting lower-cost intermediate goods and services imports for higher-cost domestic inputs can raise firms' markup over costs as well as the economy-wide profit share of national income.

Define the markup, $m = (P - C)/C$, where P is price and C are variable costs. If we reduce these costs to just labor costs, then we can write $m = (P - wa)/wa$, where w represents the wage and a is the labor coefficient. Stated equivalently, we can write $P = (1 + m)wa$. Because the pre-tax profit share PS is defined as $PS = (P - wa)/P$, this implies that the profit share, $PS = ((1 + m)wa - wa)/((1 + m)wa) = m/(1 + m)$. This gives $dPS/dm = 1/(1 + m)^2 > 0$, that is, an increase in the markup yields an increase in the profit share. The focus in the literature has been on the ability of firms to raise P, subject to various constraints. In neoclassical theory, the markup is constrained by the elasticity of substitution in demand. In the Post Keynesian theory, which forms the basis of the analysis here, the constraints include substitution by consumers, entry by new rival firms, the possibility of government intervention, labor union strength, branding effort, and the cost structure of the firm.[1]

Oligopoly models predict that the degree to which cost changes are passed through to product prices – and thus the degree to which markups remain constant – will vary directly with the degree of competition, usually measured by the price elasticity of demand for the final good. Under perfectly competitive product markets, the markup of price over marginal costs is zero and thus all cost savings would be passed through to consumers. In oligopoly, if rivals are likely to follow price drops by any one firm, then the cost-reducing firm will retain product price and thus raise its cost markup.[2] Even when all rivals experience a cost decline, say because of an exchange rate appreciation that lowers the domestic currency cost of imported inputs, there is likely to be incomplete pass-through of the cost savings to the product price.

This is clear in the Kaleckian markup pricing formulation. At the level of the firm, corporate profits depend on the ability of corporations to raise their markup prices above average costs. Kalecki (1971, 1991[1954]) models the markup as a function of "the degree of monopoly of the firm position"

---

[1] Following Kalecki (1991[1954]), Post Keynesian pricing models emerged in the 1970s. See Eichner (1976), Wood (1975), and Harcourt and Kenyon (1976). For an overview of the Post Keynesian theory, see Shapiro and Mott (1995). See Shapiro and Sawyer (2003) for a discussion of "administered costs" in oligopoly firms' markup pricing strategies.

[2] This is a version of the traditional kinked demand curve analysis of oligopoly pricing, based originally on Sweezy (1939). For a more formal rendering with econometric tests, see Cowling and Sugden (1989).

(Kalecki 1991[1954], 18), where the degree of monopoly is determined by a set of environmental or institutional factors, including industrial concentration, advertising expenditure levels, the influence of labor unions, and changes in the ratio of fixed to variable costs. In order to determine their output price, P, firms markup over average prime costs and take into account the output-weighted average price charged by rival firms in the industry, giving firm price, $P = \alpha u + \beta \overline{P}$, where $\overline{P}$ denotes the output-weighted average price in the industry, u the average prime costs, and α and β coefficients reflecting the degree of monopoly.

The markup is an increasing function of $\overline{P}/P$ because a larger deviation between the firm's price, P, and the average industry price, $\overline{P}$, reflects less competition among firms in the industry and is associated with a higher markup. If prime costs (for example, unit labor costs) fall by the same amount for all firms in the industry, then prices for all firms fall accordingly with no change in the markup. But if costs fall for one firm alone, the result of, for example, efficient value chain management, then that firm's price will not fall in the same proportion as its costs, implying an increase in the markup.[3]

Post Keynesian models of markup pricing have two important features. One is that they link the firm to the macroeconomy, because firm pricing decisions are seen as determined by investment demand and thus have an effect on investment expenditures. Second, and related to the first, is that prices are not understood as signals of efficiency or inefficiency. That is, firm pricing decisions do not serve the role of bringing efficient market outcomes, but rather are driven by firm long-term objectives for investment and growth. Prices serve these firm objectives rather than that of allocative efficiency, as in traditional theory. From this perspective, offshoring is a means for the maintenance of oligopoly power under conditions of product price competition. Just as Hymer (1972) described the rise of foreign direct investment (FDI) by U.S. firms beginning in the 1920s as "a new weapon in the arsenal of oligopolistic rivalry" (Hymer 1972, 44), so has offshoring played a similar role in the new wave of globalization.

There are three channels to maintaining or raising the markup over costs: (i) raising the product price, (ii) lowering input prices, and (iii) raising productivity. Raising the product price is the traditional channel for firms with product market power. Demand-side conditions have been the focus of the theory of oligopoly pricing (see traditional models of imperfect competition, such as Dixit and Stiglitz 1976, or with international trade, such as Krugman 1979). Despite this theoretical focus on product markets and the

---

[3] Milberg (2009) gives an algebraic demonstration.

Table 4.1. _Prices and Money Supply, Average Annual Growth, United States, 1986–2006_

	1986–1990	1991–1995	1996–2000	2001–2006
Consumer Prices	4.4%	3.5%	2.4%	2.1%
Import Prices	5.4%	2.0%	−1.4%	0.7%
Money Supply (M2)	5.7%	1.8%	8.6%	6.2%

Source: Own illustration: Data and notes: Consumer price index data are from the Bureau of Labor Statistics and refer to the base consumer price index for all urban consumers for all items less food and energy. Import prices are from the Bureau of Labor Statistics and refer to the import price index for all items less petroleum. Money supply (M2) is from the International Monetary Fund International Financial Statistics Database and comprises the sum of currency outside banks, demand deposits other than those of the central government, and the time, savings, and foreign currency deposits of resident sectors other than the central government.

demand elasticity, it would appear that over the past ten years the rising profit share has not depended on rising final goods and services prices. An increase in price competition in product markets among oligopoly firms – especially in the retail sector, but also in sectors as technologically diverse as automobiles and computers – has made the firm's implicit cost of raising the price prohibitively high. Inward foreign investment, foreign capacity expansion, changing consumer attitudes, and slow growth in the global economy appear to have rejuvenated price competition among oligopoly firms (Crotty 2005).

Recent popular writings have highlighted the increased intensity of price competition in U.S. product markets and the unprecedented power of consumers in demanding variety and low prices (for example, Reich 2008 and Cassidy 2005). Consumer price inflation (especially prices of non-energy goods and services) has fallen steadily from its post-War peaks in the 1970s, and remained low across industrialized countries during the same period that the profit share has been rising. Over the past twenty-five years, growth in U.S. consumer prices fell constantly from 4.4 percent during the second half of the 1980s to only 2.1 percent during the early 2000s (see Table 4.1). At the same time U.S. monetary policy – the usual first explanation of price level trends – has not been particularly tight. Growth in import prices declined at an even faster pace and actually fell during the second half of the 1990s. Input costs, including the cost of labor and non-labor inputs, have risen very slowly, with the exception of occasional commodity price surges.

Offshoring and the Profit Share

To add the offshoring of inputs to the model, suppose $C = vw^*a^* + (1-v)wa$, where v is the share of inputs produced offshore, w and a denote the wage rate and the labor coefficient, an asterisk designates foreign, and assume that foreign production costs are lower than U.S. costs, that is $dC/dv < 0$. Offshoring to lower costs can also help to dampen domestic costs, because the move offshore or even its threat can lower wage demands and dampen domestic wages. That is, if $w = w(v)$, and $dw/dv < 0$, then as offshoring rises and U.S. wages fall, the positive relation between offshoring and the markup is reinforced.

Note that while our pricing theory is Post Keynesian, the macroeconomic implications are not. From a Keynesian or Kaleckian macroeconomic perspective, the shift to more intensive use of imports would, *ceteris paribus*, reduce growth and the profit share. Kalecki's analysis is particularly relevant here, because he saw the trade surplus as the basis for expanding the profits through a profits multiplier:

$$\Pi = \frac{1}{1 - C_\Pi} \left(AC + I - S_W + (G - TR) + (EX - IM)\right) \quad (4.1)$$

where Π designates total profits, AC autonomous capitalists' consumption, I total private investment, S_w total savings out of wage income, G total government spending, TR total tax revenue, EX total exports, and IM total imports. $(G - TR)$ is the government deficit, $(EX - IM)$ the trade surplus, and C_Π the marginal propensity to consume out of profit income. $1/(1 - C_\Pi)$ represents the "profit multiplier."

Kalecki felt that by linking the expansion of export markets with the attainment of higher profits, he had "finally solved the puzzle of 'economic imperialism'" (Blecker 1999, 121). Blecker (1989) sought to place this Kaleckian view in the context of modern trade competition among industrialized countries, and identified import competition as an important force mitigating the power of oligopoly to raise markups. In the presence of import competition, domestic cost increases (such as a wage increase) would reduce firms' markup over costs, reducing the profit share and leading to a reduction in investment and economic growth. Blecker's insight seems to have been borne out, with one unpredicted twist in the U.S. case at least: about half of the imports are being driven by U.S. firms themselves in their effort to cut costs by importing low-cost inputs of goods and services. In the process, these firms have also reduced the demand for and cost of U.S. labor, further easing the costs of production. The result is that, *ceteris paribus*, expanded offshoring is not inconsistent with higher markups, profits, and the profit share.

We can broaden the Kaleckian analysis, however, to capture the distinction between different types of imports. Kalecki wrote in the 1930s about an economy like the United Kingdom where imports were heavily oriented towards primary commodities and exports were largely manufactures and services. Competitive imports lower both profits and wages in domestic competing firms. Non-competitive imported inputs – that is, inputs that do not compete with a domestic producer – would depress wages or employment, whereas boosting profit rates and the profit share.[4]

The implication is that when imports are non-competitive imports, then the trade deficit can have a different impact on profits and the profit share than envisioned in the Kaleckian framework. A mechanical way to think about this is that if imports do not constitute competition with domestic producers then such imports do not lower industrial concentration ratios. Cowling et al. (2000) do precisely this calculation for the case of the U.K. motor vehicles sector (car, vans, trucks, and buses). Traditional measures of concentration show a steady decline in concentration beginning in the mid-1970s through 1995. When they recalculate the concentration figures to account for non-competitive imports (by adding a certain percentage of the imports to the sales of the top five firms), they find that concentration ratios in all product categories returned in the 1980s and 1990s almost to the levels of the early 1970s. The authors write:

UK imports of manufactures should not be construed as independent of the domestic structure of production... Previous measures of concentration, which have adjusted domestic concentration ratios for imports, have been made, for the most part, under the assumption that all imports are competitive. In a world of transnationally organized production and trade, where dominant domestic producers may act to control imports strategically, this can no longer be considered an acceptable working assumption (Cowling et al. 2000, 47, 52).

There is a growing body of research on the issue of the impact of offshoring on profits, including our own econometric analysis presented in Chapter 5, which shows that in the United States at the sectoral level offshoring has significantly contributed to lower labor shares and hence higher profit shares across manufacturing and service sectors in the period from 1998 to 2006. Dossani and Kenney (2003) report that a 40 percent cost saving represents the hurdle rate of return on services offshoring. Firm level surveys, such as McKinsey Global Institute (2003), for example, find that offshoring reduces costs to the firm by around 40 percent for the foreign sourced activity. A number of large firms they survey reported savings considerably higher than this. Lazonick (2007) cites reports of 50 to 60 percent cost saving for offshoring of business, professional, and technical services.

Görg and Hanley (2004), using a sample of twelve Irish electronics subsectors, find that firm-level profits are directly related to offshoring for large

[4] We are grateful to Malcolm Sawyer for bringing this point to our attention.

firms (in employment terms) and not significantly related for the small firms in the sample. In a study of small- and medium-size Japanese firms, Kimura (2002) finds no relation between subcontracting and profitability. In a study of German manufacturing firms, Görzig and Stephan (2002) find outsourcing of materials (including domestic purchases) to be associated with higher profits but outsourcing of services (including domestic purchases) to be associated with lower profits. In Chapter 5, our econometric analysis shows that the effects vary by country and in particular depend on the labor market institutions in place.

4.1.2 The Persistence of Oligopoly

The implication of these developments is that the globalization of production has not occurred simply as a generalized increase in the degree of competition among firms. Rather, globalization has occurred instead within GVCs, in which the lead firms, and in some cases supplier firms, are oligopolistic. Oligopoly power in the United States continues to appear as a much higher markup over costs than is found in more competitive sectors. A recent study finds that the oligopoly premium averaged 15 percent in U.S. manufacturing between 1981 and 2004 (see Table 4.2). Although we lack information on market structure in services, the average markup across all service sectors over the same period was 68 percent (see Table 4.3).

Oligopoly power has been affirmed through product and process innovation, as firms have turned to product differentiation and branding to solidify their product market power. The proliferation of varieties in consumer products began with Toyota's introduction of more models in a given year than any of its competitors. This capacity is typically associated with changes in the management of the assembly line, the introduction of just-in-time inventory control, and with a system of industrial relations that promotes flexibility and production worker cooperation. The introduction of information technology (IT) has affected not only productivity, but also the variety of products offered. Mass customization – the rapid proliferation of varieties without sacrificing scale economies – has been an effective corporate response to rising consumer power and the heightened demand for variety and quality (Pine 1993; Blecker and Friedrich 2010).

Computer aided design and computer aided manufacturing have changed firms' ability to vary product lines and rapidly introduce new designs. Computerized inventory controls such as stock keeping units have

Table 4.2. *Markups in the Manufacturing Sectors, United States,*
1981–2004

Industry	1981–2004 United States
Competitive Industries[a]	
Food products & beverages	1.12
Textiles	1.07
Wearing, Dressing & Dying of Fur	1.14
Wood, Wood Products & Cork	1.15
Printing, Publishing & Reproduction	1.30
Chemicals & Chemical Products	1.31
Rubber & Plastics	1.19
Other Non-Metallic Mineral	1.26
Fabricated Metal	1.20
Machinery, nec.	1.25
Electrical Machinery & Apparatus, nec.	1.20
Average Markup in Competitive Industries[b]	**1.20**
Oligopoly Industries[a]	
Tobacco	1.61
Leather, Leather & Footwear	1.21
Paper & Pulp	1.21
Coke, Refined Petroleum & Nuclear Fuel	1.09
Basic Metals	1.10
Office, Accounting & Computing Machinery	1.19
Radio, Television & Communication Equipment	1.29
Medical, Precision & Optical Instruments	1.35
Motor Vehicles, Trailers & Semi-Trailers	0.98
Other Transport Equipment	2.79
Average Markup in Oligopoly Industries[b]	**1.38**
Oligopoly Premium	**15.3%**

Source: Own illustration. Data: Christopoulou and Vermeulen (2008), Table A1.c.

[a] The authors use concentration ratios for 2002 from the Economic Census to differentiate competitive from oligopoly sectors for the United States. Specifically, the authors looked at the Herfindahl-Hirschman index for the 50 largest companies in the industry and classified indexes larger than 130 as oligopoly sectors. The 2002 Herfindahl-Hirschman indexes for our industries ranged from 32 (rubber & plastics) to 2,905 (tobacco).

[b] Unweighted average.

led to rapid and detailed collection of sales and inventory information. Firms can now regulate inventory with precision. Giant retail firms boast of a designer line of consumer goods, changing as seasons and fashions change. In the apparel industry, "fast fashion" is the name given

Table 4.3. *Markups in Selected Service Sectors, United States, 1981–2004*

Industry	1981–2004 United States
Electricity & Gas	1.44
Water Supply	n.a.
Construction	1.31
Sale, Maint. & Repair of Motor Vehicles & Motorcycles; Retail Sale of Fuel	1.02
Wholesale Trade & Commission Trade, except of Motor Vehicles & Mot/cles	1.31
Retail Trade, except of Motor Vehicles & Mot/cles; Repair of Household Goods	1.19
Post & Telecommunications	1.38
Financial Intermediation, except Insurance & Pension Funding	1.39
Insurance & Pension Funding, except Compulsory Social Security	1.14
Activities Related to Financial Intermediation	n.a.
Real Estate Activities	3.77
Renting of Machinery & Equipment	3.21
Computer & Related Activities	1.78
Research & Development	1.62
Other Business Activities	1.26
Average Markup[a]	**1.68**
Average Markup[a] without Real Estate Activities and Renting of Machinery & Equipment	**1.35**

Source: Own illustration. Data: Christopoulou and Vermeulen (2008), Table A1.c.
[a] Unweighted average.

to those firms that are able to alter each store's offerings within days, based on the latest trends and buying patterns at that particular store (Abernathy et al. 1999). Variety in consumer goods – from fancy coffees to household appliances to cell phones – has exploded, in part the result of greater flexibility in production, improvements in the logistics of transportation and inventory management, and with massive improvements in data collection on consumption patterns.

The result of many of these changes has been a consolidation of power by large firms, indicated by a rise in industrial concentration since the mid-1990s. Nolan et al. (2002) characterize the increase in industrial concentration internationally as a "global business revolution," which, they write, "produced an unprecedented concentration of business power in large corporations headquartered in the high-income countries" (Nolan et al. 2002, 1).

They identify a broad range of industries with high degrees of concentration as measured by market share, including commercial aircraft, automobiles, gas turbines, microprocessors, computer software, electronic games, and even consumer goods, including soft drinks, ice cream, film and cigarettes, and services such as brokerage for mergers and acquisitions (M&As) and insurance. A selection of this market share evidence is presented in Table 4.4.

Over the past ten years, the surge of cross-border M&As has contributed to the global consolidation of industry. In the face of an unprecedented globalization of production over the past twenty-five years, with an historic increase in international trade, a steady decline in levels of trade protection, market-friendly policies throughout the world, a global IT "revolution" with its creation of new hardware and software megacorps, still most of the world's largest firms are based in developed countries. Of the top 100 companies, as ranked in the Financial Times 500 for 2012, 16 are from emerging markets (eight from China, four from Brazil, three from Russia, and one from Mexico). Of these sixteen firms, six are banks and five are oil and gas producers. Of the remaining large firms from emerging markets two are in mining and one each is in beverages, life insurance and mobile telecommunications (from http://www.ft.com/companies/ft500).

While branding and product variety have figured in corporate strategies to maintain markups, higher profits have also come from dramatic efforts to control costs. To maintain the markup without the traditional ability to raise product prices, unit costs must be reduced, with the typical strategic options being lower compensation or higher productivity. As has been well documented, hourly U.S. wages and even total compensation (wages, salaries, and benefits) have risen more slowly than productivity growth since the early 1980s (see Figure 4.2). Median hourly compensation of male workers even declined between 1989 and 1999. Recent research has explained this as a result of the collapse of labor-supporting institutions in the United States, as labor union membership has continued to decline (as Chapter 5 discusses) and the real minimum wage has fallen.[5] While these are no doubt of major importance, here we explore the possibility of another source, which is offshoring, that is, the effective management of GVCs.

---

[5] On U.S. wage stagnation and institutional shifts, see Temin and Levy (2007). On the issue of the distribution of productivity gains, see Dew-Becker and Gordon (2005).

Table 4.4. *Global Market Shares for Selected Business Activities*

Firm	Business activity	Market share	Source
Aerospace			
Boeing	commercial aircraft deliveries (100 + seats)	47	FT, 28 July 2005
Airbus	commercial aircraft deliveries (100 + seats)	53	FT, 28 July 2005
Autos			
GM	automobiles	16	DaimlerChrysler, 2005
Toyota	automobiles	13	DaimlerChrysler, 2005
Ford	automobiles	12	DaimlerChrysler, 2005
VW	automobiles	9	DaimlerChrysler, 2005
Renault – Nissan	automobiles	9	DaimlerChrysler, 2005
DaimlerChrysler	automobiles	8	DaimlerChrysler, 2005
Fast-moving consumer goods			
Coca-Cola	carbonated soft drinks	51	Annual report, 1998
Proctor & Gamble	fine fragrances	15	FT, 15 December 2005
L'Oréal	fine fragrances	14	FT, 15 December 2005
Gillette	razors	70	MSDW 1998
Nike	athletic foot wear	33	FT, 4 August 2005
Adidas/Reebok	athletic foot wear	25	FT, 4 August 2005
Philip Morris	cigarettes[a]	27	FT, 7 June 2008
BAT/BAT Associates	cigarettes[a]	24	FT, 7 June 2008
IT/electronics hardware and software			
Intel	micro-processors	80	FT, 20 January 2006
AMD	micro processors	15	FT, 20 January 2006
Microsoft	PC operating systems	85	FT, 29 April 2000
Sony	digital cameras	18	FT, 15 December 2004
Canon	digital cameras	16	FT, 15 December 2004
Samsung	NAND flash memory chips	60	FT, 17 May 2005
Toshiba	NAND flash memory chips	23	FT, 15 December 2005
Hewlett-Packard	notebooks and desktop PCs	17	FT, 28 May 2003
Dell	notebooks and desktop PCs	16	FT, 28 May 2003
Palm	hand held computers	32	FT, 7 August 2001
Compaq	hand held computers	16	FT, 7 August 2001
Sony	electronic games	67	FT, 29 March 2000
Nintendo	electronic games	29	FT, 29 march 2000
Samsung	flat screen TVs	17	FT, 12 June 2003
LG Philips	flat screen TVs	17	FT, 12 June 2003
Nokia	mobile phones	34	FT, 29 September 2006
Motorola	mobile phones	22	FT, 29 September 2006
Samsung	mobile phones	11	FT, 29 September 2006
Matsushita	DVD recorders	30	FT, 6 August 2004
Sony	LCD TVs	15	FT, 27 April 2006
Sharp	LCD TVs	14	FT, 27 April 2006
Philips/Magnavox	LCD TVs	14	FT, 27 April 2006

Source: Own illustration. Data: Nolan (2008). Note: The market share figures given are by various types of measures (volumes, sales etc.) and are intended only as a rough guide. FT is the Financial Times, MSDW is Morgan Stanley Dean Witter published reports.

[a] excluding China.

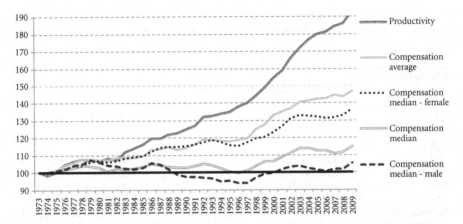

Figure 4.2. Productivity Growth and Hourly Compensation, Index (1973=100), United States, 1973–2009. *Source*: Own illustration. Data: Economic Policy Institute analysis based on Bureau of Labor Statistics and Bureau of Economic Analysis data. Note: Compensation = hourly compensation, Productivity = Output per hour.

4.1.3 Global Value Chains and Heightened Competition among Suppliers

There is less evidence available on markups and market structure at upstream points in the GVC compared to the information available on lead firms and performance of developed country sectors. To the extent that markups are associated with firm size, we would expect lower markups among developing country firms since, as we have seen, the world's largest firms are mostly based in developed countries. Although size no doubt matters, it is the structure of markets and the investment strategies of firms that determine markups. Following Mayer et al. (2002), we measure the concentration ratio of supplier markets in terms of the number of countries involved in export.

The pattern of increased spatial dispersion of supply sources has long been identified in the textiles and apparel sector and the consumer electronics sector. In these two sectors there have been regular waves of new, lower-cost entrants over time seeking to capture market share. Not coincidentally, capacity in these sectors is often located in export processing zones (EPZs), the establishment of which represents the policy aimed at gaining export market access through GVCs (see Chapter 7). Here we note simply that in the presence of considerable excess capacity in these sectors, new entrants often engage in trade diversion rather than trade creation. The point is that over time there has been continual entry by new firms into production of especially low- and medium-technology goods and services that serve as inputs to lead firm outputs.

We measure GVC structure using a modified version of the Herfindahl-Hirschman Index (HHI) calculated for each product category by taking the total sum of the squared market shares of all countries exporting that product and multiplying the sum by 10,000, thus:

$$HHI_i = \sum_c \left(\frac{EX_{ci}}{EX_{Wi}} \right)^2 * 10,000 \qquad (4.2)$$

where the term in parentheses designates a country c's exports of product i as a percentage of world exports of product i, (EX_{Wi}).[6] The HHI can range between $1/n * 10,000$ (if each of the n countries has the same share), and 10,000, if one country exports all, where n designates the total number of countries exporting this product. A decline reflects a decrease in "concentration," or, more accurately, a greater degree of spatial dispersion of export sourcing in that sector. The U.S. Department of Justice Antitrust Division considers HHIs between 1,500 and 2,500 points to be moderately concentrated, and those exceeding 2,500 points to be concentrated.[7] Although this rule of thumb refers to the original HHI, that is, to firms' market shares in a particular market rather than to the market shares of exporting countries, it provides a convenient benchmark for judging export market concentration. Figure 4.3 shows the graph of the index of industrial concentration for a selection of three-digit sectors using the Standard International Trade Classification (SITC) for selected years from 1970/1971 to 2005/2006.

Most of the product areas experience a spatial dispersion of trade although there are a number of exceptions. Moreover, most sectors except for machinery and transportation already start at a relatively low level of concentration in 1970/1971. While materials and articles of rubber experienced a strong dispersion of exports, leather products showed signs of increased concentration, especially in fur skins. In textiles, we see the strongest dispersion in textile yarn and thread or special textile fabrics and related products, whereas made up articles and to a lesser extent cotton experience a concentration of trade. In iron and steel, most sub-sectors show a clear dispersion in exports except for hoop and strip of iron and steel that experienced a strong consolidation.

Machinery shows a clear trend of spatial dispersion in exports, especially in textile and leather machinery and machines for special industries. Office

---

[6] This measure was used by Mayer et al. (2002) and Milberg (2004b).
[7] See http://www.justice.gov/atr/public/testimony/hhi.htm.

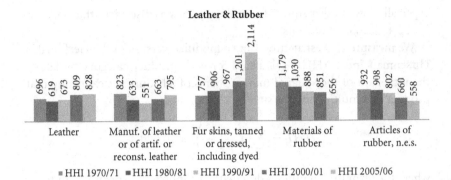

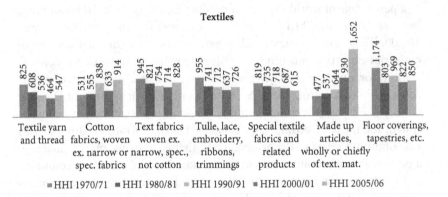

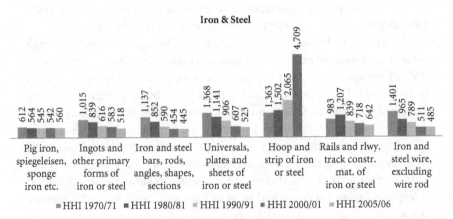

Figure 4.3. Herfindahl-Hirschman Index in Manufacturing by Standard International Trade Classification, 1970/71–2005/06. *Source*: Own illustration. Based on Milberg and Winkler (2010a, 49–51). Data: UN Comtrade. Note: The Standard International Trade Classification used was Revision 1. HHI = Herfindahl-Hirschman Index.

Machinery

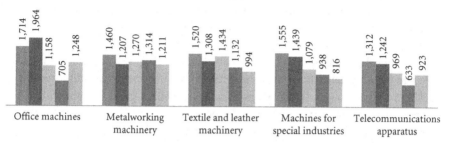

■ HHI 1970/71 ■ HHI 1980/81 ▨ HHI 1990/91 ■ HHI 2000/01 ▨ HHI 2005/06

Transportation

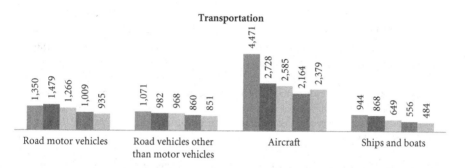

■ HHI 1970/71 ■ HHI 1980/81 ▨ HHI 1990/91 ■ HHI 2000/01 ▨ HHI 2005/06

Furniture, Travel Goods, Clothing

■ HHI 1970/71 ■ HHI 1980/81 ▨ HHI 1990/91 ■ HHI 2000/01 ▨ HHI 2005/06

Figure 4.3 (*continued*)

machines and telecommunication products followed a similar trend until 2000/2001, but show signs of consolidation since then. Transportation follows a constant trend of trade dispersion which was weaker in vehicles, ships, and boats, but much stronger in aircraft. Interestingly, furniture, travel goods, and clothing have seen an increase in concentration of export sourcing, especially travel goods and handbags, fur clothing, and footwear. These are sectors in which China made enormous gains in world market share, pushing out competitors, especially those from Africa and Latin America, but also those from smaller East and South Asian countries.

This direct evidence of greater dispersion of production across a wide variety of generally low value added manufacturing sectors is consistent with previous econometric studies of competition in developing countries. Roberts and Tybout (1996) present a series of country studies that focus on market entry and exit conditions. They present evidence on Chile, Columbia, Mexico, Morocco, and Turkey for the 1970s and 1980s. Summarizing the studies, Roberts and Tybout (1996) write that

entry and exit rates are substantial . . . Despite the popular perception that entry and the associated competitive pressures are relatively limited in developing countries, these entry figures exceed the comparable figures for industrial countries (Roberts and Tybout 1996, 191).

Another study focuses on profitability and its persistence in seven developing countries – Brazil, India, Jordan, South Korea, Malaysia, Mexico, and Zimbabwe – and compare that to estimates for industrialized countries. The authors find that,

Surprisingly, both short- and long-term persistence of profitability for developing countries are found to be lower than those for advanced countries (Glen et al. 2002, 1).

Finally, a study from the labor market perspective also confirms the competitive picture in developing countries. Brainard and Riker (1997) estimate the wage elasticity of labor demand across affiliates of U.S. multinational corporations (MNCs). A drop in the wage in a low-wage affiliate has little effect on employment in the home operation, but a large and significant effect on employment in other low-wage affiliates of the same firm (Brainard and Riker 1997).

In services, we see a similar trend of spatial dispersion. Figure 4.4 shows the HHI for selected service sectors between 1980/81 and 2005/06. Communication services, financial services, computer and information services, royalties and license fees, and other business services all experienced a dispersion over this period, with the highest degree in dispersion in computer

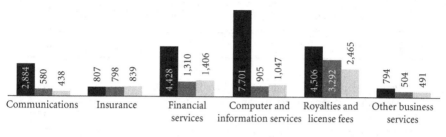

Figure 4.4. Herfindahl-Hirschman Index in Selected Service Sectors, 1980/81–2005/06. *Source*: Own illustration. Data: UNCTAD. Note: Many countries did not have data available, especially in earlier years. Therefore, the high concentration indexes can be somewhat distorted and must be interpreted with caution.

and information services and communication services. Only insurance services show a slight increase in concentration of trade.

The oligopsonistic conditions in supplier markets that emerged in the 1990s and largely persist today are reflected in falling import unit values relative to final goods and services prices. Excluding food and oil, U.S. import prices have fallen slightly on average since the mid-1990s. Import price deflation is more pronounced in those sectors in which dispersion was greatest, which is where GVCs are most developed. Recall that a greater dispersion in a given product, that is, a falling HHI, reflects that more countries export this product than previously. As a result, wider participation of many developing countries in global trade increases the price competition and should lower the import price of this product. Table 4.5 shows U.S. import prices relative to U.S. domestic consumer prices in the period from 1986 to 2006 for two-digit SITC industries. Only six sectors – and those most closely associated with commodities (specifically petroleum and iron) rather than manufactures – experienced relative import price increases.

Relative import price declines were smallest in manufacturing sectors most intensive in foods, metals, and wood, that is, industries characterized by more competition and lower markups (see Table 4.4). Relative import price declines were greatest in those sectors which have both the technological and the value chain characteristics identified with profitable offshoring – computers, electrical and telecommunications products, that is, oligopoly industries characterized by higher markups (see Table 4.4). But many of the non-electronics manufacturing sectors also showed large and persistent relative import price declines, especially those with well-developed GVCs and high rates of import penetration in the United States. Clothing, footwear,

Table 4.5. *Relative Import Prices, CAGR, United States, 1986–2006*

Sectors	CAGR
1986–2006	
33 – Petroleum, petroleum products and related materials	7.45%
28 – Metalliferous ores and metals crap	3.34%
68 – Nonferrous metals	3.14%
25 – Wood pulp and recovered paper	1.15%
24 – Cork and wood	1.07%
67 – Iron and steel	0.83%
54 – Medicinal and pharmaceutical products	− 0.01%
63 – Cork and wood manufactures other than furniture	− 0.21%
73 – Metalworking machinery	− 0.23%
72 – Machinery specialized for particular industries	− 0.25%
11 – Beverages	− 0.41%
74 – General industrial machinery, equipment, & machine parts	− 0.55%
66 – Nonmetallic mineral manufactures	− 0.55%
05 – Vegetables, fruit and nuts, fresh or dried	− 0.58%
01 – Meat and meat preparations	− 0.62%
52 – Inorganic chemicals	− 0.86%
03 – Fish, crustaceans, aquatic invertebrates, and preparations thereof	− 0.91%
51 – Organic chemicals	− 1.02%
64 – Paper and paperboard, cut to size	− 1.03%
69 – Manufactures of metals	− 1.03%
59 – Chemical materials and products	− 1.05%
78 – Road vehicles	− 1.11%
83 – Travel goods, handbags and similar containers	− 1.16%
87 – Professional, scientific and controlling instruments and apparatus	− 1.36%
65 – Textile yarn, fabrics, made-up articles, n.e.s., and related prod	− 1.43%
89 – Miscellaneous manufactured articles	− 1.49%
82 – Furniture and parts thereof	− 1.60%
55 – Essential oils; polishing and cleansing preps	− 1.63%
85 – Footwear	− 1.64%
84 – Articles of apparel and clothing accessories	− 1.84%
81 – Prefabricated buildings; plumbing, heat & lighting fixtures	− 1.96%
88 – Photographic apparatus, equipment and supplies and optical goods	− 2.13%
62 – Rubber manufactures	− 2.23%
77 – Electrical machinery and equipment	− 2.89%
07 – Coffee, tea, cocoa, spices, and manufactures thereof	− 3.27%
76 – Telecommunications & sound recording & reproducing apparatus & equipment	− 4.81%
75 – Computer equipment and office machines	− 7.81%

Source: Own illustration. Data: Bureau of Labor Statistics. Note: Import price movements are calculated as relative to changes in U.S. consumer prices. Sector numbers listed are two-digit SITC. CAGR = Compound annual growth rate.

textiles, furniture, miscellaneous manufactures (which includes toys), and chemicals all experienced import price declines (relative to U.S. consumer prices) over two decades of more than 1 percent per year on average, or 40 percent in the period from 1986 to 2006. This occurred despite the apparent consolidation in textiles and apparel, for example, due to Chinese market share growth. This provides further support for Appelbaum's (2008) findings that scale of production has not been associated with a proportional increase in markup pricing power in China. Although these data do not prove the existence of oligopsony power in the GVCs, they are consistent with it. They are also compatible with a number of studies that have identified the declining terms of trade of developing country manufactures as the consequence of a "fallacy of composition," whereby the expansion of manufacturing export capacity in one country makes sense for that country alone, but when many countries expand at the same time, the resulting system-wide excess capacity creates declining prices globally. The greater the capacity overhang, the greater is the ability of lead firms to exert oligopsony power in input markets.

4.2 Endogenous Asymmetry of Market Structure in Global Value Chains

4.2.1 Power and the Distribution of Valued Added

We discerned two, seemingly incongruous, tendencies in the evolving structure of global industry. On one side, there continues to be a high degree of markup pricing power and concentration of industry for global lead firms. On the other side, there is evidence of persistently high levels of dispersion as more developing countries entered lower- and medium-tech industries in manufacturing and services through the 1990s and continued (although at a much slower pace) through the mid-2000s. The result is an asymmetry of market structures within GVCs, with oligopolistic lead firms at the top, and competitive markets among the lower-tier suppliers.

The asymmetry of market structures found in many value chains – powerful lead firms able to maintain and increase markups and competitive supplier firms subject to pressure from buyers on supply price, delivery time, quality, and payment schedule at the bottom – is not some natural outcome, but the result of the competitive process itself. The apparent paradox is resolved when we see that it is precisely this asymmetry of market structures in GVCs, and the ability of lead firms to generate and maintain the asymmetry, that is at the core of the oligopoly firms' cost-cutting strategy that has helped them maintain their cost markups. That is, it is endogenous to the formation and governance of some GVCs. Product market pricing power *per se* is no longer crucial to maintaining markups. This is now accomplished by mass customization and by cutting costs, both of which are managed increasingly through offshore sourcing in GVCs. From the lead firm perspective, excess capacity and the steady arrival of new entrants in supplier markets serve the purpose both of cost reduction and of greater flexibility (with the possibility of multiple suppliers). According to Lynn (2005):

A growing number of large firms today view the rise and fall of prices for inputs like labor and raw materials not as a problem to be smoothed out by shelling out capital to bring more activities under the direct control of the firm's management, but rather as a never-ending opportunity to ratchet down costs and hence perpetuate profit margins. And so today's top firms are increasingly designed to play country against country, supplier against supplier and worker against worker. General Electric CEO Jeffrey Immelt put it succinctly in a recent annual report. The "most successful China strategy," he wrote, "is to capitalize on its market growth while exporting its deflationary power (Lynn 2005, 153).

In this section, we discuss a series of firm offshoring strategies aimed at raising competition among suppliers and limiting entry to lead firm markets.

The asymmetry of market structure in global supply chains may take a variety of forms distinguished by the markup over costs and the share of value added at different points in the chain. Four hypothetical cases are depicted in Figure 4.5. In all cases, value added is shown as rising at higher levels of the supply chain, reflecting the standard view that "moving up the value chain" implies moving into higher value added production activities. This is a highly simplified depiction, especially because at lower ends of the value chain there are likely to be multiple suppliers, possibly reflecting great variation in organization, from assembly-line factories, to agglomerations of craft-like production, to small-scale, home-based work.

The point of the stylized representation in Figure 4.5 is to illustrate varieties of vertical arrangements and their implications for markup pricing and the distribution of value added. Each box in the diagram represents the possibility of a different owner and a different location from the other boxes in the chain. Case I in Figure 4.5 is labeled "Vertical Competition" because it depicts that of uniform markups at each point in the chain. A variant of this form is the entry of U.S. MNCs in the IT services exports sector in India and China. IBM, for example, employed 283,455 people outside the United States in 2008 compared to 115,000 employees in the United States and competed with Wipro and Infosys for contracts.

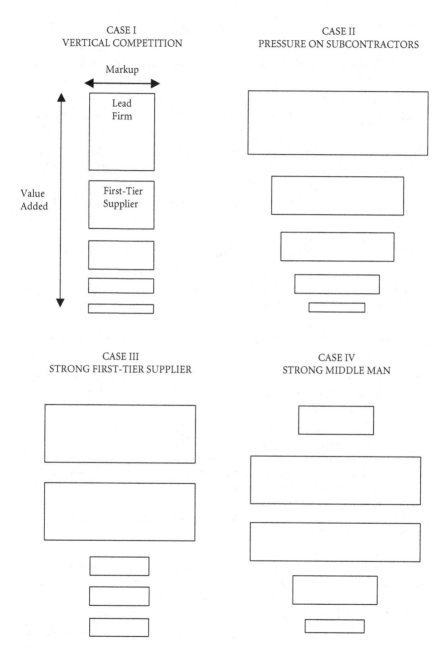

Figure 4.5. Cost Markups and Value Added in the Global Supply Chain: Four Hypothetical Cases. *Source*: Own illustration, based on Milberg (2004b).

Case II is titled "Pressure on Subcontractors" because it shows declining markups and declining value added offshoring (less value added) and the ability to squeeze suppliers (lower markups over costs). Case II describes an oligopolistic market structure at the top of the chain and a highly competitive structure at the bottom. The asymmetry occurs for reasons both technological and institutional, related both to the product side (the purchase of intermediates) and the factor side (the determination of wages). As buyers and (usually) product designers, lead firms often dictate the terms of supply. As Sturgeon and Memedovic (2011) write, "Lead firms tend to have power in GVCs, in part because they select and place orders from suppliers. Because suppliers tend to produce to the specifications of the lead firms, they have unique competencies, tend to exert less power in the chain, and earn lower profits" (Sturgeon and Memedovic 2011, 9).

The ability to divide the production process into numerous steps and tiers creates both a distance between lead firm rents and suppliers, and a greater ability to weaken labor bargaining power by creating more competition in segmented labor markets. Nathan and Sarkar (2011) note that the "splintering" of production in GVCs has two advantages for lead firms. One, with each additional tier of arm's length supplier, the lead firm is able to distance input producers from the rents earned by the lead firm and thus reduce their claims on that rent. Second, the greater the depth of the supply chain, the greater is the capacity to exploit the segmentation of labor markets. They write:

Efficiency wages can be paid to those whom it is important to retain and who can be expected to provide greater productivity with higher wages. Usually unorganized workers, such as homeworkers, women or those required in peak seasons, can be paid less if the labour markets in which they operate can be separated out. The splintering of production and outsourcing of tasks enables employers to utilize to the fullest the segmentation of the labour force, and that too on a global scale (Nathan and Sarkar 2011, 54).

Gimet et al. (2011) refer to the downward pressure on wages from the supplier's use of segmented labor as "immiserizing specialization." Case II most clearly reflects the asymmetry associated with the increasing volume of arm's-length offshoring.

Case III is that of the "Strong First-Tier Supplier," typically in a developed or newly industrialized country, for example car parts producers in Brazil, semiconductor firms in South Korea, or even some apparel producers in Mexico (see, for example, Bair and Gereffi 2001; Sturgeon 2002). Case IV is titled "Strong Middle Man," reflecting a bloated markup in the middle of the chain, resulting from the ability of traders to both squeeze suppliers below them and to retain proprietary advantages not appropriable by demanders to whom they sell. Examples of this are the cut flower industry, the Hong Kong apparel trade, and the cocoa and coffee trade.[8] According to Feenstra and Hanson (2004), Hong Kong-based firms earned an average markup of 24 percent on re-exports from China. In the apparel sector, Li & Fung is a buyer for major Western apparel manufacturers and retailers such as Wal-Mart and Target. Li & Fung has such power as a buyer, mainly because of the magnitude of its orders, that it is able to charge a 5 percent fee to suppliers desperate to maintain Li & Fung contracts. According to Tommy Hilfiger CEO Fred Gehring,

Li & Fung has an incredible amount of buying power. When they go to a factory and place orders, they get better clout than if we went on our own (Kapner 2009).

Endogenous asymmetry can take a variety of forms depending on the strategic focus of the lead firm. Four strategies stand out in the recent case study literature on GVCs: (i) inducing competition among suppliers, (ii) offloading risk to suppliers, (iii) erecting entry barriers through branding, and (iv) minimizing technology sharing. Some sectors lend themselves to only one or the other of these mechanisms. In many sectors, lead firms engage in more than one form at a time.

Inducing competition is the process of diversifying among suppliers in order to spur competition among them. Playing one supplier off another, working with multiple suppliers, and even creating new supplier firms has become a standard strategy of lead firms in GVCs, and is a major technique for keeping input prices low. Of course this diversification also reduces risk, in the event of political, economic, or natural disaster in any particular country, or of a unionization effort or work protest at any particular location. It is easiest where global capacity is already excessive (for example, see Gibbon and Ponte 2005; Lynn 2005). The offloading of risk has been documented in a variety of industries, including apparel (Abernathy et al. 1999) and electronics (Kaplinsky 2005). Nolan et al. (2002) analyze the careful control of technology by Boeing in its sourcing with Japanese, British (and American) parts producers.

Branding activity is a textbook example of constructing an entry barrier (see, for example, Bagwell 1989; Porter 1998). There is considerable theoretical analysis of entry barriers, but limited study of the economics of branding *per se* within value chains. Branding tilts bargaining power

---

[8] On cut flowers, see Ziegler (2007). On Hong Kong apparel trade, see Feenstra et al. (1998). Regarding coffee, see Fitter and Kaplinsky (2001) and Fafchamps and Hill (2008), and on cocoa, see Cowell (2002). McMillan et al. (2003) find a similar asymmetry in Mozambiquan cashews.

in the production process to the firm that holds the brand design. In industries in which production technology is standardized, for example apparel, footwear, airlines, and now even some computers, consumer electronics and even to some extent automobiles, branding is a key part of lead firm strategy. Davis (2009) cites the following exchange between the founder of a Chinese auto manufacturer and the Chairman of Ford Motors:

The firm's founder stated, "How to make cars is no longer a big secret. The technologies are widely used and shared." Tellingly, Ford Chairman William Clay Ford Jr. responded, "It's easy to build a car. It's harder to build a brand" (Davis 2009, 200).

Heintz (2006) explicitly models "unequal exchange" within GVCs as a function of brand power by the lead firm. Bardhan et al. (2010) model so-called "middlemen margins" as rising from buyer pressure to ensure (supplier) brand reliability. Thus the importance of branding can apply to both cases II and IV in our taxonomy, but in both cases branding serves as an entry barrier and as a source of unequal distribution of value added in the GVC. As Bardhan et al. (2010) point out, the preset of these middle men in developing countries can explain the rise in inequality there, a finding that is contrary to the prediction of the Stolper-Samuelson theorem. Brand power is not attained costlessly, and can be associated with considerable technological design content (such as Apple or Toyota) or with considerable marketing and advertising effort (such as Nike or J. Crew). But in either case, the maintenance of brand loyalty can become the main focus of operation and origin of rent generation, whereas production can be fully outsourced at arm's length. Even the emergence of large contract manufacturers, who produce multiple brands within the same plant, has not cut significantly into the power of branding. According to an executive of Hewlett-Packard,

The consumer doesn't care if all the computers [bearing different brands] were made on the same production line. The only thing that matters is who will stand behind it (Davis 2009, 94).

4.2.2 Sustainability of the Asymmetry

At least four factors make the asymmetry of the type depicted in case II to be sustainable over time. First is the nature of entry barriers, which we have seen are formidable at the high end of the value chain and non-existent at the low end. At all levels of the global supply chain, scale economies may deter entry. In addition to the barrier from branding, which makes market access difficult at the top of the supply chain, scale economies may deter entry especially for lead firms and many first-tier suppliers. Even "fab-less" firms (those who do no fabrication) limit market access by innovative product design and marketing activity. In this environment, it is difficult for developing country firms to develop their own brands. The exception is when buyers themselves demand supplier reliability, creating the need for high-reputation middle men.

A second factor is capital mobility, which affects the low value added operations much more significantly than the high value added ones. Gereffi (1999) shows how apparel production has moved over time to lower and lower cost (such as wage) locations. There is evidence that this mobility is affected even when the supply chain is organized within a single firm. Brainard and Riker's (1997) finding that the elasticity of labor demand is much greater for low-wage affiliates of MNCs with respect to other low-wage operations than it is between a high-wage and low-wage location suggests that capital mobility creates competition among low-wage locations.

A third factor is political. Tariffs have fallen most in low value added sectors. This is true generally, but has also been an explicit policy goal, as seen in the tariff policies that promote low-wage offshore assembly operations, such as the duty drawback clause (Section 9802) of the Harmonized Tariff Schedule of the United States, rule of origin principles of the African Growth and Opportunity Act and the Central American Free Trade Agreement and the Lomé Convention, and the establishment of EPZs in many developing countries. These programs are highly concentrated in the garment and electronics sectors. Textiles and apparel are traditionally one of the lowest value added sectors in manufacturing. The electronics parts and components that dominate in EPZs are at the low end of the spectrum of value added for electronics goods.

A fourth factor sustaining the asymmetry is the persistence and growth of global excess capacity in many industries. Freeman (2007) describes the entry of China, India, and Eastern Europe into the world capitalist economy as a historic, "great doubling" of the world's labor force, adding enormous productive power and greatly lowering the world's capital-labor ratio. This competitive pressure on suppliers translates into pressure on labor costs or on labor standards. Similarly, arm's-length relations with suppliers reduce the buyer firms' responsibility for standards in the supplying firm. A company is less likely to be held accountable for standards if the supplier is independently owned than if it is an affiliate of the buyer firm. We do not have good information on the extent of excess capacity globally in different industries. What is clear is that the drop in income and thus import demand in the industrialized countries beginning in 2007 and accelerating through 2009 has led to a surge in excess capacity. Small and large exporting firms across the globe have had to shut down. Recent reports claim that the downturn had resulted in 10 million new unemployed workers in China alone by mid-2009 (Hurst et al. 2009).

4.2.3 What Drives Foreign Direct Investment?

The logic of endogenous asymmetry of market structures is that global production is increasingly coordinated externally rather than within firms if offshoring can create competition among suppliers, reducing costs and raising flexibility beyond what could be accomplished with internalized operations. Externalization is the result of successful creation of asymmetries in market structure across GVCs. Thus we shouldn't be surprised, even in the age of MNCs, that the share of intra-firm trade in total U.S. trade has not increased. The MNC is often viewed as a key driver of the process of the globalization of production. This is understandable, since the existence of the MNC is, by definition, premised on some previous and significant (controlling) foreign investment.[9] Moreover, the past twenty years have seen an explosive rise in the activities of MNCs, despite a huge drop-off in FDI in 2009.

According to the World Investment Report there were about 82,000 transnational corporations with around 850,000 foreign affiliates worldwide in 2008. Between 1990 and 2010, the stock of outward FDI increased from $2.1 trillion to $20.4 trillion. Foreign affiliates employed over 68 million workers in 2010, compared to only 21 million in 1990. Their sales were almost $33 trillion, more than five times of their sales in 1990. In 2010, foreign affiliates accounted for more than one-tenth of global GDP and one-third of world exports (UNCTAD 2010, 2011).

Globally, FDI skyrocketed in the 1990s, although it dipped suddenly in 2001 as a result of world recession, asset deflation (especially stock market declines), and consequently a decline in value of a number of large mergers, mainly in Europe. This drop-off in FDI flows was skewed toward developed countries. Average FDI flows to non-developed countries (developing countries and countries in transition) rose from $6.3 billion in the 1970s to $140 billion in the 1990s to $394 billion in the 2000s. The non-developed country share of global FDI rose from 22 percent in the 1970s to 27 percent in the 1990s to almost 35 percent in the 2000s (Table 4.6). This has not been

---

[9] The convention for measurement purposes continues to be greater than ten percent ownership in a foreign asset. With the growth of stock markets in even many developing countries in the 1990s, the liquidity of FDI was raised, further blurring the distinction between portfolio investment and FDI. See Milberg (1999) for a more detailed discussion.

Table 4.6. *Distribution of World Foreign Direct Investment Flows, Averages,*
1971–2010

	1971–1980	1981–1990	1991–2000	2001–2010
FDI Inflows (in B. $)				
Developed economies	21.8	84.9	381.3	741.2
Non-developed economies	6.3	23.3	140.3	394.4
Shares (% of World FDI Inflows)				
Developed economies	77.6%	78.4%	73.1%	65.3%
Non-developed economies	22.4%	21.6%	26.9%	34.7%

Source: Own illustration. Data: UNCTAD Handbook of Statistics.

enough of an increase, however, to make a change in the non-developed countries' share of the world stock of foreign investment, which has fluctuated around 28.5 percent for the past 30 years.

While the developing country share of world FDI flows has increased slightly, the role of FDI in the total inflow of foreign capital to low- and middle-income countries has risen dramatically (see Table 4.7). Since the debt crises of the 1980s, direct investment has supplanted private debt,

Table 4.7. *Long-Term Net Resource Flows to Low- and Middle-Income Countries,*
1970–2010

	1970	1980	1990	2000	2010
B. $					
Long-term net resource flows	*16.2*	*123.0*	*173.3*	*383.1*	*1,305.4*
FDI, net inflows	1.5	8.0	21.5	149.1	509.2
Profit remittances on FDI	1.0	11.1	16.1	67.8	342.9
Portfolio equity flows	0.0	0.1	3.4	14.0	128.4
Net flows on debt, total long-term	7.5	57.7	42.6	16.5	212.9
Interest payments, total long-term	2.5	28.8	48.9	93.9	111.9
Grants	3.5	17.2	40.9	41.8	106.3[a]
Percentage					
Long-term net resource flows	*100.0%*	*100.0%*	*100.0%*	*100.0%*	*100.0%*
FDI, net inflows	9.5%	6.5%	12.4%	38.9%	39.0%
Profit remittances on FDI	6.3%	9.0%	9.3%	17.7%	26.3%
Portfolio equity flows	0.0%	0.0%	2.0%	3.7%	9.8%
Net flows on debt, total long-term	46.7%	46.9%	24.6%	4.3%	16.3%
Interest payments, total long-term	15.6%	23.4%	28.2%	24.5%	8.6%
Grants	21.9%	14.0%	23.6%	10.9%	7.5%[a]

Source: Own illustration. Data: Global Development Finance, World Bank.
[a] 2009 data.

equity, and government grants as the major channel of foreign capital inflows into developing countries.

To understand what is motivating such high levels of FDI, it is useful to distinguish vertical and horizontal FDI. Horizontal FDI is associated with "market-seeking" in that it involves a replication of productive capacity in the foreign location, presumably to better promote sales in that location. Two conditions are necessary to induce such FDI. First the foreign market must already exist or be about to develop. Second, replication of production on foreign soil must be preferable to export from home.

Typically, this second condition depends on an absence of significant economies of scale and the presence of high tariffs in the foreign market, and for this reason such horizontal FDI is often termed "tariff hopping." Certainly, most FDI to developed countries is aimed at better serving host markets, and some FDI in developing countries is driven by similar reasoning – Brazil being a well-documented example. Thus, studies looking at all FDI will likely find host-market GDP as the most significant determining variable.

Backward vertical FDI involves capital movement mostly aimed at more efficient linkages, either in production or in natural resources.[10] Efficiency-seeking vertical FDI is the movement abroad of productive resources with the aim of lowering costs. It can be driven by a variety of factors, including lower labor costs, lower taxes on profits, and low or lax standards on labor or the environment. These advantages must more than offset the tariffs and transportation costs incurred as a result of the international movement of any parts, components or assembled goods. Efficiency-seeking FDI is typically viewed as investment in low-wage countries, but it is not exclusively so. Considerable U.S. direct investment in Canada, for example, serves to produce or assemble parts used in goods sold in the United States. Japanese direct investment in Ireland has been understood as driven by that country's relatively efficient labor force and proximity to the EU market.

Resource-seeking vertical FDI is driven by the desire of lead firms to control supplies of natural resources or primary commodities used in the production of other goods. This motivated the traditional structure of colonial and neocolonial foreign investment, led by Britain between 1870 and 1913, and by the United States after World War II, but continues to be a factor in FDI today for sectors which are resource-intensive, such as steel or fabricated metal products. Some analysts have recently added "strategic-asset seeking" as an additional motive for FDI, where firms are

---

[10] One could also envisage the case of forward FDI (such as retail, wholesale), which is more likely to serve the purpose of market-seeking abroad.

Table 4.8. *Horizontal versus Vertical FDI Stocks Abroad, United States, 1985–2010*

	1985	1990	1995	2000	2005	2008	2010
U.S. FDI Stocks (M. $)							
Horizontal[a]	28,069	84,369	166,253	329,133	580,227	958,095	1,101,934
Vertical[b]	82,430	148,468	215,462	304,553	426,151	510,841	625,241
U.S. FDI Shares (%)[c]							
Horizontal[a]	25.4%	36.2%	43.6%	51.9%	57.7%	65.2%	63.8%
Vertical[b]	74.6%	63.8%	56.4%	48.1%	42.3%	34.8%	36.2%

Source: Own illustration. Data: Bureau of Economic Analysis, U.S. Direct Investment Position Abroad on a Historical-Cost Basis.

[a] Horizontal sectors include: Utilities; Food and beverage and tobacco products; Paper products; Printing and related support activities; Petroleum and coal products; Nonmetallic mineral products; Broadcasting and telecommunications; Information and data processing services; Federal Reserve banks, credit intermed. & related activ.; Securities, commodity contracts, and investments; Funds, trusts, and other financial vehicles; Rental & leasing services and lessors of intangible assets; Computer systems design and related services.

[b] The remaining sectors of Table 4.8 are rather characterized by vertical FDI stocks.

[c] Share of considered FDI stocks abroad.

seeking skilled labor, specialized knowledge, or knowledge spillovers abroad, referring to cases such as European investment in Silicon Valley, IBM's investment in Southern India, or Microsoft investment in research and development facilities in China (Dunning 2000).

Table 4.8 provides a crude breakdown of global FDI, between horizontal and vertical FDI. The calculation of U.S. FDI stocks does not include all FDI positions abroad. We focused on the twenty-one manufacturing sectors and fourteen service sectors, for which offshoring intensities are available. We used sectoral materials (services) offshoring intensities of 1998 (see Figures 2.10 and 2.11), as defined in Chapter 2, to determine the type of FDI for manufacturing (service) sectors. Sectors with offshoring intensities that exceeded the weighted average across all thirty-five sectors were classified as vertical FDI as they show a high proportion of imported inputs. Sectoral offshoring intensities below the weighted average were considered horizontal FDI.

The table shows that the accumulated stock of vertical FDI has increased gradually over time, although at a much lower rate as horizontal FDI, resulting in a substantial decline in its share from 75 percent in 1985 to 35 percent in 2008.[11] The dominance of horizontal FDI would explain why

---

[11] Hanson et al. (2001) find evidence of increased verticality in U.S. outward FDI in the 1990s compared to the 1980s.

Table 4.9. *Return on Foreign Assets (ROFA), United States vis-à-vis Region (%),*
1985–2010

	1985	1990	1995	2000	2005	2007	2010
All countries	12.1%	13.5%	12.5%	10.2%	12.1%	12.5%	10.5%
Canada	10.8%	6.9%	10.5%	12.2%	8.9%	8.4%	10.0%
Europe	13.1%	15.2%	11.9%	9.5%	11.2%	11.4%	9.1%
Latin America and Other Western Hemisphere	8.9%	12.2%	12.3%	7.4%	12.7%	14.1%	12.4%
Africa	15.7%	24.7%	29.9%	16.9%	23.2%	21.7%	13.6%
Middle East	8.9%	27.1%	19.1%	20.9%	24.2%	25.3%	25.1%
Asia and Pacific	14.2%	15.0%	14.8%	13.5%	15.1%	15.4%	12.3%
OPEC	23.8%	39.9%	25.5%	16.6%	25.0%	29.8%	19.4%

Source: Own illustration. Data: Bureau of Economic Analysis, Balance of Payments and Direct Investment Position Data. ROFA = FDI income / FDI stock, OPEC = Organization of the Petroleum Exporting Countries.

horizontal investment swamps the dynamics of vertical investment in most econometric studies. Another reason these studies have often not found cost differences to be a significant driver of globalized production is that such movements in relative costs may trigger production sharing through external rather than intra-firm channels, an issue we consider in detail in the following section.[12]

The asymmetry of lead and supplier market structures, we have argued, has created the conditions for greater returns from externalization than internalization. That is, externalization is a rational governance strategy if the return on offshore-outsourcing – implied by the cost reduction it brings to the buyer firm – exceeds that on internal vertical operations. The return on vertical FDI suggests a lower bound on cost saving from offshore-outsourcing.

To get a simple measure of implicit profit flows from FDI, we can apply the return on foreign assets (ROFA) to all trade in intermediate goods. We calculated the *ex-post* rate of return on U.S. operations abroad, by dividing foreign income earned on U.S. FDI by the corresponding accumulated stock of foreign investment in various countries and regions in the period from 1985 to 2010. The results are presented in Table 4.9. For the aggregate of U.S. investment abroad, this return was 12.5 percent on a foreign capital stock of $2.8 trillion in 2007. Compared to 1985, this return remained

---

[12] See Feenstra (1998) for a similar criticism of studies of offshoring that only include foreign investment data, that is that exclude arm's-length subcontracting.

relatively stable over time, but was slightly lower in 2010 with a ROFA of 10.5 percent.

At the regional level, however, we see strong differences. The average ROFA of U.S. FDI in developed countries such as Canada and Europe declined during the period of 1985 to 2007, although Canada's ROFA increased again in 2010. In contrast, the average return on assets increased in developing regions, especially in the Middle East, Latin America and Africa. Asia's development seems relatively low, which is because of the many developed countries in the region. The return in China, for instance, grew from 7 percent in 1995 to 21 percent in 2007. Between 1985 and 2007, the average ROFA in developed countries was 9.1 compared to 9.82 in developing countries. When we break out the vertical from the horizontal investment in all countries, the gap widens further, at 10.96 for vertical and 8.45 for horizontal. In principle, the return on offshore-outsourcing must exceed that on vertical FDI, implying considerable cost savings from externalization. Previously we saw that cost savings from offshore-outsourcing are reported at between 40 and 60 percent.

In Chapter 7, we explore the extent to which this competitive pressure on suppliers translates into downward pressure on developing countries' terms of trade, wages, and labor standards as managers in supplier firms themselves seek to retain their slim cost markups in the face of oligopsony power from lead firm buyers. We note here only that arm's-length relations with suppliers reduces the buyer firm responsibility for standards in the supplying firm. A company is less likely to be held accountable for standards if the supplier is independently owned than if it is an affiliate of the buyer firm.

The managerial focus on core competence is the mirror image of the picture we have presented here of the development of oligopsony markets for inputs which no longer yield rents and thus are, from the lead firm perspective, better subcontracted at arm's length. The point is that offshoring has had a dual role for lead firms, one being the support of cost markups, the other being the reduction of the scope of productive activities of the firm.

4.3 Determinants of Global Value Chain Structure

4.3.1 Transactions Cost–Based Theories

Because of its concern with the governance of production, GVC analysis is often associated with the transactions cost theory of the firm, which focuses on transactions costs and the specificity of a firm's assets. In transactions cost analysis, firms are a governance structure of contractual relations that focuses on attracting orders, reducing conflicts, and thus realizing profits by minimizing transactions costs.[13] The existence of the firm itself is the result of its efficiency compared to market relations. The transactions cost approach thus departs from the neoclassical conception of the firm, where the latter is essentially defined by a production function and an objective of profit maximization. According to Ronald Coase (1937):

The main reason why it is profitable to establish a firm would seem to be that there is a cost of using the price mechanism. The most obvious cost of "organizing" production through the price mechanism is that of discovering what the relevant prices are (Coase 1937, 4).

Transactions costs comprise all sacrifices and disadvantages that arise for the involved parties when exchanging goods and services. They include all information and communication costs that are associated, *ex ante*, with the initiation (for example, travel, communication, and consulting costs), the agreement (for example, contract arrangement costs, legal advice), the transaction (for example, management costs for leadership and coordination) and, *ex post*, with the control (for example, control of quality and date) and adjustment (extra costs due to subsequent changes in amount and dates) of an exchange that is perceived as fair (see, for example, Picot 1982, 1991).

Williamson (1985, 1996, 2002) has extended Coase's framework in a number of ways relevant to the study of globalized production. First, Williamson specifies why the firm might be more efficient than a market. Williamson (1996) attributes a firm's decision for in-house production (vertical integration) to market failure, especially of product and capital markets. Firms exist because they economize on transactions costs more effectively than markets. Thus, Williamson rejects the neoclassical model of the firm in which competition promotes efficiency in product and capital markets by squeezing out inefficient firms.

Firms have informational advantages over markets, therefore, according to Williamson, the corporate head office can coordinate the firm's divisions more efficiently than the capital market would if these divisions were each independent firms. Hierarchy can also be more efficient than the external market solution because of the existence of incomplete contracts. According to Williamson (2002),

---

[13] See Winkler (2009) for a longer discussion of transactions costs considerations in the theory of offshoring.

All complex contracts are unavoidably incomplete. For this reason, parties will be confronted with the need to adapt to unanticipated disturbances that arise by reason of gaps, errors and omissions in the original contract (Williamson 2002, 174).

Because the environment in which transactions occur is uncertain and because agents have bounded rationality, a "complete" contract is not attainable.

Williamson (1975) emphasizes the specificity of assets as another factor favoring internalization. He differentiates among specialized physical assets, specialized human assets, site specificity, dedicated asset specificity, and brand capital. Specific transactions thus depend on site-specific facilities, specialized machines and technologies, specialized and qualified employees, or on buyer-specific investments. The higher the degree of asset specificity for a particular production process, the greater is the efficiency of hierarchy compared to market-based organization. This focus on asset specificity leads to the possibility of hybrid forms of governance, characterized as "market-preserving credible contracting modes that possess adaptive attributes located between classical markets and hierarchies" (Williamson 2002, 181).

Hybrid forms of governance are particularly relevant in the study of GVCs. Lead firms cooperate, train, and provide support to supplier firms even in the absence of an ownership stake, and certainly in the absence of a controlling authority. Gereffi et al. (2005) identify three hybrid forms common to GVCs. "Modular" governance involves numerous suppliers of components and materials and a large turn-key assembler supplying the lead firm. A "relational" GVC has considerable interaction and technological sharing between the lead firm and first-tier supplier. In a "captive" GVC structure, the lead firm contracts directly with an array of much smaller supplier firms.

Figure 4.6 maps the comparative costs of governance in markets, $M(AS)$, and in hierarchies, $H(AS)$, both being functions of asset specificity. When asset specificity is low or even zero, the costs of governance with hierarchy are higher because costs of bureaucracy are not offset by any particular advantages compared to markets, such as $H(AS) > M(AS)$. As asset specificity rises, the more the initial cost advantage of the market solution falls and at some point the hierarchy becomes more advantageous than the market because of its savings on transactions costs. For $0 \leq AS < AS_1$, the market solution dominates the two other options. For $AS_1 < AS < AS_2$, the hybrid solution is preferred, whereas if $AS > AS_2$, hierarchy is the best option (Williamson 2002).

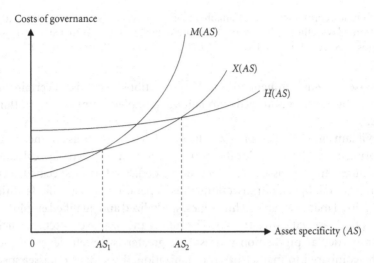

Figure 4.6. Externalization – A Transactions Costs Perspective. *Source*: Modified from Williamson (2002, 181), permission granted by the American Economic Association.

The transactions cost approach gives a number of insights into the latest wave of globalized production. Improvements in transportation and communications may well have reduced the cost of market-based organization (although they have reduced costs of hierarchy as well). The GVC focus described by Gereffi et al. (2005) can be depicted as hybrid forms. We can also see how suppliers would be inclined to move toward modular production platforms, because customer-specific investments leave the supplier bargaining power vis-à-vis the buyer (from the perspective of pricing or delivery times) greatly reduced (Sturgeon 2002). Because the subcontractor can already anticipate such a situation, he is tempted to make more general investments, which could be used more widely (such as with a lower asset-specificity), but would be less efficient than the optimal investment. We can also use Figure 4.6 to describe the basic notion that technological change has led to greater market-based governance.

Langlois (2003), following Coase (1937), attributes the rise in arm's-length international transactions to a decline in transactions costs in market exchange resulting from technological change as well as a reduction in asset specificity of a variety of tasks in the production process. This is the result of the improved functioning of markets that reduce the efficacy of vertically integrated firms.

The transactions cost approach has informed a generation of sophisticated mathematical models of outsourcing. Incomplete contracts have been used in several models to explain the make-or-buy decision of a firm (for example, Antràs 2003). Grossman and Helpman (2002, 2005) emphasize the search costs of finding a supplier and the degree of incompleteness of contract between buyer and supplier. Outsourcing (which can be domestic or international) occurs when the cost savings to the lead firm buying from "specialized input producers" exceed the costs resulting from search and incomplete contracting, where the latter is associated with a higher potential for holdup (that is, a broken contract), or with a greater difficulty of convincing suppliers to customize products to the buyer firm's needs and to deliver inputs of acceptable quality. In sum, the firm's "make or buy" decision is

a trade-off between the transactions costs that stem from search and incomplete contracts on the one hand and the extra governance costs associated with vertical integration on the other... [W]hen product markets are highly competitive... the occurrence of outsourcing requires a large per-unit cost advantage for specialized input producers relative to integrated firms. This advantage must be large enough to overcome search frictions and the pricing disadvantage that stems from the holdup problem. In contrast, when markets are not highly competitive, the viability of outsourcing hinges mostly on a comparison of the fixed costs that must be borne by an integrated firm and those that are paid by specialized producers (Grossman and Helpman 2002, 118).

Therefore, Grossman and Helpman (2002) see entry in the supplier market as raising the likelihood of outsourcing, not because it increases the cost savings for lead firms by adding additional capacity at the supplier level, but because it reduces search costs by adding to the number of potential suppliers.

4.3.2 Resource-Based Theories and the Shift to Core Competence

GVC analysis is compatible with the transactions cost approach to corporate governance, but value chain research extends beyond the make-or-buy decision, to questions of the distribution of value added both within and across links in the chain, and especially to the ability of supplier firms to upgrade their role within the value chain. Value chain analysis in its full scope requires a broader conception of the firm. The tradition of Penrose and Chandler, focusing on corporate strategy, provides a more fruitful foundation.[14]

In her *Theory of the Growth of the Firm*, Penrose (1959) describes the firm as a collection of productive resources that have the capability to generate services. Productive resources are managed within an administrative organization, which can determine the amount and type of these services.

---

[14] See Winkler (2009) for a longer discussion of resource-based theories of the firm.

Productive resources are similar to what later writers refer to as "firm-specific" or "knowledge-based" assets (for example, Amsden 2001). Such resources are the basis of the firm's productive services that are the source of rents for the firm. According to Penrose:

A firm may achieve rents not because it has better resources, but rather the firm's distinctive competence involves making better use of its resources (Penrose 1959, 54).[15]

Penrose focuses on the need for firms to create a sustainable competitive advantage over competitors, including technological superiority, strong marketing, and operational scale effects. Penrose also provides an early statement of the advantages of mass customization and core competence. Customization is an aspect of "diversification." A firm is diversified when it offers new and sufficiently different products in addition to its already existing product range of intermediate and final goods. The "diversification of... activities, sometimes called 'spreading of production' or 'integration'" increases the variety of final goods, vertical integration, and the number of basic business areas (Penrose 1959, 104).

According to Penrose (1959), efficient production at a given product variety is only possible for large firms with strong diversification and integration because only high product variety can protect a firm from major demand shifts – neither monopoly power nor technological progress alone will do. Distributing productive resources to a larger variety of goods can thus be more profitable in certain periods. Second, and more important, is the fact that diversification extends the production and investment possibilities into new areas, while maintaining or even expanding the existing production lines (Penrose 1959).

Core competence in the Penrosian firm means divesting those resources which are "excess," meaning those that do not generate rents. The main limitation on firm's growth is the shortage of managerial resources, which Slater (1980) calls the "Penrose effect" (Slater 1980, 521). According to Penrose,

The Schumpeterian process of 'creative destruction' has not destroyed the large firm; on the contrary, it has forced it to become more 'creative' (Penrose 1959, 106).

If offshoring can create competition among suppliers, reduce costs and raise flexibility beyond what could be accomplished within the realm of

---

[15] Also see Wernerfelt (1984) and Foss (1997, 1998).

internal operations, then globalized production will be increasingly coordinated externally rather than within firms. Thus, an additional consequence of globalized competition is that the scope of the firm has in many cases narrowed. In knowledge-based theories, a separate school of thought among the resource-based theories, this is presented as a focus on "core competence," and management reviews are filled with advice on how to focus on core competence (Prahalad and Hamel 1990). A core competence should at least have three features:

First, a core competence provides access to a wide variety of markets.... Second, a core competence should make significant contribution to the perceived customer benefits of the end product... Finally, a core competence should be difficult for competitors to imitate (Prahalad and Hamel 1990, 83–84).

From an economic perspective, core competence is a synonym for a rent-generating proprietary asset, and as competition in other aspects of production has increased, lead firms have outsourced the non-rent-generating parts of their operation, further encouraging competition among suppliers and lowering prices for purchased inputs. Thus, the flip side of the asymmetry of market structures is the externalization of global supplier relations. We saw previously that despite the growth of MNCs over the past twenty years in terms of assets, sales, and employment, intra-firm trade has remained constant as a share of U.S. trade.

In the Coase tradition, as discussed previously, internalization is explained as the result of firms seeking to minimize transactions costs in situations in which organizing production within the firm is more efficient than by means of the market. With the current trend apparently in the opposite direction, that is, with more arm's-length relationships within the value chain for particular commodities, the Coasian logic would imply that there has been a reduction in transactions costs for market-based relations. Langlois (2003) attributes this to technological and legal developments that make markets more efficient, and he posits that this increased market efficiency has brought the end of the Chandlerian era of complex multidivisional corporate structures. The situation could be represented in Figure 4.6 as a downward shift in the $M(AS)$ curve, leading to a greater share of organization being governed by the market.

An alternative interpretation is that externalization has developed from the logic of vertically integrated markets, with continued pressure on competition among suppliers, offloading of risk, and increased focus on core competence, all part of business strategy whose financial dimension is the focus of Chapter 6. Specifically, when suppliers have the capacity to act as monopolists there is a greater incentive for buyers to internalize supply production. When there is a high degree of competition among suppliers, then arm's-length relations between buyer and supplier are more likely. At issue is the ability of suppliers to capture value added in the GVC.

Grossman and Helpman (2002, 2005) and Antràs (2003) among others follow Coase in identifying the logic of outsourcing in transactions costs. There is no doubt some truth to this, but the approach should be expanded to comprise the perspective of Hymer (1976), according to whom it is the market power of corporations rooted in the ownership of knowledge-based assets that results in FDI. In the current context, with some transactions costs declining due to information and computer technology, and productive capacity and skill in developing countries rising, lead corporations have successfully encouraged competition among suppliers while limiting channels for upgrading that would threaten their own position.

4.3.3 Beyond Transactions Cost Minimization: Global Value Chain Governance Strategies

The prevalence of externalization in offshoring is consistent with different theories of the firm and thus should not simply be read as a decline in transactions costs as argued by Langlois and depicted in Figure 4.6. The power of lead firms in GVCs can make such relative cost profiles endogenous to the process of GVCs themselves with implications for the scope of lead firms and their suppliers.

Transactions cost economics are very useful in thinking about the governance of GVCs. But the focus on the transaction leaves the analysis largely one of constrained optimization in which (transactions) costs are minimized, subject to given technology, input prices, and market prices. From this perspective, the firm does not have a strategy for growth – in size, market share, or profits – other than transactions cost minimization under given constraints. Even asset specificity is assumed given.

In transactions cost economics, structure (that is, the structure of transactions costs) drives strategy. In this view, the constellation of transactions costs determines the relative efficiency of different structures, that is, vertically integrated or not. The governance structure that emerges in transactions cost economics is by definition efficient and thus optimal.

An alternative perspective on the firm is that the firm's strategy for growth is aimed precisely at overcoming constraints, whether it is in terms of product or process innovation, investment in asset specificity, factor or input prices, or even markets. As Lazonick (1991) writes, strategic firms "seek to generate a new cost structure" (Lazonick 1991, 288). The shift to core competence also is a strategic move to raise the intensity of asset specificity for the firm.

To put it in Chandlerian (1962) terms: strategy drives structure. Today this is not the multidivisional structure that was the concern of Chandler. The structure is the GVC, and it is driven by a strategy of governance emphasizing shareholder value from within a context of technology, transportation, communication, and global capacity in which vertical disintegration is feasible in a variety of forms.[16] In the GVC approach, lead firm strategy and the institutional context in which strategy is developed, determines value chain structure. Firms are profit-oriented, but maximization of shareholder value and long-run growth – two strategic objectives that are by no means necessarily consistent with each other – rather than simply the presence of transactions costs, result in a particular GVC structure. In the strategic approach, there is no reason that a particular structure (of the GVC, for example) is optimal in the sense of Pareto.[17]

The strategic perspective provides a different understanding of the apparent reemergence of arm's-length transactions in the global economy. The notion of corporate strategy connotes more than in the negative sense of simply protecting rents, but in the positive sense of innovating for growth and even altering market conditions. Offshoring is driven centrally by such corporate strategy, and the observed persistence of arm's-length trade in a world in which MNCs are larger than ever. While the firm in both conceptions is rational, the firm approaches the issue of profit maximization differently in the two conceptions. In the transactions cost approach, the firm is a transactions cost minimizer. For the strategic firm, offshoring is a means to cost reduction, flexibility enhancement, entry deterrence, and at the same time serves the broader strategy of focusing on core competence and shareholder value. Offshoring allows diminished obligations to domestic labor and poses a threat to the ongoing domestic employees. Bas and Carluccio

---

[16] For Chandler, vertical integration is not the result of high transactions costs, but of profit opportunities from large-scale production, the exploitation of which required specialized managerial expertise.

[17] Thus Pitelis (1991) writes about market and non-market failures. See also Cowling and Sugden (1987).

(2009), for example, find that offshoring by French corporations is much more likely to be at arm's length when unions are strong in the supplier country:

Multinational firms use their organizational structure strategically when sourcing intermediate inputs from unionized markets... International outsourcing provides a strategic way of accessing the higher productivity workers in [the supplier country] while avoiding the exposure of worldwide profits to extraction by the union... [W]hen union bargaining power is sufficiently strong, subcontracting is chosen despite the inefficiencies it entails (Bas and Carluccio 2009, 1–2).

Supplier firms are not simply given as part of a menu of production options, but are nurtured and encouraged, both for the purpose of increasing the reliability and precision of supply and also as a means to enhance competition among supplier firms. To the extent that such inducements are effective, then more arm's-length transactions are the rational result of lead firm strategy. Hymer's (1972) theory of the MNC stresses oligopoly internalization as the means to preserve rent-generating proprietary assets. The logic also predicts externalization when supplier operations are no longer rent-generating. What matters strategically is control, not ownership. Lead firms may induce more competition among suppliers. They also may work extensively with suppliers to improve quality, design, and reliability of supply and logistics. They take great pains to retain brand identity and to create other barriers around self-identified core competence. They may exploit segmentation in labor markets to further increase flexibility and reduce production costs.

If the strategic approach to understanding the firm emphasizes the effort to overcome constraints and produce a new cost structure rather than accept that which is given, this does not imply that strategic choices are infinite. From a strategic perspective, businesses have a finite set of options. One reason for this is that the cost of knowing the effectiveness of different production techniques can be prohibitive (Rosenberg 1982). According to Piore (1998), the institutionalist approach sees choice as narrower, discrete and the result of ongoing conflict and dialogue. He writes:

It is as if the isoquant were to collapse into a few widely dispersed points on the capital-labor map. We can talk about those alternatives as business strategies... [T]he discrete alternatives that the economic agents face are not worked out in advance... It is a product... of the understandings about the constraints and opportunities that emerge as the actors talk to each other (Piore 1998, 261).

Another reason is that business culture is just that – a culture – and certain strategies take hold and are emulated. Rubery et al. (2009) note the "fad" nature of offshoring, that firms see others doing it and decide they do not want to be left behind. Moreover, the options are path dependent and may emerge as the strategy is implemented.

The transactions cost and the corporate strategy approaches may not be incompatible, but the latter emphasizes the dynamics of firm behavior and sheds more light on the social conflicts inherent in the offshoring decision, that is on the welfare consequences of particular outcomes. Both the transactions cost and the resource-based theories clearly have some explanatory power regarding the expansion of arm's length trade in intermediates. The latter would seem to be the result of a combination of declining transactions costs because of digitization and the expansion of manufacturing and services productive capacity, and continued power of lead firms in their ability to retain rent-generating assets in-house and to encourage competition among suppliers. The governance structure that emerges in transactions cost economics is by definition efficient and thus optimal. In the strategic approach, there is no reason that a particular structure (of the GVC, for example) is optimal in the economics sense of Pareto. We have argued that both transactions costs and corporate strategy-based theories of the firm help to explain the expansion of globalized production and this also includes the motives for FDI.

There is a commonality across the three motives for FDI in the traditional taxonomy. In all cases, firms have decided to maintain the foreign operation within the firm. This is the process of internalization, according to which firms will expand their own operations when they control an asset – often an intangible or knowledge-based asset – that allows them to earn above-normal profits rather than seek another firm to supply the downstream, upstream, or horizontal product or service. The internalization motive is rooted in the very logic of the firm itself: firms are organizations that exist distinct from markets precisely because they can organize production at a lower cost than would be incurred if all aspects of the production process took place in markets. Coase (1937) identified lower transactions costs as the source of the advantage of firm rather than market-based organization of production. This rationale for the existence of the firm was extended to explain FDI, that is, as the simultaneous desire of firms to expand markets and retain the benefits of the firm organization.

Coase's insights have formed the basis for the theory of the MNC for the last three decades. Hymer (1976), and later others, described the multinational firm as a non-market institution in the Coasian sense: The international extension of the firm reflects its apparent organizational superiority, perhaps because of the transactions cost savings it brings compared to market transactions. Such savings, or rents, could result from the firm's intangible assets related to technology, production process, product design, management, labor relations, marketing, service, or any other dimension of the production or delivery of a good or service. While the internalization of international operations through foreign investment is a result of the relative inefficiency of the market, the strategic protection of such knowledge assets by keeping them internal to the firm is widely recognized as the prime reason for firms to invest abroad rather than serve foreign markets in other ways, such as exports or even through licensing or subcontracting. Today, the advantages of internalization strategies are still seen as the key explanation of FDI.[18]

The relative gain from vertical disintegration make apparent some limitations of the vertical organization that characterized successful firms for the entire twentieth century. Powell (1990) mentions three weaknesses of vertically integrated firms:

An inability to respond quickly to competitive changes in international markets; resistance to process innovations that alter the relationships between different stages of the production process; and systematic resistance to the introduction of new products (Powell 1990, 318–319).

Trade patterns may be a function of global production location strategies of firms, but does the ownership structure within these global production systems matter? We have argued that this structure is partly endogenous to the dynamics of international competition itself. Specifically, if intra-firm trade is the result of firm internalization strategies, then the observed rise in arm's-length subcontracting requires a theory of externalization. Firms internalize an international production process to protect rents that accrue to their firm-specific (often knowledge-based) assets. Such rents are possible only in an oligopolistic industry, in which economies of scale and market power can both foster the development of such assets and permit their continued profitability.

Conversely, firms will externalize a portion of the operation if the expected cost savings exceed the expected rent accrual. This is more likely to be the case when (intermediate) product markets are competitive. That

[18] Dunning (2000) has for many years embellished the internalization theory with two other types of advantages that would explain FDI: ownership and location.

is, firm strategy is to externalize whenever downstream markets are competitive. If externalization itself fosters downstream competition, the asymmetry of market structures along the global supply chain can be considered endogenous to lead firms' competitive strategies.

To the extent that the asymmetry in market structures is endogenous, then by the same reasoning so is the rising incidence of externalization. Competition among suppliers is beneficial to lead firms not only because of its cost implications. It also enhances the flexibility of lead firm supply conditions. Lead firms can set relatively short-term subcontracts, allowing the ability to more rapidly respond to changes in final good demand conditions or changes on the supply side, on issues ranging from changes in product design, to changes in wage, exchange rate or policies in the countries with suppliers or potential suppliers. According to Strange and Newton (2006):

If there are a large number of competitive suppliers of raw materials and/or intermediate goods, then the corporation might well choose to externalize production in order to (a) reduce the risks associated with the commitment of resources, and (b) save capital for other activities. One might also put forward a further advantage, namely that a monopsonistic buyer would be able to push down the prices of supplies to marginal cost and thus extract the full profits from the sales of the final goods from a smaller capital stake – i.e. the buyer would show a higher return on capital. If there were but a few suppliers, in contrast, then there would be a situation of bilateral monopoly (or oligopoly) and conventional internalization arguments might dictate vertical integration (Strange and Newton 2006, 184).

Externalization also results from the firms' tendency to focus on core competence and to otherwise rely on arm's length offshoring. Such a shift permits firms to focus on aspects of the process in which entry is difficult, mainly because of the skill and technology they require. Firms reduce their scope to their core competence not only for the obvious reason that this is what they are best at, but also because this is the aspect of the integrated production process that generates rents and which maximizes the possibility of retaining those rents over time. Thus core competence is difficult to isolate from market power. Discussing Hewlett-Packard personal computers, one Hewlett-Packard executive is quoted:

We own all of the intellectual property; we farm out all of the direct labor. We don't need to screw the motherboard into the metal box and attach the ribbon cable (quoted in Davis 2009, 94).

Another factor driving such externalization is policy, both in the developed and developing countries, in particular the establishment of EPZs, that is special areas in which goods may be imported duty free and most output is for export. EPZs are most common in East Asia and Latin America and are largely concentrated in just two sectors, apparel and electronics. Electronics is considerably more capital-intensive than apparel. The degree of foreign ownership of EPZ-based firms varies across regions, and is much higher in Latin America than in East Asia. Yeats (2001) finds that "much of the offshore assembly processing activity is by locally owned producers rather than with foreign owned manufacturing activities" (Yeats 2001, Box 2). We return to the role of EPZs in GVC upgrading when we analyze economic development in Chapter 7.

4.4 A Classical Approach to Offshoring

4.4.1 Relevance of Ricardo's Dynamic Gains from Trade

What exactly is at stake in the demotion of the principle of comparative advantage, a doctrine that is almost 200 years old?[19] The principle of comparative advantage is one of the great insights in the history of economics since, as Samuelson (1969) has written, it is logically true – ignoring the conceptual issues previously raised – and it is not intuitively obvious. To suggest limits to the relevance of this principle is to open up the enormous question of what determines the international division of labor in a world characterized by historically unprecedented levels of trade and international capital mobility, in which globalized production is a standard feature of business strategy and in which productive capacity globally continues to expand despite already existing excess capacity. And to reduce the relevance of the positive dimension of the principle of comparative advantage – that is, its relevance as a predictor of the direction and commodity composition of trade – is also to reduce the relevance of its normative flip

---

[19] There is some debate about the exact origins of the principle of comparative advantage. Thweatt (1976) shows that the idea of comparative advantage predated Ricardo and that it was only on James Mill's urging that Ricardo included the passages most explicit about comparative advantage. An implication of this is that Ricardo's central purpose in Chapter 7 was not to explain the efficiency gains from specialization according to comparative advantage but to analyze the implications of trade liberalization for the determination of rent and profit.

side, which is the notion of the optimality and mutual beneficence of free trade.

Whereas economists cite the famous Ricardian principle of comparative advantage to show the static benefits of offshoring to all countries, in our view the case that offshoring benefits the U.S. economy overall relies more firmly on another argument found in Ricardo – his theory of economic growth and especially of the link between international trade and domestic investment.[20] In Ricardo's view, the importance of trade liberalization was through its impact on the profit rate. He saw agricultural protectionism in his day as keeping the price of food high, and, as a consequence, pushing up the cost of subsistence and thus the real wage. Relatively cheap food imports would lower the real wage paid by employers and thus raise the rate of profit. A higher profit rate would induce a more rapid rate of investment, which in turn would generate a higher rate of economic growth. As Ricardo writes,

Foreign trade... increases the amount and variety of objects on which revenue may be expended, and affords, by the abundance and cheapness of commodities, incentives to saving and to the accumulation of capital (Ricardo 1981[1817], 133).

Ricardo emphasizes that the increase in profits due to trade results from real wage declines that come with lower priced consumer goods. We refer to the investment and innovation that results from the higher profits from trade as "dynamic gains" from trade. Maneschi (1983, 1992, 1998) emphasizes the importance of this dynamic interpretation of the classicals. In this view, free trade can have both dynamic and static efficiency benefits.

Ricardo's point is that trade liberalization can raise the profit rate if it reduces the cost of wage goods, and that this leads to investment and growth. Maneschi's interpretation is summarized in Figure 4.7, which shows a one-sector model (corn as the good, made with labor and corn inputs), with a diminishing marginal product of labor (curve *A*) and rising corn demand with labor force growth (curve *B*). With no international trade (autarky) and labor demand *E*, the profit rate is the ratio of total value of profits minus the total wage bill per unit of output, or *CD/DE* in the figure. With

---

[20] The original statement is Ricardo (1981[1817]).

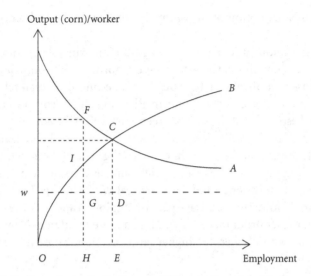

Figure 4.7. Trade and the Profit Rate in Ricardo's Corn Model. *Source*: Modified from Maneschi (1998, 70), *Comparative Advantage in International Trade: A Historical Perspective*, Cheltenham, UK and Northampton, MA: Edward Elgar Publishing Ltd.

trade liberalization and the inflow of imports and assuming no change in the wage, then the firm's wage bill relative to revenues falls, and the profit rate rises to *FG/GH*.

Ricardo was not alone in emphasizing the role of cost reduction, profits and investment in the analysis of international trade. It was common across the classical economists. Only with the modern neoclassical theory does the focus of the analysis shift to the static gains from trade, that is the productivity gains from a more efficient international division of labor. Marx includes foreign trade as one of five "counteracting factors" that slow or halt the tendency of the rate of profit to fall. According to Marx, foreign trade "cheapens commodities and the means of subsistence" (Marx 1991[1894], 351), and this can raise the rate of profit by raising the rate of surplus value and reducing the cost of circulating capital required for production.

John Stuart Mill (1968[1848]) was also concerned with the tendency of capital accumulation to lower the rate of profit and thus the incentive for further investment and growth, potentially leading from a progressive state of economic growth to what he termed a "stationary state." Mill identified a series of forces that would hold off the arrival of this stationary state by keeping profit rates up. One channel is productivity growth that, by lowering the cost of production of consumer goods, could lower wages and thus push up the profit rate. Another channel is "imports of cheap necessaries" that Mill understood as equivalent to "an improvement in production." This idea is very similar to Ricardo's notion that cheap imports of consumer goods could prop up the profit rate (and reduce rents in agriculture).[21]

Mann (2003, 2006) is among the few contemporary analysts to emphasize the dynamic effects of offshoring, associated with downstream effects of input price declines. She looks at offshoring of IT, and argues that the globalization of IT hardware production has contributed to a decline in IT hardware prices, which is equivalent to an increase in productivity and, *ceteris paribus*, has raised the profit margin. This in turn has led to greater quantity of IT hardware being demanded by business, further raising productivity. Because of this higher return on investment, firms undertake more investment generally, because

relatively lower prices for IT products due to the globalization of production raises the rate of return to IT investment, and more projects achieve internal benchmarks that firms use to decide whether to invest (Mann 2006, 18–19).

The positive outcome is the result of the capital deepening that comes from increased business purchases of IT hardware in response to the price reduction from cheap imports. Mann estimates that imports of IT hardware between 1995 and 2002 accounted for 20 percent of the observed decline in IT hardware prices and as a result raised U.S. real GDP by 0.3 percentage points over what it would have been otherwise.[22]

Her analysis shows that the strongest case for services offshoring is not found in the static efficiency gains identified in the traditional theory of international trade, but in the dynamic process of capital deepening that can occur when the offshored good is an input to production. Imported intermediates raise profit margins directly and then indirectly through resulting

---

[21] Note that Mill did not think that the stationary state was such a bad thing, since it would allow a greater focus on "human improvement" and for a policy goal of reducing inequality through redistributive tax policy, including an estate tax.

[22] Mann's estimate has been lauded by many as proof of the positive long-term effects of offshoring and has been criticized by others for overstating the share of IT capital income in total national income and thus for overstating the implications for GDP growth. For praise, see Bhagwati et al. (2004). For a critique, see Bivens (2005).

productivity gains from greater use of IT hardware. The higher capital intensity of production following the price decline leads to higher productivity, spurring demand, output and employment. Thus the dynamic gains from the globalization of production of IT hardware are the result of the productivity gains made by firms that face lower costs due to relatively inexpensive imports. One can question the elasticity and rate of return estimates cited by Mann, and especially her effort to generalize the IT hardware example to the case of software and business services generally, but her focus on the effect of offshoring on firms' return on investment highlights that dynamic effects of trade may be greater than the static, efficiency effects.[23]

Rodríguez-Clare (2007) has a similar finding in the context of a multicommodity Ricardian model. He shows that the "rich country" will experience a wage decline in the short-run, but that a "research effect", whereby rich country firms invest gains from cost saving due to offshoring into research, increases wages for research workers. Akyuz and Gore (1996) emphasize the "nexus" between profits and investment in East Asian development. In this more conventional case, profits are tied to export performance.

4.4.2 Static and Dynamic Gains from Offshoring

The focus on dynamic effects of offshoring puts profitability at the center of the analysis of welfare, in contrast to approaches using social indifference curves or a social welfare function. It goes beyond the focus on direct welfare gains from specialization and improved terms of trade and emphasizes instead the effects of trade on the return on investment and the subsequent impact on investment demand. We have seen that our approach is in the spirit of classical economics, with labor demand affected by trade through its "cheapening of commodities," outsized profits, capital investment, and possible leakages to the financial sector. The classicals did not foresee the development of GVCs and the outsized development of the financial sector, but by placing international trade in the context of investment and economic growth, the classical economists provided a useful starting point for the analysis of offshoring.

The static and dynamic effects of offshoring are summarized in Figure 4.8, which adopts domestic labor demand as the outcome variable. The

---

[23] See also Amiti and Wei (2009). For a critique of the elasticity assumptions, see Mahoney et al. (2007). For doubts about the magnitude of the productivity growth estimates see Houseman et al. (2010).

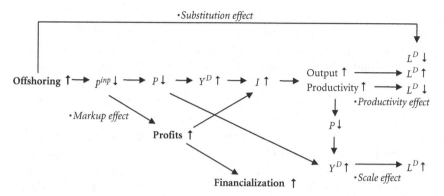

Figure 4.8. Gains and Losses from Offshoring. *Source*: Milberg and Winkler (2010c, 278). Note: p^{inp} = intermediate input price, P = output price, Y^D = demand for output, I = investment, and L^D = demand for labor.

figure is a simplification that considers all labor as one type, and leaves out some potentially significant indirect effects; for example, the increased sensitivity of labor demand to wage changes at home and abroad (that is, an increase in the wage elasticity of labor demand), and the greater use of company threats to move production abroad that reduce wage bargaining power and wages.

Weakening labor demand results from the direct replacement of foreign for domestic labor (the "substitution effect") and the "productivity effect" which involves reduced demand for labor for each unit of output. Productivity gains from offshoring can occur through various channels, including specialization in more efficient, core aspects of production, and mechanization that can result from increased expenditure on cheaper – imported – inputs. Another important channel is the "scale effect," where lower intermediates prices are passed on to the consumer in the form of lower output prices, resulting in higher demand for final goods. Labor demand increases with the scale of production, offsetting the negative labor demand effects from substitution and productivity. Whereas the scale effect raises labor demand, scale economies lead, by definition, to less labor demand per unit of output.

The productivity and scale effects are filtered through by a "markup effect," according to which lead oligopoly firms in GVCs are able to raise the markup over costs, not in the traditional oligopoly fashion of raising product prices, but through the control of input costs. If product markets are purely competitive, then the cost decline is passed through entirely to lower product prices with no change in the markup. In oligopoly product markets, however, the pass-through is incomplete. With heterogeneous oligopoly firms, the result could be different cost savings through offshoring and different degrees of pass-through across firms in the same industry.[24] This effect is implicit in the productivity effect, but in the dynamic approach it is assumed that the productivity gain will lead to higher rates of firm investment in the cheaper inputs as well as in other inputs, and new plant and equipment.

The markup effect is particularly important in light of the creation of oligopsonistic buyer relations in global supply chains that underpinned some shifting in the source of corporate profits, from traditional oligopoly pricing power in product markets to oligopsony power in global supply chains in which lead firms have greater control over input prices and greater flexibility because of the presence of multiple, competing suppliers.

The markup effect, however, leaves open the possibility that not all of the rise in profits results in new investment and labor demand. Corporations may also choose to return their net gains immediately to shareholders through higher dividend payments and share buybacks that create capital gains by reducing the supply of outstanding equity and raising share prices. This is the financialization of the nonfinancial corporate sector, and it constitutes a leakage in the nexus between profits and investment in the analysis of offshoring. This leakage is especially important because recent studies have established that financialization has come at the expense of investment, implying that offshoring has enabled financialization and, in turn, financialization has reduced the dynamic gains from offshoring. Pressures for greater shareholder value – financialization pressures – can thus be connected to the lead firm strategy of promoting market structure asymmetry across GVCs.

Expansion of global production networks has served a dual purpose in the evolving corporate strategy. Cost reductions from the globalization of production have supported the financialization of the non-financial corporate sector, both by raising profits, and by reducing the need for domestic reinvestment of those profits, freeing earnings for the purchase of financial assets and raising shareholder returns. It should not be surprising, then, that the emphasis on maximizing shareholder value and aligning management interests with those of shareholders emerged around the same time – the

---

[24] We are grateful to David Kotz for emphasizing the disequilibrium nature of this process. On partial pass-through of cost changes under conditions of oligopoly, see Blecker (2012) and Arestis and Milberg (1993–1994).

late 1980s – that management experts advised corporations to reduce the scope of corporate activity to focus on core competence. In addition to the direct cost reduction, the move offshore or even its threat can lower wage demands and dampen domestic wages, reinforcing the positive relation between offshoring and the markup.

4.4.3 Conclusion

The scale and productivity effects are both premised on a "markup effect," according to which the lead firm in the GVC is able to raise the markup over cost, not in the traditional oligopoly fashion of raising product prices, but through the control of input costs. The markup effect, however, leaves open the possibility of financialization, which represents a drain on labor demand and, as we discuss in Chapter 6 may play an important role in the link between globalization and economic insecurity. Therefore, the central question from the classical, dynamic perspective is whether offshoring is leading to higher profits, and if these profits are then being invested and bringing higher productivity and output, or if they are leaking into the purchase of financial assets. The evidence on the United States presented in Chapters 5 and 6 is that the dynamics are being only partially captured. Offshoring is contributing to lower costs of production, higher profits, and a higher profit share, but this is not being matched by a rise in investment that would spur productivity gains and economic growth. Instead, firms in the United States have invested in financial assets and focused on returning value to shareholders through dividend repayments and share buybacks in particular.

The key to the markup effect is the asymmetric nature of market structures along the global supply chain. The effect is enhanced by the ability of the lead firm to successfully induce oligopsonistic input markets along GVCs. Specifically, we have argued that the creation of oligopsonistic buyer relations in GVCs has allowed some shifting in the source of corporate profits: from traditional oligopoly pricing power in product markets to oligopsony power in global supply chains in which lead firms have greater control over input prices and greater flexibility due to the presence of multiple, competing suppliers. We should note again that in addition to the direct cost reduction, the move offshore or even its threat can lower wage demands and dampen domestic wages, reinforcing the positive relation between offshoring and the markup. That is, embedded in the markup effect is the "threat effect" of offshoring, according to which the threat of offshoring leads to a dampening of wage demands in the domestic labor market. This may be an important aspect of the economic insecurity felt by many workers in the industrialized countries under the new wave of globalization. We turn now to an analysis of the relation between globalization and economic insecurity.

FIVE

Economic Insecurity in the New Wave of Globalization

The financial collapse of 2008, the catalyst for the worldwide economic downturn that ensued, has introduced a new element of economic insecurity – the collapse of home prices and retirement incomes – into industrialized countries. In the United States, over 8 million homes went into foreclosure, as families were unable to meet their mortgage debt obligations. Credit card debt defaults followed a similar, and historic, trajectory. But heightened economic insecurity in these countries – whether measured by greater volatility of household incomes, a slowdown in wage growth, rising income inequality, growing unemployment, a rise in the incidence of long-term unemployment or involuntary part-time employment, a decline in labor's share of national income – preceded the financial crash by years, if not decades. Arguably, the rise in inequality and the expansion of corporate profits foreshadowed the crisis itself, by encouraging excessive financial speculation among higher earners and unsustainable borrowing by those at the lower end of the income distribution.

A factor in both the pre-crisis and crisis periods has been economic openness, with goods and services trade, foreign direct investment (FDI) and financial flows rising to unprecedented levels in relation to economic activity. There is overwhelming evidence that offshoring has for decades had an adverse impact on low-skill workers in industrialized countries, both in terms of pay and employment, in both absolute and relative terms. Recent papers now find a negative impact of offshoring on high-skill workers as well. This has especially been associated with the expansion of services offshoring. As supply chains extend to high-tech goods and higher-skill services, there are massive possibilities for the expansion of offshoring in the future.

In this chapter, we explore the relation between growing economic insecurity in industrialized countries and the growth in offshoring. Our analysis is premised on a distinction between economic vulnerability and economic insecurity. Economic vulnerability is the risk of a negative shock to household income or of losing a job. Economic insecurity is the result of this risk, mitigated by any buffer or insurance enjoyed by households, either privately on their own behalf or from public programs, including labor market support and health insurance. From this perspective, countries subject to the same degree of economic vulnerability because of globalization, may experience very different levels of economic insecurity due to social protection provided by the state or insurance obtained by households. We focus on the United States and five other industrialized countries: Denmark, France, Germany, Japan, and the United Kingdom. These countries represent a broad spectrum of the advanced industrialized world, and although all have expanded their exposure to international trade and investment in the past fifteen to twenty years, they have not all experienced the same degree of increased economic insecurity.

In Section 5.1, we present indicators of economic insecurity and how insecurity has risen since the 1980s across these major industrialized countries. Section 5.2 considers the role of government, and specifically labor market regulation, in mediating the effect of markets on incomes and shifting the burden of risk from rapid income decline. In Section 5.3, we analyze the relation between globalization and economic security. In the econometric analysis presented in Section 5.4, we first estimate the effect of offshoring on employment for the United States between 1998 and 2006. Second, we estimate the impact of offshoring on the labor share in the United States for the same period. Finally, we look at a sample of fifteen Organisation of Economic Co-operation and Development (OECD) countries and estimate the effect of offshoring on the labor share covering the period from 1991 to 2008. In order to detect differential effects of labor market regimes, we interact offshoring with policy indicators of labor market flexibility and labor support. In a second step, we relate our estimated effects to the perceptions of globalization that we discussed in Chapter 1.

5.1 Economic Insecurity

The period from 1950 to 1973 is widely referred to as the "Golden Age" of capitalism, but it might be better termed the period of rising economic security for people in the industrialized countries. Not only did the OECD countries experience rapid growth in real gross domestic product (GDP), but this was reflected in rising median wages, even more rapid improvements

Table 5.1. *Economic Performance, Golden Age versus Post–Golden Age, Selected Countries*

	Denmark	France	Germany	Japan	United Kingdom	United States
Gross Domestic Product[a] (CAGR)						
1950–1973	3.8%	5.0%	6.0%	9.3%	2.9%	3.9%
1980–2011	1.7%	1.8%	1.7%	1.6%	2.1%	2.7%
GDP per Person Employed[a] (CAGR)						
1950–1973	2.9%	4.5%	4.7%	7.5%	2.4%	2.3%
1980–2011	1.4%	1.3%	1.3%	1.4%	1.7%	1.6%
Average Unemployment Rate (Percent of Labor Force)						
1956–1973	1.1%[b]	1.9%	1.3%	1.5%	1.8%	5.0%
1980–2010	6.8%	9.7%	7.3%	3.5%	7.9%	6.3%

Source: Own illustration. Data: The Conference Board and Groningen Growth and Development Centre, Total Economy Database. OECD Labor Force Statistics. Note: CAGR = Compound annual growth rate.
[a] Converted at Geary Khamis PPPs.
[b] Average based on 1960, 1965, 1967, 1969–1973.

in median family income, relatively low rates of unemployment, falling inequality, and improvements in the post-Great Depression system of social protection in most countries.

Since 1973, the major industrialized economies have grown more slowly, as productivity growth has diminished. Over the entire OECD, total factor productivity growth fell to 1.5 percent per annum on average after 1985, from rates more than twice that during the twenty years before 1973 (Howell 2005). As seen in Table 5.1, our six countries had higher rates of average annual GDP growth for the period from 1950 to 1973 than they did over the period from 1980 to 2011. In some cases (Japan, Germany and France), the growth rate fell by more than half. Note that the United States showed the highest average annual GDP growth rate in the post-1973 period. Labor productivity growth follows a similar pattern. Thus, GDP per person employed fell in all six countries, but most dramatically in Japan, Germany, and France.

The post-1973 period has seen a significant increase in worker insecurity in many industrialized countries. The average rate of unemployment (on a standardized basis) has been significantly higher in the post-Golden Age era compared to the period between 1956 and 1973, ranging from slightly higher in the United States to more than five times higher in France, Germany, and Denmark (see Table 5.1). The incidence of long-term unemployment, defined as unemployment duration greater than one year, also rose over

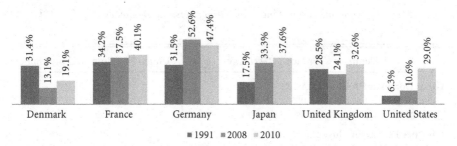

Figure 5.1. Long-Term Unemployed (% of Total Unemployed), Selected Countries and Years. *Source*: Own illustration. Data: OECD Labor Force Statistics. Note: Long-term unemployed refers to more than one year.

the post-Golden Age in many industrialized countries. France, Germany, Japan, and the United States all saw long-term unemployment higher in 2008 compared to 1991, while Denmark and the United Kingdom saw a decline (see Figure 5.1).[1] The global economic crisis of 2008 resulted in increasing long-term unemployment rates in all countries except for Germany. In the United States, the percentage of long-term unemployed almost tripled to 29 percent in 2010. Whereas the United States still has lower long-term unemployment rates than most other countries, it now shows higher rates than Denmark and is almost on pair with the United Kingdom.

The post-Golden Age period of slower GDP and productivity growth and higher rates of unemployment also involved a slowdown in the growth of wages and the labor share. Beginning in the early 1980s, the labor share of national income began to fall across many industrialized countries (see Figure 5.2). Since most labor force participants are not owners of capital, this trend in the labor share captures in a broad way the growing economic insecurity in the industrialized world. In Figure 5.2, we see two turning points. At the beginning of the 1980s, the increases in the labor share from the early 1970s began to level off. This can be associated with the advent of neoliberal policies, labor market deregulation and the retreat of the welfare state in some countries. The second turning point occurs at the end of the 1990s, with a clear downward trend in the labor share across the sample except for Denmark. This second shift has been linked to financialization and globalization, and in particular the emergence of China, India, and other low-wage exporting countries.

Equally dramatic is the rise in inequality across wage earners, documented in Table 5.2, which shows the ratio of wages in the top decile to the bottom decile for 1985, 1991, and 2008. Over the entire period, U.S. income

---

[1] We have used 1991 as a start point in much of the analysis so that German data reflect unification.

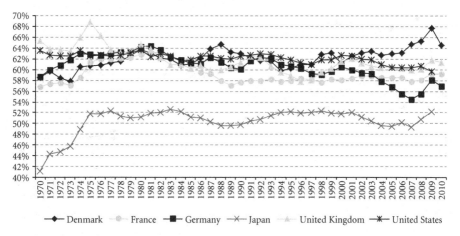

Figure 5.2. Labor Compensation (% of Gross Value Added), Selected Countries, 1970–2009/10. *Source*: Own illustration. Data: OECD Annual National Accounts Statistics.

inequality has been far above the others, and compression of incomes much greater in Denmark than in all the rest. Since 1985, France and Japan were the only countries of these six not to experience an increase in inequality. Japan's slow growth seems to have affected all groups proportionally. France underwent a large increase in the minimum wage, which served to compress the wage distribution (Howell and Okatenko 2008). The percentage increase

Table 5.2. *Wage Inequality, Selected Countries, 1985–2008*[a]

	1985	1991	2008
Denmark	2.2	2.2[b]	2.7
France	3.1	3.3	2.9[c]
Germany	2.9[d]	4.3	3.3
Japan	3.1	3.1	3.0
United Kingdom	3.2	3.4	3.6
United States	4.1	4.3	4.9

Source: Own illustration. Data: Wages per full-time employee are calculated based on the OECD Labor Force Statistics. Note: Wage inequality is measured as P90/P10, where P90 are the wages of top 10 percent earners and P10 the wages of bottom 10 percent earners. Wages are averages of women and men.

[a] Ratio of wages of top 10 percent of earners to bottom 10 percent of earners.

[b] 1990 wages for Denmark.

[c] 2007 wages for France.

[d] 1985 wages only for West Germany.

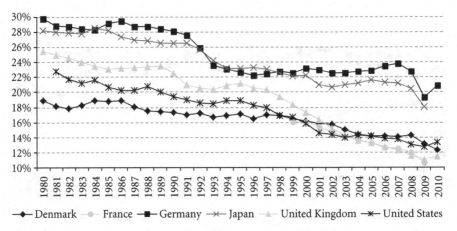

Figure 5.3. Manufacturing Value Added (% of Total Gross Value Added), Selected Countries, 1980–2009/10. *Source*: Own illustration. Data: OECD National Accounts Statistics.

in inequality between 1985 and 2008 was greatest in the United States and Denmark.

The productivity growth slowdown, as shown in Table 5.1, occurred as the process of deindustrialization continued in all countries in our sample except Germany, and in many cases the rate of deindustrialization accelerated (see Figure 5.3).[2] Manufacturing now accounts for between 11 and 13 percent of total gross value added in the United States, United Kingdom, Denmark, and France. The two trends are not unrelated, as services productivity, while difficult to measure, is widely recognized to be lower than productivity in manufacturing. Thus the increase in the importance of services in economic activity relative to manufacturing contributed to reductions in economy-wide rates of productivity growth.

By some accounts, formalized in Verdoorn's Law, manufacturing output growth is a main driver of productivity growth. Moreover, the manufacturing sector in industrialized countries traditionally offered jobs with high pay and employment protection, often the result of oligopoly product market power and effective union wage bargaining. Service sector jobs are quite varied in their productivity, skill requirements and pay, but offer lower pay and less job security and employee benefits, partly because of low rates of unionization in services industries, an issue we return to in the following

---

[2] According to Kalmbach et al. (2005), the German data overstate the size of the manufacturing sector because many services are counted in manufacturing.

section. As services have grown as a share of employment and value added, productivity growth has been relatively low, certainly as compared to the "Golden Age." The development of modern business services, however, counterbalanced this effect to some extent, as these are characterized by higher productivity, skills, and pay.

5.2 Varieties of Capitalism and the Burden of Economic Risk

5.2.1 Strictness of Employment Legislation versus Labor Support

There are private and public responses to rising economic vulnerability for workers. Despite the general rise in economic insecurity after 1980 in our sample of industrialized countries, governments have generally reduced social and labor market protections. The neoliberal move to deregulate markets has involved efforts to increase labor market flexibility in Europe, to bring greater fiscal constraint in the Eurozone, and to reduce the role of labor unions in the United States. Within these broad trends, there is still considerable variation across industrialized countries in the amount and form of social protection they provide. We focus on three aspects of social protection – the gross unemployment replacement rate, public expenditures on active labor market programs, and the strictness of employment protection legislation (EPL). By these measures there remain clear differences in government response to economic insecurity.

In fact, all countries except France have reduced unemployment benefits since 1981 and in France after 2001 (see Table 5.3). The United States showed the second lowest gross unemployment replacement rate after Japan, which is less than a third of Denmark's rate. Only Denmark and France among our sample of countries increased spending on active labor market programs as a percentage of GDP since 1990, with France again showing a decline after 2000. Active labor market programs include expenditures related to worker placements: worker training; job rotation and sharing; employment incentives, employment support, and rehabilitation; direct job creation; and, start-up incentives. The low expenditures on active labor market programs in the United Kingdom, Japan, and the United States stand out in our country sample.

There has been a different pattern of change in terms of strictness of EPL, which measures the regulation of hiring and firing. The OECD uses the term EPL to refer to all types of employment protection measures, whether grounded primarily in legislation, court rulings, collectively bargained

Table 5.3. *Labor Market Policy Indicators, Selected Countries and Years*

		Denmark	France	Germany	Japan	United Kingdom	United States
Gross	1981	54.2%	31.3%	29.3%	8.8%	24.2%	14.6%
Unemployment	1991	51.9%	37.6%	28.8%	9.9%	17.8%	11.1%
Replacement	2001	50.9%	43.5%	29.4%	9.1%	16.6%	13.5%
Rate (%)	2005	48.9%	39.0%	24.2%	7.7%	15.6%	13.5%
Short-term Net	2001	80.1%	73.9%	68.5%	61.4%	49.4%	58.8%
Unemployment							
Replacement	2007	77.8%	71.4%	66.5%	59.7%	57.1%	55.7%
Rate (%)							
Long-term Net	2001	76.8%	53.6%	65.0%	55.4%	60.9%	28.9%
Unemployment							
Replacement	2007	74.1%	53.0%	59.5%	55.9%	58.9%	24.3%
Rate (%)							
Public Expenditures	1985	4.7%	2.1%	1.7%	n.a.	2.3%	0.8%
for Active							
Labor Market	1991	5.9%	2.3%	2.9%	0.6%	1.5%	0.9%
Programs	2001	4.1%	2.6%	3.2%	0.8%	0.6%	0.7%
(% of GDP)	2008	2.6%	2.0%	1.9%	0.6%	0.5%	1.0%

Source: Own illustration. Data: Based on Milberg and Winkler (2011a) and OECD Social Expenditures and OECD Tax-Benefit Models. Note: Gross unemployment replacement rate: The OECD summary measure is defined as the average of the gross unemployment benefit replacement rates for two earnings levels, three family situations and three durations of unemployment.

conditions of employment, or customary practice.[3] These are combined into an index in which six represents the most strict regulation and zero the least strict. A less strict EPL would indicate that employers would have more flexibility to hire and fire. EPL is particularly strict in France and Germany, at a medium level in Denmark and Japan, and very low in the United Kingdom and the United States. The United States shows a constant EPL between 1991 and 2008, Denmark, Germany, and Japan became less strict, and France and to some extent the United Kingdom became more strict (see Table 5.4).

Using 2001 and 2007 data, we calculated an index of the strictness of EPL by setting the U.S. level of EPL equal to one and recalculating the relative levels for other countries. We constructed an index of "labor support" by again setting U.S. levels of net unemployment replacement rates and public expenditures on active labor market programs equal to one and (with equal

---

[3] See http://stats.oecd.org/glossary/detail.asp?ID=3535.

Table 5.4. *Strictness of Employment Protection Legislation, Selected Countries and Years*

	1991	2001	2008
Denmark	2.40	1.50	1.50
France	2.98	3.05	3.05
Germany	3.17	2.34	2.12
Japan	1.84	1.43	1.43
United Kingdom	0.60	0.68	0.75
United States	0.21	0.21	0.21

Source: Own illustration: Based on Milberg and Winkler (2011a, 154). Data: OECD Labor Statistics. Note: Higher values indicate stricter regulation on hiring and firing.

weights on each variable) combining them into a single index. A scatter plot of these two indexes for twenty-two OECD countries is shown in Figure 5.4.

Five distinct "models" of labor market regulation and support emerge, and they follow closely the groupings presented in recent discussions of "varieties of capitalism" (for example, Boeri 2002; Sapir 2006; Hancke et al. 2007). On the lower left, we can identify an "Anglo-Saxon model" of low levels of regulation on hiring and firing and low levels of worker support.

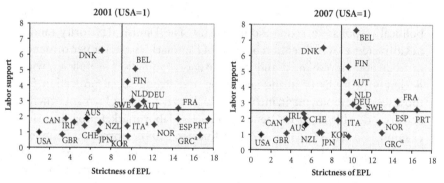

Figure 5.4. Different Labor Market Regimes, 2001 versus 2007. *Source*: Own calculations. Data: OECD Labor Force Statistics and OECD Going for Growth 2010 Database. Note: Labor support is an index (using equal weights) composed of the indexed (USA=1) public expenditures on labor market programs (as % of GDP) as well as the indexed (USA=1) short-term net unemployment replacement rate. See Appendix 5.1 for country abbreviations. See Appendix 5.2 for data description.

[a] Public expenditures on labor market programs include all measures except for "public employment services and administration."

This group includes the United States, the United Kingdom, Canada, Australia, Ireland, and New Zealand. Countries on the lower right follow the "Mediterranean model" that combines relatively strict employment legislation and low levels of worker support. This group includes Greece, Portugal, Spain, and France. Countries on the upper right of the scatter plot – "the Rhineland model" – combine medium to strict EPL and medium to high levels of worker support. Here we find Sweden, Belgium, Germany, and Austria. In the upper left are countries with relatively flexible labor markets and high levels of worker support. We call this the "flexicurity model," and its followers include Denmark, Belgium, Finland, and the Netherlands.

Japan has always been difficult to categorize in these schemes because although the state supports only low levels of labor market and social protection, the private sector had traditionally supported long-term employment security. Based on our two variable characterization, we can identify an "East Asian model" including Japan and South Korea, who both have greater employment protection than those in the Anglo-Saxon group but have less labor support than most European countries. It would seem that the traditional role for the private sector in Japan has given way to a great extent, as seen by the increase to European levels of Japanese long-term unemployment and involuntary part-time employment.

5.2.2 The Burden of Economic Risk

Denmark and the United States represent polar opposites in terms of the political response to economic insecurity. The Danish flexicurity model has attracted a lot of attention because of Denmark's superior performance in trade and employment and the unusual combination of policies, with flexibility in terms of hiring and firing and strong social protection for those seeking employment, including a high level of unemployment benefits and considerable levels of spending on active labor market programs (for example, Gazier 2006; Clasen 2007; Kuttner 2008). Moreover, Denmark greatly exceeds the other countries in terms of pension benefits relative to lifetime earnings (Figure 5.5). This system of flexicurity is in part the reason for Denmark's attainment of a high level of economic security, which is measured by changes in the labor share and wage inequality.

Over the past twenty-five years, the United States has experienced a dramatic shift in the burden of risk, from government to the households themselves. This has resulted from a combination of more volatile household income and an increase in health insurance costs, a greater reliance on

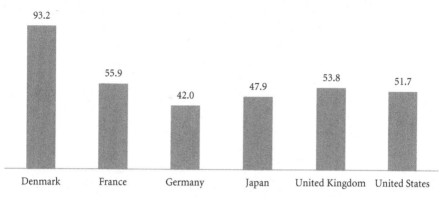

Figure 5.5. Gross Pension Replacement Rates by Earnings (% of Median Earnings), Selected Countries, Based on 2008 Rules. *Source*: Own illustration, Data: OECD Pensions at a Glance. Note: For median income earner. The figures show future entitlements for single workers who entered the labor market in 2008 and spend their entire working lives (starting at age 20) under the same set of rules.

private (as opposed to public) pensions, and a continuation of policies of low levels of unemployment benefits. Hacker (2006) describes these political changes as "the great risk shift" as governments and employers shifted the burden of insuring against a rapid decline in income to the employees and households themselves (see also Gosselin 2008).

Households may borrow in order to insulate their spending patterns from earnings volatility, which is one of the reasons for the rise in home equity loans in the United States and consumer credit in the United Kingdom.[4] Household saving rates out of disposable income fell over the 1990s for the major OECD countries (Germany and France being the exceptions), indicating the need for households to limit saving in order to maintain economic security and to incur debt for the same purpose (OECD 2007a).

Economic security is by many measures lowest in the United States and this is supported by the unusually high perception of insecurity and fear of globalization in the United States discussed in Chapter 1. We have seen that the United States, often lauded for the degree of flexibility in its labor markets, stands out in terms of its low levels of unemployment benefits and limited state spending on active labor market programs (Table 5.3). In their long-term historical analysis of U.S. income distribution, Temin and Levy (2007) argue that this deterioration of the social safety net, combined with

---

[4] Barbosa et al. (2005) find that the deterioration in the U.S. current account between 1995 and 2003 closely tracks the rise in health care spending by Americans.

Table 5.5. *Union Members as Share of Total Labor Force (%), Selected Countries and Years*

	1981	1991	2001	2008
Denmark	79.9	75.8	73.8	67.6
France	17.8	10.0	8.0	7.7
Germany	35.1	36.0	23.7	19.1
Japan	30.9	24.8	20.9	18.2
United Kingdom	50.0	38.2	29.6	27.1
United States	21.0	15.5	12.8	11.9

Source: Own illustration. Based on Milberg and Winkler (2011a, 256), Data: OECD Trade Union Statistics.

the decline of other institutions such as trade unions, has been a source of the bifurcation in the growth of productivity and the growth of wages:

The recent impacts of technology and trade have been amplified by the collapse of these institutions, a collapse which arose because economic forces led to a shift in the political environment over the 1970s and 1980s. If our interpretation is correct, no rebalancing of the labor force can restore a more equal distribution of productivity gains without government intervention and changes in private sector behavior (Temin and Levy 2007, 5).

As an indication of the changes in the United States, Table 5.5 shows union density in our sample countries since 1981, with Denmark remaining at very high levels and the United States experiencing the greatest decline. The United Kingdom, following a similar model, is second in the extent of decline of unionization, but remained still in 2008 at a much higher level than the United States. France's low rate of unionization would seem to be deceptive, because bargaining coverage of union agreements has remained very broad.

The United States also stands out in the area of health insurance. The United States, alone among our sample countries in not having universal health insurance coverage, had almost 50 million people uninsured in 2010, reflecting a steady increase in the number and percentage uninsured since the late 1980s (Figures 5.6 and 5.7). This situation may change dramatically by 2014 if the healthcare reform law of 2009 is fully implemented.

5.3 Connections between Globalization and Economic Insecurity

Before moving on to econometric analysis of the role of offshoring for economic insecurity in the United States and of the importance of institutional

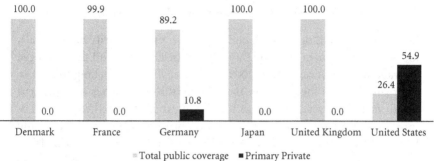

Figure 5.6. Public and Primary Private Health Insurance Coverage (% of Population), Selected Countries, 2009. *Source*: Own illustration, Data: Health at a Glance 2011: OECD Indicators.

context (and especially government policy) in mitigating this effect, we first provide an overview of the channels through which the new wave of globalization affects economic insecurity, beginning with the one that has received most attention from economists: skills-biased shifts in labor demand, and then moving to those that encompass the institutional context, including bargaining power, threat effects, and re-employment rates.

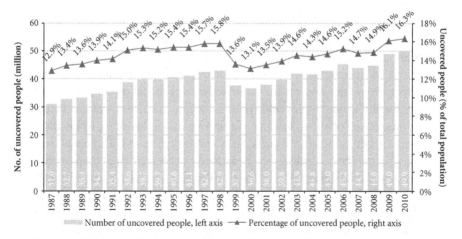

Figure 5.7. Number and Percentage of People without Health Insurance, United States, 1987–2010. *Source*: Own illustration. Data: U.S. Census Bureau, Current Population Survey, 1987 to 2010 Annual Social and Economic Supplements. People as of March of the following year. Taken from: Income, Poverty, and Health Insurance Coverage in the U.S.: 2010, 77.

5.3.1 Skill-Biased Shifts of Labor Demand

Economic research on the link between trade and insecurity has generally focused on wage inequality and the skill-bias of labor demand shifts induced by trade liberalization (Crinò 2009). Labor economists seeking to explain the rising income inequality in the industrialized countries over the past fifteen to twenty years looked to technological change as the culprit. The introduction of information and communication technology (ICT) and ICT-enabled tasks was said to have brought a bias to changes in labor demand, according to which the labor demand for higher-skill workers would grow faster than that for low-skill workers. The result of such "skills-biased technological change" was to raise income inequality as higher-paid workers saw gains whereas lower-paid workers experienced smaller gains or even, in some cases, decline.

According to the Stolper-Samuelson theorem, trade liberalization should benefit an economy's abundant factor relative to its scarce factor. In a world of high- and low-skill labor, the industrialized countries were clearly relatively abundant in skilled labor and thus could expect to see the returns to skill rising in relative terms. In sum, trade liberalization and technological change were both expected to contribute to rising wage inequality in the industrialized countries. The debate at the time was thus about the relative contribution of these two forces to the observed increases in inequality.

Table 5.6 presents a summary of selected econometric studies across OECD countries on the effects of offshoring on the relative wage bill of heterogenous labor, which can be interpreted as relative wages or relative labor demand. Most econometric studies confirm the inequality-enhancing effect of offshoring. Focusing on the relative demand for labor, another recent study for the United States finds that, since the late 1980s, less productive portions moved offshore, leading to a decline in employment, while maintaining higher value added parts. As a consequence, overall productivity rises, whereas the tradable sector generated only incremental employment (Spence and Hlatshwayo 2011). Thus offshoring may have partly offset the decline in productivity growth experienced after the Golden Age.

The most recent studies indicate that offshoring may no longer have such a skills bias in its impact on labor demand. Geishecker (2008) finds that employment duration and thus economic security is negatively affected by offshoring in Germany across all skill levels. Winkler (2009, 2013) reports that the effect of services offshoring in Germany was negative for the relative demand for high-skill German labor from the period 1995 to 2004. Interestingly, Autor (2010) suggests that job opportunities in the United States only

Table 5.6. *Offshoring and the Relative Demand for Skilled Labor*

Source	Country	Unit of analysis	Years	Measure of offshoring	Effect
Offshoring and the relative demand for skilled labor in studies with two labor inputs					
Feenstra and Hanson (1996)	United States	435 mfg. ind.	1977–1993	imported material inputs (broad) / output	+
Anderton and Brenton (1999)	United Kingdom	11 textiles and non-electr. machinery ind.	1970–1986	imports from low-income countries / output	+
Feenstra and Hanson (1999)	United States	447 mfg. ind.	1979–1990	imported material inputs (narrow and broad) / total non-energy inputs	+
Hansson (2000)	Sweden	34 mfg. ind.	1970–1993	imports from non-OECD countries / domestic demand	+
Slaughter (2000)	United States	32 mfg. ind.	1977–1994	affiliate employment / total employment	no ev.
Anderton et al. (2002)	Sweden	41 mfg. ind.	1975–1993	imports from low-income countries / output	+
Head and Ries (2002)	Japan	1,070 mfg. MNCs	1965–1989	affiliate employment / total MNC's employment	+
Strauss-Kahn (2004)	France	50 mfg. ind.	1977–1993	imported material inputs (narrow and broad) / output	+
Egger and Egger (2005)	Austria	20 mfg. ind.	1990–1998	imported material inputs (narrow)	+
Hansson (2005)	Sweden	73 mfg. MNCs	1990–1997	affiliate employment in non-OECD countries / total MNC's employment	+

(continued)

Table 5.6 (continued)

Source	Country	Unit of analysis	Years	Measure of offshoring	Effect
Helg and Tajoli (2005)	Italy	13 mfg. ind.	1988–1996	outward processing trade imports / output	+
	Germany	20 mfg. ind.	1993–1997	outward processing trade imports / output	no ev.
Hsieh and Woo (2005)	Hong Kong	54 mfg. ind.	1971–1996	(i) imports from China / consumption, (ii) imported intermediates from China / consumption	+
Lorentowicz et al. (2005)	Austria	15 mfg. ind.	1995–2002	imported material inputs (narrow) / value added	–
	Poland	23 mfg. ind.	1994–2002	(i) foreign fixed assets / domestic fixed assets, (ii) number of foreign firms / number of domestic firms	+
Geishecker (2006)	Germany	23 mfg. ind.	1991–2000	imported material inputs from CEECs (narrow and broad) / output	+
Minondo and Rubert (2006)	Spain	12 mfg. ind.	1986–1994	imported material inputs (narrow and broad) / total non-energy inputs	+
Yan (2006)	Canada	81 mfg. ind.	1981–1996	imported intermediates (broad)	+
Becker et al. (2009)	Germany	1,266 mfg. and serv. plants in 490 MNCs	1998–2001	affiliate employment / total MNC's employment	+

Study	Country	Industries	Period	Measure	Result
Winkler (2009)	Germany	28 mfg. ind.	1991–2000	imported service inputs (broad) / total non-energy inputs	+
				imported material inputs (broad) / total non-energy inputs	+
Winkler (2009, 2013)		35/31 mfg. ind.	1995–2004	imported service inputs (broad) / total non-energy inputs	−
				imported material inputs (broad) / total non-energy inputs	no ev.

Offshoring and the relative demand for the highest skill category in studies with more than two labor inputs

Study	Country	Industries	Period	Measure	Result
Morrison and Siegel (2001)	United States	450 mfg. ind.	1959–1989	imports / output	+
Falk and Koebel (2002)	Germany	26 mfg. ind.	1978–1990	imported material inputs	no ev.
Hijzen et al. (2005)	United Kingdom	50 mfg. ind.	1982–1996	imported material inputs (narrow) / value added	+
Ekholm and Hakkala (2006)	Sweden	20 mfg. ind.	1995–2000	imported material inputs (narrow and broad) / output	+
Crinò (2010)	United States	144 mfg. and serv. ind.	1997–2006	imported service inputs (broad) / total non-energy inputs	+
Crinò (2012)	9 EU	20 mfg. and serv. ind. / 13 mfg. ind.	1990–2004	imported service inputs (broad) / total non-energy inputs	+

Source: Winkler (2013). This material was originally published in *The Oxford Handbook of Offshoring and Global Employment*, edited by Bardhan, A., D. Jaffee, and C. Kroll (2013), and has been reproduced by permission of Oxford University Press [http://www.oup.com/us/catalog/general/series/OxfordHandbooks/]. Based on Crinò (2009) and own revisions and updates. Note: MNCs = Multinational corporations, CEECs = Central and Eastern European Countries, narrow = imports from the same industry, broad = imports from more or all industries.

fell for middle-wage, middle-skill jobs since the last 1980s, whereas high-skill, high-wage and low-skill, low-wage employment expanded, which he relates, among other factors, to offshoring of middle-skill "routine" tasks that were formerly performed mainly by workers with moderate levels of education.

5.3.2 Overall Labor Demand

The increased magnitude of – and public concern over – offshoring has spurred further empirical research on the employment effect of offshoring where labor is considered homogenous. Some of the most recent research focuses for the first time on services offshoring and considers its effect on overall employment. This focus is important because it gets away from the narrow theoretical confines of the Stolper-Samuelson theorem and the difficulty of testing it, and asks a more general question.[5] Their results are not fully conclusive, but they broadly indicate that across the OECD offshoring has led to reductions in overall employment.

The OECD (2007b) measures the effects of offshoring for twelve OECD countries (Austria, Belgium, Denmark, Finland, France, Germany, Greece, Italy, South Korea, Norway, Sweden, and the United States). Three types of models are estimated, which all cover 26 manufacturing and service industries for the two years 1995 and 2000, that is, growth rates from 1995 to 2000 are used in the regressions. The results indicate a significantly negative effect of materials and services offshoring on manufacturing and service employment, respectively.

Amiti and Wei (2006) find that services offshoring in the United States between 1992 and 2001 reduced manufacturing employment by 0.4 to 0.7 percent per year. At a more aggregated level (96 industries), the negative effect disappears. Materials offshoring shows significantly positive coefficients at the aggregated level, which become insignificant using 450 industries.[6]

---

[5] The theory has not gone uncriticized, both on the grounds of relevance (see Samuelson 2004) and on the grounds of the difficulty of measuring high-skill and low-skill labor (see Howell 2005), and its weak predictive power for the case of developing (low-skill abundant) countries (see, for example, Berg 2005).

[6] Most studies on the employment level effects of offshoring refer to the labor demand specification of Hamermesh (1993), where conditional labor demand is derived from a cost function using Shephard's Lemma whereby factor demand is given by the partial derivative of the cost function with respect to the corresponding factor price, regardless of the functional form of the production function.

Amiti and Wei (2005) test the impact of materials and services offshoring on home employment for the United Kingdom between 1995 and 2001. Including 69 manufacturing industries, they find a significantly positive impact of services offshoring on employment. Thus, a 1 percent increase of services offshoring led at least to a 0.085 percent increase in employment. The impact of materials offshoring on employment is ambiguous and insignificant. The study also focused on the effects in nine service industries for the same period. Here, materials and services offshoring both show negative coefficients which are significant in most specifications. However, due to the small sample size the results are less reliable.

Winkler (2009) analyzes the impact of services offshoring on German employment between 1991 and 2000 for 36 manufacturing industries and finds evidence of a negative impact. There is also some evidence for a negative influence of materials offshoring. In a second study from the period 1995 to 2006, Winkler (2010) confirms that services offshoring reduced manufacturing employment in Germany.

The perceptions of a strong link between globalization and economic insecurity discussed in Chapter 1 are likely driven both by current reality and by predictions of the future of globalized production. A number of recent studies project potentially very significant expansion of services offshoring. Blinder (2007, 2009) has done a detailed analysis of the U.S. labor force, looking especially at services jobs and the extent to which they are "personally-delivered" or "impersonally-delivered" (see Chapter 3). Personally-delivered services cannot be delivered electronically, such as child care or garbage collection. Impersonally-delivered services are those that can be delivered electronically without a significant loss of quality. These would include travel reservations and computer support. Blinder estimates that 30 to 40 million current jobs are likely in the future to involve impersonally-delivered services and thus be potentially subject to offshoring. This estimate is equivalent to 22 to 29 percent of the current American workforce (Blinder 2009).

Blinder's analysis is notable not just because the potential labor market displacement is large, but because the displacement affects all skill levels of the U.S. labor force. Blinder sees the potential wave of offshoring as driving a new industrial revolution:

The sectoral and occupational compositions of the U.S. workforce are likely to be quite different a generation or two from now. When that future rolls around, only a small minority of U.S. jobs will still be offshorable; the rest will have already moved off shore (Blinder 2005, 18).

Blinder's research shows that the distinction between high-skill versus low-skill labor which characterizes most of the research to date, may be much less relevant in the near future.

5.3.3 Labor Share of Income

A reasonable summary measure of economic security is the labor share of national income, because it captures both employment and wage effects in relation to a variety of factors, including offshoring. Previously we saw that the labor share of national income has fallen in many industrialized nations (Figure 5.2). Does offshoring play a role in this? A number of recent papers have taken up the question of trade and the profit share at the aggregate level. Harrison (2002) studies the relation between trade openness and the functional distribution across a large number of countries and finds (contrary to the prediction of Heckscher-Ohlin theory) that openness is generally associated with a lower labor share of national income. Harrison concludes that "rising trade shares and exchange rate crises reduce labor's share, while capital controls and government spending increase labor's share" (Harrison 2002, 1).

Guscina (2006) finds that three aspects of globalization (related to prices, offshoring and immigration) combined to play a large role in explaining the declining labor share for a group of six OECD countries between 1960 to 2000, although the effect of offshoring *per se* is relatively small. The International Monetary Fund (IMF) (2007) estimates that offshoring and immigration have reduced the labor share in continental Europe over the period from 1982 to 2002, while in the Anglo-Saxon countries the effect of offshoring is smaller. These studies may understate the impact of offshoring, since they include both trade and import prices. A study by the IMF (2005) finds that offshoring is a small, but nonetheless negative and significant factor in the determination of the labor share of income for a group of OECD countries.

Ellis and Smith (2007) find no connection between imports from emerging markets and the profit share (and thus the labor share as well), but link the rising profit share in nineteen OECD countries between 1960 to 1995 to increased "churning" in the labor market. They write that "This greater churn strengthens firms' bargaining positions and allows them to capture a larger share of factor income" (Ellis and Smith 2007, 18). Whereas the authors attribute this to technological change, we have previously argued that it is very difficult to distinguish the technological change and offshoring parts of the corporate decisions. In any case, it seems likely that the effect of such churning might vary depending on labor market institutions.

5.3.4 Displacement from Trade

Another measure of the effects of trade on economic insecurity is the replacement of earnings for those displaced by import competition. Kletzer (2001) has done the most extensive analysis of the re-employment rate and replacement wage for workers displaced as the result of foreign trade (see Chapter 1). In a study of the United States in the period from 1979 to 1999 she finds that earnings losses of job dislocation are large and persistent over time. Specifically, she finds that 64.8 percent of manufacturing workers displaced between 1979 and 1999 and one-fourth of those re-employed suffered earnings declines of greater than 30 percent. Workers displaced from non-manufacturing sectors did a little better: 69 percent found re-employment, and 21 percent suffered pay cuts of 30 percent or more.

OECD (2005) did a similar study for fourteen European countries between 1994 to 2001 and finds that while re-employment rates in Europe were lower than in the United States, a much lower share had earnings losses of more than 30 percent upon re-employment and a slightly higher share had no earnings loss or were earning more than before displacement, further evidence that labor market institutions and policies result in different outcomes with respect to insecurity even in the face of similar pressures on vulnerability. This cross-country comparison also indicates the usefulness of looking at the effect of trade on the labor share of national income. The European experience has been larger employment losses and smaller declines in wages compared to the United States.

5.3.5 Elasticity of Labor Demand and the Threat Effect

In addition to labor demand shifts and job displacement, greater openness to international trade can also raise the sensitivity of labor demand to changes in domestic or foreign wages, that is, the wage elasticity of labor demand. This sensitivity of employment to both domestic and foreign wage movements is further increased as global supply chains become more developed and offshoring increases. According to Anderson and Gascon (2007),

disaggregating the value chain has allowed U.S. business to substitute cheaper foreign labor, increasing firms' own price elasticity of demand for labor, raising the volatility

Table 5.7. *Adjustment Costs of Trade-Displaced Workers, Europe versus United States*

Industry	14 European countries: 1994–2001[a]			United States: 1979–1999		
	Share re-employed two years later (%)	Share with no earnings loss or earning more (%)	Share with earnings losses > 30% (%)	Share re-employed at survey date (%)	Share with no earnings loss or earning more (%)	Share with earnings losses > 30% (%)
Manufacturing	57.0	45.8	6.5	64.8	35.0	25.0
High International Competition	51.8	44.0	5.4	63.4	36.0	25.0
Medium International Competition	58.7	45.7	7.0	65.4	34.0	25.0
Low International Competition	59.6	47.3	6.8	66.8	38.0	26.0
Services and Utilities[b]	57.2	49.6	8.4	69.1	41.0	21.0
All sectors	57.3	47.1	7.5	–	–	–

Source: Own illustration. Based on Milberg and Winkler (2011a, 162). Data: OECD (2005), Table 1.3, 45; and Kletzer, L.G. (2001), Job Loss from Imports: Measuring the Costs, Institute for International Economics, Washington, DC, Table D2, 102.

[a] Secretariat estimates based on data from the European Community Household Panel (ECHP) for Austria, Belgium, Denmark, Finland, France, Germany, Greece, Ireland, Italy, Luxembourg, the Netherlands, Portugal, Spain and the United Kingdom.

[b] Services for Europe.

of wages and employment, which increase worker insecurity (Anderson and Gascon 2007, 2).

There have been very few estimates of the relation between trade openness and the wage elasticity of labor demand. Slaughter (2001) studies U.S. manufacturers in the period from 1960 to 1991 and finds that the labor demand elasticity rose for U.S. production workers (a proxy for lower-skill workers) and not for non-production workers over this time. The demand for production workers rose most in those sectors with the greatest increases in offshoring, as well as those with more technical change in the form of more computer-related investment. Scheve and Slaughter (2003) find that FDI is the key aspect of globalization that raises the elasticity of labor demand. In a study of outward FDI by U.K. firms, they find that more foreign investment is associated with a higher labor demand elasticity, and more volatility of wages and employment. Senses (2010) shifts the focus to offshoring in U.S. manufacturing industries between 1972 and 2001, and confirms that offshoring increased the elasticity of labor demand, both in the short-run and in the long-run. This relationship doesn't change when controlling for skill-biased technical change.

The higher elasticity of labor demand can have an indirect effect on wage formation, because it enhances the threat effect, whereby the mere threat by companies to move production overseas influences wage demands. Discussing trade openness in the U.S. toy industry, Freeman (1995) notes,

It isn't even necessary that the West import the toys. The threat to import them or to move plants to less-developed countries to produce toys may suffice to force low-skilled westerners to take a cut in pay to maintain employment. In this situation, the open economy can cause lower pay for low-skilled westerners even without trade (Freeman 1995, 21).

A few researchers have explored the importance of firms' threats to move production abroad on the bargaining power and demands of labor. According to Piore (1998):

Merely management's credible threat of moving production offshore in response to import competition can induce vulnerable workers or their unions to settle for wage concession or benefit reductions. Management need only point to a few compelling examples of where labor's wage demand led to job loss to obtain this outcome (Piore 1998, 289).

This issue has received considerable attention by theorists, but has undergone little empirical analysis. Choi (2001) looks at detailed, sectoral data on outward FDI by U.S. manufacturers and finds that increased outward investment was associated with a lower wage premium for union members during the period from 1983 to 1996. Bronfenbrenner and Luce (2004), studying the United States between 1993 and 1999, focus more narrowly on unionization campaigns as opposed to wages. They find that a firm's mobility did raise the credibility of the threat to move production offshore and that this influenced union elections, with unionization drives having a much lower rate of success in firms with a credible threat of mobility than in those considered immobile.

5.4 Offshoring and the Labor Market: Econometric Evidence

We turn now to our own analysis of offshoring and the labor market in industrialized countries. We begin with employment effects and then turn to the labor share generally, before exploring the impact of different labor market regulations on the outcome.

5.4.1 Offshoring and Labor Demand in the United States

We look first at the question of labor demand. We adopt a very traditional model so that our results are easily comparable with existing studies of labor demand.

A firm's linearly homogeneous cost function, conditional on the level of output Y, is the following:

$$C = C(Y, w, r, p^{INP}, T) \frac{\partial C}{\partial c_1} > 0, \frac{\partial C}{\partial c_1 \partial c_2} > 0 \text{ with } c_1, c_2 = w, r, p^{INP}, T$$

(5.1)

where Y designates the output, w wages, r the rental rate on capital, and p^{INP} the prices for intermediate inputs. Following Feenstra and Hanson (2003), any structural variables that shift the production function and, thus, affect costs can be included into the cost function. Therefore, we include the technology shifter $T = T(OSS, OSM)$ to equation (5.1), which is a function of services and materials offshoring intensities OSS and OSM.

Using Shephard's Lemma, the conditional labor demand function L in log-linear form is given as follows:

$$\ln L_{it} = \beta_0 + \eta_Y \ln Y_{it} + \eta_L \ln w_{it} + \eta_K \ln r_{it} + \eta_{INP} \ln p_{it}^{INP}$$
$$+ \eta_{OSS} \ln OSS_{it} + \eta_{OSM} \ln OSM_{it}$$

(5.2)

where i designates the sector dimension, t the time dimension, and β_0 the constant.

Offshoring intensities enter the labor demand function through the technology shifter in the form of services offshoring intensity OSS, and materials offshoring intensity OSM, as defined in Section 2.1.3.[7] However, the effect of offshoring might be exaggerated due to omitted correlated variables. We address this problem by adding the shares of total imports in total output,

---

[7] Appendix 5.2 contains a full description of the data used for estimation.

as suggested by Amiti and Wei (2005, 2009). A higher import share could be related to higher offshoring intensities.

We estimate the following specification of equation (5.2):

$$\ln L_{it} = \beta_0 + \eta_Y \ln Y_{it} + \eta_L \ln w_{it} + \eta_K \ln r_{it} + \eta_{INP} \ln p_{it}^{INP}$$
$$+ \eta_{OSS} \ln OSS_{it} + \eta_{OSM} \ln OSM_{it} + \eta_{IM} \ln(IM/Y)_{it}$$
$$+ D_i + D_t + \varepsilon_{it} \tag{5.3}$$

where D_i denotes fixed sector effects, D_t fixed year effects, such as common shocks influencing all sectors, and ε_{it} the random error term.

We expect higher output to have a positive effect on labor demand ($\eta_Y > 0$), while an increase in wages will lower labor demand ($\eta_w < 0$). An increase in capital and intermediate input prices might have a positive ($\eta_K, \eta_{INP} > 0$) or negative ($\eta_K, \eta_{INP} < 0$) effect on labor demand, depending on whether capital stock or intermediate inputs are substitutes or complements for labor. Analogously, the effect of the import share on labor demand can be positive ($\eta_{IM} > 0$) or negative ($\eta_{IM} < 0$).

The expected effects of offshoring on labor demand were discussed in Chapter 4 (Figure 4.5). Weakening labor demand results from the direct replacement of foreign for domestic labor (the "substitution effect") and the "productivity effect," which involves reduced demand for labor for each unit of output. Labor demand increases with the scale of production ("scale effect"), offsetting the negative labor demand effects from substitution and productivity. But the conditional labor demand function in equation (5.3) only captures the productivity and substitution effect. Scale effects are taken into account when the output price is substituted for the quantity of output (Amiti and Wei 2009). Allowing for scale effects, the unconditional labor demand equation can be written as follows:

$$\ln L_{it} = \beta_0 + \eta_P \ln P_{it} + \eta_L \ln w_{it} + \eta_K \ln r_{it} + \eta_{INP} \ln p_{it}^{INP}$$
$$+ \eta_{OSS} \ln OSS_{it} + \eta_{OSM} \ln OSM_{it} + \eta_{IM} \ln(IM/Y)_{it}$$
$$+ D_i + D_t + \varepsilon_{it} \tag{5.4}$$

We have estimated the effect of offshoring on both the conditional and unconditional labor demand function (see Appendix 5.2 for data description). Table 5.8 presents the results of the consistent fixed effects estimator. All estimations produce standard errors robust to heteroscedasticity (Huber-White sandwich estimators). All regressions control for industry

Table 5.8. *Offshoring and Labor Demand, Regressions, United States, 1998–2006*

Dependent variable: $\ln L_t$	Manufacturing and service sectors				Manufacturing sectors				Service sectors			
	Conditional		Unconditional		Conditional		Unconditional		Conditional		Unconditional	
	(1)	(2)	(3)	(4)	(5)	(6)	(7)	(8)	(9)	(10)	(11)	(12)
$\ln Y_t$	0.4499*** (0.000)				0.6091*** (0.000)				0.0741 (0.493)			
$\ln Y_{t-1}$		0.3886*** (0.000)				0.5511*** (0.000)				−0.1307 (0.273)		
$\ln P_t$			0.3141* (0.084)				0.0088 (0.975)				0.3474 (0.154)	
$\ln P_{t-1}$				0.3559** (0.041)				0.2267 (0.360)				0.2724 (0.329)
$\ln w_t$	−0.2930*** (0.000)	−0.2683*** (0.000)	−0.1186* (0.073)		−0.2649*** (0.000)		−0.1852* (0.042)		−0.2192* (0.096)		−0.0611 (0.673)	
$\ln w_{t-1}$				−0.1039* (0.099)		−0.2565*** (0.000)		−0.1257 (0.109)		−0.1294 (0.359)		−0.1133 (0.480)
$\ln r_t$	0.4107** (0.010)	0.3056** (0.048)	0.0496 (0.722)		0.4334 (0.293)		−1.2048* (0.062)		0.2219** (0.030)		0.2256** (0.036)	
$\ln r_{t-1}$				0.0522 (0.688)		0.1182 (0.814)		−1.2510 (0.101)		0.1052 (0.258)		0.1700 (0.119)
$\ln p_t$	−0.1893*** (0.002)	−0.1046 (0.106)	−0.3529** (0.024)		−0.1262* (0.090)		0.0316 (0.889)		−0.2945 (0.443)		−0.6159* (0.097)	
$\ln p_{t-1}$				−0.3173** (0.041)		−0.0435 (0.556)		−0.0690 (0.744)		−0.2386 (0.593)		−0.5560 (0.275)

lnOSS_t	−0.1988*** (0.001)		−0.3372*** (0.001)		−0.0314 (0.792)		−0.4916** (0.015)		−0.1725* (0.055)		−0.1330 (0.155)	
lnOSS_{t-1}		−0.1961*** (0.002)		−0.3321*** (0.000)		−0.0132 (0.921)		−0.4764** (0.023)		−0.1258 (0.171)		−0.1292 (0.138)
lnOSM_t	−0.1744** (0.029)		−0.4270*** (0.000)		−0.2177* (0.097)		−0.7417*** (0.001)		0.0022 (0.982)		0.0324 (0.751)	
lnOSM_{t-1}		−0.1183 (0.193)		−0.3402*** (0.002)		−0.2449* (0.059)		−0.6414*** (0.003)		0.1579 (0.150)		0.1210 (0.284)
ln(IM/Y)_t	0.0016 (0.954)		−0.0986*** (0.002)		−0.0791** (0.014)		−0.0911* (0.084)		0.0353 (0.401)		0.0226 (0.607)	
ln(IM/Y)_{t-1}		−0.0049 (0.866)		−0.0677** (0.031)		−0.0487 (0.155)		−0.0549 (0.280)		−0.0019 (0.962)		0.0119 (0.796)
Fixed sector effects	Yes	Yes	Yes	Yes	Yes	Yes	Yes	Yes	Yes	Yes	Yes	Yes
Fixed year effects	Yes	Yes	Yes	Yes	Yes	Yes	Yes	Yes	Yes	Yes	Yes	Yes
Observations	297	264	297	264	189	168	189	168	108	96	108	96
R-squared (within)	0.77	0.74	0.60	0.61	0.90	0.89	0.75	0.76	0.42	0.42	0.43	0.41

Source: Own calculations. $p^* < 0.1$, $p^{**} < 0.05$, $p^{***} < 0.01$ (p-values in parentheses).

Note: L = labor demand, Y = real output, P = output price, w = real wage rate, r = capital price, p = intermediate input price, OSS = services offshoring intensity, OSM = materials offshoring intensity, and (IM/Y) = import share.

fixed effects and year fixed effects. Columns 1 to 4 consider the 33 manufacturing and service sectors simultaneously.[8] Columns 1 and 2 focus on conditional labor demand given by equation (5.3). Output and capital prices have a positive effect on conditional labor demand, whereas wages, intermediate input prices, and services and materials offshoring show a negative impact on employment, with all coefficients statistically significant (column 1). Using one-period lags of each explanatory variable only (column 2) confirms the results, although intermediate input prices and materials offshoring narrowly miss the 10 percent significance level, which indicates that the contemporaneous effect is stronger for these variables.

When output prices P are substituted for the amount of output (columns 3 and 4), the negative wage effect becomes smaller, whereas the negative impact of services and materials offshoring increases. Output prices have a positive and significant effect on unconditional labor demand, whereas intermediate input prices show a statistically significant negative effect on unconditional labor demand. Capital prices are no longer significant, whereas import shares now have a significantly negative effect on unconditional labor.

Columns 5 to 8 present estimates for the 21 manufacturing sectors only. Columns 5 and 6 show the results for the conditional labor demand regressions. The positive effect of output and the negative effect of materials offshoring is larger in the manufacturing sample, whereas the negative wage effect is slightly smaller. Services offshoring shows no impact, while the import share has a negative impact on conditional labor demand (column 5). Focusing on unconditional labor demand (columns 7 and 8) shows that both materials and services offshoring have a strongly negative (and significant) effect. Columns 9 to 12 show the results for the 12 service sectors only. Wages significantly lower conditional labor demand, whereas capital prices increase it (column 9). Interestingly, services offshoring shows a negative impact on both conditional (columns 9 and 10) and unconditional labor demand (columns 11 and 12), although it narrowly misses the 10 percent significance level in columns 10 to 12.

Focusing on the specifications covering the full sample with contemporaneous effects, we can offer the following interpretation: Holding all variables constant, a 10 percent increase of services and materials offshoring intensity

---

[8] We deleted the outliers "federal reserve banks, credit intermediation and related activities" due to extremely low *OSM* intensities and "motion picture and sound recording industries" due to extremely high *OSS* intensities relative to employment.

reduced conditional labor demand by 2.0 and 1.7 percent, respectively, in the period from 1998 to 2006 (column 1). This can be explained as the result of a combination of a negative productivity effect and a negative substitution effect due to offshoring. Allowing for scale effects we can say that a 10 percent increase in services and materials offshoring intensity lowered unconditional labor demand by 3.4 and 4.3 percent, respectively (column 3). Focusing on the more conservative results, this implies a drop in employment of approximately 3.5 million full-time equivalent jobs between 1998 and 2006.

How can the even stronger negative effects of offshoring be explained when one allows for scale effects? Theory would suggest positive scale effects and thus either an overall positive effect or a weaker negative effect. The first would be the case when positive scale effects dominate negative productivity and substitution effects, whereas the second would occur when negative productivity and substitution effects dominate the positive scale effects. Our results suggest negative scale effects, that is lower intermediate input prices do not result in higher labor demand (see Figure 4.8), which could be confirmed in our regressions. There are three possible direct leakages in the schema presented in Chapter 4: (i) Lower (foreign) input prices and thus higher profits do not lead to lower output prices; (ii) Lower output prices do not result in higher output demand; (iii) Higher output demand does not lead to higher labor demand. There might be indirect leakages as well, for example, when higher investment or productivity does not result in higher output and employment.

Note that the results of services offshoring in the unconditional labor demand regressions are in contrast to the findings of Amiti and Wei (2009) who find no negative impact of services offshoring on U.S. manufacturing employment in the period from 1992 to 2001 at an aggregated industry-level. Moreover, this study finds a positive effect of materials offshoring at the aggregated industry-level, whereas we find a negative effect.

In Chapter 6 we explore the first possible leakage, according to which cost savings from offshoring are passed on to shareholders – what we call financialization – rather than to consumers in the form of price cuts. But first we estimate the effect of offshoring on the labor share of income. We then consider two questions: The first is the issue of how labor market institutions, and in particular government intervention in labor markets, affect the impact of offshoring on economic security. The second is how these estimated effects of offshoring on the labor share are related to the perceptions of globalization that we discussed in Chapter 1.

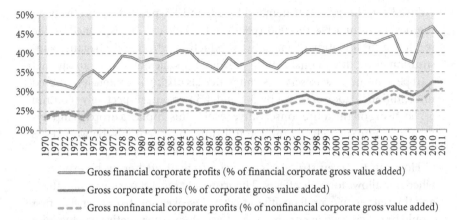

Gross financial corporate profits (% of financial corporate gross value added)

Gross corporate profits (% of corporate gross value added)

Gross nonfinancial corporate profits (% of nonfinancial corporate gross value added)

Figure 5.8. Corporate Profit Shares, United States, 1970–2010. *Source:* Own illustration. Data: U.S. Bureau of Economic Analysis, National Income and Product Accounts. Note: Gross profits are calculated by summing up net operating surplus and consumption of fixed capital and dividing their sum by GVA. Gray bars correspond to U.S. business cycles recessions according to the definition of the National Bureau of Economic Research.

5.4.2 Offshoring and the Labor Share in the United States

We see that the expansion of offshoring (as shown in Figure 4.3 and discussed more broadly in Chapter 2) has corresponded to a slow but steady rise in the share of corporate profits in corporate gross value added (GVA), which reached levels shortly before the global financial crisis not seen in 30 years (see Figure 5.8). The gray area in Figure 5.8 shows that corporate profit shares in the United States correspond to recessions and have a clear cyclical pattern. The profit share generally rises well into the cycle and then begins to fall as the downturn approach, bottoming out during the recession. After stagnating in the 1980s, the profit share recovered beginning in the early 1990s. It has been higher during the last two business cycles than at any time since the 1970s. Corporate profits of financial industries, in particular, skyrocketed to almost 45 percent before the financial crisis, but sharply fell in 2007 and 2008 before quickly recovering to historic highs.

The profit share and offshoring seem to rise together, but can we establish that offshoring is in part responsible for this rise in the U.S. profit share? To address this question we begin with a very standard model of the profit share and then integrate changes in offshoring into the model. Following Bentolila and Saint-Paul (2003), we adopt a model of the labor share which assumes constant elasticity of substitution technology, and gives the following expression for the labor share of income *LS*:

$$LS = \frac{(1 - \alpha)(T^L \cdot L)^\gamma}{\alpha(T^K \cdot K)^\gamma + (1 - \alpha)(T^L \cdot L)^\gamma} = 1 - \alpha(T^K \cdot k)^\gamma \quad (5.5)$$

where *K* and *L* denote capital and labor, while T^K, T^L and γ represent technological parameters. Capital intensity *k*, i.e. the capital-output ratio, is defined as:

$$k = \left(\frac{K^\gamma}{\alpha(T^K \cdot K)^\gamma + (1 - \alpha)(T^L \cdot L)^\gamma} \right)^{1/\gamma} \quad (5.6)$$

The profit share, *PS*, is defined analogously, and thus

$$PS + LS = 1 \quad (5.7)$$

Equation (5.5) shows that there is a stable relationship between the labor share and capital intensity *k*. This relationship does not change if there are changes in factor prices (wages or interest rates), quantities or labor-augmenting technological progress T^L, because these will only result in movements along the curve described in equation (5.5). However, Bentolila and Saint-Paul (2003) identify two sources of deviation from the relationship in equation (5.5), which result in shifts of the curve: (i) capital-augmenting technological progress T^K induced changes, for example as a result of import price fluctuations, and (ii) divergence between wages and productivity, brought on, for example, by a shift in labor bargaining power *LBP*. This leaves four explanatory variables in the model: technological progress T^K, capital intensity *k*, import prices *MP* and labor bargaining power *LBP*. Taking natural logarithms we obtain:

$$\ln LS_{it} = \beta_0 + \beta_1 \ln T_{it}^K + \beta_2 \ln k_{it} + \beta_3 \ln MP_{it} + \beta_4 \ln LBP_{it} \quad (5.8)$$

where *i* designates sectors, *t* the time dimension, and β_0 the constant.

Capital intensity can have a positive or negative impact on the labor share depending on the sign of γ in equation (5.5): (i) If labor and capital are substitutes, that is, $\gamma < 0$, a higher capital intensity will reduce the labor share; (ii) If labor and capital are complements, that is, $\gamma > 0$, a higher capital intensity will increase the labor share; (iii) In the Cobb-Douglas case, i.e. $\gamma = 0$, the labor share is $LS = 1 - \alpha$. If the technological parameter T^K is strictly capital-augmenting, it should have the same coefficient sign as capital intensity. If this is not the case, it suggests a more complex relation between productivity and output.

Prices of imported materials can have a positive or negative influence on the labor share, depending on three effects: (i) If import prices decline, the labor-capital ratio must fall in order to maintain a constant capital intensity, which lowers the labor share. (ii) The second effect is an indirect consequence of the first effect. It captures a rise in the wage rate induced by the lower labor-capital ratio, which has a positive effect on the labor share. (iii) If imported materials increase the marginal product of labor, a lower import price raises material imports, which increases the marginal product of labor and, thus, wages and the labor share. The net effect of import prices on the labor share is ambiguous.

The effect of increased labor bargaining power depends on the underlying bargaining model. (i) In the first model, firms and unions first bargain over wages and then firms set employment unilaterally, taking wages as given. An increase in labor's bargaining power results in a higher wage rate, which increases the capital intensity as firms substitute capital for labor. But the labor share may rise or fall depending on the elasticity of substitution between labor and capital (see discussion above). (ii) In the second model, firms and workers bargain over both wages and employment and will set employment in an efficient way. For a given level of capital intensity, higher labor bargaining power increases the labor share, because labor is paid more than its marginal product. Capital intensity remains unchanged, because of the equality between marginal product and the alternative wage (Bentolila and Saint-Paul 2003).

The labor share is measured as a sector's compensation of employees in value added, or wL/VA, where w denotes the wage rate and VA value added. The technology parameter in the model is captured with labor productivity (LP). Capital is made up of its subcomponents "private equipment and software" and "private structures." Because we believe that their respective effects on labor shares are different, we include two measures of capital intensity in our estimations (k^{equip} and k^{struc}).

Sectoral import prices MP are captured by using sectoral services, materials and energy offshoring intensities, which represent the proportion of imported inputs used in home production (see Section 2.1.3 for the definition of sectoral offshoring intensities). Energy offshoring intensity OSE is used as a proxy for the prices of imported energy inputs[9], that is, a

---

[9] We focus on three energy inputs that are associated with imported oil prices, namely "oil and gas extraction," "electric power generation, transmission and distribution" and "natural gas distribution."

higher intensity reflects *higher* imported energy input prices. Whereas firms generally depend on foreign energy inputs, imported service and material inputs are mostly chosen for cost reasons. Thus, services and materials off-shoring intensities, *OSS* and *OSM*, serve as inverse proxies for the prices of imported service and material inputs, that is, a higher intensity reflects lower imported service and material input prices. We adopt union density *UND* as a proxy for labor bargaining power. The data description can be found in Appendix 5.2.

This gives the follow equation for estimation:

$$\ln LS_{it} = \beta_0 + \beta_1 \ln LP_{it} + \beta_2 \ln k_{it}^{equip} + \beta_3 \ln k_{it}^{struc} + \beta_4 \ln OSS_{it}$$
$$+ \beta_5 \ln OSM_{it} + \beta_6 \ln OSE_{it} + \beta_7 \ln UND_{it}$$
$$+ D_i + D_t + \varepsilon_{it} \tag{5.9}$$

where β_0 denotes the constant, D_i and D_t fixed sector and year effects, and ε_{it} the random error term.

Table 5.9 shows the results using the consistent fixed effects estimator. All estimations produce standard errors robust to heteroscedasticity (Huber-White sandwich estimators).[10] All regressions control for industry fixed effects and year fixed effects. We first show the results for the whole sample (columns 1 to 3), before analyzing the results for the manufacturing (columns 4 to 6) and service sectors (columns 7 to 9) separately.

Column 1 considers only the instantaneous effects on the labor share, whereas column 2 considers only the lagged effects. The results show clearly that increases in services and materials offshoring are associated with a lower labor share between 1998 and 2006, while energy offshoring has a positive relation. However, only the lagged effect is statistically signifi-cant for services offshoring (column 2), while only the contemporaneous effect shows statistically significant results for materials offshoring (column 1). Labor productivity has a negative (and statistically significant) effect on the labor share. Interestingly, the capital intensity of equipment and software has no impact, whereas the capital intensity of structures has a positive (and statistically significant) one. Higher union density is asso-ciated with a higher labor share, which is insignificant. In column 3, we combine instantaneous and lagged effects. Whereas the overall trends of

---

[10] We deleted the outliers "federal reserve banks, credit intermediation and related activities" due to extremely low *OSM* intensities and "motion picture and sound recording industries" due to extremely high *OSS* intensities relative to labor share.

columns 1 and 2 can be confirmed, the F-tests show that the null hypothesis of no joint influence on the labor share cannot be rejected for capital intensity of equipment and software, materials offshoring intensity, and union density.

Isolating the manufacturing sectors (columns 4 to 6) confirms the trends described above. However, some of the coefficient sizes change. The positive effect of capital intensity of structures as well as the negative effects of materials and services offshoring are bigger now. The positive impact of energy offshoring becomes smaller. Union density now has a statistically significant effect (column 4).

Columns 7 to 9 show the estimations for service sectors only. The combined effect of capital intensity of equipment and software becomes significantly positive in column 9, whereas the effect of capital intensity of structures becomes much smaller but statistically insignificant (columns 7 and 8) or even negative (column 9). The negative coefficient of services offshoring is smaller than in the manufacturing sector and narrowly misses the 10 percent significance level, whereas the negative effect of materials offshoring is bigger and significant. The positive impact of energy offshoring becomes insignificant, whereas the lagged union density variable again shows a positive and statistically significant effect (columns 8 and 9).

Interpreting the more conservative results of column 3, we can say that, holding all other variables constant, a 10 percent increase of services offshoring – reflecting lower imported service input prices – reduces the labor share in the manufacturing and service sectors by 0.8 percent between 1998 and 2006. A 10 percent increase of materials offshoring – reflecting lower imported material input prices – leads to an average labor share decline of 1.8 percent (column 1).

5.4.3 Offshoring and the Labor Share: The Role of Labor Market Support

In this section we consider the issue of how labor market institutions, and in particular government intervention in labor markets, affects the impact of offshoring on economic security. In the next section we consider how these estimated effects of offshoring on the labor share are related to the perceptions of globalization that we discussed in Chapter 1. We adopt Bentolila and Saint-Paul's (2003) model of the labor share as specified in equation (5.5). The labor share is measured as a sector's compensation of employees in value

Table 5.9. *Offshoring and the Labor Share, Regressions, United States, 1998–2006*

Dependent variable: $\ln LS_t$	Manufacturing and service sectors			Manufacturing sectors				Service sectors	
	(1)	(2)	(3)	(4)	(5)	(6)	(7)	(8)	(9)
$\ln LP_t$	-0.6045***		-0.6712***	-0.5908***		-0.6244***	-0.6404***		-0.7320***
	(0.000)		(0.000)	(0.000)		(0.000)	(0.000)		(0.000)
$\ln LP_{t-1}$		-0.4326***	0.0363		-0.3452***	0.0664		-0.6474***	-0.0581
		(0.000)	(0.305)		(0.002)	(0.182)		(0.000)	(0.601)
$\ln(k^{equip})_t$	0.0023		-0.0241	-0.0382		0.0987	0.0051		-0.1599*
	(0.945)		(0.813)	(0.394)		(0.662)	(0.921)		(0.072)
$\ln(k^{equip})_{t-1}$		0.0803	0.0046		0.1646	-0.1298		0.0756	0.1802**
		(0.225)	(0.957)		(0.224)	(0.527)		(0.147)	(0.020)
$\ln(k^{struc})_t$	0.0840***		0.0693	0.1608***		0.0264	0.0256		0.1151
	(0.001)		(0.282)	(0.000)		(0.895)	(0.651)		(0.163)
$\ln(k^{struc})_{t-1}$		0.1439***	0.0133		0.0850	0.1283		0.0519	-0.1338*
		(0.002)	(0.857)		(0.316)	(0.525)		(0.457)	(0.080)
$\ln OSS_t$	-0.0536		0.0602	-0.1531*		-0.0106	-0.1094		0.0414
	(0.187)		(0.138)	(0.052)		(0.913)	(0.100)		(0.602)
$\ln OSS_{t-1}$		-0.1400*	-0.1340***		-0.1589	-0.1512*		-0.0867	-0.1307
		(0.060)	(0.001)		(0.353)	(0.090)		(0.245)	(0.134)
$\ln OSM_t$	-0.1791***		-0.1276	-0.2212***		-0.2923***	-0.2837***		-0.0747
	(0.001)		(0.189)	(0.007)		(0.007)	(0.001)		(0.410)
$\ln OSM_{t-1}$		-0.0561	0.0834		0.1846	0.1715		-0.1582**	-0.1001
		(0.498)	(0.350)		(0.365)	(0.145)		(0.042)	(0.358)

(continued)

Table 5.9 (continued)

Dependent variable: $\ln LS_t$	Manufacturing and service sectors			Manufacturing sectors			Service sectors		
	(1)	(2)	(3)	(4)	(5)	(6)	(7)	(8)	(9)
$\ln OSE_t$	0.0862***		0.0786***	0.0458**		0.0376	0.0464		−0.0127
	(0.000)		(0.000)	(0.039)		(0.123)	(0.653)		(0.863)
$\ln OSE_{t-1}$		0.0981***	0.0120		0.1696***	0.0213		−0.1000	0.0887
		(0.000)	(0.502)		(0.001)	(0.404)		(0.173)	(0.348)
$\ln UND_t$	0.0206		0.0142	0.0525*		0.0224	0.0175		0.0072
	(0.277)		(0.226)	(0.084)		(0.425)	(0.514)		(0.701)
$\ln UND_{t-1}$		0.0123	0.0310		−0.1104	0.0180		0.0674**	0.0403**
		(0.637)	(0.143)		(0.148)	(0.655)		(0.047)	(0.045)
Fixed sector effects	Yes	Yes	Yes	Yes	Yes	Yes	Yes	Yes	Yes
Fixed year effects	Yes	Yes	Yes	Yes	Yes	Yes	Yes	Yes	Yes
Joint significance:									
$\ln LP_t + \ln LP_{t-1} = 0$			p>F=0.0000			p>F=0.0000			p>F=0.0000
$\ln(k^{equip})_t + \ln(k^{equip})_{t-1} = 0$			p>F=0.9292			p>F=0.6348			p>F=0.0641
$\ln(k^{struc})_t + \ln(k^{struc})_{t-1} = 0$			p>F=0.0687			p>F=0.0059			p>F=0.2093
$\ln OSS_t + \ln OSS_{t-1} = 0$			p>F=0.0032			p>F=0.1408			p>F=0.3165
$\ln OSM_t + \ln OSM_{t-1} = 0$			p>F=0.4164			p>F=0.0236			p>F=0.1040
$\ln OSE_t + \ln OSE_{t-1} = 0$			p>F=0.0006			p>F=0.0720			p>F=0.5699
$\ln UND_t + \ln UND_{t-1} = 0$			p>F=0.2256			p>F=0.6706			p>F=0.1305
Observations	297	264	264	189	168	168	108	96	96
R-squared (within)	0.83	0.56	0.86	0.87	0.56	0.89	0.78	0.75	0.88

Source: Own calculations. p* < 0.1, p** < 0.05, p*** < 0.01 (p-values in parentheses).

Note: LS = labor share, LP = labor productivity, k^{equip} = capital intensity of equipment and software, k^{struc} = capital intensity of structures, OSS = services offshoring intensity, OSM = materials offshoring intensity, OSE = energy offshoring intensity, and UND = union density.

added, or wL/VA, where w denotes the wage rate and VA value added. The technology parameter in the model is captured with labor productivity LP, measured as value added per employee (VA/L). Capital intensity is obtained by dividing a sector's capital stock by value added (K/VA). Import prices MP are captured by using goods offshoring intensities as inverse proxies for the prices of imported goods, that is, a higher intensity reflects lower imported goods prices. Offshoring (OSG) is measured as the share of sectoral manufacturing imports from low- and middle-income countries (LMICs) in a sector's total manufacturing imports, as defined in Section 2.1.2. We adopt union density UND as a proxy for labor bargaining power, which measures the percentage of union affiliation in total employment, but is only available at the country level. Detailed data description can be found in Appendix 5.3.

This gives the following equation for estimation:

$$\ln LS_{it} = \beta_0 + \beta_1 \ln LP_{it} + \beta_2 \ln k_{it} + \beta_3 \ln OSG_{it} + \beta_4 \ln UND_{ct}$$

$$+ D_i + D_t + \varepsilon_{it} \tag{5.10}$$

where β_0 denotes the constant, D_i fixed sector effects, D_t fixed year effects, and ε_{it} the random error term.

This completes the basic model of the labor share, expanded to allow estimation of the impact of offshoring. But recall that we also want to explore empirically the effects of offshoring under different labor market regimes. Specifically, we interact offshoring with policy indicators of labor market flexibility and labor support to detect differential effects of offshoring. Interacting offshoring in equation (5.10) with a policy indicator at the country level yields the following equation:

$$\ln LS_{it} = \beta_0 + \beta_1 \ln LP_{it} + \beta_2 \ln k_{it} + \beta_3 \ln OSG_{it} + \beta_4 \ln UND_{ct}$$

$$+ \delta_1 \ln OSG_{it} * policy_{ct-1} + \delta_2 \, policy_{ct-1} + D_i$$

$$+ D_t + \varepsilon_{it} \tag{5.11}$$

where the total effect of exports on the labor share is given by $\beta_3 + \delta_1 policy_{ct-1}$. By definition, the value of policy is positive in our sample ($policy_{t-1} > 0$). As a consequence, the total effect ($\beta_3 + \delta_1 policy_{ct-1}$) will be smaller (larger resp.) than β_3 if the coefficient of the interaction term is negative (positive resp.), that is, $\delta_1 < 0$ ($\delta_1 > 0$ resp.). We use different policy indicators to capture labor market flexibility and labor support at the country level, because comparable indicators are unavailable at the sectoral level. Labor market flexibility is measured using the EPL index previously discussed (see Table 5.4).

We expect that the effects of offshoring on a country's labor share are lower the more protective is its labor market, because firms are more likely to use offshoring mainly to complement existing, domestic operations. Winkler (2009), for instance, finds that offshoring has negative employment effects in Germany, while Amiti and Wei (2005, 2006) find positive effects for the United Kingdom and the United States. Winkler (2010) attributes these differences to different degrees of labor market flexibility. Firms in more rigid labor markets, such as Germany, do not create new jobs when they expand their offshoring despite efficiency gains. The net result is a decline in employment. Moreover, re-employment rates of laid-off workers tend to be higher in the United States compared to Europe (Table 5.7). As a consequence, we expect the interaction term of EPL with offshoring to be negative. That is, the overall effect of offshoring on the labor share is smaller the more protective a country is in terms of hiring and firing regulation.

We capture labor support with three different policy indicators: (i) First, we use the share of a country's public expenditure on labor market programs as percentage of GDP. (ii) Second, we interact offshoring with a country's short-term net unemployment benefits as percentage of earnings for benefits paid in the first year of unemployment. (iii) We also use a country's long-term net unemployment benefits, that is, unemployment benefits that are paid after five years of unemployment. The second and third indicators are only available between 2001 and 2007. In general, we expect that more labor support should positively influence the effect of offshoring on the labor share. Thus, we hypothesize that the coefficient on the interaction variables will have a positive coefficient sign, i.e. $\delta_1 > 0$. This hypothesis is supported by a study showing at a cross-country level that for the countries providing more labor support – based on an index (using equal weights) composed of spending on labor market programs and unemployment replacement benefits – offshoring has a less unfavorable or more favorable effect on the labor share of national income (Milberg and Winkler 2010b).

Regression Results

Our regression analysis covers twenty-one manufacturing sectors (at the two-digit International Standard Industrial Classification (ISIC) level; see Appendix 5.4 for a sectoral classification) in fifteen OECD countries over the period 1991 to 2008. Unfortunately, many countries did not report information on capital stock (such as Belgium, Canada, France, Greece,

Ireland, and Luxembourg), which restricted our country sample to these fifteen countries. However, our country sample still includes a variety of labor market regimes, which allows us to detect the differential effect of offshoring on the labor share. In a first step, we examine the effects of offshoring on the labor share using the whole country and sector sample. In a second step, we focus on the effects of offshoring by country and country grouping following our grouping of five different labor market regimes previously developed (see Figure 5.4).

The regression results using the consistent fixed effects estimator are reported in Table 5.10. All regressions correct for industry fixed effects and year fixed effects, are robust to heteroscedasticity, and include country-year clusters. The results for the whole period from 1991 to 2008 are reported in columns 1 to 5. Capital intensity is positively and significantly associated with the labor share, suggesting that labor and capital are complements. Labor productivity does not show the same coefficient sign as capital intensity, but it is negative and statistically significant. At a given wage rate, higher productivity *per se* lowers the labor share. This suggests that the direct effect of the productivity change is dominating any indirect wage effect with a more complex effect of productivity on the production function.

The variable of most interest, offshoring, has a positive and statistically significant coefficient. This finding is the opposite from what we reported above for the United States (Section 5.4.2). But given the heterogeneity of labor markets in our sample – what has been termed by others the "varieties of capitalism" – as well as the different measure of offshoring (import share from LMICs as opposed to input-output based measures) the discrepancy between these results and those of the U.S. study is not surprising.

We use interaction terms to capture the combined effect of offshoring and the particular structure of labor market regulation on the labor share. Specifically, we are interested in the interaction of offshoring with EPL and public expenditure on labor market programs. As hypothesized, the positive effect of offshoring on the labor share is significantly reduced the more protective a country is in terms of hiring and firing (column 4). Surprisingly, more public expenditure on labor market programs significantly reduces the positive impact of offshoring on the labor share (column 5).

We explored the issue further by splitting the time series into two separate periods, 1991 to 1999 and 2000 to 2008. The results for 1991 to 1999 are shown in columns 6 and 7. In this case, the results from the full period sample estimation are confirmed. Most importantly, interacting offshoring with the variable on labor market programs still shows a negative effect, and

Table 5.10. Offshoring and the Labor Share, Regressions, 15 OECD Countries, 1991–2008

Dependent variable: $lnLS_t$	1991–2008					1991–1999			2000–2008		
	(1)	(2)	(3)	(4)	(5)	(6)	(7)	(8)	(9)	(10)	(11)
$lnLP_t$	−0.0434***	−0.0370**	−0.0370**	−0.0596***	−0.0438**	−0.1020***	−0.1290***	−0.0936**	−0.1200***	−0.0332	−0.0339
	(0.006)	(0.016)	(0.017)	(0.000)	(0.014)	(0.001)	(0.000)	(0.039)	(0.009)	(0.601)	(0.601)
lnk_t	0.0904***	0.0978***	0.0978***	0.0883***	0.1096***	0.1207***	0.1117***	0.1658***	0.1649***	0.2484***	0.2508***
	(0.000)	(0.000)	(0.000)	(0.000)	(0.000)	(0.003)	(0.011)	(0.000)	(0.000)	(0.000)	(0.000)
$lnOSG_t$		0.0292***	0.0292***	0.1154***	0.0620***	0.0759***	0.0620***	0.0208	−0.0172	−0.1235	0.0039
		(0.000)	(0.000)	(0.000)	(0.000)	(0.002)	(0.001)	(0.556)	(0.499)	(0.173)	(0.931)
$lnUND_t$			0.0004	0.0969**	−0.0059	0.0203	−0.0701	0.3280	0.4158**	0.1023	0.2197
			(0.994)	(0.060)	(0.918)	(0.774)	(0.348)	(0.124)	(0.049)	(0.611)	(0.297)
$lnOSG_t * EPL_{t-1}$				−0.0333***		−0.0262***		0.0006			
				(0.000)		(0.002)		(0.964)			
EPL_{t-1}				−0.0442***		−0.0312		−0.0317			
				(0.007)		(0.302)		(0.328)			
$lnOSG_t * LMP_{t-1}$					−0.6950***		−1.1893***		1.9128*		
					(0.006)		(0.001)		(0.053)		
LMP_{t-1}					−2.6858***		−5.0643***		−1.3638		
					(0.005)		(0.000)		(0.631)		
$lnOSG_t * URB\_ST_{t-1}$										0.2366*	
										(0.067)	
URB_ST_{t-1}										0.5585*	
										(0.078)	

											lnOSG_t*URB_LT_t-1

$lnOSG_t^\star URB\_LT_{t-1}$

URB_LT_{t-1}

	(1)	(2)	(3)	(4)	(5)	(6)	(7)	(8)	(9)	(10)	(11)
$lnOSG_t^\star URB\_LT_{t-1}$											0.0602
											(0.422)
URB_LT_{t-1}											−0.0599
											(0.887)
Observations	4,443	4,234	4,234	4,073	3,665	2,201	1,918	1,570	1,486	1,268	1,268
R-squared (within)	0.11	0.09	0.09	0.11	0.1	0.16	0.18	0.16	0.19	0.18	0.18
Countries	15	15	15	15	15	15	15	15	15	15	15
Fixed sector effects	Yes	Yes	Yes	Yes	Yes	Yes	Yes	Yes	Yes	Yes	Yes
Fixed year effects	Yes	Yes	Yes	Yes	Yes	Yes	Yes	Yes	Yes	Yes	Yes
Country-year clusters	Yes	Yes	Yes	Yes	Yes	Yes	Yes	Yes	Yes	Yes	Yes
F-test of joint significance: $lnOSG_t + lnOSG_t^\star policy_{t-1} = 0$			p > F = 0.0000	p > F = 0.0001	p > F = 0.0001	p > F = 0.0051	p > F = 0.0013	p > F = 0.5269	p > F = 0.1060	p > F = 0.0366	p > F = 0.1574

Source: Own illustration. Calculations based on Milberg and Winkler (2011a, 173). $p^\star < 0.1$, $p^{\star\star} < 0.05$, $p^{\star\star\star} < 0.01$ (p-values in parentheses).

Note: LS = labor share, LP = labor productivity, k = capital intensity, OSG = goods offshoring intensity, UND = union density, EPL = employment protection legislation, LMP = labor market programs, URB_ST = short-term unemployment replacement benefits, and URB_LT = long-term unemployment replacement benefits.

it is even larger for the sub-sample period of 1991 to 1999 than for the full period.

Columns 8 to 11 show the results for the period 2000 to 2008. The results are different, in three important ways: First, offshoring no longer has an effect on the labor share. Second, the interaction with EPL is no longer significant (column 9). And third, the interaction with public expenditure on labor market programs is now significantly positive. While the effect of offshoring is insignificant, there seems to be a joint significance with the interaction variable (column 10).

Finally, we include other variables of labor support, namely short-term and long-term net unemployment benefits as a percentage of earnings, which are only available for the period 2001 to 2007 (columns 10 and 11). Short-term net unemployment benefits show a positive and statistically significant effect. Moreover, the interaction of offshoring with short-term unemployment benefits is also positive and statistically significant (column 10).

To sum up, regression analysis in the period from 1991 to 2008 shows that offshoring significantly increases the labor share. The positive effects from offshoring on the labor share are significantly less, however, the more protective a country is in terms of EPL and the higher a country's public expenditure on labor market programs. However, splitting the sample into the periods 1991 to 1999 and 2000 to 2008 shows that the overall results seem to be driven by the first period. Between 2000 and 2008, a country's public expenditure on labor market programs increases the effect from offshoring on the labor share. We then added a country's short-term and long-term net unemployment replacement benefits as percentage of earnings as alternative measures of labor support. We find that higher short-term net unemployment benefits positively influence the effect of offshoring on the labor share, whereas such an effect cannot be confirmed for long-term net unemployment benefits.

Regression Results by Country Groupings and Country

We saw previously that breaking down our sample into sub-periods gave some important insights about the change over time in the relation between offshoring and economic security (captured by the labor share), especially as mediated through labor market institutions. In this section, we look more carefully at the country coverage, and especially the varieties of countries contained in the sample according to the taxonomy of labor market regimes discussed in Section 5.2.1. Therefore, we run the labor share regressions by country and then by country groupings.

Table 5.11. *Rank of Labor Support Index, 15 OECD Countries, 2001 versus 2007*

2001		2007	
Country	Index	Country	Index
Denmark	3.82	Denmark	3.95
Netherlands	3.02	Netherlands	3.57
Germany	2.97	Finland	3.31
Finland	2.78	Spain	3.18
Sweden	2.71	Germany	2.95
Spain	2.22	Austria	2.80
Portugal	1.88	Sweden	2.71
Austria	1.87	Portugal	2.59
Norway	1.50	Italy	1.91
Italy	1.41	Norway	1.79
Australia	1.38	Australia	1.26
Japan	1.10	Japan	1.11
United States	1.00	United Kingdom	1.08
United Kingdom	0.86	United States	1.00
South Korea	0.73	South Korea	0.91

Source: Own calculations. Data: OECD Labor Force Statistics and OECD Going for Growth 2010 Database. Note: Labor support is an index (using equal weights) composed of the indexed (United States = 1) public expenditures on labor market programs (as % of GDP) as well as the indexed (United States = 1) short-term net unemployment replacement rate. Public expenditures on labor market programs include all measures except for "public employment services and administration." See Appendix 5.3 for data description.

Recall that we defined labor support in Figure 5.4 as an indexed combination of public expenditure on labor market programs and the net unemployment replacement benefit level as a share of earnings. Table 5.11 shows the levels of labor support for our sample of fifteen OECD countries including their ranks for 2001 and 2007. We see that Anglo-Saxon, East Asian, and Mediterranean countries show a low labor support, whereas Rhineland and "Flexicurity" countries are characterized by a medium to high labor support.

Table 5.12 gives a summary of our analysis of Figure 5.5 for the sample of fifteen OECD countries, which is the groupings of countries according to the combination of labor support and strictness of EPL. We identify five labor market regimes, presented in Figure 5.5, which shows the countries in our sample that comprise each regime. Italy and Norway cannot be classified into any one of these regimes, as they are both characterized by a medium

Table 5.12. *Taxonomy of Labor Market Regimes*

Model	Anglo-Saxon	Mediterranean	Rhineland	Flexicurity	East Asian
Labor support	low	low	medium to high	high	low
Labor flexibility	high	low	medium to low	medium to high	medium
Countries	Australia Canada Ireland New Zealand United Kingdom United States	France Greece Portugal Spain	Austria Germany Sweden	Belgium Denmark Finland Netherlands	Japan South Korea

Source: Own illustration. Based on Milberg and Winkler (2011a, 176). Data: OECD Labor Force Statistics and OECD Going for Growth 2010 Database. Note: See footnote of Table 5.11 on labor support. Labor flexibility is calculated based on the EPL index.

degree of labor market flexibility and medium level of labor support. As a result, we have left them out of the country groupings.

The results of the country-based regressions are shown in Table 5.13. As specified in column (2) of Table 5.10 we used the consistent fixed effects estimator. We report the instantaneous effect of offshoring on the labor share unless only the lagged value of offshoring had a significant impact on the sectoral labor share. In these cases, the level of significance is indicated with crosses instead of stars.

The results in Table 5.13 indicate that offshoring has no clear effect on the labor share at the country level. The results for the whole period from 1991 to 2008 are reported in columns (1) and (2). Offshoring has a significantly positive impact in Australia, Austria, Finland, Germany, Italy, the Netherlands, and Norway. Note that these are mostly countries characterized by a medium to high level of labor support (see Table 5.12). In contrast, the effect of offshoring is significantly negative in Japan, Spain, and the United States, all countries with medium to low levels of labor support. We again break the time period into two parts, and columns (3) and (4) report the results for the period from 1991 to 1999. Now, Australia, Denmark, Germany, and South Korea show a significantly positive relation between offshoring and the labor share, whereas Italy, Portugal, and Spain show a significantly negative effect. While Portugal and Spain belong to the Mediterranean model with a medium to low labor support, the first group includes countries

Table 5.13. *Offshoring and the Labor Share, Country Regressions, 1991–2008*

Dependent variable: $\ln LS_t$	1991–2008		1991–1999		2000–2008	
	Offshoring (1)	p-value (2)	Offshoring (3)	p-value (4)	Offshoring (5)	p-value (6)
Australia	0.1268***	0.0010	0.1404***	0.0060	−0.0414	0.3400
Austria	0.1246**	0.0140	0.0099	0.5270	0.3045+++	0.0080
Denmark	−0.0021	0.8490	0.0283++	0.0480	0.0363	0.4560
Finland	0.0396+	0.0780	0.0406	0.3650	−0.0989	0.1660
Germany	0.1255***	0.0000	0.1179***	0.0070	0.1484++	0.0430
Italy	0.0503+	0.0170	−0.0449*	0.0680	−0.0435	0.2550
Japan	−0.0277+	0.0700	0.0088	0.6390	−0.0868+	0.0770
Netherlands	0.1390***	0.0080	0.0611	0.1860	0.2340++	0.0120
Norway	0.0803**	0.0480	0.0139	0.7670	0.0045	0.9410
Portugal	−0.0269	0.1880	−0.0595**	0.0420	−0.0769**	0.0200
South Korea	0.0139	0.3400	0.0502*	0.0860	−0.0307	0.1720
Spain	−0.0331**	0.0420	−0.0653**	0.0310	−0.0931***	0.0000
Sweden	0.0436	0.1140	−0.0009	0.9810	0.1715*	0.0730
United Kingdom	0.0001	0.9980	0.0139	0.7800	0.0589	0.4770
United States	−0.1369**	0.0140	−0.0609	0.2050	−0.2268+	0.0950

Source: Own illustration. Calculations based on Milberg and Winkler (2011a, 177). Note: p* < 0.1, p** < 0.05, p*** < 0.01 for instantaneous effect of offshoring ($\ln OSG_t$). p+ < 0.1, p++ < 0.05, p+++ < 0.01 for lagged effect of offshoring ($\ln OSG_{t-1}$).

with both a high (Denmark, Germany) and low degree of labor support (Australia, South Korea).

In the country-level estimations of the labor share for the more recent period from 2000 to 2008, only four countries show a positive and statistically significant coefficient on the offshoring variable, namely Austria, Germany, the Netherlands, and Sweden. All of these countries have a medium to high level of labor support. Four countries have a significantly negative effect, namely Japan, Portugal, Spain and the United States, all countries with a low to medium labor support. The negative impact of offshoring on the sectoral labor share in the United States stands out in terms of coefficient size and confirms the findings by Milberg and Winkler (2010c) for thirty-five manufacturing and service industries between 1998 and 2006 as well as our findings in Section 5.4.2 of this chapter. The country-level regressions are suggestive, but our presentation above on economic security and its regulatory dimension focused on a set of five distinct labor market "regimes," defined by the two dimensions of labor market protection and by spending on labor support, and summarized in Table 5.12.

We estimated the labor share regression as specified in column (3) of Table 5.10 for the different labor market regimes. Column (1a) of Table 5.14 shows the results for the "Anglo-Saxon model," which includes Australia, the United Kingdom, and the United States. The results of the "Mediterranean model," which includes Portugal and Spain are shown in column (2). Column (3) focuses on the "Rhineland model" including Austria, Germany, and Sweden. Column (4) shows the results of the "Flexicurity model" covering Denmark, Finland, and the Netherlands, whereas column (5) shows the results of Japan and South Korea, the "East Asian model." We also recognize that Australia is dissimilar from the other countries in the Anglo-Saxon group because of its position in global trade. Australia's trade structure differs from the United Kingdom and the United States, as Australia is a commodity exporter and manufacturing goods importer, and thus cannot be expected to be affected by offshoring in the same way as most OECD countries. Thus, column (1b) is estimated for the Anglo-Saxon group excluding Australia.

Once again, this is a very standard specification of a model of the labor share, and our main interest is in the offshoring variable. Offshoring has a positive and statistically significant impact on the labor share in the Anglo-Saxon, Rhineland, and Flexicurity model. The coefficient is negative and statistically significant in the Mediterranean model and negative but statistically insignificant in the East Asian sample. For the Anglo-Saxon sample, the offshoring coefficient is positive and significant when Australia is included (column (1a)), but the coefficient becomes negative and statistically significant when Australia is excluded (column (1b)). In sum, these findings show that more offshoring is associated with less economic insecurity in those countries with more supportive labor market regimes (Rhineland and Flexicurity) and is associated with greater economic insecurity in areas characterized by less supportive labor market institutions (Mediterranean and Anglo-Saxon). The findings support the view that labor market institutions matter in mediating the effects of globalization on workers in OECD countries.

Regarding the other variables in the model, labor productivity has a negative and statistically significant effect on the labor share for all groups except in the East Asian model. The size of the coefficient, however, seems to increase with the degree of labor support, ranging from -0.028 in the Anglo-Saxon model to -0.2606 in the Flexicurity model. What would be an explanation for that? Recall that labor productivity is defined as value added per employee (VA/L), whereas the labor share is defined as the compensation of employees in value added wL/VA. By definition, an increase of labor productivity lowers the labor share to the same extent holding the wage rate

Table 5.14. *Offshoring and the Labor Share by Labor Market Regime, Regressions, 1991–2008*

Dependent variable: lnLS_t	Anglo-Saxon		Mediterranean	Rhineland	Flexicurity	East Asian
	(1a)	(1b)	(2)	(3)	(4)	(5)
lnLP_t	−0.0280*	−0.0109	−0.1298**	−0.1971***	−0.2606***	0.0048
	(0.098)	(0.499)	(0.024)	(0.001)	(0.000)	(0.772)
lnk_t	−0.0503	−0.1129***	0.1378*	−0.0233	0.1434***	0.1224***
	(0.113)	(0.000)	(0.089)	(0.412)	(0.000)	(0.000)
lnOSG_t	0.0472**	−0.0425*	−0.0316***	0.0741***	0.0330**	−0.0029
	(0.018)	(0.078)	(0.004)	(0.000)	(0.030)	(0.798)
lnUND_t	0.2498**	0.8931**	−0.1387	0.3408**	0.2680*	0.6473***
	(0.014)	(0.019)	(0.100)	(0.015)	(0.093)	(0.000)
Observations	875	560	533	827	856	620
R-squared (within)	0.08	0.21	0.13	0.31	0.33	0.17
Countries	Australia, United Kingdom, United States	United Kingdom, United States	Portugal, Spain	Austria, Germany, Sweden	Denmark, Finland, Netherlands	Japan, South Korea
Fixed sector effects	Yes	Yes	Yes	Yes	Yes	Yes
Fixed year effects	Yes	Yes	Yes	Yes	Yes	Yes
Country-year clusters	Yes	Yes	Yes	Yes	Yes	Yes

Source: Own illustration. Calculations based on Milberg and Winkler (2011a, 179). $p^* < 0.1$, $p^{**} < 0.05$, $p^{***} < 0.01$ (p-values in parentheses).

Note: LS = labor share, LP = labor productivity, k = capital intensity, OSG = goods offshoring intensity, and UND = union density.

w constant. A simultaneous increase in the nominal wage rate, on the other hand, can counterbalance this drop in the labor share. Capital intensity significantly increases the labor share in the Mediterranean, Rhineland, and East Asian model with coefficient sizes of similar magnitudes. Union density has a significantly positive effect on the labor share in all models except for the Mediterranean one. Moreover, the coefficient size is highest in the Anglo-Saxon model without Australia (column 1b) and Asian model. This suggests that the positive effect of union density is stronger the more flexible labor markets are, and would contradict the Calmfors-Driffill hypothesis that the effect of an increase in the degree of cooperativeness is more effective only if a country is in the more cooperative range (see Chapter 3).

5.4.4 Actual and Perceived Effects of Offshoring

Do the perceptions of the effect of globalization on economic security bear any relation to the actual impact of trade and FDI on industrialized countries? Here we compare surveys of the perception changes of globalization-induced economic insecurity with the results of our own econometric estimates of the impact of offshoring on the labor share of sectoral income by country. Because offshoring involves both trade and FDI, we can assume that the term "globalization" in these surveys is conceptually close to our notion of offshoring.

Perceived insecurity due to cost-oriented offshoring is based on the Eurobarometer survey that asked, "What comes first to mind when you hear the word 'globalisation'?" Possible answers included: (i) "opportunities for domestic companies in terms of new outlets," (ii) "foreign investments in country," (iii) "relocation of some companies to countries where labor is cheaper," (iv) "increased competition for country," and (v) "other." Answer (iii) reflects perceived worker insecurity with regard to cost-oriented offshoring. Figure 5.9 shows the percentage change of perceived insecurity because of cost-oriented offshoring (on the x-axis), while the y-axis shows the regression coefficients from the country regressions over the period from 2000 to 2008. There is a weakly negative correlation, that is, countries with a growing fear of globalization-induced job relocations tend to be those that we previously identified as characterized by a weaker or negative connection between offshoring and the labor share. There are a few outliers. In Germany, Netherlands, and Austria, the fear of offshoring has grown, although the actual effect of offshoring on the labor share is positive.

The Eurobarometer survey also asked the following question, "Which of the following two propositions is the one which is closest to your opinion with regard to globalization?" Possible answers included: (i) "good

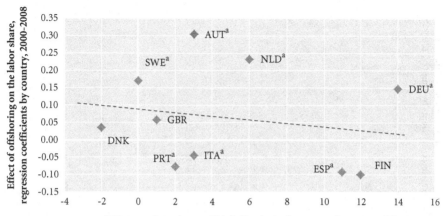

Figure 5.9. Correlation of Actual and Perceived Insecurity due to Offshoring. *Source:* Own illustration. Based on Milberg and Winkler (2011a, 85). Survey data: Eurobarometer, *Public Opinion in the EU*, various surveys. [a]Significant estimates. Dashed line is OLS regression line. See Appendix 5.1 for country abbreviations.

opportunity for domestic companies," (ii) "threat to employment and companies," and (iii) "don't know." Answer (ii) reflects perceived fears of globalization. Figure 5.10 shows the percentage change of perceived insecurity because of globalization on the x-axis. The correlation with the regression coefficients in the labor share equations is again weakly negative, that is, countries with a growing fear of the negative effects of globalization on companies and employment generally have a lower or negative link between offshoring and labor's share of national income. Outliers include Austria, where fear of globalization fell only by a small percentage, whereas offshoring led to actual gains for workers in terms of the labor share. Similar developments can be observed in Sweden and the Netherlands. The negative correlation shows that perceptions of offshoring are not rooted in myth or unfounded fears as so much of the economics literature insists. As we argued in Chapter 3, the problem lies in the difficulty of squaring the Panglossian economics models of offshoring with their measured impact.

We have focused here on relatively short-term effects of globalization on economic insecurity. Long-term gains from trade liberalization can come from the reinvestment of the higher profits that result from lower costs due to effective supply chain management. It is to this question that we turn in the next chapter.

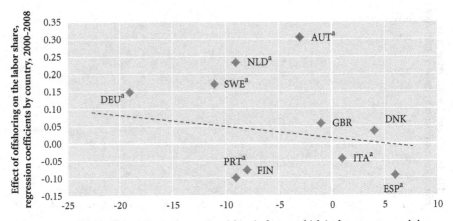

"Which of the following two propositions is the one which is closest to your opinion
with regard to globalisation?" Answer: "Threat to employment and companies"
% points change, Spring 2006-Fall 2008

Figure 5.10. Correlation of Actual and Perceived Insecurity due to Globalization. *Source*:
Own illustration. Based on Milberg and Winkler (2011a, 186). Survey data: Eurobarometer, *Public Opinion in the EU*, various surveys. [a]Significant estimates. Dashed line is OLS
regression line. See Appendix 5.1 for country abbreviations.

APPENDIX 5.1. COUNTRY CODES, OECD COUNTRIES

Country code	Country
AUS	Australia
AUT	Austria
BEL	Belgium
CAN	Canada
DNK	Denmark
FIN	Finland
FRA	France
DEU	Germany
GRC	Greece
IRL	Ireland
ITA	Italy
JPN	Japan
KOR	South Korea
NLD	Netherlands
NZL	New Zealand
NOR	Norway

PRT	Portugal
ESP	Spain
SWE	Sweden
CHE	Switzerland
GBR	United Kingdom
USA	United States

APPENDIX 5.2. DATA DESCRIPTION, UNITED STATES

Services and materials offshoring intensities *OSS* and *OSM* are based on Annual I/O Accounts, The Use of Commodities by Industries after Redefinitions from the U.S. Bureau of Economic Analysis (BEA), available for the period 1998 to 2006 (downloaded on October 14, 2008). For a description of the offshoring measures, see section 2.1.3. Sectoral definitions follow the 1997 North American Industry Classification System, primarily at the three-digit level. For energy offshoring (*OSE*), we also used KLEMS Annual I/O Accounts, in order to detect specific energy inputs related to imported oil prices. Calculations follow Feenstra and Hanson (1996). *OSS* and *OSM* have total non-energy inputs in the denominator, whereas *OSE* uses total inputs.

Sectoral employment and wage data were obtained from the BEA Annual Industry Accounts, Gross Domestic Product by Industry. We used the number of full-time equivalent employees for our analysis. Sectoral wage rates were not directly available, but could be calculated by dividing sectoral compensation by the sectoral number of employees, both available from the BEA Annual Industry Accounts.

Output, value added and intermediate input prices were obtained from the BEA Annual Industry Accounts, Gross Domestic Product by Industry and Value Added by Industry with 2000 as the base year. We calculated real wages using value added deflators and real output using output deflators.

The additional control variable import share, measured as imports by output, was obtained from the BEA Annual I/O Accounts, The Use of Commodities by Industries after Redefinitions.

Labor shares *LS* are defined as compensation of employees as share of total value added. Both are from the Annual I/O Accounts, The Use of Commodities by Industries after Redefinitions from the BEA.

Labor productivity *LP* is value added as share of full-time equivalent employees, from the Annual Industry Accounts, Gross Domestic Product by Industry.

Capital intensity is capital stock as share of total output. The capital stock data (equipment and software, private structures) are from the BEA, measured as net stock of private fixed assets by industry. Total sectoral output is taken from the Annual I/O Accounts, The Use of Commodities by Industries after Redefinitions from the BEA. We multiplied chain-type quantity indexes for net stock of private fixed assets from BEA (with 2000 as the base year) with the nominal capital stock data of 2000 and divided that product by 100 to obtain real capital stock. We then obtained capital prices by dividing nominal capital stock by real capital stock and multiplying that quotient with 100.

Union density is defined as the percentage of union members in employed wage and salary workers, from the U.S. Bureau of Labor Statistics monthly Current Population Survey. Since the data begin in 2000, we extrapolated back to the years from 1998 to 1999.

APPENDIX 5.3. DATA DESCRIPTION, OECD COUNTRIES

We estimate the effect of offshoring on the labor share at the two-digit ISIC Rev. 3 sectoral level for the period from 1991 to 2008 using a sample of twenty-one manufacturing sectors for fifteen OECD countries. Offshoring is defined as the share of manufacturing imports from LMICs in total manufacturing imports. We obtained sectoral import data from UN Comtrade.

The sectoral labor share is calculated as total compensation (nominal) in value added (nominal). We obtained the data for all countries from the OECD STAN Database except for Australia and Japan which we retrieved from the European Union (EU) KLEMS Database. Labor productivity is measured as GVA (in constant prices) divided by the number of persons engaged (in 1000s). The data are obtained from the EU KLEMS Database except for Norway (OECD STAN Database). We used GVA price indexes with 1995 as the base year. Since value added was reported in national currencies, we converted these into U.S. dollars using exchange rates from the Economist Intelligence Unit Database.

Capital intensities are obtained by dividing the sectoral net capital stock (constant prices) by sectoral value added (constant prices). Many countries did not report capital stock data (that is, Belgium, Canada, France, Greece, Ireland and Luxembourg), which restricted our sample to fifteen countries. Only Austria and Germany had capital stock data available at the two-digit ISIC Rev. 3 classification. Other countries reported capital stock at the two-digit level for some sectors only. We captured missing sectors by calculating capital intensities at a more aggregated level (at most three two-digit sectors by country) for which capital stock data were available. This follows the assumption that capital intensities at a higher aggregation are similar to capital intensities at the disaggregated two-digit level. For example, in many countries we had to use the same capital intensity for sectors 17 to 19 (textiles, textile and leather, and footwear), because capital stock data were not available for the individual sectors. We obtained capital intensities from the OECD STAN Database and the EU KLEMS Database.

Union density, defined as the number of union members in total employment, is based on the OECD Labor Force Statistics and is available at the country level only. The policy indicators are also only available at the country level. The EPL indicator and public expenditure on labor market programs as percentage of a country's GDP are retrieved from the OECD Labor Force Statistics. We obtained net unemployment replacement benefits as percentage of earnings from the OECD Going for Growth 2010 Database. The data are available for the period from 2001 to 2007 only. Short-term benefits refer to unemployment benefits that are paid within the first year of unemployment. Long-term refer to unemployment benefits which are paid after five years of unemployment.

APPENDIX 5.4. SECTORAL CLASSIFICATION

ISIC Rev. 3	Sector Name
15	Food products and beverages
16	Tobacco products
17	Textiles
18	Wearing apparel, dressing, and dying of fur
19	Leather, leather products, and footwear
20	Wood and products of wood and cork
21	Pulp, paper, and paper products
22	Printing and publishing
23	Coke, refined petroleum products, and nuclear fuel
24	Chemicals and chemical products
25	Rubber and plastics products
26	Other non-metallic mineral products
27	Basic metals
28	Fabricated metal products, except machinery and equipment
29	Machinery and equipment, nec
30	Office, accounting, and computing machinery
31	Electrical machinery and apparatus, nec
32	Radio, television, and communication equipment
33	Medical, precision, and optical instruments
34	Motor vehicles, trailers, and semi-trailers
35	Other transport equipment
36	Manufacturing nec

SIX

Financialization and the Dynamics of Offshoring

In the immediate wake of the collapse of the U.S. financial sector in 2008, a number of commentators pointed to the non-financial sector as a potential source of demand growth and innovation that could lead a recovery and long-term economic expansion (see, for example, Mandel 2008). This view was justified by the fact that non-financial corporate profits for years provided savings and liquidity for the rest of the economy. These profits offset the low levels of personal saving and the large deficits on the government and foreign accounts, and also created the possibility that these firms could finance investment out of internal funds, that is without seeking access to frozen credit markets (see Figure 6.1 for U.S. net savings and current account balance as a percentage of gross domestic product (GDP)). Despite U.S. monetary policy in its most expansionary mode in recent history, nonetheless the private investment growth since 2009 has been inadequate to create a typical recovery in employment.

This prospect should be viewed in some historical perspective. Beginning in the 1980s and gaining strength in the 1990s, American corporate strategy began to shift, focusing more on the maximization of shareholder value and less on long-term growth. The transformation involved less investment out of retained earnings and, instead, a financialization of the non-financial corporate sector, driven by an increased offering of financial services, an increase in the purchase of financial assets, and, more recently, the massive purchase of their own shares aimed at raising stock prices.

This chapter focuses on the real-side aspects of this corporate shift to financialization, and in particular on its relation to globalized production. We argue that potential dynamic gains of offshoring, associated with reinvestment of higher profits, have not been fully realized. To the extent that corporations have become financialized – mainly through an increase in dividend payments and share repurchases, but also with increased merger

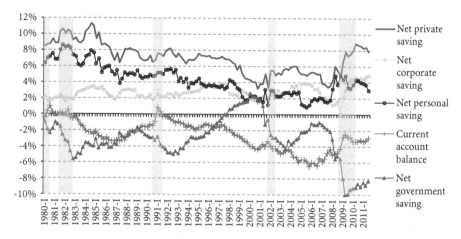

Figure 6.1. Net Savings and Current Account Balance (% of GDP), United States, 1980–2011 (Quarterly Data), United States *Source*: Own illustration. Data: U.S. Bureau of Economic Analysis, National Income and Product Accounts, Tables 4.1, 5.1 and 1.1.5. Note: Quarterly figures are seasonally adjusted annual rates. Gray bars correspond to U.S. business cycles recessions according to the definition of the National Bureau of Economic Research.

and acquisition (M&A) activity and large executive compensation packages involving stock options – this has diminished the capture of dynamic gains from offshoring. Offshoring has played a dual role in the financialization of the non-financial sector: First, as we have emphasized, offshoring has been a strategy of cost reduction, which has provided an important source of new profits. Second, offshoring, and especially arm's-length contracting, reduces the need for investment spending by turning potentially large parts of production over to foreign companies.

Therefore, financialization and globalization have reinforced each other for U.S. corporations and, despite the corporate sector's contribution to national savings over the past decade, the offshoring-financialization linkage creates a structural limit on the capacity of non-financial corporations to act as engines of economic growth and innovation. Having narrowed their scope of operations and innovative activity in the move into core competence and global offshoring beginning in the early 1990s, U.S. non-financial corporations are today ill-equipped to serve as the driver of the recovery from the economic crisis that hit in 2008.

The situation is depicted in Figure 6.2. To the extent that profits are channeled into investment, the dynamic gains from offshoring are captured. Financialization, on the other hand, results in a failure to fully capture the dynamic gains.

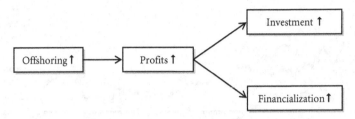

Figure 6.2. The Offshoring-Financialization Nexus. *Source:* Own illustration. Based on Figure 4.8.

This chapter is concerned with the extent to which financialization has diminished the realization of dynamic gains from offshoring. Section 6.1 considers the shift in corporate strategy from "retain and reinvest" to "downsize and distribute" and its consequences for offshoring, profits, investment, and financialization. In Section 6.2, we estimate the effect of offshoring on U.S. capital accumulation and look explicitly at the link between offshoring and financialization. Section 6.3 assesses the extent to which this link is replicated outside the United States and how sustainable it is globally. We conclude with a discussion of the future of the globalization-financialization link in the face of the collapse and subsequent recovery of the financial sector in the United States and some other industrialized countries.

6.1 The Shift to Core Competence, Offshoring, and Financialization

We have seen that the motives for offshoring range from the pursuit of greater flexibility, to diversification of location in order to reduce risk, to the lowering of production costs. Although all of these goals have been cited in studies of offshoring, the importance of cost reduction is unmistakable. Over the past twenty-five years, U.S. corporations faced price competition in product markets and thus slow-rising product prices at home. U.S. import prices fell by almost 2 percent per year in the late 1990s and were essentially flat in the 2000s (see Table 4.1). At the extreme, this has promoted the creation of manufacturing firms that do no manufacturing at all, such as the Gap, Dell Computers, or Cisco Systems.

We have also argued in Chapter 4 that the shifting patterns of U.S. international trade – more intermediates and more exports of manufactures and services from developing countries – have been part of a broader corporate strategy adopted by many larger firms in the industrialized countries, which emphasizes a focus on core competence and a greater attention to shareholder value. This has driven firms to break up the production process and take advantage of low-cost offshore production for all but the highest value added aspects of production to maintain their cost markups and profits. Such offshoring accounts for up to 27 percent of goods input purchases in some U.S. industries, 50 percent or more of U.S. imports, and provides reported cost savings of 40 to 60 percent. Over the 2000s, U.S. corporate profits rose and the profit share of national income reached a 40-year high, in part due to the markup effect of offshoring as discussed in Chapter 4 and estimated in Chapter 5[1]. The new corporate strategy has a human resource dimension as well, in which there has been in many cases a backing away from traditional commitments to long-term employment, and a reduction in pension and health insurance benefits. We discussed the observed increase in economic insecurity across industrialized countries in Chapter 5.

Offshoring has thus served the new business model in two ways: First, it has led to cost reductions and thus increased firms' markup over cost, despite the fact that they face price competition in product markets. Second, by limiting the scope of the firm and especially its domestic operations, offshoring has reduced the investment needs of firms, increasing their ability to return value to shareholders. That is, the expansion of offshoring supported a financialization of non-financial corporations in many industrialized countries. As Watson (2007) writes,

Disinvestment is the only certain way of increasing shareholder value: that is, selling off or closing down all but the most profitable parts of the business. This is guaranteed to generate higher returns on capital employed, thus providing a rationale for an increase in the stock price (Watson 2007, 4).

Financialization and the expansion of global value chains (GVCs) are thus mutually supporting processes: Pressures for short-run increases in stock prices have encouraged the shift to core competence and offshoring that Watson describes. And offshoring has raised profits and permitted a shift of resources from long-term investment in firm growth to financial assets (Milberg 2008).

6.1.1 Decline in Investment

In Chapter 4 (Figure 4.1), we saw how since the 1970s the U.S. profit share has risen to new highs in each successive business cycle. At the same period, the import share from developing countries was steadily rising and capital formation (as a share of GDP) has been stagnant since the early 1980s, and

---

[1] In Chapter 5, we showed that offshoring lowered the labor share in U.S. manufacturing and service sectors over the period from 1998 to 2006. Since the profit share equals 1 minus the labor share, this implies a positive effect of offshoring on the profit share.

down from its levels in the late 1970s. With a higher profit share – partly the result of offshoring – U.S. non-financial companies have been awash in cash. Bates et al. (2006) report a 129 percent increase in the cash ratio of U.S. industry over the period from 1980 to 2004.

The traditional managerial strategy of using retained earnings to finance new investment had resulted in relatively high levels of investment out of profits and considerable power for top-level managers in the 1960s and 1970s. Studies of industrial organization in these years stress that managers preferred internal funds to external borrowing because it raised managerial discretion over the allocation of funds and allowed managers to focus on company growth over the long-term rather than on short-term shareholder returns (see, for example, Marris 1964; Eichner 1976).

The problem is that while profits and profit shares increased fairly steadily beginning in the early 1980s, this generally did not translate into higher rates of investment. The decline in investment spending in the corporate sector is tied to the shift in corporate strategy that occurred during the 1980s as the revolution in the assertion of shareholder rights took hold in the United States and subsequently elsewhere. Pressure on management was to downsize the corporation and distribute profits at a greater pace back to shareholders. This process was supported by the possibility of moving operations abroad through foreign direct investment (FDI) or arm's-length subcontracting. By focusing increasingly on "core competence" and contracting out (both domestically and internationally) the remainder of the operation, corporate managers were able to reduce domestic investment needs and meet shareholder demands for improvements in shareholder value.

The relative stagnation of U.S. investment in relation to profits and domestic income is shown in Figure 6.3. Gross private fixed investment as a share of gross domestic income has recovered from its low levels in the early 1990s, but with the recent economic crisis has dropped to the lowest levels in forty years. Fixed investment of non-financial corporations as share of gross profits has, with the exception of the period of the information technology (IT) boom, been below the levels of the 1970s. If investment growth did not rise in proportion with profits growth, then what did the corporations do with their earnings? For an explanation, we look to the issue of financialization.

6.1.2 Increase in Financialization

Financialization is defined in three ways in the recent literature: (i) A greater share of GDP or net worth in the industrialized countries is accounted for

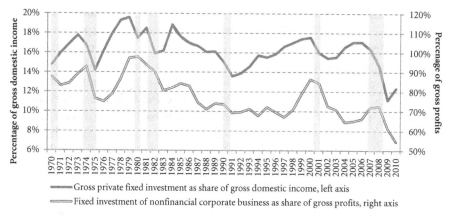

Gross private fixed investment as share of gross domestic income, left axis

Fixed investment of nonfinancial corporate business as share of gross profits, right axis

Figure 6.3. Investment Shares, Total and Non-Financial Corporations, United States, 1970–2010. *Source:* Own illustration. Data: U.S. Bureau of Economic Analysis, National Income and Product Accounts. U.S. Federal Reserve Bank, Flow of Funds Account, Schedule Z.1. Note: Gross profits of non-financial corporate business are calculated by summing up net operating surplus and consumption of fixed capital. Gray bars correspond to U.S. business cycles recessions according to the definition of the National Bureau of Economic Research.

by the financial sector.[2] (ii) Gross international capital flows have grown much faster than world output and faster than trade in goods and services (see, for example, Eatwell and Taylor 2002). (iii) Non-financial firms have increasingly used finance rather than production as both a source and a use of their funds (see, for example, Stockhammer 2004; Crotty 2005).

Here we are mainly interested in (iii), that is, the increasingly financial emphasis of non-financial corporations or, as Stockhammer (2004) puts it "the engagement of non-financial businesses in financial markets" (Stockhammer 2004, 7). This new focus is not just the provision of financial services as part of the corporations' product lines, but the increase in the share of assets of the firm that are financial and the increased use of firm profits to raise shareholder returns, either through dividend payments, share buybacks, and even through M&As.

Explanations for Financialization

Many analysts see financialization as the defining characteristic of the world economy of the last twenty-five years, and offer at least two explanations of the surge in the importance of finance in the macro economy at the level of the non-financial firm. The most fully developed explanation is the

---

[2] Epstein and Jayadev (2005), for example, define financialization as a rise in the rentier share of national income, where rentier share is the profits of financial firms plus interest income earned in the rest of the economy.

shareholder value revolution, according to which the assertion of shareholder rights in the late 1970s and 1980s shifted power in corporate governance from managers to shareholders, bringing to the fore a concern for raising shareholder value. This resulted in a change in corporate strategy from the Chandlerian concern with firm growth through retaining profits and reinvesting them, to an emphasis on shareholder value and short-run return on investment through downsizing the firm and distributing a greater percentage of profits back to shareholders with the use of higher dividend payments and an increased volume of share buybacks. As Davis (2009) writes about the shareholder value revolution in the 1980s:

Financial considerations – market valuation – would drive choices about the boundaries and strategies of the firm. Firms would focus on doing one thing well, and that one thing was often determined by the stock market (Davis 2009, 93).

Share buybacks raise share prices by reducing the supply of outstanding shares. With the collapse of the stock market in 2008/2009 it would appear that share buyback strategies were hugely unsuccessful. Nonetheless, as the economic recovery began in 2009, share buybacks again turned up, indicating that the pre-crisis strategy has started up again. While the boosting of chief executive officer compensation with stock options was intended to better align manager and shareholder interests, it has led instead to greater incentives for managers to focus on short-term movements in share prices. Only if these options vest over the course over several years will executives have personal incentive to focus beyond the short-term.

The situation is depicted in Figure 6.4, in which the investment bias toward share buybacks will, *ceteris paribus*, raise the return on equity (ROE), thus generating higher shareholder (and stock option) returns without any resources allocated toward process or product innovation, skills development, efficiency wages, or even marketing. Analogous to the skills-biased labor demand shift explanation of rising wage inequality, here we have a finance-biased capital supply shift explanation for rising ROE (from S_0 to S_1). Net of a shift of the demand curve D, the rise in the ROE must be due to a negative supply shift of outstanding equity (share buybacks), which we define as a finance-biased capital allocation.

A second explanation for financialization – and not incompatible with the first – is that financialization resulted from a change in the gap between the rate of return on manufacturing investment and the rate of return on investments in financial assets (Dumenil and Levy 2005; Crotty 2005). On

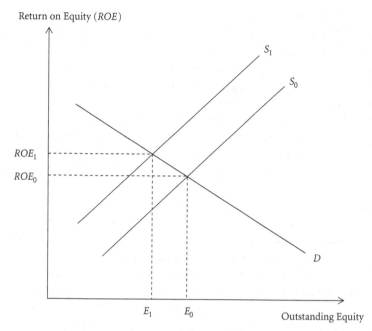

Figure 6.4. Finance-Biased Return on Non-Financial Corporate Equity. *Source:* Own illustration.

the side of returns in finance, real interest rates got a boost in the late 1970s with tight monetary policy and the deregulation of financial markets. Interest rate ceilings on deposits were removed, encouraging banks and money market funds to invest in higher return (and riskier) assets such as "junk bonds" (Lazonick and O'Sullivan 2000). On the side of manufacturing, the emergence of Japan as a major U.S. competitor beginning in the late 1970s cut into profits directly, especially in automobiles and electronics. Indirectly, the increased investment in manufacturing, beginning with Japan and then across East Asia, eventually brought chronic global excess capacity, lowering the rate of return on manufacturing and services investments.

With both sides of the finance-industry divide moving in favor of finance, the incentives for investment switched from industry to finance. According to Dumenil and Levy (2005),

The rise of interest rates biased capital allocation in favor of financial investment... capitals 'rushed' toward financial corporations when the profit rate in this sector soared (Dumenil and Levy 2005, 39).

There were two dimensions of the transformation. One is that the net worth of financial corporations rose steadily relative to the net worth of non-financial corporations. Second, traditionally non-financial firms became more like financial holding companies, with a spectrum of financial services and financial investments swamping production in terms of their contribution to company revenues.

The relative stagnation of investment in relation to profits and domestic income is well documented but not well theorized. According to Van Treek (2008), "the diverging development of accumulation and profitability since the early 1980s remains unexplained" (Van Treek 2008, 378), although there have been numerous efforts to integrate financialization forces into Post Keynesian growth models (see, for example, Onaran et al. 2011; Skott and Ryoo 2007; Van Treek 2008; Badhuri 2011). Most pose it as a puzzle to be resolved, because the premise of previous work was the classical one embedded in the Cambridge growth equation that "workers spend all and capitalists save all" and in equilibrium savings equal investment and thus all profits are presumed reinvested. But, as Lazonick (2008) emphasizes, the changed structure of executive compensation in the United States brought greater concern with shareholder value, beginning in the 1980s but surging the 2000s.

In this environment, increases in profitability (and in stock prices) will not automatically raise investment, and financialization of the non-financial corporate sector may have negative implications for investment and labor demand. It will also have consequences for firm innovation. A number of studies show the extensive industrial innovation in the 1920s and its connection to the stock market boom of that decade. While innovation in the 1990s was largely in the emerging IT sector, the role of new equity issues was clear. In the 2000s, innovation occurred mainly in the financial sector itself, with the explosive creation of new derivatives (in particular mortgage backed securities) and an apparent hedge in the form of credit default swaps.

With financial innovation driving an expansion of the financial sector and the volume of speculative activity, there was a conflation of the important dichotomy that Keynes (1964[1936], 158) draws between enterprise ("the activity of forecasting the prospective yield of assets over their whole life") and speculation ("the activity of forecasting the psychology of the market"). Therefore, the bull market in the 2000s has not to date been associated with the innovative effort as both Tobin's (1969) "q" theory of investment and the historical precedent would indicate. In Tobin's theory of the relation between the stock market and firm investment, a heightened market valuation of the firm is a signal to the firm to raise investment, because it constitutes an assessment that additional capital will bring higher returns than is reflected in its current cost.

Innovative effort by firms often relies heavily on equity (as opposed to debt) finance. Shapiro and Milberg (2012) show that both the 1920s and the 1990s were periods of considerable innovation in which rising stock prices may have served as both cause and effect of innovation. By the mid-2000s, economists recognized that higher share prices were associated not with more investment and expenditure on innovative effort (for example, research and development (R&D) spending) on the part of firms, but with an increase in demand for financial assets, including shares of the firm itself (share buybacks).

To be clear, the bull market of the 2000s was not without a rise in business spending and in innovation. But the upturn in spending was focused on housing construction, which is not the same as an increase in productive capacity as envisioned in Tobin's q theory. And the innovation was largely concentrated in the financial sector, with the invention of new financial instruments (many tied to the housing market), new marketing techniques for financial products, and the innovative application of new IT that brought down financial transactions costs and raised the prospect for national and international arbitrage opportunities to be exploited.

Key Indicators of Financialization

A key indicator of the financialization of the non-financial sector is the upward trend in dividend payments and share buybacks as a share of internal funds. These rose in the early 1980s from a plateau of around 20 percent and reached over 100 percent in recent years (see Figure 6.5). The ratio collapsed in the recent recession, as the macroeconomic forces driving down stock prices made buybacks unthinkable. But buybacks have quickly rebounded, just as corporate profits have rebounded very early in the recovery.

There are no readily-available data on imports or offshoring by individual firms, but the financial data suggest that firms with extensive global supply chains undertook massive share buybacks in the 2000s (see Table 6.1). IT hardware and software manufacturers (Cisco, Microsoft, Hewlett-Packard, Dell, and Intel), retailers (Wal-Mart and Home Depot), and consumer non-durables firms (Procter & Gamble) that rely heavily on sophisticated GVC arrangements, were among those returning the highest levels of dividends and share buybacks. Table 6.1 lists the top thirty non-financial

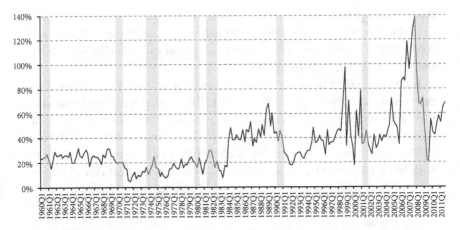

Figure 6.5. Net Dividends Plus Share Buybacks (% of Internal Funds), Nonfarm Non-financial Corporate Business, United States, 1960–2011 (Quarterly Data). *Source*: Own illustration. Data: U.S. Federal Reserve Bank, Flow of Funds Account, Schedule Z.1. Note: Quarterly figures are seasonally adjusted annual rates; share buybacks correspond to negative net new equity issues. Internal funds = gross saving including foreign earnings retained abroad less net capital transfers paid. Gray bars correspond to U.S. business cycles recessions according to the definition of the National Bureau of Economic Research.

firms in terms of share buybacks over the period from 2000 to 2007 and 2010.

Cisco Systems was among the first U.S. manufacturers to largely abandon manufacturing through the use of foreign contract manufacturers in order to focus on sales and service. Already by the late 1990s, Cisco owned only two of the thirty-four foreign plants it contracted for manufacturing. Microsoft has well-established offshore software development, including in India, and the design and manufacture of its XBOX video game consoles has been managed by the Asian contract manufacturer Flextronics. Dell, the personal computer (PC) assembler that revolutionized mass customization in the PC market, purchases 4,500 different parts from 300 suppliers. Hewlett-Packard purchases some of its highest technology components from Taiwanese suppliers (Lynne 2005).

Wal-Mart is the leading importer from China, with reported imports of $9.5 billion in 2001 and $27 billion in 2006 (Scott 2007). From the perspective of share buybacks between 2000 and 2007, Wal-Mart ranks twenty-eighth among Standard & Poor 500 firms, with share buybacks and dividends equal to 57 percent of net income. Wal-Mart's pressure on its suppliers to deliver at low cost and its pitting of suppliers against each other

Table 6.1. *Repurchases and Dividend Payments (% of Company Net Income), Top 30 Nonfinancial, Nonenergy Corporations, 2000–2007 versus 2010*

Rank		2000–2007			2010		
2000–2007		Stock repurchases	Cash dividends	Sum	Stock repurchases	Cash dividends	Sum
1	Hewlett-Packard Co.	134.0	26.5	160.5	126.0	8.5	134.5
2	Microsoft Corp.	99.6	57.3	156.9	60.1	24.2	84.3
3	Pfizer Inc.	82.2	65.9	148.1	12.1	72.2	84.3
4	Cisco Systems Inc.	140.3	0.0	140.3	101.2	0.0	101.2
5	Dell Inc.	139.7	0.0	139.7	30.4	0.0	30.4
6	Texas Instruments Inc.	123.4	11.6	135.0	76.0	18.3	94.3
7	Amgen Inc.	133.3	0.0	133.3	81.8	0.0	81.8
8	Disney (Walt) Co.	107.5	23.0	130.5	67.3	16.7	84.0
9	Procter & Gamble Co.	74.5	43.6	118.1	54.9	49.9	104.8
10	United Parcel Service Inc.	74.6	41.6	116.2	23.4	54.7	78.1
11	McDonald's Corp.	79.5	36.3	115.8	54.6	48.7	103.3
12	Anheuser-Busch	77.2	38.0	115.2	0.0	21.3	21.3
13	UnitedHealth Group Inc.	105.9	0.8	106.7	54.3	9.7	64.0
14	Intel Corp.	85.2	20.5	105.7	15.1	30.6	45.7
15	AT&T Inc.	37.5	67.2	104.7	0.0	52.3	52.3
16	3M Co.	61.9	41.4	103.3	20.9	36.7	57.6
17	PepsiCo Inc.	66.2	36.1	102.3	78.8	47.9	126.7
18	Boeing Co.	69.1	31.9	101.0	0.0	37.6	37.6
19	WellPoint Inc.	98.6	0.0	98.6	151.0	0.0	151.0
20	Home Depot Inc.	79.1	19.0	98.1	78.1	47.0	125.1
21	Intl Business Machines Corp.	82.2	15.7	97.9	103.7	21.4	125.1
22	Merck & Co.	34.7	56.2	90.9	185.0	549.4	734.4
23	Altria Group Inc.	23.2	57.7	80.9	0.0	78.0	78.0
24	Allstate Corp.	55.3	25.6	80.9	16.4	46.7	63.1
25	Oracle Corp.	79.9	0.0	79.9			
26	Johnson & Johnson	41.2	38.4	79.6	21.0	43.5	64.5
27	General Electric Co.	27.6	49.8	77.4	10.0	43.7	53.7
28	Wal-Mart Stores Inc.	35.6	21.4	57.0	96.2	28.9	125.1
29	Time Warner Inc.	−84.5	−7.4	−91.9	78.2	37.7	115.9
30	CBS Corp.	−93.3	−13.1	−106.4	5.1	19.2	24.3

Source: Own illustration. Methodology based on Lazonick (2009), Table 7. Data: Compustat. Note: Stock repurchases = repurchases of common and preferred stock, cash dividends = common and preferred cash dividends, net income = net after-tax income. Ranked by total repurchases in 2000–2007.

are well documented.[3] Retailer Home Depot ranks above Wal-Mart in total repurchases. Its dividends and share buybacks were equal to 98 percent of net income between 2000 and 2007.

Procter & Gamble ranks ninth over the period, with dividends and share buybacks equal to 118 percent of net income. This reflected a shift in discretionary cash distribution compared to the 1990s. In the 1990s, capital expenditure accounted for 46 percent of Procter & Gamble's discretionary cash distribution, whereas share buybacks were 13 percent. Between 2000 and 2007, capital expenditure was 21 percent (Andersson et al. 2008) while share buybacks rose to 74 percent (Table 6.1). The pressures to financialize were more severe due to Procter & Gamble's purchase of Clairol, Wella, and Gillette since 2000. According to Procter & Gamble's annual reports, the firm turned to heighten its offshoring operations in an effort to cut costs in the past eight years (see Procter & Gamble's annual report 2007, cited in Andersson et al. 2008).

Another potential use of corporate funds is for M&As. Like dividends and share buybacks, M&A activity reached record levels over the last two business cycles. For the first five months of 2007, global M&A transactions valued $2 trillion, almost double the value for the same period in 2006. But it is not just the value of these transactions that has hit historic highs. As a recent report in *The Financial Times* notes,

Not only has the overall volume of M&A been rising, but the proportion of those deals funded entirely by cash is on the rise as well. In the first quarter of 2004, all-cash deals were less than a third of all M&A by value. By the first quarter of this year they accounted for half (Larsen 2007).

Heightened M&A activity is not just an indicator of financialization and (in this case) liquidity, but also a cause of financialization itself. It was the hostile takeover movement in the 1980s that solidified the shift to a "portfolio view" of the large non-financial corporation. Finally, with domestic requirements for plant and equipment investment reduced, non-financial corporations have diversified into finance itself. Since the early 1980s, non-financial corporations have increased their relative investment in financial assets. This financial investment picked up in the late 1990s, and by around 2000, non-financial corporations as a whole held more than half of their assets in the form of financial assets.

---

[3] Studies of European retailers show that those firms under more pressure to deliver immediate returns to shareholders are more likely to intensify pressure on foreign suppliers. See Gibbon (2002) and Palpacuer et al. (2005).

6.2 Offshoring, Capital Accumulation, and Financialization: Econometric Evidence

In this section, we test econometrically whether the decline in investment and the increase in financialization can be related to offshoring in the United States. We find evidence that both services and materials offshoring lowered capital accumulation. We then present estimates of the impact of services and materials offshoring on financialization. Our results indicate that materials offshoring increased financialization, while services offshoring had the opposite effect.

6.2.1 Offshoring and Capital Accumulation in the United States

To further analyze the issue of dynamic gains from offshoring, we again adopt a very traditional model of production and costs to estimate the relation between offshoring and capital accumulation at the sectoral level for the United States between 1998 and 2006. A firm's linearly homogeneous cost function, conditional on the level of output Y, is described as in equation (5.1). Using Shephard's Lemma[4], the conditional capital function K in log-linear form is derived as follows:

$$\ln K_{it} = \beta_0 + \eta_Y \ln Y_{it} + \eta_L \ln w_{it} + \eta_K \ln r_{it} + \eta_{INP} \ln p_{it}^{INP}$$
$$+ \eta_{OSS} \ln OSS_{it} + \eta_{OSM} \ln OSM_{it} \qquad (6.1)$$

where w designates wages, r the rental rate on capital, p^{INP} the prices for intermediate inputs, and OSS and OSM services and materials offshoring intensities. i denotes the sector dimension, t the time dimension, and β_0 the constant.

Equation (6.1) is specified as in equation (5.3) and specializes to:

$$\ln K_{it} = \beta_0 + \eta_Y \ln Y_{it} + \eta_L \ln w_{it} + \eta_K \ln r_{it} + \eta_{INP} \ln p_{it}^{INP}$$
$$+ \eta_{OSS} \ln OSS_{it} + \eta_{OSM} \ln OSM_{it} + \eta_{IM} \ln(IM/Y)_{it}$$
$$+ D_i + D_t + \varepsilon_{it} \qquad (6.2)$$

where (IM/Y) designates the import share, D_i and D_t denote fixed sector and year effects, and ε_{it} the random error term. See Appendix 5.2 for a data description.

We expect higher output to have a positive effect on capital accumulation ($\eta_Y > 0$) and higher capital prices to have a negative effect ($\eta_K > 0$).

---

[4] According to Shephard's Lemma factor demand is determined by the first partial derivative of the cost function with respect to the corresponding factor price, regardless of the functional form of the production function.

An increase in wages has no clear effect on capital, as this depends on the relationship between labor and capital. If they are complements, we expect a decline in capital accumulation ($\eta_w < 0$), but the inverse if they are substitutes ($\eta_w > 0$). An increase in intermediate input prices might have a positive ($\eta_{INP} > 0$) or negative ($\eta_{INP} < 0$) effect on capital stock, depending on whether intermediate inputs are substitutes or complements for capital. Similarly, the effect of the import share on capital can be positive ($\eta_{IM} > 0$) or negative ($\eta_{IM} < 0$).

Analogously to the case of labor demand, we identify three effects of offshoring on capital accumulation. A decline in capital stock can result from the direct replacement of foreign for domestic capital stock (the "substitution effect"). A lower capital stock also results from the reduced demand for capital for each unit of output produced ("capital productivity"). Capital accumulation increases with the scale of production ("scale effect"), offsetting the negative effects from substitution and productivity. As in Section 5.4.1, scale effects are taken into account when the output price is substituted for the quantity of output. Allowing for scale effects, the unconditional capital function can be written follows:

$$\ln K_{it} = \beta_0 + \eta_P \ln P_{it} + \eta_L \ln w_{it} + \eta_K \ln r_{it} + \eta_{INP} \ln p_{it}^{INP}$$
$$+ \eta_{OSS} \ln OSS_{it} + \eta_{OSM} \ln OSM_{it} + \eta_{IM} \ln(IM/Y)_{it}$$
$$+ D_i + D_t + \varepsilon_{it} \tag{6.3}$$

In the following, we estimate the effect of offshoring on the capital function. Table 6.2 presents the results of the consistent fixed effects estimator. All estimations produce standard errors robust to heteroscedasticity (Huber-White sandwich estimators) and control for fixed sector and year effects. Columns 1 to 6 consider the thirty-three manufacturing and service sectors simultaneously.[5]

Columns 1 and 2 focus on the conditional capital function given by equation (6.3). Output has a positive effect on real capital stock, whereas wages, capital prices, intermediate input prices, and materials offshoring show a negative impact. Services offshoring shows no effect. Using one-period lags of each explanatory variable only (column 2) confirms most of the results. When output prices P are substituted for the amount of output (columns 3 and 4), the negative wage and intermediate price effects become statistically insignificant, whereas the negative impact of capital prices and

---

[5] Again, we deleted the outliers "federal reserve banks, credit intermediation and related activities" due to extremely low *OSM* intensities and "motion picture and sound recording industries" due to extremely high *OSS* intensities relative to capital stock.

Table 6.2. *Offshoring and Capital Accumulation, Regressions, United States, 1998–2006*

Dependent variable: $\ln K_t$	Manufacturing and service sectors				Manufacturing sectors				Service sectors			
	Conditional		Unconditional		Conditional		Unconditional		Conditional		Unconditional	
	(1)	(2)	(3)	(4)	(5)	(6)	(7)	(8)	(9)	(10)	(11)	(12)
$\ln Y_t$	0.4349*** (0.000)				0.1609*** (0.000)				0.7895*** (0.000)			
$\ln Y_{t-1}$		0.4187*** (0.000)				0.1715*** (0.000)				0.6769*** (0.000)		
$\ln P_t$			0.3599 (0.187)				-0.2196 (0.232)				0.6069 (0.161)	
$\ln P_{t-1}$				0.3131 (0.166)				-0.1141 (0.503)				0.3913 (0.246)
$\ln w_t$	-0.1572*** (0.000)		0.0300 (0.758)		-0.0252 (0.304)		-0.0686 (0.238)		-0.2600* (0.087)		0.4278* (0.093)	
$\ln w_{t-1}$		-0.1450*** (0.000)		0.0096 (0.907)		-0.0309 (0.157)		-0.0418 (0.428)		-0.0752 (0.572)		0.3529 (0.107)
$\ln r_t$	-0.7596*** (0.002)		-1.1077*** (0.001)		-0.5224 (0.292)		-1.0576** (0.023)		-0.8161*** (0.000)		-1.0199*** (0.000)	
$\ln r_{t-1}$		-0.4751** (0.014)		-0.7511** (0.012)		-0.4838 (0.321)		-1.0333** (0.025)		-0.5101*** (0.002)		-0.6655*** (0.005)
$\ln p_t$	-0.1282* (0.055)		-0.3262 (0.127)		0.0657 (0.325)		0.2794* (0.086)		0.5156 (0.351)		0.2962 (0.654)	
$\ln p_{t-1}$		-0.0668 (0.258)		-0.2456 (0.183)		0.1057* (0.078)		0.2412 (0.117)		0.8821** (0.045)		0.4841 (0.437)
$\ln OSS_t$	-0.0033 (0.964)		-0.1366* (0.070)		-0.0110 (0.907)		-0.1103 (0.263)		-0.0889 (0.444)		0.0421 (0.701)	

(continued)

225

Table 6.2 (continued)

Dependent variable: $\ln K_{it}$	Manufacturing and service sectors				Manufacturing sectors				Service sectors			
	Conditional		Unconditional		Conditional		Unconditional		Conditional		Unconditional	
	(1)	(2)	(3)	(4)	(5)	(6)	(7)	(8)	(9)	(10)	(11)	(12)
$\ln OSS_{t-1}$		-0.0311 (0.673)		-0.1768** (0.018)		-0.0177 (0.848)		-0.1413 (0.160)		-0.1184 (0.270)		0.0415 (0.700)
$\ln OSM_t$	-0.2233** (0.047)		-0.4684*** (0.000)		-0.0859 (0.472)		-0.1915* (0.067)		-0.1777 (0.206)		0.0495 (0.757)	
$\ln OSM_{t-1}$		-0.1299 (0.156)		-0.3369*** (0.001)		-0.0040 (0.972)		-0.0925 (0.404)		-0.0533 (0.692)		0.1778 (0.185)
$\ln(IM/Y)_t$	-0.0048 (0.904)		-0.1006** (0.042)		-0.0945*** (0.005)		-0.1121*** (0.002)		0.1721*** (0.007)		0.0568 (0.412)	
$\ln(IM/Y)_{t-1}$		-0.0136 (0.654)		-0.0827** (0.045)		-0.0792*** (0.009)		-0.0927*** (0.006)		0.1272** (0.016)		0.0276 (0.634)
Fixed sector effects	Yes	Yes	Yes	Yes	Yes	Yes	Yes	Yes	Yes	Yes	Yes	Yes
Fixed year effects	Yes	Yes	Yes	Yes	Yes	Yes	Yes	Yes	Yes	Yes	Yes	Yes
Observations	297	264	297	264	189	168	189	168	108	96	108	96
R-squared (within)	0.69	0.65	0.54	0.44	0.378	0.41	0.32	0.32	0.87	0.85	0.78	0.75

Source: Own calculations. p* < 0.1, p** < 0.05, p*** < 0.01 (p-values in parentheses).

Note: K = capital stock, Y = real output, P = output price, r = real wage rate, w = real wage rate, r = capital price, p = intermediate input price, OSS = services offshoring intensity, OSM = materials offshoring intensity, and (IM/Y) = import share.

materials offshoring increases. Services offshoring (column 4) and import share (columns 3 and 4) also show a significantly negative effect.

Columns 5 to 8 present estimates for the twenty-one manufacturing sectors only. Columns 5 and 6 show the results for the conditional capital function. The positive coefficient on output is smaller in the manufacturing sample. Higher intermediate input prices now affect capital stock positively (column 6), while a higher import share shows a significantly negative impact. Focusing on the capital function unconditional on output (columns 7 and 8) shows that capital prices, materials offshoring and import share significantly reduce the capital stock. Services offshoring also shows a negative coefficient sign, but narrowly misses the 10 percent significance level. Intermediate input prices, on the other hand, increase capital stock (column 7).

Columns 9 to 12 show the results for the 12 service sectors only. Output significantly increases real capital stock, whereas wages reduce capital stock only in the conditional capital function (column 9), but show a positive and statistically significant effect when we allow for scale effects (column 11). Capital prices significantly reduce capital stock both conditional and unconditional on output. Intermediate input prices (column 10) and, surprisingly, import share (columns 9 and 10) have a positive effect on the conditional capital function. The negative effect of import share is in contrast to the manufacturing and overall samples, indicating that imports seem to be complements for capital in services industries, but substitutes in manufacturing sectors. Services and materials offshoring show no effects on capital stock.

Holding all variables constant, a 10 percent increase of materials offshoring intensity reduces the capital stock conditional on output by 2.2 percent (column 1) in the manufacturing and service sector. Allowing for scale effects, a 10 percent increase of services and materials offshoring intensity lowers the capital stock unconditional on output by 1.4 and 4.7 percent, respectively (column 3). Interestingly, these negative effects are only significant for materials offshoring in the manufacturing sectors when we allow for scale effects, while they are not statistically significant in service sectors.

The results show that higher offshoring did not lead to higher capital accumulation between 1998 and 2006, but reduced it significantly. The dynamic gains from offshoring were not being fully realized. Without investment gains from offshoring, there are no scale effects, or even worse, when offshoring reduces real capital stock, negative scale effects can be the result.[6]

---

[6] This could explain why offshoring had a more negative effect on labor demand when we allowed for scale effects (see Table 5.8 and the discussion).

A number of econometric and accounting studies have confirmed that rising financialization is associated with declining investment. Stockhammer (2004) finds a statistically significant negative association between financialization of non-financial businesses (measured by interest and dividends as a share of value added) and investment by this sector in the United States and France between the early 1960s and the mid-1990s. The relation is negative also for Germany and the United Kingdom, but not statistically significant. Orhangazi (2008) uses firm-level data for the United States in the period from 1973 to 2000 and again finds a negative and significant relation. Andersson et al. (2007) make a similar finding for the non-financial Standard & Poor 500 firms in the period from 1990 to 2006.

This finding is at odds with the conclusion of those who claim that more outward FDI is associated with more domestic investment (Kimmitt and Slaughter 2010). While this result may be correct, its narrow focus on intra-firm purchases rather than on all offshoring – arm's-length and non-arm's-length – appears to bias the result.

6.2.2 Offshoring and Financialization in the United States

We turn now to the relation between offshoring and financialization. If we assume a Cobb-Douglas production function with constant returns to scale:

$$Y = TL^\alpha K^\beta \quad \frac{\partial Y}{\partial x_1} > 0, \frac{\partial^2 Y}{\partial x_1^2} < 0, \frac{\partial^2 Y}{\partial x_1 \partial x_2} > 0 \text{ with } x_1, x_2 = L, K, T \quad (6.4)$$

where output Y is produced by the input factors labor L, capital K, and technology T. α and β designate the shares of labor and capital in output. Then, under perfect competition, the profit maximizing amount of capital is the following:

$$\frac{\partial Y}{\partial K} = \beta TL^\alpha K^{\beta-1} = (r/P) \quad (6.5)$$

where (r/P) denotes the rental rate on capital in real terms and can be considered our financialization variable FIN. The financialization function in log-linear form is derived as follows:

$$\ln FIN = \ln \beta + \ln T + \alpha \ln L + (\beta - 1) \ln K \quad (6.6)$$

Substituting $T = T(OSS, OSM)$ into T and renaming the coefficients yields a fully specified model:

$$\ln FIN_{it} = \beta_0 + \beta_1 \ln OSS_{it} + \beta_2 \ln OSM_{it} + \beta_3 \ln L_{it}$$
$$+ \beta_4 \ln K_{it} + D_i + D_t + \varepsilon_{it} \quad (6.7)$$

where OSS and OSM denote services and materials offshoring intensities, i and t the sector and time dimension, β_0 the constant, D_i and D_t sector and year fixed effects, and ε_{it} the random error term.

Our measure of financialization focuses on publicly listed firms only, that is, firms that repurchase stocks and pay dividends. Therefore, we use a firm-level measure of financialization from Compustat, which we aggregated to the sectoral level in order to match the data with our measures of services and materials offshoring (see Appendix 5.2 for data description of offshoring variables). Our measure of financialization is the sum of (i) common dividend payments, (ii) purchase of preferred/preference and common stock, and (iii) net interests in natural logarithms. Analogously, our measures of employment and capital stock are the respective sectoral aggregates over all firms in the Compustat database in natural logarithms. We used value added deflators from the Bureau of Economic Analysis (BEA) with 2000 as the base year to calculate real financialization and capital prices from BEA with 2000 as the base year to obtain real capital stock (see Appendix 5.2).

Table 6.3 shows the results in the period from 1998 to 2006 using the consistent fixed effects estimator.[7] All estimations produce standard errors robust to heteroscedasticity (Huber-White sandwich estimators). Columns 1 to 3 show the results for all manufacturing and service sectors. The regression results indicate that while services and materials offshoring have a statistically significantly positive impact on financialization when we only control for fixed sector effects (columns 1 and 2), they only show a significant impact for services offshoring when we additionally control for fixed year effects (column 3). A higher sectoral employment or capital stock both are associated with an increase in financialization when we control for both fixed industry and year effects (column 3).

In manufacturing (columns 4 to 6) both services and materials offshoring are positively associated with financialization when fixed year effects are not included (columns 4 and 5). Controlling for fixed year effects confirms a positive effect for services offshoring (which narrowly misses the 10 percent significance level), whereas the impact of materials offshoring reverses (column 6).

In service sectors (columns 9 to 12) we find positive effects for both materials and services offshoring when fixed year effects are not included (columns 7 and 8). The impact of services offshoring, however, reverses

---

[7] We didn't have any financialization data for "federal reserve banks, credit intermediation, and related activities" and "management of companies and enterprises." We dropped extreme outliers "motion picture and sound recording industries," "securities, commodity contracts, and investments," "funds, trusts, and other financial vehicles," and "legal services."

Table 6.3. *Offshoring and Financialization, Regressions, United States, 1998–2006*

Dependent variable: $\ln FIN_t$	Manufacturing and service sectors			Manufacturing sectors				Service sectors		
	(1)	(2)	(3)	(4)	(5)	(6)	(7)	(8)	(9)
$\ln OSS_t$	0.7656**	1.0124***	0.7995**	0.5920	0.9114**	0.6490	0.8351*	1.0207*	0.0059
	(0.012)	(0.001)	(0.022)	(0.120)	(0.032)	(0.129)	(0.083)	(0.056)	(0.992)
$\ln OSS_{t-1}$		0.0832	−0.2774		0.5256	0.1260		−0.1888	−1.2829*
		(0.824)	(0.529)		(0.275)	(0.831)		(0.785)	(0.068)
$\ln OSM_t$	0.6974***	0.9097***	−0.4613	0.4533**	1.0342**	−1.1069*	1.5324**	1.1212	0.1563
	(0.001)	(0.017)	(0.351)	(0.022)	(0.023)	(0.093)	(0.016)	(0.182)	(0.857)
$\ln OSM_{t-1}$		−0.1369	−0.3637		−0.9330*	−1.1901		1.1579	0.1545
		(0.719)	(0.470)		(0.074)	(0.127)		(0.128)	(0.868)
$\ln L_t$	0.0375	0.0230	0.1933**	−0.0784	−0.2125	−0.0450	0.0737	0.1040	0.1367*
	(0.620)	(0.747)	(0.013)	(0.515)	(0.237)	(0.802)	(0.411)	(0.240)	(0.082)
$\ln L_{t-1}$		0.3179*	0.2026		0.3179*	0.2848		0.4765	0.0867
		(0.054)	(0.211)		(0.083)	(0.170)		(0.171)	(0.714)
$\ln K_t$	0.8955***	0.6837***	0.5066***	0.7492***	0.8537***	0.6805***	0.8891***	0.6605***	0.6987***
	(0.000)	(0.000)	(0.000)	(0.000)	(0.000)	(0.004)	(0.000)	(0.000)	(0.000)
$\ln K_{t-1}$		−0.1272	0.1123		−0.2835	−0.2016		−0.3390	0.0893
		(0.487)	(0.544)		(0.295)	(0.490)		(0.307)	(0.750)
Fixed sector effects	Yes	Yes	Yes	Yes	Yes	Yes	Yes	Yes	Yes
Fixed year effects	No	No	Yes	No	No	Yes	No	No	Yes
Joint significance:									
$\ln OSS_t + \ln OSS_{t-1} = 0$		p>F=0.0057	p>F=0.0683		p>F=0.0721	p>F=0.2461		p>F=0.1558	p>F=0.0940
$\ln OSM_t + \ln OSM_{t-1} = 0$		p>F=0.0164	p>F=0.1969		p>F=0.0713	p>F=0.0208		p>F=0.0240	p>F=0.9334
$\ln L_t + \ln L_{t-1} = 0$		p>F=0.1006	p>F=0.0035		p>F=0.2200	p>F=0.2529		p>F=0.1798	p>F=0.1975
$\ln K_t + \ln K_{t-1} = 0$		p>F=0.0000	p>F=0.0000		p>F=0.0000	p>F=0.0004		p>F=0.0001	p>F=0.0000
Observations	254	225	225	189	168	168	65	57	57
R-squared (within)	0.55	0.53	0.67	0.20	0.22	0.46	0.78	0.78	0.91

Source: Own calculations. p* < 0.1, p** < 0.05, p*** < 0.01 (p-values in parentheses).
Note: FIN = financialization, OSS = services offshoring intensity, OSM = materials offshoring intensity, L = employment, and K = real capital stock.

230

when we control for fixed year effects (column 9). The results are merely suggestive, but tend to support the view that services offshoring increases financialization in the overall sample.

6.3 Sustainability and Replicability of the Globalization-Financialization Link

The analysis so far has largely focused on the United States and the period since the mid-1980s. This raises the question of whether the analytical framework is relevant in different contexts. Therefore, before drawing any general conclusions about the relation between value chain governance and the process of financialization, in this section we briefly address the question of the sustainability of the relation and then turn to the issue of the extent to which it is found in countries other than the United States. In the subsequent and concluding section, we take up these same issues briefly in the context of the current economic downturn that also began in the United States and appears to have spread to different degrees to a number of other industrialized countries.

6.3.1 Sustainability

The literature on financialization to date has left unanswered the question of how the financialized non-financial corporate system sustains itself. Lazonick and O'Sullivan (2000) are skeptical that U.S. corporations have the long-term ability to support stock prices through "downsize and distribute strategies." They write:

> The experience of the U.S. suggests that the pursuit of shareholder value may be an appropriate strategy for running down a company – and an economy. The pursuit of some other kind of value is needed to build up a company and an economy (Lazonick and O'Sullivan 2000, 33).

Boyer (2000) notes that while his simulation model of U.S. economic growth is profit-led and stable, nonetheless:

> The more extended the impact of finance over corporate governance ... the more likely is an equity-based regime to cross the zone of structural stability (Boyer 2000, 142).

This pessimism is reflected in the literature on the effects of financialization. We saw previously that Stockhammer (2004) and Orhangazi (2008) find a negative relation between financialization and investment in the United

States, and our own regression results confirmed these findings. A large literature on finance and economic development attributes slow growth in developing countries and the recurrence of financial crises on excessive financial liberalization and the financialization it has brought, especially to emerging market economies (see, for example, Arestis 2005).

Sustainability can be addressed at a number of levels. One implication of our discussion of GVCs and financialization is that the current global payments imbalances are mutually reinforcing, as reduced (imported) input prices support cost markups and rates of return that attract capital inflows from abroad. Specifically, imported inputs raise profits and profit margins which in turn attracts (domestic and foreign) capital. On the flip side, imported inputs increase supplier country (such as Chinese) exports, creating an expansion of foreign reserves holdings by those countries.

This link among globalized production, corporate rates of return and international payments has not been adequately acknowledged by those who have predicted an imminent hard landing for the dollar. The argument here is that because of these connections between trade and profitability, the international payments imbalances may be more sustainable than standard debt-to-GDP-ratio calculations would indicate. Some have also pointed to the nature of financialization in the state-owned enterprise sector in China, in particular the large undistributed profits that have brought excessive saving and a higher Chinese current account surplus. One response, proposed by those on both sides of the Western political spectrum, would be more government spending out of these profits, for example on a greater public provision of social protection (Kujis 2005; Hung 2008).

The process described here may be sustainable from the point of view of the dynamics of foreign debt, but it is clearly not desirable from a social perspective. In particular, the situation has contributed to rising inequality in both the industrialized countries and in much of the developing world, and certainly in China. Most studies of trade and income distribution focus on the increase in the ratio of wages of skilled to low-skill workers. The focus here has been on the share of national income going to wages as compared to profits. We saw that globalized production is contributing to a rising profit share in the United States and to an accumulation of profits in the form of foreign exchange reserves in China. Such heightened inequality may not be sustainable, and gets to the heart of political debates and struggles over the effects of globalization. Shareholder value strategies are likely to become a "site of political struggle" (Watson 2007, 17) for similar reasons, that is heightened income and wealth inequality. Further revaluation of the Renminbi against the dollar might simply trigger a shift in sourcing from China to other locations, perhaps raising costs to U.S. firms and thus the value of U.S. imports, lowering Chinese exports and raising exports by other countries (such as Vietnam). In effect, this would be a transfer of rents from U.S. company stockholders to producers in the other countries who capture the export markets.

6.3.2 Replicability

In the dynamic model of offshoring discussed in Chapter 4, the gains from the new wave of globalization require the reinvestment of profits gained through cost-reducing offshoring. The rise in the profit share of national income observed across the industrialized countries is thus consistent with this dynamic. Figure 5.2 shows the inverse of this, which is the decline in the share of labor compensation in GDP for six Organisation for Economic Co-operation and Development (OECD) countries. Note that by this very broad measure the labor share in the United States has declined less than in some of the others, in particular the United Kingdom and Germany.

The key to the attainment of dynamic gains is that the efficiency gains from offshoring be shared between consumers and producers and that both these channels (a rise in quantity demanded due to the price decline and a rise in the cost markup) lead to greater investment, which in turn generates higher productivity growth, output, and employment. The problem is that while profits and profit shares are up across the OECD, this has generally not been associated with higher rates of investment. In many cases, the demand for domestic investment relative to GDP and to profits has fallen.

Figure 6.6 shows the rate of investment out of GDP in the industrialized countries and China since 1970. As investment rates generally fell in the industrialized countries, the rate of investment in China steadily increased. There are a number of explanations for the decline in investment out of GDP. With respect to the globalization of production, the simple fact is that less investment is needed when significant portions of the production process (goods and services) are moved offshore.

The decline in investment spending is also an indication that the strategic shift from "retain and reinvest" to "downsize and distribute" which began in force in the United States in the 1980s appears to have taken hold in other industrialized countries. By focusing increasingly on "core competence" and contracting out (both domestically and internationally) the remainder of the operation, corporate managers have been able to reduce domestic investment needs and meet shareholder demands for improvements in shareholder value, that is, the financialization of the non-financial corporate sector.

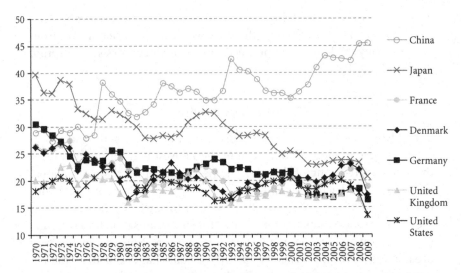

Figure 6.6. Gross Capital Formation (% of GDP), Selected Countries, 1970–2009. *Source:* Own illustration. Data: United Nations Conference on Trade and Development.

Stockhammer (2004) documents a marked increase in the share of non-financial corporations' value added going to interest and dividends between 1978 and 1995 in the United States, United Kingdom, France, and Germany. He finds this measure of "financialization" to be associated with declines in business investment. A pair of studies of U.K. and Danish retail GVCs show that the greater shareholder pressure on the U.K. firms led to much stricter conditions being imposed on foreign suppliers to these firms compared to Danish firms. U.K. retailers were more aggressive in seeking low-cost suppliers and in pressuring suppliers to reduce prices. The relation between the globalization of production and financialization thus appears to go in both directions (Palpacuer et al. 2005; Gibbon 2002).

6.4 Conclusion: Interdependence of Globalization and Finance in the Global Crisis

Analysis of GVCs often leaves aside the financial implications. Studies of financialization tend to leave as implicit the link to production and investment. In this chapter, we focused on the United States to demonstrate that there is a link between the globalization of production and financialization, although not a simple causal relation from one to the other. The globalization of production and in particular the governance structure of GVCs have clear implications for pricing, profits, wages, and investment at the level of the firm and these have supported the process of financialization.

Pressures for financialization and increased short-run shareholder returns have, in turn, spurred greater globalization of production, as firms have divested the less competitive aspects of their production or relocated parts of the production process in order to lower costs. Corporate governance and GVC governance are linked and our understanding of each of these processes can be strengthened by a deeper exploration of this interdependence.

Changes in the structure of production, and specifically the rise of GVCs, have provided the continued capacity of the major industrialized countries to sustain profit growth within the confines of a financialized system. Therefore, while a common presumption in the financialization literature is that finance is the "tail" wagging the production "dog," it is not possible to make the case that the revolution in corporate governance or the liberalization of capital accounts *caused* the international vertical disintegration of production because it preceded it chronologically.[8] The two processes emerged in force in the past twenty-five years – the same period in which the profit share in most industrialized countries rebounded to new highs – and it is more reasonable to see the two as interdependent tendencies.[9]

Financialization has encouraged a restructuring of production, with firms narrowing their scope to core competence. And the rising ability of firms to disintegrate production vertically and internationally has allowed these firms to maintain cost markups – and thus profits and shareholder value – even in a context of slower economic growth. The point is not that globalized production necessarily triggered financialization, but that global production strategies have helped to sustain financialization.

Sustainability in terms of profits and international capital flows is not synonymous with social sustainability. We have seen the social conflict created as a result of the interdependence of financialization and GVC governance. Although we have explored this dynamic mainly in terms of the United States, we have also argued that the dynamic appears to operate

---

[8] Note also that there is an older literature on the relation between financial institutions and production relations based on Gershenkron's (1962) study of the institutional foundations of economic development, according to which financial institutions are the result of the specific production system. Zysman (1983) filled out this picture and identified different sets of financial institutions as enabling of three distinct systems of industrial relations, the Anglo-Saxon, the Japanese, and the French. Palpacuer et al. (2005) provide a rare recent sectoral analysis along these lines.

[9] Montgomerie (2007) also questions the idea of a single direction of causation, arguing that financialization is "an entry point into an analysis of a dynamic system of social interaction, rather than a static description of unitary will and collective logic" (Montgomerie 2007, 6). On the long-run shifts in the profit share, see Wolff (2003) and Glynn (2006), who link it specifically to financialization and globalization.

broadly in the U.S. non-financial sector and there are indications of its operation across the OECD.

The GVC-financialization link has been especially effective under conditions of slow but positive economic growth in the United States and Europe. With the collapse of the housing and mortgage derivatives markets in the United States, bringing severe losses to the financial sector in the United States and other major industrialized countries, the link between the governance of GVCs and financialization will likely change. With the financial sector reduced in size and scope, the behavior of the non-financial corporate sector has come into the spotlight, with a number of articles in the popular press positing that activity in the non-financial corporate sector will be crucial in the return to more rapid economic growth rates in the United States.

Our findings indicate that this is unlikely. On the one hand, many non-financial corporations are lead firms in GVCs and may simply intensify their sourcing strategy to raise markups. Product markets are likely to be depressed given that consumer confidence and demand and debt levels have continued to fall along with housing prices. The offshoring strategy is complicated by the fact that the dollar began to weaken against the Chinese Renminbi in the middle of 2005 and has depreciated just over 15 percent from its fixed level of the 1990s, making it more difficult for U.S. lead firms to reduce costs through GVCs. But the dollar's depreciation vis-à-vis the Chinese Renminbi has been slow and steady, reducing the likelihood of a run on the dollar and dollar assets. Also, a number of foreign firms have provided capital for ailing U.S. financial firms. On the other hand, surprising strength of the Euro against the Renminbi – largely maintaining its value from the early 2000s despite the Eurozone's fiscal turmoil – increased the likelihood that the GVC-financialization interdependence could gain strength in Europe.

Some analysts have argued that the financial crisis that erupted in 2008 would be contained within the financial sector, with few serious real-side consequences. The premise of this argument was that non-financial corporations had generated high profits over the previous ten years and could finance their investment out of these profits rather than returning them to shareholders as they have done at increasing rates over this same period. The argument ignores that consumer demand in the United States fell drastically and has recovered at well below historical rates, because of unemployment and uncertainty of employment security in the future, wealth effects resulting from the moribund housing market, and a collapse of household access to credit. It also fails to come to terms with the fact that the traditional business model of retaining profits to finance growth through investment has been giving way to a strategy of focusing on core competence and maximizing shareholder value.

The new model has been built on the strategy of lead firm governance of global production networks, aimed at cutting costs and reducing production-side risk. This has permitted the U.S. non-financial corporate sector to behave increasingly like the financial sector, purchasing more financial assets and raising dividends and executive compensation rather than investing in the real economy. The dynamic gains from offshoring have not been fully realized because firms have purchased financial assets rather than investing in productive assets that raise productivity, growth, employment, and income. The financialization of non-financial firms reduces the dynamic gains from offshoring by reducing reinvestment out of profits.

Imports are linked to higher cost markups and firm profits, and the gains from such non-competitive imports – the result of offshoring – are increasingly associated with the reinvestment of these higher profits. Our approach constitutes a shift in the study of trade, away from questions of skills-biased labor demand, and toward the distribution of income between profits and wages and their macroeconomic effects. The approach connects in this sense to structuralist macroeconomic models in which economic structure affects economic growth.[10]

As concerns over shareholder value have dominated over concerns with growth and innovation, the non-financial corporate sector has acted more and more like the financial sector itself, and in the process has lost productive capacity and innovativeness. Assuming that innovation is embodied in new investment, then the long-term effects of financialization on productivity growth may be significant.

---

[10] See Taylor (2004) and Nastepaad and Storm (2006/2007). Recent efforts introduce financialization into these models. See Hein and Stockhammer (2009) and Van Treek (2008).

SEVEN

Economic Development as Industrial Upgrading in Global Value Chains

Our main focus in this book until now has been the industrialized countries and especially the United States. Even when we considered foreign direct investment (FDI) in Chapter 4, it was to further our understanding of lead corporation strategies. In this chapter, we look more closely at the implications of the steady increase in industrialized country offshoring for the developing countries. Most research on global value chains (GVCs) has in fact focused on developing countries. As we see in this chapter, the expansion of GVCs amidst a global push to trade liberalization and export orientation has rendered the goal of "industrial upgrading" within GVCs to be nearly synonymous with economic development itself. If economic development in the mid-twentieth century was driven by strategies of import substitution, and the later part of the century by a clear export orientation, the last twenty years could be said to be characterized by vertically-specialized industrialization efforts.

Section 7.1 discusses the transition to vertically-specialized industrialization (VSI). We focus on the growth of export processing zones (EPZs), an important entry point for developing economies into GVCs. In Section 7.2, we propose simple and operational measures of upgrading. Here we add the notion of "social upgrading," relating to wages, employment, and social standards, to the standard notion of industrial or economic upgrading. We show that surprisingly few developing countries satisfy some simple criteria of upgrading. Export growth alone, we find, is not a guarantee of industrial upgrading. We explore the extent to which economic upgrading results in social upgrading, looking at both the national and GVC level. Section 7.3 considers the gender segmentation of labor markets that has resulted in a rising female intensity of employment, followed by a surprising decline in female intensity as industrial upgrading has occurred in some regions. We conclude in Section 7.4 with a summary of the challenges of upgrading, characterizing the situation as akin to that in the 1950s, when structuralist development economists warned of the development trap from a commodity-based production pattern. A similar "Prebisch-Singer trap" can be found in the manufacturing-oriented trade profile of developing countries today as a result of the asymmetric relations under GVC-based development.

The purpose of this chapter is neither to give a full-blown theory of economic development, nor to "explain" the development experience of any particular country. It is to explore the implications of the prominence of GVCs for the development process and in fact to question the overuse of the concept of economic or industrial upgrading as a proxy for economic development. There are problems of both theory and measurement in the use of upgrading as a proxy for economic development, and the purpose of this chapter is to elucidate those so we can better understand the usefulness and limitations of using the GVC as a starting point in the study of economic development.

7.1 Vertically-Specialized Industrialization

7.1.1 From Import Substitution to Export Orientation to Vertical Specialization

Since the mid-1970s, developing country exports have grown (as a share of gross domestic product) by more than exports in industrialized countries, reflecting the shift from import substitution industrialization (ISI) to export-oriented industrialization (EOI) strategies adopted by many developing country governments, promoted by the international financial institutions, and governed by the dynamics of GVCs. This structural change accelerated during the 1980s, as shown in Figure 7.1. While in 1985 only 24 percent of low- and middle-income countries' (LMICs) exports were manufactures, by 2000 this share had risen to 52 percent. Therefore, not only has there been a shift in the composition of exports by LMICs out of commodities and into manufactures, but these countries have expanded their share of world exports of intermediates goods in manufacturing, as implied by the rising goods offshoring intensities of industrialized countries in Figure 2.5.

Focusing simply on the shift from import substitution to export expansion veils the fact that the new wave of globalization has altered the nature of economic development. The massive globalization of production, led by large firms in industrialized countries and facilitated by new communication technologies, has combined with the policy shift in developing

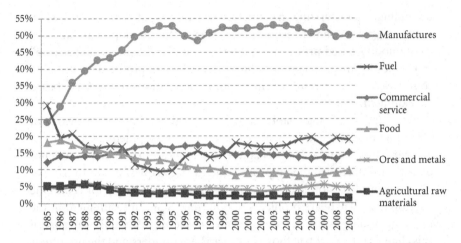

Figure 7.1. Exports from LMICs by Product Group (% of Total Exports from LMICs), 1985–2009. *Source*: Own illustration. Data: World Development Indicators. Note: The sum of manufactures, fuel, food, ores and metals, and agricultural raw materials does not fully capture total merchandise exports, especially in 1985 and 1986, hence, the sum of product groups presented here does not total 100 percent.

countries to make efforts at "upgrading" within GVCs central to any strategy of economic development. The globalization of production has made industrialization today different from the final goods, export-led process of just twenty-five years ago.

Now the issue facing firms and governments is less that of finding new, more capital-intensive goods to sell to consumers in foreign countries. Instead, it requires moving up through the chain of production of a particular commodity or set of commodities into higher value added activities. This involves raising productivity and skills through mechanization and the introduction of new technologies. It also requires fitting into existing corporate strategies or, as Gereffi (1999) writes, "to establish close linkages with a diverse array of lead firms" (Gereffi 1999, 38). We might say that in the same way the ISI strategies gave way to EOI, the latter has now given way to VSI efforts aimed at upgrading within GVCs.

The expansion of GVCs has meant that about 50 percent of the value of international trade in goods and services is in intermediates rather than in final goods and services (see Chapter 2). Moreover, a growing share of intermediates exports have come from developing countries. With the great opportunities for developing country export expansion have come a number of new challenges to economic development. The challenges arise from the fact that while global production sharing has apparently helped developing countries expand manufacturing export activity, the value added from that activity has not generally increased proportionally.

In Chapter 4 we argued that lead firms in GVCs seek to induce competitive conditions in supplier markets and thus that the asymmetry of market structures in GVCs is endogenous to the dynamics of GVC governance. Lead firms in GVCs offshore lower value added activities, retaining control over production in the higher value added aspects of business. These areas are often characterized by higher technological and skill requirements, but also are commonly oligopolistic and are susceptible to the construction of significant barriers to entry. These areas may even involve no production at all, but instead be focused on high value added functions such as product design, branding, marketing, finance, and retailing. The lead firm focus on core competence is consistent with a strategy of retaining rents through the encouragement of oligopsony input markets.

The lower value added portions of many GVCs have low entry barriers. We saw in Chapter 4 that entry by countries into producing components of a variety of manufacturing sectors has been massive since the early 1980s and generally continued, although at a slower pace, through the mid 2000s (see Figure 4.3). Competition at the lower levels of the GVC can be so intense as to keep cost markups very low and impose intense downward pressure on wages and labor conditions. While wage stagnation affects the standard of living today, it is the difficulty of capturing rents for future reinvestment that poses the greatest challenge to economic development, because it is the socially productive reinvestment of these rents – the dynamic gains from trade once again – on which economic development crucially hinges.

Since GVCs are largely driven and designed by lead firms, the strategic focus is not industrial upgrading in the developing supplier country, but the profitability and flexibility of the lead firm. The profitability or even efficiency of the supplier is not necessarily a consideration in the construction of the global production network (GPN), although reliability and quality of supply are crucial. Industrial upgrading requires capital investment that is usually generated from oligopoly profits, not the competitive conditions that increasingly characterize supplier markets. But the growth of FDI in developing countries has in most cases not solved the problem, because profits are often repatriated and FDI tends to lag rather than lead economic development. This macroeconomic view admittedly neglects spillovers of technology and knowledge (such as management and organizational practices) to local firms and workers which, in the long-run, can foster economic development by raising the level of domestic firm productivity.

Upgrading within GVCs does not obviate the traditional need for developmental state policy. In most cases, the effort was underpinned by an industrial policy that, building on prior industrial experience, selectively targeted and subsidized certain sectors and activities, building a base of technology, labor skills and management that led to a slow climb up the global supply chain. In the Korean case, for example, industrial policy included export subsidies, import and foreign investment controls, production targets, low-interest credit and technical support, in order to generate the long-run efficiency previously defined (Amsden 1989). This was supplemented by an expanding educational system that raised the average skill-level of the workforce.

The export-based industrial upgrading path to economic development is difficult and risky. Mexico, with its considerable links to multinational corporations and to the U.S. market through geographic proximity and preferential trading relations under the North American Free Trade Agreement, has achieved a huge expansion of exports but suffered a broad-based decline in real wages. After the transition to capitalism, a number of Eastern European countries, for all their skill accumulation and proximity to the rich EU market, saw their presence across supply chains reduced to the lower end.[1] Global integration thus brings an opportunity of upgrading, but also a risk of industrial or social "downgrading."

Our analysis of the obstacles to upgrading in GVCs focused on lead firm strategy. This is appropriate in that these firms have generally been the drivers of the construction and operation of GVCs. But developing country firms, policies, and institutions have also played an important part in giving GVCs their particular form and dynamics.

7.1.2 Entering Global Value Chains through Export Processing Zones

If there is one institution associated with development policy aimed at connecting domestic labor to GVCs, it is the EPZ, and the establishment of EPZs has been driven in part by the recognition of the importance of collaboration with GVC lead firms in order to reach their markets and to have a chance for industrial upgrading. EPZs are those regulatory spaces in a country aimed at attracting export-oriented companies by offering these companies special concessions on taxes, tariffs, and regulations.

Some of the typical special incentives offered under EPZs include exemption from some or all export taxes, exemption from some or all duties on imports of raw materials or intermediate goods, exemption from direct taxes such as profits taxes, municipal and property taxes, exemption from

---

[1]　This was the case of the garment sector in Romania, for example. See Staritz (2010).

indirect taxes such as value added taxes on domestic purchases, exemption from national foreign exchange controls, free profit repatriation for foreign companies, provision of streamlined administrative services especially to facilitate imports and exports, and free provision of enhanced physical infrastructure for production, transport, and logistics.

There are other less transparent features of EPZs that are sometimes used to provide further incentives for firm investment and export. One is a relaxed regulatory environment, including with respect to the enforcement of labor rights and standards (notably the right to unionize), foreign ownership regulations and on the leasing or purchasing of land.[2] Another feature (although not available to all countries simultaneously) is an undervalued currency that renders costs lower (in foreign currency terms) and raises export competitiveness.

EPZs take a variety of names in different countries, and here we use the shorthand of "EPZ" to designate a wide variety of regulatory frameworks that contain some or all of the special concessions previously listed. Singa Boyenge (2007) lists thirty-two different titles used for such zones around the world, each indicating slight differences in terms of concessions, subsidies, and regulations. In manufacturing, EPZs range from "Special Economic Zones" (SEZs) that comprise entire provinces of China, offering reduced business taxes and foreign exchange controls and lax labor codes, to the classic "fenced-in" EPZs of Ireland, Malaysia, Mexico, Dominican Republic, Mauritius, and Kenya that offer a fifteen-year tax exemption, relief from exchange controls, free profit repatriation, and limits on trade union freedom, to enterprise zones such as those in Indonesia and Senegal focused on reviving depressed municipal areas through the development of small and medium enterprises. Thus, EPZs may be of the traditional geographically self-contained variety or they may apply to single factories operating in different geographical locations.

EPZs have been extended from goods production and assembly to services, and thus include information processing zones in India and the Caribbean, that offer tariff exemptions on information technology required for services provision, and even financial services zones, such as those in Dubai, Turkey, and the Cayman Islands, offering tax relief and free repatriation of profits to financial corporations (Engman et al. 2007).

EPZs have grown in terms of their number, in terms of the number of countries offering them, in terms of their size and in terms of the scope

---

[2] On labor rights enforcement, see ILO (2002). On foreign ownership and property issues, see Engman et al. (2007).

Table 7.1. The Development of Export Processing Zones, 1975–2006

	1975	1986	1995	1997	2002	2006
No. of countries with EPZs	29	47	73	93	116	130
No. of EPZs	79	176	500	845	3,000	3,500
Employment (millions)	n.a.	n.a.	n.a.	22.5	43	66
– of which China	n.a.	n.a.	n.a.	18	30	40
– of which other countries for which figures are available	0.8	1.9	n.a.	4.5	13	26

Source: Own illustration. Data: Milberg (2007).

of industries they comprise. According to Milberg (2007), the number of countries using EPZs increased to 130 in 2006, up from 116 in 2002 and 29 in 1975 (see Table 7.1). These 130 countries operated 3,500 EPZs, employing 66 million people. China has been by far the major country of expansion of EPZ activity. China is now estimated to have 40 million people working in EPZs or EPZ-like operations, an increase of 10 million since 2002. Outside of China, employment in EPZs doubled between 2002 and 2006, from 13 to 26 million.

By 2006, all of the regions of the world with the exception of South America had a fairly large presence of EPZs in terms of employment. The active use of EPZs in East Asia, Central America, and the Caribbean has been widely known and studied since they were created in the 1970s and 1980s. Today there are over ninety EPZs in sub-Saharan Africa and in the transition economies of Eastern and Central Europe, including those accounting for a significant share of country exports in Gabon, Ghana, Kenya, Lesotho, Mali, Mozambique, Nigeria, Zimbabwe, the Czech Republic, and Lithuania (Milberg 2007).

EPZs continue to contribute a major share of national exports in many countries. During the 1990s, many countries expanded EPZ exports considerably. Costa Rica's EPZs accounted for 10 percent of manufactured exports in 1990 and reached 50 to 52 percent in the early 2000s (Engman et al. 2007). Bangladesh saw its EPZ exports rise from 3.4 percent in 1990 to 21.3 percent in 2003 (Aggarwal 2005). Table 7.2 shows EPZ exports as a share of national exports for 2002 and 2006. In many countries, EPZ exports continued in 2006 to account for 80 percent or more of exports. A number of countries had a decline in the EPZ share of exports, including Mauritius, Mexico, the Philippines, and Tunisia. A few countries experienced an increase from 2002 to 2006, from already high levels, in the EPZ share of exports, including Bangladesh, Colombia, Kenya, Madagascar, the Maldives, and Sri Lanka.

Table 7.2. *EPZ Share of Total Exports, Selected Countries, 2002 versus 2006*

Country	2002	2006
Philippines	87.0	60.0
Malaysia	83.0	83.0
Mexico	83.0	47.0
Gabon	80.0	80.0
Macao, China P.R.	80.0	80.0
Zimbabwe	80.0	80.0
Vietnam	80.0	80.0
Dominican Republic	80.0	80.0
Tunisia	80.0	52.0
Kenya	80.0	86.9
Senegal	80.0	n.a.
Mauritius	77.0	42.0
Morocco	61.0	61.0
Bangladesh	60.0	75.6
Costa Rica	50.0	52.0
Haiti	50.0	50.0
Madagascar	38.0	80.0
Sri Lanka	33.0	38.0
Cameroon	32.0	33.0
Maldives	13.2	47.7
Colombia	9.3	40.0

Source: Own illustration. Data: Milberg (2007). Note: Countries are ranked by 2002 EPZ shares of total exports.

It has been recognized for decades that for EPZs to contribute to sustained economic development, they would have to be linked to the rest of the economy. Jenkins (2005) puts it succinctly:

The strength of the linkages between EPZs and the rest of the domestic economy seems to play an essential role in determining whether, and to what extent, the host nation benefits from opening EPZs (Jenkins 2005, 24).

The problem has always been that by their nature EPZs resist such links. For one, EPZs are generally created precisely to attract foreign firms because domestic firms are not competitive internationally and are not able to generate foreign exchange. Schrank (2001) sees EPZs as reconciling the disparate interests of governments seeking to promote jobs and exports, foreign firms seeking profitable production conditions and domestic firms who are not internationally competitive. Thus, from the start, domestic firms are behind in their capacity to provide low-cost, high-quality inputs to production in EPZs. Second, EPZs are generally defined by an allowance of duty-free imports of material inputs. Non-EPZ firms cannot import inputs duty free.[3] This puts domestic firms at a cost disadvantage in input production. According to Madani (1999),

> the tariff free inputs for the firms in the zone act as import subsidies competing against domestic input production and discouraging creation of backward linkages (Madani 1999, 28).[4]

Add to this factor that EPZs are dominated by foreign firms with well-established relations with foreign input producers. In many cases, foreign firms may follow a co-sourcing strategy, relying on imported inputs from established suppliers abroad. Alternatively, foreign firms may follow co-location strategies requiring established foreign input suppliers to also enter EPZs. Most studies of the amount of backward linkages find them to be minimal, with domestic orders remaining at a very low level and technology spillovers rare.

There are some important exceptions, including South Korea, where the share of inputs purchased from the domestic economy rose from 13 percent in 1972 to 32 percent in 1978 and remained at that high level through the 1980s (Kusago and Tzannatos, 1998). The Korean EPZs were established to attract foreign investment and promote the electronics sector. Thus the level of integration is particularly impressive given that about 80 percent of investment in the EPZs was foreign. The state played an important role in fostering the linkage by providing duty drawbacks to non-EPZ firms in its "equal footing policy" (Engman et al. 2007, 39). Taiwan experienced a similar transformation, with domestic inputs accounting for only 5 percent of inputs in 1967 and rising to 27 percent by 1978 (Heron 2004). In Mauritian EPZs, 41 percent of material inputs were purchased domestically (Willmore 1995). Domestic Mauritian firms have invested in EPZs at higher rates than in most countries, introducing stability in the EPZ sector and creating the foundation for technology and knowledge internalization (Baissac 2003).

The South Korea, Taiwan, and Mauritius examples of considerable linkage between the EPZs and the rest of the economy are exceptional. More

---

[3] Thus to protect domestic producers, a number of countries (Kenya and Tanzania, for example) limit the amount that EPZ-based firms can sell to the domestic economy.

[4] Heron (2004) makes this argument for the case of Caribbean exporting companies operating under the U.S.9802.00 tariff scheme that provides tariff- and duty-free treatment only for products made from U.S. components. The African Growth and Opportunity Act (AGOA) suspended rules of origin stipulations on low-income countries. See Gibbon and Ponte (2005).

common is the range of 3 to 9 percent of inputs purchased domestically, reported for Sri Lanka, the Philippines, Guatemala, and El Salvador in the mid to late 1990s. In the Dominican Republic in 2004, after thirty years of EPZ presence and robust growth in EPZ exports and employment, EPZs purchased 0.0001 percent of material inputs from the domestic market (Engman et al. 2007).

Technology spillovers are also limited, as the low-skill assembly type production so common in EPZs is simply not conducive to technology transfer. And the higher skill-intensive EPZs, such as those involving software or other business services, are often enclaves and de-linked from the rest of the economy except for their high-skill labor force.[5] The technology is embodied in imported capital and the knowledge is embodied in management. Evidence shows, for example in the case again of South Korea in the mid-1980s, that knowledge transfers increase when the skill intensity of production rises (Engman et al. 2007).

In sum, EPZs have provided an entry point into GVCs, a way for the state not just to attract foreign capital but also to connect the local labor force to established GVCs. This has provided a boost to exports, which in many countries come overwhelmingly from EPZs. As we further show in this chapter, export growth is unevenly correlated with economic upgrading and the latter even more loosely connected to social upgrading. Thus within the framework of the new wave of globalization, EPZs have a clear rationale.

Three problems remain, however, from the perspective of economic development. First, EPZs do not resolve, and in fact may exacerbate the problem of a lack of backward linkages from a successful export operation. Second, EPZs play an important role in the asymmetry of market structures that has underpinned the terms of trade weakness for developing country manufactures exports. Third, while EPZs have created employment and pay average wages slightly above those in similar jobs outside EPZs, they have not been associated with significant improvement in wages and labor standards.

The remainder of this chapter is dedicated to the underlying issue raised by our overview of EPZs in the era of VSI. This is the issue of upgrading in GVCs, how common it is and what its implications are for social improvement, all of which are crucial for sustainable development.

---

[5] Most studies of EPZs address this issue in some way. See, for example, Heron (2004) on Jamaica, Armas and Sadni-Jallab (2002) on Mexico, Aggarwal (2007) on India and ILO (2005) on Madagascar.

7.2 Economic Upgrading versus Social Upgrading

7.2.1 Upgrading Defined and Measured

Economic upgrading – often referred to as "industrial upgrading" or simply "upgrading" – is defined as the ability of producers "to make better products, to make products more efficiently, or to move into more skilled activities" (Pietrobelli and Rabellotti 2006, 1). The focus of most studies of upgrading is on the degree of technological sophistication of production and especially on value added. In the terminology of GVCs, upgrading is defined as

the possibility for (developing country) producers to move up the value chain, either by shifting to more rewarding functional positions or by making products that have more value added invested in them and that can provide better returns to producers (Gibbon and Ponte 2005, 87–88).

Humphrey (2004) and Humphrey and Schmitz (2002) identify four distinct types of economic upgrading, including: (i) process upgrading, (ii) product upgrading, (iii) functional upgrading, and (iv) intersectoral (or chain) upgrading. Process upgrading is productivity growth in existing activities in the value chain. Product upgrading is the move into more higher value added products within the same value chain. Most case study work has been on functional upgrading, defined as the move into more technologically sophisticated or more integrated aspects of a given production process. Intersectoral upgrading – moving into new, higher value added supply chains – is perhaps the most important in terms of overall development trajectory, but has received the least attention in the value chain case study literature.

The key steps in the functional upgrading process are from assembly to original equipment manufacture to original design manufacture and to original brand manufacture (see Humphrey 2004 for an overview). Bair and Gereffi (2001), for example, identify upgrading among denim jeans producers in Torreon, Mexico, as the move from cutting, assembly, laundry and finishing, to design, distribution, and marketing. Mortimer (2002) describes the move by Asian apparel manufacturers to "full package" production, which includes almost all aspects of production including the logistics of managing the process itself. Sturgeon (2002) finds this "modular" supply capacity by large first-tier supplier firms in Asia to be a hallmark of GPNs in consumer electronics. Dolan and Humphrey (2000) describe functional upgrading among Kenyan producers of fresh vegetables, who have tried to move into more processing and packaging of foods for sale to U.K. retailers.

Schmitz (1999) argues that the limited functional upgrading by Brazilian footwear manufactures (in particular the failure to attain design capacity) led to that sector's decline when American firms began sourcing from China in the 1990s.

Despite the numerous case studies, functional upgrading is hard to measure and often seems relegated to the category of "you know it when you see it." However, quantification might be helpful to know, for example, how much upgrading has occurred, which sectors in a country have experienced relatively more or less upgrading, which country's sector has experienced more upgrading compared to a competing sector in other countries, or even which policies are more conducive to upgrading. These are hard issues to address without agreed-upon observable measures of upgrading.

If there is a possibility of economic upgrading, is there also a possibility of downgrading? If international competitiveness depends in part on production costs, then there are two routes to raising international competitiveness: lower the payment to factors of production (in particular, labor and capital) or raise productivity. Leaving capital costs aside for the moment, we can simplify the issue as between lowering wages and raising labor productivity – a "low-road" and a "high-road." Whereas the high-road does not guarantee that wage growth (part of "social upgrading" discussed later in this section) will follow, there are nonetheless limits to the low-road strategy of lowering wages based on considerations of political stability and mere human subsistence.[6]

The study of economic upgrading has emphasized technology and management capacity. There is a presumption in these studies that such upgrading translates straightforwardly into social improvement. We find, to the contrary, that the translations are quite varied across countries and GVCs. In theory, there are four combinations of outcomes, as illustrated in Figure 7.2. Economic upgrading may be combined with social upgrading or downgrading. Thus, it is possible for social upgrading to occur in the absence of economic upgrading as well as for a country to experience simultaneous "downgrading" in economic and social terms.

Most of the massive amounts of research done on upgrading in GVCs has been the study of individual cases of countries or sectors organized in international networks, how the networks are governed, and how the governance structure influences the upgrading process. Different case studies have different foci and cover different time periods, so it is difficult to

---

[6] Amsden (1989), for example, argues that given the productivity advantages of industrialized countries with whom Korean industry competed in the 1970s and 1980s, wage cuts could not possibly have gone far enough to make Korean production competitive.

		Social realm	
		Upgrading	Downgrading
Economic realm	Upgrading	*High-road growth*	*Low-road growth*
	Downgrading	*High-road decline*	*Low-road decline*

Figure 7.2. Upgrading and Downgrading. *Source:* Own illustration. Based on Milberg and Winkler (2011b, 345).

compare across case studies. Thus, for example, it is hard to compare the South African experience in auto parts production (Kaplinsky 2005) with the Costa Rican case of semiconductors (Sanchez-Ancochea 2006), even though both are examples of upgrading efforts within producer-driven GVCs.

The problem of comparability due to the different emphasis of the case studies is compounded by the fact that there is such a wide variety of variables adopted to measure economic and social upgrading. Table 7.3 shows a list of measures of economic and social upgrading that have been used in past studies done at different levels of analysis: the nation, the sector or GVC, and the firm or the plant. It shows a dizzying variety of measures across levels of analysis, but even across studies done at the same level. Most of the variables listed in Table 7.3 are self-explanatory.

The focus on value added and its expansion in the definition and analysis of upgrading has some limitations. For one, it leaves aside the question of the distribution of value added among profits, wages, and taxes, not to mention among different types of labor. If value added is defined as wage income plus profit income plus tax payments, then simply identifying an increase in value added obviously gives no information on its distribution. When there are many types of labor – skilled, low-skill, formal, informal, home-based, contract, or seasonal – then even knowing changes in labor income *per se* might indicate very little about social upgrading. This distribution is essential to the analysis of the extent to which economic upgrading is associated with social upgrading. As Gereffi et al. (2001) write:

Profitability has limitations for GVC analysis because capital (whose reward is profit) is only one factor of production. Profits do not tell us anything about the returns to labor or the general productivity of the economy at large (Gereffi et al. 2001, 5).

Table 7.3. *Proxy Measures of Economic and Social Upgrading*

Level of aggregation	Economic	Social
Country	– Productivity growth – Value added growth – Profits growth – Export growth – Growth in export market share – Unit value growth of output – Unit value growth of exports – Reduced relative unit labor costs – Increased capital intensity	– Wage growth – Employment/population growth – Growth in labor share – Formal employment – Decline in youth unemployment – Gender equality of employment and wages – Poverty reduction – Share of wage employment in non-agricultural employment – Improved labor standards, including FACB, job safety, child labor, forced labor, employment discrimination – Regulation of monitoring – Improved political rights – Human development index
Sector or GVC	– Productivity growth – Value added growth – Profits growth – Export growth – Growth in export market share – Unit value growth of output – Unit value growth of exports – Reduced relative unit labor costs – Increased capital intensity – Increased skill intensity of functions – Increased skill intensity of employment – Increased skill intensity of exports	– Wage growth – Employment growth – Improved labor standards, including FACB, job safety, child labor, forced labor, employment discrimination
Firm	– Increased skill intensity of functions (assembly/OEM/ODM/OBM/full package) – Developing skills to manage the supply chain – Composition of jobs – Increased capital intensity/mechanization – Product, process, functional, chain	– Improved standards in plant monitoring (e.g., M-audit criteria) – Number of workers per job

Source: Own illustration. Based on Milberg and Winkler (2011b, 349).
Note: FACB = freedom of association and collective bargaining, OEM = original equipment manufacture, ODM = original design manufacture, and OBM = original brand manufacture.

Putting this more formally, we can define value added *VA* as follows:

$$VA = WI + \Pi + TR \qquad (7.1)$$

where *WI* is wage income, Π is profit income and TR is tax revenue. But we can break *WI* into different varieties of labor:

$$WI = wL = \sum_v w_v L_v \qquad (7.2)$$

where $v = 1, \ldots, n$ denotes varieties of labor by skill, gender, ethnicity or other distinctions.

Upgrading might lower total employment by increasing demand for more skilled labor and reducing demand for low-skill labor by even more, for example. It might raise demand for very high-skill labor but raise demand for home-based or informal workers even more. It is thus difficult to construct a single indicator of social upgrading. In addition, there are qualitative aspects of social upgrading – the incidence of informality in labor markets, aspects of worker rights and labor standards, gender equity – that obviously cannot be extracted even from the most detailed information on value added.

Improved international competitiveness can also be a misleading indicator of upgrading, as it can be the result of a number of factors. Competitiveness is often measured by relative unit labor costs, *RULC*, as follows:

$$RULC = WI(1/LP)E \qquad (7.3)$$

where *RULC* designates relative unit labor costs, *WI* wage income, *LP* labor productivity, and *E* the nominal exchange rate.

From equation (7.3) we see that improvements in international competitiveness (a decline in *RULC*) can result from a decline in wages, an increase in labor productivity, or from a currency devaluation. To associate an increase in trade performance with "upgrading" veils the contribution of these different aspects of competitiveness. Studies of Chinese and Mexican export expansions, for example, show that all of these factors played some role. In both of these cases, productivity growth outpaced wage growth, leading to declining *RULC*.[7]

Careful analysis of trade performance can help. Amighini (2006) decomposes the change in a sector's exports into three components: (i) external market conditions; (ii) change in market share; (iii) change in product price.

---

[7] On China, see Ceglowski and Golub (2005). On Mexico, see Palma (2003).

Kaplinsky and Readman (2004), in a study of the wood furniture industry, develop a similar framework, focusing on market share and export unit value as indicators of upgrading. Upgrading occurs when there is relatively good price performance and stable or growing market share. Amighini (2006) defines upgrading similarly, that is, when there is a rise in product price with an increase (or no decrease) in market share. This is a particularly important approach to analyzing upgrading on the basis of trade data, and we adopt it in our analysis below of economic upgrading in four GVCs: horticulture, apparel, mobile phones, and tourism. In the following, we focus on the relationship between economic and social upgrading first at the national level and then at the level of the GVC.

7.2.2 Economic and Social Upgrading at the National Level

Economic Upgrading
Beyond the question of variable choice is the issue of magnitude. How much change in a given variable is enough to constitute upgrading or its opposite, downgrading? The starting point here is the analysis of economic growth. Kaldor (1954) posits that manufacturing productivity growth serves as the driver for economic growth generally across the economy because of scale economies and learning in manufacturing that raise productivity throughout the economy. The growth in labor productivity is by definition equal to the difference in the growth of output and the growth of employment. Kaldor theorized that output growth is itself a function of the growth of output in the manufacturing sector, giving the Kaldor-Verdoorn "law": productivity growth in manufacturing is a function of the growth in manufacturing output (Pieper 2000).

Kaldor's law leads us to a central question in the era of EOI: Does export growth generate economic growth? Empirical research gives conflicting results (see, for example, the extensive literature review in Harrison and Rodríguez-Clare 2009). Earlier cross-sectional or pooled studies generally support the export-led growth hypothesis, but have well-known econometric weaknesses. Frankel and Romer (1999) find a clear and positive link between exports and economic growth for a sample of 63 countries for the year 1985. But cross-country growth regressions are notoriously difficult to interpret. Sali-i-Martin (1997) identifies 22 of the 59 variables tested as reasonably robust in his (two million!) cross-country growth regressions. Trade openness is not one of the 22 variables. Rodrik et al. (2002) argue that institutions are more important than exports and "location." They write that:

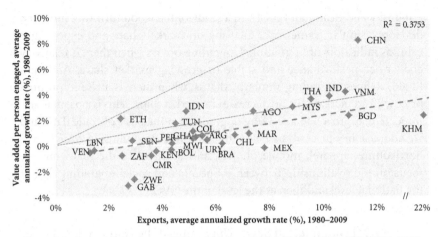

Figure 7.3. Growth in Export and Value Added per Person Engaged (CAGR), 1980–2009. *Source*: Own illustration. Based on Milberg and Winkler (2011b, 352). Data: United Nations Conference on Trade and Development (UNCTAD) Handbook of Statistics, World Bank World Development Indicators and Groningen Growth and Development Centre Total Economy Database. Countries above upper dotted line = "strong absolute upgrading"; countries above middle dotted line = "weak absolute upgrading"; countries above dashed OLS regression line = "relative upgrading". Note: Exports and value added at 2005 prices. CAGR = Compound annual growth rate.

Once institutions are controlled for, integration has no direct effects on income, while geography has at best weak direct effects. We find that trade often enters the income regression with the "wrong" (i.e. negative) sign, as do many of the geographical indicators (Rodrik et al. 2002, 4).

Hausmann et al. (2006), on the other hand, develop a measure of the income content of exports using the concept of revealed comparative advantage and find this measure to be statistically significantly related to economic growth, indicating that countries exporting a higher value added bundle of goods and services are likely to have a higher rate of economic growth. They conclude that "what you export matters."

Figure 7.3 is a scatterplot of export growth and the growth in value added per worker (labor productivity) in the period 1980 from 2009 for a sample of 30 developing countries (see Appendix 7.1 for the country sample). Our analysis is simply suggestive – a rigorous test would require considerably more attention to sectoral and firm-level patterns – that even at very aggregate levels some of the basic presumptions about the connections between trade and economic upgrading and social upgrading may not hold. We have drawn the ordinary least squares (OLS) regression line in Figure 7.3, and we see that export growth is on average associated with higher

Table 7.4. *Classification of Upgrading, Thirty-Country Sample, 1980–2009*

Strong absolute upgrading $z > 1$	Weak absolute upgrading $z > 1/3$	Relative upgrading $z > 1/\beta + c$
	Angola	Angola
	China	China
	Ethiopia	Colombia
	India	Ethiopia
	Indonesia	India
	Malaysia	Indonesia
	Thailand	Malaysia
	Tunisia	Senegal
	Vietnam	Thailand
		Tunisia
		Vietnam

Source: Own illustration. Based on Milberg and Winkler (2011b, 353). Data: Based on Figure 7.3.

value added per worker. A similar pattern emerges when we look at high-tech exports as a share of exports in relation to value added per worker (not shown here). These scatterplots indicate in general that export growth is associated with economic upgrading.

A closer look at the data in Figure 7.3 shows this. We calculate an "upgrading ratio," z, as the ratio of the growth in value added to the growth in exports and define three measures of upgrading as follows:

If $z > 1$, then "strong absolute upgrading" (upper dotted line);

If $z > 1/3$ then "weak absolute upgrading" (middle dotted line);

If $z > 1/\beta + c$ (where β is the slope coefficient and c is the constant of the regression line), then "relative upgrading" (dashed OLS regression line).

Table 7.4 shows the countries in the sample that satisfy each of the criteria for upgrading.

Notably, no countries in the thirty-country sample satisfy the criterion for absolute upgrading and only nine satisfy the criterion for "weak absolute upgrading" and eleven surpass the criterion for "relative upgrading." Perhaps as expected, many of the upgrading countries are Asian (Vietnam, India, China, Indonesia, Thailand, and Malaysia) and none are from Latin America. This is consistent with the case study literature, especially as it relates to apparel and electronics.

Even if we accept a low threshold for economic upgrading, the simple correlation analysis does not provide an explanation of causation. Does exporting raise productivity ("learning-by-exporting") or is there self-selection by high productivity growth firms into export markets? Once again, research is inconclusive, with different studies drawing opposite conclusions depending on the country and time period under study (see also the literature review in Wagner 2007).

Social Upgrading

None of this is very promising for our understanding of the broad correlates of economic upgrading. In particular, we find that economic upgrading is not guaranteed, even with successful export performance. Here we take the analysis one step further by asking what such upgrading means for living standards, including wages, work conditions, economic rights, gender equality, and economic security. We refer to improvements in these aspects of economic and social life as social upgrading. As a first exercise we concentrate on the most basic expressions of this: employment and pay.

Despite the paucity of successful cases of economic upgrading identified in our previous cross-national sample, we found that in general export growth performance and economic upgrading were positively correlated. Still, if we go back to our cross-country evidence on upgrading, we can quickly see (Figure 7.3) that Mexico, Peru, Bolivia, and Peru can be characterized by economic downgrading over the sample period, because they are not only below the three lines, but experienced positive export growth and negative growth in per worker value added.

The link between economic upgrading and social upgrading is even weaker, and there is a great need for an improved understanding of the connection. Neither of the well-developed empirical literatures on economic upgrading – that is, neither the vast array of econometric and accounting work on the causes of economic growth, nor the value chain case study research on industrial upgrading – have clearly identified, much less theorized, the connection between economic and social upgrading.

The link between economic upgrading and social upgrading is rooted in economic theory that sees wage growth closely tied to productivity growth. If we accept productivity growth (such as changes in output per worker) as a proxy for economic upgrading and wage growth as a reasonable representation of social upgrading, then we can look to economic theory for an explanation of the relation between economic and social upgrading. As is often the case in economics, there are competing theories – in this case mainly neoclassical and institutionalist – and no clear consensus view on which theory is better.

In neoclassical theory, wages in a competitive market are given by the marginal revenue product of labor, a function both of the marginal productivity of labor and of the product market price of labor's output. This implies that wages rise as the marginal productivity of labor rises, assuming the price of the good produced remains constant. For our purposes here, the theory implies that, other things equal, social upgrading is the result of industrial upgrading (a rise in productivity). Flanagan (2005) analyzes pay and productivity growth in a 45-country sample for the apparel and the footwear sectors in the period from 1995 to 1999 and shows an extremely high correlation. This gives support to the marginal productivity theory of income distribution and the notion that economic upgrading drives social upgrading in individual sectors. Van Biesebroeck (2011) tests the theory for three countries (Kenya, Tanzania, and Zimbabwe) and finds the theory supported only in the case of Zimbabwe. He attributes the failure to "localized labor markets and imperfect substitutability of worker-types" (Van Biesebroeck 2011, 1333).

In a monopsony labor market, firms are still assumed to be profit maximizing, but because the labor force faces a single employer the result is a "margin of exploitation," which is the amount that the wage falls below the marginal revenue product of labor. This implies a constant deviation between productivity and pay (Manning 2005). There are few empirical studies of the margin of exploitation in developing countries. One study of manufacturing firms in Indonesia finds that more than half have a "significant amount of market power" rooted mainly in the characteristics of the firms rather than in the overall labor market conditions (Brummund 2011).

From an institutionalist perspective, wages are understood to be a function of the relative power of labor versus management and in which labor market regulations and their enforcement play an important role in determining outcomes. Union density, bargaining rights, minimum wages, and active labor market policies have been found to be significant determinants of labor market outcomes in developed and developing economies.[8] Here the tight connection between productivity growth and wages is not guaranteed but will depend on the context: Wages are the outcome of a bargaining process whose outcome depends on the relative strength of the two sides and with labor market institutions informing the relative position of the two sides. In such a context, social upgrading is delinked from technological change *per se* and associated also with social institutions.

---

[8] On developed countries, see Howell (2005). On developing countries, see Berg and Kucera (2007).

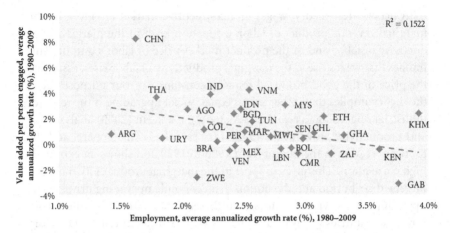

Figure 7.4. Growth in Value Added per Person Engaged and Employment (CAGR), 1980–2009. *Source*: Own illustration. Based on Milberg and Winkler (2011b, 359). Data: United Nations Statistics Division (National Accounts Main Aggregates Database), UNCTAD Handbook of Statistics, Groningen Growth and Development Centre Total Economy Database. Countries above dashed OLS regression line = "relative upgrading". Note: Value added at 2005 prices. CAGR = Compound annual growth rate.

By definition, a growing gap between productivity and wages is equivalent to a rise in the share of national income going to profits. As we saw in Chapter 5, the profit share has risen in the major industrialized countries since the mid-1980s. Less well documented is a similar pattern in developing countries. Harrison (2002) finds that trade openness has been associated with a rising profit share across a large sample of developing countries. This finding does not directly contradict the neoclassical theory, but it raises questions about the extent to which social upgrading is accomplished through trade liberalization.

Analysis of our sample of thirty developing countries reveals that the connection between economic and social upgrading is weaker than the connection between export growth and economic upgrading. At the simplest level, higher exports, all other things equal, are generally associated with higher employment. This is borne out by the positive correlation between export growth and employment growth in our sample (not shown here), although when we look just at high-tech exports, there is no measurable employment effect across countries (Milberg and Winkler 2011b). Figure 7.4 shows the relation between the growth in value added per worker and the growth in employment. The correlation is very low, and the OLS regression line slopes negatively – indicating that higher labor productivity growth is associated with lower employment growth.[9] Employment, too, can be a deceptive measure of social upgrading, because it doesn't account for pay, the quality of work, the standards of employment, or the degree of informal or unpaid labor.

The data thus suggest that economic upgrading does not instantly translate into social upgrading. Since simple correlations say nothing about causality, we must also consider the inverse relation. That is, does social upgrading adversely affect international trade performance? Social upgrading (higher pay or labor standards) is typically thought to raise production costs and by implication reduce international competitiveness (for an overview of the "conventional wisdom," see Kucera 2001).

If adopted in one country, social upgrading should lead to reduced international competitiveness. This implies a feedback from economic upgrading in GPNs to social upgrading to a deterioration in international trade performance and a reduction in inward FDI. But the conventional wisdom is not supported by the evidence across a broad sample of developing countries. Kucera (2001) models labor costs and FDI flows as a function of a series of indicators of core labor standards for a sample of 127 countries. His findings fail to confirm the view that adherence to higher labor standards raises labor costs and reduces inward FDI. If social upgrading does not adversely impact trade performance then it may be the result of improved productivity and product quality that results from improved pay and work conditions. A similar dynamic emerges in research on gender and trade, as we show in Section 7.3.

In addition to the extensive evidence on social upgrading at the national and sectoral levels is an accumulating body of research on the monitoring of labor standards. These studies are based on both interviews with auditors and on independent observation. The research gives varied results. Piore and Schrank (2008) observe that labor monitors in the Dominican Republic have used a variety of techniques to make a marked difference on the enforcement of labor standards there. Locke et al. (2007a, 2007b) conclude that Nike's "management audit" had a minimal and inconsistent impact on labor standards over repeated audits. Locke et al. (2007a) find that it is the commitment over time of the supplier to the buyer firm rather than coercion *per se* that supports upgrading.

The premise of the research on plant-level monitoring of labor standards is that social upgrading can be attained through regulation and monitoring

---

[9] A similarly ambiguous result is found in the correlation between growth in the intensity of high-technology exports and employment (Milberg and Winkler 2011b).

and thus does not require economic upgrading or even economic growth as a prerequisite. This view is at odds with most of economic theory – both neoclassical and Keynesian – in which social upgrading is viewed as endogenous to the process of economic and productivity growth. In the neoclassical view, higher marginal productivity results in higher wages. In the Keynesian view, higher levels of aggregate demand lead to greater labor demand and (other things equal) higher wages. These two perspectives on social upgrading – call them sociological and economic – not only indicate very different research programs, they also give very different policy conclusions. It is likely that there is some truth in both views. Kucera and Sarna (2004), for example, propose that some labor standards (such as child labor) are a function of per capita income and others (for example, freedom of association and collective bargaining rights) are not (Polaski 2008). Robertson et al. (2011) find that Cambodian apparel firms that complied with labor standards under the International Labor Office "Better Work" program also saw improved performance in terms of productivity and exports.

7.2.3 Economic and Social Upgrading in Global Value Chains[10]

The analysis so far in this chapter is at the level of countries, while throughout this book we have insisted that the appropriate unit of analysis for the study of dynamics of trade and distribution is the GVC. Data availability is a problem at the level of the GVC, so we confine our analysis to a few sectors and a very parsimonious definition of economic and social upgrading.[11] Even more than in the aggregate analysis, the GVC-level evidence shows that there is considerable slippage between the cup of economic upgrading and the lip of social upgrading.

Bernhardt and Milberg (2011) study four GVCs – apparel, horticulture, mobile phones, and tourism – and ten to twenty countries in each GVC. They find that in only half the cases of economic upgrading is there also social upgrading, but that when social upgrading occurs it is almost invariably accompanied by economic upgrading. Thus, economic upgrading seems to be a necessary but not sufficient condition for social upgrading. This begs the question: what policies and institutions strengthen the connection

---

[10] This section draws on Bernhardt and Milberg (2011).
[11] The selection of sectors is based on ongoing research project, "Capturing the Gains from Globalization." See www.capturingthegains.org for a full description of the program.

between the two dimensions of upgrading? We leave this important question for Chapter 8. Our discussion below focuses on social and economic upgrading and downgrading in apparel and mobile phones, although we briefly mention also the findings for horticulture and tourism.[12]

Economic Upgrading

Bernhardt and Milberg (2011) define economic upgrading/downgrading as the result of changes in export market share and changes in export unit value. The interpretation of the four quadrants of the diagrams is the following: The upper right and the lower left quadrants represent instances of clear economic upgrading and clear economic downgrading, respectively, whereas the remaining two quadrants include the intermediate cases. Note that this definition of upgrading is less strict than the definition of economic upgrading at the national level (see Section 7.2.2). A country experiences upgrading in a sector if export unit values and export market shares show positive growth over a given period. In contrast to our three measures of upgrading at the national level, upgrading doesn't require one measure to be larger than the other.

In the apparel sector, none of the countries in the sample experienced clear-cut economic downgrading over the period from 1990 to 2009 (see Figure 7.5). However, if we look just at the 2000s, then both El Salvador and Guatemala were clear downgraders. The ending of the Multi-Fiber Arrangement in 2005 played an important role, as China and a few other countries captured a much bigger share of world exports. Nicaragua's export market share shot up in the period from 1990 to 2009, but with a significant slowdown of market share gains in the second half of the period. It also experienced a slight fall in export unit values over the period. In sum, Bernhardt and Milberg (2011) find that export market share growth is generally associated with less-than-proportional growth or declines in export unit values at the GVC level.

The mobile phone sector (see Figure 7.6) came into being in the period under study and thus the growth rates are from extremely low levels. Nonetheless, aspects of the industry exhibit enormous competitive pressure among suppliers and rapidly changing technological demands. In this environment, most of the countries in the Bernhardt and Milberg sample were able to achieve economic upgrading with both gains in export market

---

[12] Results for all sectors and countries, along with a test of the robustness of the results, can be found in Bernhardt and Milberg (2011).

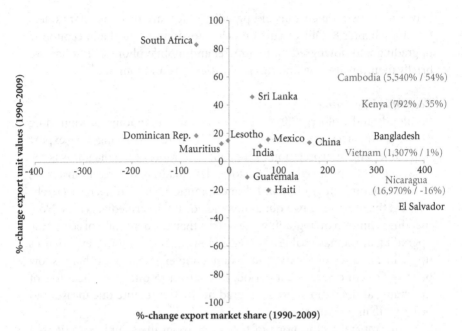

Figure 7.5. Economic Upgrading in Apparel, 1990–2009 (%-change in market share and unit values, 3-year moving averages). *Source*: Bernhardt and Milberg (2011).

share and export unit value growth. There are only three developing countries among the fifteen leading exporters in the sector. These three countries, however, occupy top spots. China ranks first, whereas Mexico and Malaysia are the world's fifth- and ninth-largest exporters. Apart from these exceptions, the technology intensity of the mobile telecom sector guarantees that the world market is dominated by exports from the advanced economies, and the huge majority of the countries in the sample play very small roles as exporters. Bernhardt and Milberg (2011) have not included the raw materials such as coltan in their definition of the mobile telecom sector, thus understating the importance of developing countries within the GVC.[13]

Over the last twenty years, changes in market shares were relatively minor for most Latin American and Caribbean countries. The notable exceptions are the two most competitive exporters, Mexico and Brazil, both of which managed to increase their market shares since 1990. Meanwhile, mobile telecom exports from almost all the Asian countries in the sample went up significantly – and today some of them are important players. The stellar performer is China, which managed to ramp up its market share from

---

[13] On "conflict coltan" and the mobile phone supply chain, see Nathan and Sarkar (2011).

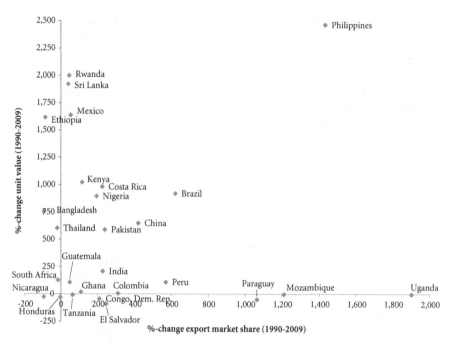

Figure 7.6. Economic Upgrading in Mobile Telecom, 1990–2009 (%-change in market share and unit values, 3-year moving averages). *Source*: Bernhardt and Milberg (2011).

2.5 percent in 1990 to 37.4 percent in 2009. Vietnam and the Philippines represent similar success stories, albeit at much lower levels (reaching export market shares of 0.18 percent and 0.39 percent, respectively, in 2009). Two-thirds of the countries in the sample recorded an increase in the unit values of their mobile telecom exports over the last decade.

In total, eighteen out of twenty-nine countries managed to economically upgrade in the mobile telecom sector during the last decade, with especially impressive performance by Brazil, Costa Rica and Haiti. The upgraders include countries from all three (sub-)continents. Between 2000 and 2009, the only countries that experienced outright economic downgrading were Honduras and Nicaragua.

In horticulture, only six out of nineteen countries studied by Bernhardt and Milberg (2011) experienced economic upgrading between 1990 and 2009. Uganda was the most impressive success story, increasing its market share seventy-eight-fold (albeit from very low levels in the early 1990s) and its export unit values six-fold during the last twenty years. Ethiopia and Kenya also stand out, as both were able to more than double the unit value of their horticulture exports while increasing their market shares more than seven-fold and three-fold, respectively. In Latin America, Chile and Ecuador were the only clear economic upgraders from 1990 to 2009, the latter recording an impressive growth in the unit values of its exports of 150 percent during this period. The only country in the sample whose horticulture sector experienced clear economic downgrading was Thailand, losing almost 40 percent of its market share and seeing its export unit values decrease by a quarter between 1990 and 2009.

On a global scale, developing countries do not (yet) play a leading role as exporters of tourism services. Among the top fifteen tourism exporters, there are only three developing countries: China is ranked sixth, while Turkey and Thailand have the tenth and eleventh largest world export market shares, respectively. The rest of the ranking is dominated by North American and European countries. The developing countries in the sample are, thus, all rather small players in the global tourism industry. Among them, the most important exporter of tourism services is China, with a world market share of 4.5 percent in 2007. Its continuous gains in market share (up from a bit more than one percent in 1990) have actually earned China a place among the top six world exporters, only slightly behind the United Kingdom. India is the only other Asian country in the sample with a world market share exceeding one percent (namely 1.3 percent in 2007). After gaining market shares in the first half of the 1990s (from 0.97 percent in 1990 up to 1.03 percent in 1994), it dramatically lost market shares until the early 2000s (down to 0.64 percent in 2002), when it started to regain ground. The same pattern (with market share losses in the 1990s and gains in the 2000s) can actually also be observed for Brazil, Kenya, Jordan, and South Africa. Meanwhile, Costa Rica and Uganda steadily increased their export market shares, whereas Indonesia's, Jamaica's, and Nepal's tourism sectors were in continuous decline.

Unlike commodities whose unit value measure is relatively straightforward, services – and tourism in particular – are not so simple. In view of the data available in UNCTAD's Handbook of Statistics 2009, Bernhardt and Milberg (2011) divided the value of tourism services exports by the number of arrivals of visitors, in order to derive a measure for export unit values, namely "travel expenditures per visitor" (in $). Using this measure of unit values in tourism exports, they find that more than half the countries in the sample experienced declines between 1990 and 2007. Among the African and Latin American and Caribbean countries in the sample, two out of three earned less in travel expenditures per foreign visitor in 2007 than in 1990 (namely Kenya and South Africa, and Brazil and Jamaica). In Africa,

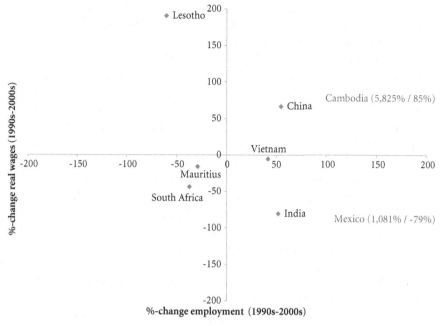

Figure 7.7. Social Upgrading in Apparel, Early 1990s-Late 2000s (%-change in employment and real wages, 3-year moving averages). *Source*: Bernhardt and Milberg (2011).

the exception to this downward trend is Uganda, whereas in Latin America the only country where visitors from abroad increased their expenditures is Costa Rica. Among the Asian countries in the sample, three countries experienced a decline in tourism export unit values (Indonesia, Jordan, Nepal) and three countries an increase (China, India, Vietnam). During 1990 to 2007, all countries in the sample experienced either clear economic upgrading or clear economic downgrading in their tourism sectors. Five countries experienced upgrading and seven experienced downgrading.

Social Upgrading

Bernhardt and Milberg (2011) define social upgrading/downgrading also as having two dimensions, employment, and real wages. The interpretation of the four quadrants of the diagrams is analogous to the case of economic upgrading, with the upper right and lower left showing cases of unambiguous upgrading and downgrading, respectively and the other quadrants representing mixed outcomes. In the apparel sector (see Figure 7.7), clearcut social upgrading was rare over the last two decades. There are only two unambiguous cases of social upgrading, Cambodia and China. However, while China's improvements in terms of employment and real wages were rather modest (around 60 percent each over two decades), Cambodia experienced a doubling of real wages and an almost sixty-fold increase in employment. At the other extreme, all the African countries in the sample recorded a decline in employment. While in Lesotho this was at least accompanied by an increase in real wages (actually the highest in the sample, reaching an impressive +191 percent between 2001 and 2007), in Mauritius and South Africa workers' pay in real terms went down too so that their apparel sectors experienced social downgrading.

A common pattern observed in the apparel sector data was increased employment and declining real wages, consistent with our analysis of the expanded use of EPZs and mostly female labor in GVC production in that sector. Mexico exhibits this in dramatic fashion, with a ten-fold increase in employment and a 79 percent decline in real wages. Only India's apparel sector witnessed a more dramatic fall in real wages (81 percent). Meanwhile, Vietnam came close to social upgrading in apparel, with a negligible fall in real wages and employment growth of 42 percent. Of course, the data sets employed here capture only formal employment, and the apparel and horticulture sectors are notorious for their use of informal labor. This would amplify the observed increase in employment and decline in real wages.

In the mobile telecom sector (see Figure 7.8), social upgrading is scarcer than in apparel, largely driven by the fact that very few countries experienced gains in real wages. The only unambiguous success story was China, where employment doubled and real wages increased by 50 percent. On the other hand, a third of all the countries experienced declines in both dimensions of social downgrading. The worst performer was South Africa where employment went down by 58 percent and real wages by 57 percent, respectively. The decline in real wages was more dramatic in both Brazil and the Philippines, the two other clear-cut social downgraders, yet they at least saw a less drastic reduction in employment (−19 and −35 percent, respectively) as compared to South Africa.

Most of the countries in the sample have to be classified as intermediate cases. Mexico again had considerable employment growth and a large fall in real wages (−71 percent). Colombia's experience is exactly reverse: while employment shrank by a record -88 percent, workers saw an increase in real wages of +12 percent. The remaining intermediate cases, all of which are Asian countries, went through less extreme changes in their social performance, with India being the only case where real wages increased (by 68

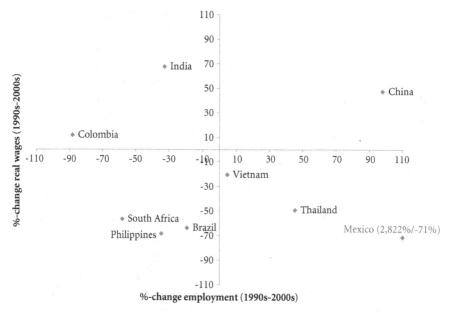

Figure 7.8. Social Upgrading in Mobile Telecom, Early 1990s-Late 2000s (%-change in employment and real wages, 3-year moving averages). *Source*: Bernhardt and Milberg (2011).

percent) whereas Thailand and Vietnam registered growth in employment but a decrease in real wages. In sum, Bernhardt and Milberg (2011) find that social downgrading is more common than economic downgrading.

Tourism and horticulture are more difficult to assess in terms of social upgrading. Employment data are not reliable in horticulture and wage data are often not available in tourism. We summarize here only the findings on tourism. Employment in the tourism sector increased in all the countries in the sample over the past two decades. In absolute terms, the two Asian giants, China and India, have the highest numbers of employees in the tourism sector. In 2009, the Indian tourism industry provided jobs for 18.4 million people, whereas the Chinese industry employed 16.7 million people. Both figures have grown considerably since 1990, when tourism employment in both countries amounted to about 11.7 million. Brazil and Indonesia rank third and fourth in terms of the number of jobs; both had more than two million employees in the tourism industry in 2009. However, they experienced much slower growth in tourism jobs than China and India.

Uganda experienced some of the most rapid increases in tourism employment (up from 43,700 jobs in 1990 to 182,500 jobs in 2009). This contrasts with the experience of the two other African countries in the sample, Kenya and South Africa, where employment growth was more moderate (from 151,000 to 197,000 and from 252,000 to 389,000, respectively, between 1990 and 2009). Similar intra-regional discrepancies can be observed in Latin America and the Caribbean. Here, Brazil and Jamaica (up from 67,900 to 85,800 jobs) experienced only sluggish job growth in the tourism sector, whereas in Costa Rica employment increased quite dramatically over the last twenty years (from 52,400 to 118,900 jobs). Meanwhile, in Asia, tourism employment growth was significant in Jordan and Nepal (from 53,800 and 141,700 to 130,400 and 274,400 jobs, respectively) but rather slow in Vietnam (from 951,000 to 1.4 million jobs).

Among those countries for which data on both wages and employment in tourism are available, three are unequivocal upgraders, whereas two represent intermediate cases, so there are no clear-cut downgraders. The top performer is China's tourism sector, where workers saw an exceptional, twenty-fold increase of their real wages; yet employment grew only by around 20 percent. Meanwhile, Costa Rica's achievements are also impressive: employment more than doubled, while real wages went up by 82 percent. In India, the number of tourism jobs grew faster than in China (+41 percent), but the rise in real wages (+40 percent) fell short of that in the two other upgraders, China and Costa Rica.

Economic versus Social Upgrading
A central purpose of this section is to analyze the relationship between economic and social upgrading. Bernhardt and Milberg (2011) have defined economic upgrading as a combination of changes in export market shares and changes in export unit values. Social upgrading is defined by changes in employment and changes in real wages. Is improved export performance associated with better labor market conditions? To begin to address this question, Bernhardt and Milberg (2011) use the data previously presented to create a single index of economic upgrading and a single index of social upgrading and the authors plot them together. This allows an analysis of the relation between economic and social upgrading in a 2 × 2 matrix, a prototype of which is depicted in Figure 7.9. Of the four different scenarios, the upper right and the lower left quadrants represent the clear-cut cases. The upper right quadrant includes those countries that combine economic upgrading and social upgrading for "overall upgrading." In the lower left quadrant, on the other hand, will be those countries that experienced both economic and social downgrading and that, therefore, have to be called "overall downgraders." Countries falling in the remaining two quadrants

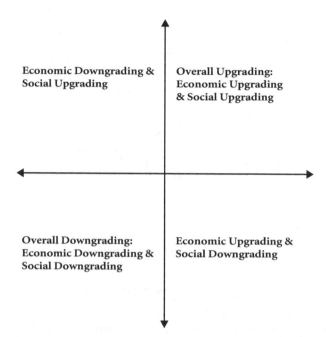

Figure 7.9. Prototype Matrix of Economic and Social Upgrading. *Source*: Bernhardt and Milberg (2013). This material was originally published in *The Oxford Handbook of Offshoring and Global Employment*, edited by Bardhan, A., D. Jaffee, and C. Kroll (2013), and has been reproduced by permission of Oxford University Press [http://www.oup.com/us/catalog/general/series/OxfordHandbooks/].

are again intermediate cases, with success on one front (either economic or social) but lack of progress on the other front. Therefore, their experiences are harder to be interpreted as either clear "overall" upgrading or downgrading.

Bernhardt and Milberg (2011) propose a simple method for combining the two variables in each realm which gives equal weight to each component. To get an indicator for economic upgrading, for example, a weight of 50 percent each is assigned to both the percentage change in export market share and the percentage change in export unit value.

The apparel sector has also many cases of overall upgrading, as shown in Figure 7.10. Five of the eight countries for which data are available appear in the upper right quadrant of clear overall upgraders. Among them, Cambodia is the prime performer with formidable upgrading in both economic and social terms. Other outstanding performers include Vietnam (on the economic front) and Mexico (on the social front). The remaining two upgraders' progress was less pronounced, particularly China's. Lesotho

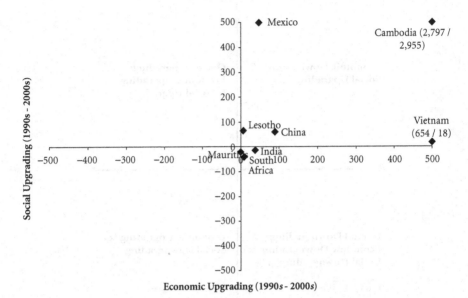

Figure 7.10. Economic and Social Upgrading and Downgrading in Apparel, 1990s–2000s. *Source*: Bernhardt and Milberg (2013). This material was originally published in *The Oxford Handbook of Offshoring and Global Employment*, edited by Bardhan, A., D. Jaffee, and C. Kroll (2013) and has been reproduced by permission of Oxford University Press [http://www.oup.com/us/catalog/general/series/OxfordHandbooks/].

exhibits social upgrading without economic upgrading. Mauritius is the single case of full-fledged overall downgrading in the apparel sector. The remaining two countries in the sample, India and South Africa, are categorized as intermediate cases. Both have experienced upgrading in the economic sphere but downgrading in the social sphere. Overall, when judged by Figure 7.10, there seems to be a positive relationship between economic upgrading and social upgrading in the apparel sector.

In the mobile telecom sector there is ubiquitous economic upgrading but very little social upgrading. As can be seen in Figure 7.11, all of the countries in the sample are located to the right of the vertical axis, implying that there is not a single case of economic downgrading. The best overall performer is clearly Mexico with spectacular upgrading on both the economic and the social fronts. Mexico's social performance is particularly noteworthy, especially when compared to the sluggish or, even more often, entirely absent social progress in the other countries. In fact, the two Asian giants, China and India, are the only other countries that qualify as overall upgraders in the mobile telecom sector. Both combine an excellent economic performance with weak social upgrading. All

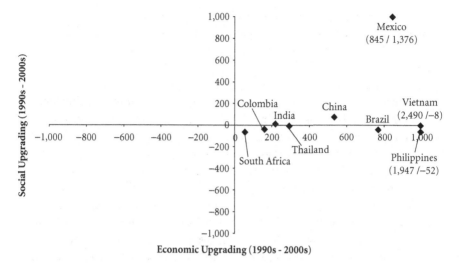

Figure 7.11. Economic and Social Upgrading and Downgrading in Mobile Telecom, 1990s–2000s. *Source*: Bernhardt and Milberg (2013). This material was originally published in *The Oxford Handbook of Offshoring and Global Employment*, edited by Bardhan, A., D. Jaffee, and C. Kroll (2013) and has been reproduced by permission of Oxford University Press [http://www.oup.com/us/catalog/general/series/OxfordHandbooks/].

the remaining countries in the sample are intermediate cases – invariably because of a lack of social upgrading. These include some very strong economic performers, however, most notably the Philippines, Vietnam, and Brazil. Brazil and Colombia experienced significant degree of total economic upgrading but also quite pronounced total social downgrading. By far the worst performer in the sample is South Africa, which recorded the smallest improvements in economic terms and the largest deteriorations in social terms.

In the tourism sector, developments are inverse of those seen in the mobile telecom sector: While there is widespread social upgrading (experienced by *all* of the countries in the sample for which data were available), there is somewhat less economic upgrading. All the countries are situated above the horizontal axis, signaling that they have registered social upgrading. Among them, three (namely China, Costa Rica, and India) also experienced economic upgrading so that we observe three instances of overall upgrading in the tourism sector. China is the premier performer with remarkable economic upgrading but even more impressive social upgrading. In Costa Rica, the pattern (economic upgrading combined with even more social upgrading) is the same, albeit at a smaller scale. In fact, this pattern – with the social performance trumping the economic performance – can also be observed for the two intermediate cases, Brazil and Jordan. These two countries recorded social upgrading but economic downgrading. The only exception to the pattern previously described is India, the third overall upgrader, which is the only country in the sample whose economic performance in tourism was better than its social performance.

In horticulture, the majority of countries in the sample exhibit both economic and social upgrading. The most outstanding performer is Belize with impressive upgrading on both the economic and the social front. It is interesting to note that Bangladesh is the second stellar performer with significant improvements in both economic and social terms. Advances were more modest in the remaining upgraders, namely Brazil, El Salvador, and Mexico, with the latter scoring high on the social front while recording only a very small improvement on the economic front. In the lower left quadrant, Honduras figures as the only straightforward overall horticultural downgrader in the sample, with regress notably in the social sphere. The two intermediate cases in the sample, Costa Rica and Nicaragua, have opposing experiences: While Costa Rica improved on the social front but did not manage to do so on the economic front (although only narrowly), Nicaragua was not able to accompany its economic success with social progress. Overall, however, there appears to be a positive correlation between economic upgrading and social upgrading in the horticulture sector.

Although we have framed the analysis in this chapter in terms of upgrading in GVCs, the findings also have implications for economic theory relating productivity growth (economic upgrading) and wages (social upgrading). Referring to the marginal productivity theory of wages (or returns to factors of production more generally), economists often claim that higher productivity also leads to higher compensation or remuneration (see section 7.2.2).[14] In the context of our analysis, this view would translate into saying that economic upgrading should lead to social upgrading.

This framework does not allow for a direct test of this relation, however, the results cast doubt on the theory. A first indication of this discordance is provided by the scatter plots previously presented, most notably for the mobile telecom and tourism sectors, where no clear pattern emerges. Across countries and sectors, Bernhardt and Milberg (2011) have a total of 30 data points or data pairs for economic upgrading/downgrading and social upgrading/downgrading; according to method 1, only 16 of these 30 data pairs have the same sign for economic upgrading/downgrading and social upgrading/downgrading. This does not make a compelling case for

---

[14] For a textbook presentation of this idea, see Mas-Colell et al. (1995) or Varian (1992).

the proposition that social upgrading goes hand in hand with economic upgrading. We should emphasize that all that these exercises can at best indicate a *correlation* between developments in the economic and social spheres. They tell us nothing about the *direction of causality* between the two. Causality may plausibly run in either direction, and there is empirical evidence on both sides, as discussed in section 7.2.2.

Contrary to the spirit of much case study of GVCs, Bernhardt and Milberg's (2011) analysis using published data and an admittedly parsimonious definition of upgrading shows that economic downgrading and social downgrading are both fairly regular occurrences, with social downgrading more common in particular because of stagnant real wages. Contrary to standard economic theory on the relation between productivity growth and wage growth, the authors find that there is a variety in the pattern observed across GVCs in the relation between economic and social upgrading: In apparel and horticulture, the authors generally find a positive correlation between economic upgrading and social upgrading. In mobile phones, there is widespread economic upgrading without social upgrading. In tourism, there are many cases of social upgrading with less economic upgrading. Overall, economic and social upgrading occurred together in fifteen to seventeen out of thirty cases. In sum, this evidence shows that economic upgrading does not automatically translate into social upgrading. Equally interesting, however, is that in all sectors except tourism (with the exception of Costa Rica in horticulture), there is no social upgrading without economic upgrading in the sample.

7.3 Gender Bias in Industrial Upgrading?[15]

The focus on social upgrading immediately raises the issue of gender and gender equity given the disproportionate role of women in the massive mobilization of labor that has occurred with EOI efforts in developing countries. Researchers have for decades found that "globalization" – an increase in trade openness, for example – is closely associated with "feminization," a rise in the female intensity of formal employment – especially in developing countries.

Women workers can create a competitive advantage for export-oriented firms that are engaged in price-cutting competition in the international market (Elson 2007). Standing (1989, 1999) attributes "global feminization" to the fact that women provide a cheaper and more flexible source of labor

[15] This section draws on Tejani and Milberg (2010).

than men and thus are preferred by employers seeking to expand exports by lowering labor costs, raise flexibility of hiring and firing in response to fluctuations in product demand, and to minimize the bargaining power of workers on issues of overtime, workplace safety, and collective bargaining. Structural adjustment in particular, Standing argues, created conditions in which firms increasingly hired women workers in order to cut labor costs and to "flexibilize" the labor force. Women were particularly suited to the task because they had lower aspirations and a lower efficiency wage, and were more easily employed as casual, contract or part-time labor with little or no benefits (Standing 1989).

Seguino (1997, 2000) also argues that the gender wage gap was an important basis for the heavy reliance on female labor in the East Asian export expansion and rapid economic growth in the 1990s (see also Carraway 2007). Busse and Spielman (2006) find that the gender wage gap is statistically correlated with higher exports of labor-intensive goods in a sample of ninety-two countries. Mitra-Kahn and Mitra-Kahn (2007) find that the relationship between gender wage inequality and growth for twenty developing countries is non-linear: low-skill export manufacturing is positively related to wage inequality while high-skill manufacturing is not.

Particularly striking is that SEZ employment – so crucial, as we previously saw, to the exports of many developing countries – has been intensively female, at levels near 90 percent in some countries (Nicaragua, Jamaica, El Salvador, and Bangladesh and near 80 percent in Sri Lanka, Honduras, and the Philippines, and in many countries at least double the level of female intensity in the overall economy (see Figure 7.12).

In contrast to these now-classic findings relating globalization and feminization, a number of recent studies have observed a defeminization of manufacturing employment in developing countries, even as globalization continues (Joekes 1999; United Nations 1999; Ghosh 2001; Cling and Letilly 2001; Jomo 2009). Tejani and Milberg (2010) consider middle-income countries and find that in the period from 1985 to 2006, Latin American and Caribbean middle-income countries continued to experience rising female intensity of manufacturing employment, but that most East Asian and Pacific countries have experienced a defeminization beginning in the mid-1980s. Western Europe and other industrialized countries also experienced a decline in the female intensity of manufacturing employment.[16]

---

[16] The focus here is on the middle-income countries of Latin America and Southeast Asia. Data are not available for many low-income countries. And the high-income countries have been the focus of study for decades. On the United States, see Black and Brainerd (2004) and Kongar (2007). On Japan and Germany, see Kucera (2001).

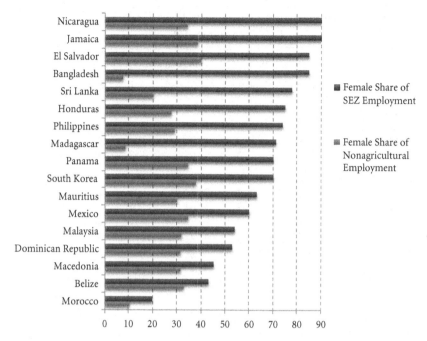

Figure 7.12. Female Share of SEZ Employment and Nonagricultural Employment, Selected Countries, 2005–2006. *Source:* Tejani (2011, 258). Note: SEZ = special economic zone. This figure has been reproduced by permission of The World Bank.

Table 7.5 shows the average level and growth rate of female intensity for all countries covered in the Tejani and Milberg (2010) sample. In general, defeminization in Southeast Asia accelerated in the period 1996 to 2007 even though Thailand was experiencing rising female labor intensity; Malaysia was defeminizing the most rapidly. The trend in the Latin American sample of large countries is exactly the reverse of that in Southeast Asia: feminization accelerated from the mid-1990s onwards in all cases except Colombia, with Brazil's female intensity of manufacturing employment growing the fastest. In the group of smaller Latin America countries, female intensity grew rapidly from 1985 to 1995 while defeminization set in during the following decade (see Table 7.5).

What can account for this pattern of feminization and defeminization? Tejani and Milberg (2010) present a model of female intensity of employment that comprises three main variables: growth in exports, growth in the capital intensity of production, and the gender wage gap. Industrial upgrading (for example, rising capital intensity) is expected to lower the female intensity of employment. A closing gender wage gap is associated

Table 7.5. *Female Intensity in Manufacturing, Selected Southeast Asian and Latin American Countries, 1985–2007*

East Asia	1985 to 1995		1996 to 2007		1985 to 2007	
	Average	Growth[c]	Average	Growth[c]	Average	Growth[c]
Indonesia	45.21	−0.52	42.59	0	43.84	−0.24
Malaysia	45.37	0	40.49	−0.65	42.83	−0.34
Philippines	46.78	0.02	45.76	−0.41	46.28	−0.21
Thailand	48.11	1.38	51.08	0.57	49.39	0.96
Latin America[a]						
Argentina	25.77	−0.41	28.08	1.24	27.36	0.8
Brazil	27.56	0.72	32.64	3.05	29.9	1.89
Chile	26.09	−0.23	26.71	0.16	26.45	−0.02
Colombia	40.11	1.56	45.21	0.53	42.77	1
Mexico	32.88	−3.67	36.95	2.12	35.76	0.67
Peru	29.23	0.03	.	.	31.96	1.57
Venezuela	27.29	1.08	30.54	2.43	28.59	1.64
Latin America[b]						
Costa Rica	36.08	1.7	32.78	−0.77	34.21	0.41
Dominican Rep.	.	.	32.87	−0.02	32.87	−0.02
El Salvador	44.85	1.76	50.75	0.12	47.8	0.9
Ecuador	35.09	2.98	34.85	−0.41	34.94	0.65
Panama	29.64	0.41	31.23	1.55	30.4	1.01

Source: Own illustration. Data: Tejani and Milberg (2010) based on ILO (2009). Note: Data availability varies by country.
[a] Large country sample. [b] Small country sample. [c] Average of annuals.

with a falling female intensity of labor as the demand for women's labor falls when they are no longer a cheap factor of production relative to men. This accords with the relation between the gender wage gap and the growth of exports implied by Becker's (1957) theory of discrimination, whereby greater competition through exports leads to the elimination of the gender wage gap. Finally, they posit that industrial upgrading is associated with more rapid growth in exports.

The model does not give a sense of the relative strength of the different factors affecting female intensity, nor the direction of causality among them. In econometric analysis, however, Tejani and Milberg (2010) find that the role of the gender wage gap is ambiguous, with the predicted inverse relation between relative wages and relative labor demand observed in some countries but a positive relation found for a number of others. In Brazil and

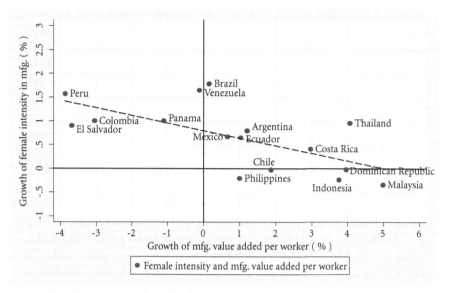

Figure 7.13. Female Intensity of Manufacturing Employment and Manufacturing Value Added per Worker, CAGR, 1985–2006. *Source*: Tejani and Milberg (2010). Data: ILO (2009) and WDI (2009). Note: a. Fitted Line: Y = 0.86 – 0.13X (Adj. R-squared = 0.24; t-stat. = –2.38). b. Data availability varies by country. See Tejani and Milberg (2010), Appendix B. CAGR = Compound annual growth rate.

Thailand, a narrowing wage gap is associated with rising female intensity; in Malaysia, the female intensity rises as the gender wage gap grows; and in Mexico, female intensity falls as the gender wage gap closes from 1996 to 2003. Costa Rica and El Salvador show no clear relationship; the same is true for Indonesia and the Philippines.

By far the most significant determinant of the change in feminization was the degree of industrial upgrading, as shown in Figure 7.13, where the growth in manufacturing value added per manufacturing worker is negatively related to the growth of female intensity. Presumably the strong correlation in Figure 7.13 is due to the fact that women have, on average, attained a lower level of skills than men and thus lose out in terms of employment when upgrading occurs. Defeminization in the presence of industrial upgrading makes economic sense if there is a skills bias to the shift in labor demand that occurs with upgrading and a distinct skill differential between men and women workers.

However, evidence on women's educational attainment relative to men does not support this view. In both East Asia and Latin America, female enrollment in tertiary education, and to a lesser extent in secondary education, generally exceeds that of males (Tejani and Milberg 2010). The gains in Latin America in tertiary education are particularly impressive – especially in Argentina, Brazil, Dominican Republic, and Panama – with Mexico and Peru being the only countries in which parity has not been achieved. In Southeast Asia, Malaysia and the Philippines have the highest level of secondary and tertiary enrollment although women in Indonesia and Thailand have also exceeded male educational attainment. Upgrading should thus not result in a defeminization due to labor supply shortages. In sum, the educational attainment of women puts into question the "skills mismatch" hypothesis regarding defeminization in middle-income countries.

As feminist accounts have emphasized for decades, the persistence of gender norms and stereotypes in the labor market is reflected directly in the segmentation of occupations by sex, which have a remarkable durability across regions and over time (Mehra and Gammage 1999). Sex segmentation of occupations is also influenced by factors such as barriers to entry because of the actions of labor market institutions, including male-dominated unions or government policy, and "pre-market discrimination" in education and training (see Milkman 1987; Rubery 1988; Badgett and Folbre 1999; ILO 2004; Williams 1991; United Nations 1999). Lower-tier supplier firms in GVCs often face severe product market competition and generally create jobs with lower pay, fewer benefits and less security (Anker 1997).

Women tend to be crowded in particular segments of the secondary sector because of gender stereotypes of women's abilities and characteristics, as well as their intermittent labor supply. Industrial upgrading in a context of gender-based labor market segmentation would appear to have a nonlinear relation to female employment, with female intensity rising as initial connections to GVCs are established within EPZs and other low-standard, low-productivity operations, and then later falling as industrial upgrading leads to a shift into primary segment activities.

7.4 Obstacles to Upgrading: Prebisch-Singer Trap for the Twenty-First Century?

We have argued that the conception of economic development has been transformed in the new wave of globalization, that is by the emergence of GVCs. Whereas previously EOI meant competing strictly according to final goods cost competitiveness, today the predominance of GPNs means that economic development is now closely tied to a nation's industries' ability to successfully enter these networks, to become a supplier in the supply chain, and then to "move up" into higher value added activities within the chain. "Industrial upgrading" is the new synonym for EOI.

There are a number of reasons why manufacturing export expansion does not translate into proportional economic upgrading. First is the fact that as GVCs become more complex, exports have greater import content, that is there is a higher level of vertical specialization, as discussed in Chapter 2. The result can be that measured export values can be associated with very different amounts of domestic value added. The Apple iPhone and iPod case studies reveal this in dramatic fashion, with Chinese domestic value added less than 5 percent of the value of Chinese exports to the United States in these products (Linden et al. 2007; Xing and Detert 2011).

A second issue is the terms of trade at which developing country exports are valued in the new wave of globalization. Chapter 4 argues that there is an asymmetry of market structures along GVCs, endogenous to lead firm corporate strategies that created GVCs, as oligopoly lead firms seek to promote competition and risk bearing among suppliers. This puts downward pressure on the price offered by supplier firms, creating another obstacle to upgrading through GVC-based exports.

Therefore, supplier firms face enormous competitive pressure from other suppliers to keep costs low, keep quality consistently high, and to keep delivering to buyers on schedule or risk losing the contract. They must bear much of the risk of carrying inventory in the face of volatile demand. They are sometimes limited in the technologies they can adapt. And they are often blocked from moving to the top of the supply chain by the expensive and successful branding strategies of the lead firms. Constraints on the expansion of value added by suppliers are felt in the limited ability to control markups over cost and through the resulting need to control labor costs.

The finding that so few countries in our thirty-country sample exhibit broad-based economic upgrading is consistent with recent studies showing that the export-led growth strategy adopted by most developing countries following the debt crisis in the 1980s (in place of the previous strategy of ISI) has suffered from a "fallacy of composition" problem. According to the fallacy of composition, it may be advantageous for one country if it alone achieves exporter status in a particular industry. But if many countries make the same calculation, all countries will be unable to capture the same advantage because of lower prices that follow from the expansion of world supply.[17]

---

[17] See Mayer (2002) and Razmi and Blecker (2008) for empirical evidence of a fallacy of composition.

The result can be a disproportionately small rise in value added. In our analysis in Chapter 4 of U.S. import prices relative to U.S. consumer prices, we found that only six sectors – and those most closely associated with commodities (specifically petroleum and iron) rather than manufactures – experienced relative import price increases. Relative import price declines were smallest in manufacturing sectors most intensive in foods, metals, and wood. Relative import price declines were greatest in those sectors which have both the technological and the value chain characteristics identified with profitable offshoring – computers, electrical, and telecommunications products. But many of the non-electronics manufacturing sectors also showed large and persistent relative import price declines, especially those with well-developed GVCs and high rates of import penetration in the United States. Clothing, footwear, textiles, furniture, miscellaneous manufactures (which includes toys), and chemicals all experienced import price declines (relative to U.S. consumer prices) over two decades of more than 1 percent per year on average, or 40 percent in the period from 1986 to 2006.

Figure 7.14 shows the lack of terms of trade improvement in some of the most important developing countries heavily involved in GVCs, including China, Mexico, Indonesia, and India. China and Indonesia show a long-term steady decline. India saw some improvement and then deterioration of late. Mexico and Brazil show only slight improvement throughout the export boom years of the 2000s.

The situation would appear to be a contemporary version of the Prebisch-Singer dilemma. In the 1950s and 1960s, development economists warned that continued specialization in commodities and agriculture would depress terms of trade and block the structural adjustments needed to raise income and industrialize (Prebisch 1949; Singer 1950). Developing country firms have successfully made the transition to manufacturing exports, yet are again suffering the terms of trade stagnation. It is not surprising that studies that focus on the terms of trade are often more pessimistic about prospects for economic upgrading than those that focus on functional upgrading, (compare, for example, Kaplinsky 2005 and Bair and Gereffi 2001). There is great irony in the recent upturn in world prices of commodities and foodstuffs, and the benefit this has brought to commodity exporters given that it was precisely this specialization pattern that Prebisch and Singer warned against.

Prebisch-Singer structural problems are today not about the nature of the product as much as they are about the governance structure within GVCs. Many lead firms in GPNs maintain markups by operating in factor or input markets that are increasingly oligopsonistic. Buying practices of lead firms

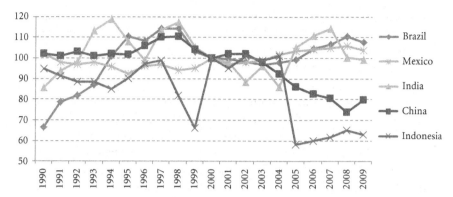

Figure 7.14. Merchandise Terms of Trade Indexes, Selected Countries, 1990–2009. *Source:* Own illustration. Data: UNCTAD. Note: The terms of trade index is defined as the ratio of the export unit value index to the import unit value index.

can lead to shaving of markups and cost cutting by suppliers that leaves them unable to innovate and resistant to improvements in wages or labor standards.

The dynamic of endogenous asymmetry may account for the continued importance of arm's-length transactions within GVCs since in such conditions supplier firms will generate little economic rent. This implies that bargaining power, not transactions costs minimization *per se*, is the driver of externalization strategies of lead firms. Whereas there is evidence of growing power of large, first-tier suppliers, who have market power of their own, there is also surprisingly little pricing power for very large scale contract manufacturers in China. Scale alone, it seems, does not guarantee the ability to raise value added per worker.[18]

In this chapter, we analyzed some of the consequences of GVCs for economic development. A few conclusions emerge. First, industrial upgrading has become the focus of contemporary development strategies, so the GVC becomes an important unit of analysis for the study of economic development. Whereas many of the institutions and forces that affect development are not determined at the level of the GVC, nonetheless the channels for attaining higher productivity and higher value added, and for generating innovation in both products and processes, increasingly occur within the confines of GVCs. Second, although the workings of the GVC revolve around international trade and thus fit nicely with the export-oriented

---

[18] See Sturgeon (2001) on the power of some first-tier suppliers. See Appelbaum (2008) on the Chinese contract manufacturers.

development strategy increasingly adopted by developmental states beginning in the 1980s, we found that export success alone does not guarantee improvements in value added per worker.

Third, increases in value added per capita do not necessarily translate into gains in employment. On average the relation goes the other way. That is, social upgrading does not immediately follow from industrial upgrading, and focusing on value added alone hides a variety of social outcomes in terms of wages, the amount of employment and even its gender distribution. This was shown with both aggregate and sectoral data. In some sectors, economic upgrading is positively associated with social upgrading, but in other sectors it is not. The policy challenge from the perspective of economic development is to identify the conditions under which economic upgrading is most likely to be associated with social upgrading. This is not a straightforward matter, because the most common policy tool for low-wage countries to enter GVCs – the establishment of EPZs – has in many cases also been part of GVC lead firm efforts to induce competition among suppliers and extend the asymmetry of GVC market structures.

APPENDIX 7.1. THIRTY-COUNTRY SAMPLE AND INCOME CATEGORY

Country	Country code	Income
Angola	AGO	Lower-middle
Argentina	ARG	Upper-middle
Bangladesh	BGD	Low
Bolivia	BOL	Lower-middle
Brazil	BRA	Upper-middle
Cambodia	KHM	Low
Cameroon	CMR	Lower-middle
Chile	CHL	Upper-middle
China	CHN	Lower-middle
Colombia	COL	Upper-middle
Ethiopia	ETH	Low
Gabon	GAB	Upper-middle
Ghana	GHA	Low
India	IND	Lower-middle
Indonesia	IDN	Lower-middle
Kenya	KEN	Low
Lebanon	LBN	Upper-middle
Malawi	MWI	Low
Malaysia	MYS	Upper-middle
Mexico	MEX	Upper-middle
Morocco	MAR	Lower-middle
Peru	PER	Upper-middle
Senegal	SEN	Low
South Africa	ZAF	Upper-middle
Thailand	THA	Lower-middle
Tunisia	TUN	Lower-middle
Uruguay	URY	Upper-middle
Venezuela	VEN	Upper-middle
Vietnam	VNM	Low
Zimbabwe	ZWE	Low

Source: Own illustration. Data: World Bank, as of July 2009.
Note: Income classification based on 2008 gross national income per capita; low-income = \$975 or less; lower-middle-income = \$976–\$3,855; upper-middle-income = \$3,856–\$11,905.

EIGHT

Outsourcing Economics

8.1 Global Business and the Polanyian Moment

In his pathbreaking work on the great economic and political crises of the twentieth century, *The Great Transformation*, Karl Polanyi (2001[1944]) writes that the history of capitalism can be characterized by a "double movement" where the policies of economic liberalism result in economic crises, which in turn provoke a political response in the other direction: government intervention in the form of regulation aimed at taming the excesses and unsustainable consequences of liberalism. For Polanyi, the classic liberal ideal of a "self-adjusting market" is a "stark utopia" bound to fail because of the burden it imposed on society. At the core of this mistaken utopianism, Polanyi argues, is the notion that labor, land, and money are pure commodities, most efficiently valued and allocated through markets. He termed them "fictitious commodities." Polanyi took this approach to economy to be both immoral and mistaken. The moral dimension refers to the burden – deprivation and insecurity – that labor (and the environment) must bear when they are subject to unregulated market forces. The mistake is not understanding that markets, especially for the fictitious commodities, invariably require government regulation and management for their functioning and stability.

Polanyi takes as his subject matter the rise of fascism in the wake of the economic liberalization of the nineteenth century and the Great Depression of the twentieth century. For him, it is impossible to imagine markets functioning in a pure sense, that is in the absence of the social and political foundation which creates markets and gives them legitimacy and stability. Therefore, he insists that markets never function in a pure sense, but are "embedded" in specific political and civil society institutions (Block 2001; Block and Evans 2005). The nature of embeddedness, of course, changes

284

through history. Polanyi's own writings describe the relation between economy and other social, cultural, religious, and political institutions in ancient Greece, early empires of Africa and the British empire in the nineteenth century. Others have extended Polanyi's framework to describe the world economy in the second half of the twentieth century. Polanyi's discussion of the embeddedness of markets is also a useful starting point for analyzing the political economy of the new wave of globalization.

After World War II, the industrialized economies were distinguished by market-oriented growth tempered by government regulation and social protections. This political arrangement has been described by Ruggie (1982, 1998, 2003) as "embedded liberalism." By this, he means that liberal tendencies in trade and investment were combined with social protections and arrangements that allowed a sharing of productivity gains, including the New Deal and labor union agreements in the United States, the strong assertion of social democracy in Europe and a system of fixed exchange rates. Embedded liberalism was largely limited to the industrialized countries, and often the social protections of embeddedness came at the expense of the developing world.

The asymmetry of trade liberalization in the General Agreement on Tariffs and Trade and subsequently in the World Trade Organization (WTO) illustrates the way the developing countries' efforts to succeed in world markets are frustrated by regulations that give an advantage to the industrialized world. Industrialized countries liberalized trade in manufactures, seeking to expand access to those markets in which they had a clear advantage, while they maintained protective barriers in agriculture, precisely the sector where developing countries were strongest and had the greatest chance of success.

Beginning in the 1980s, the disappearance of embedded liberalism coincides with what we have called the new wave of globalization. Today, global value chain (GVC) governance structures have changed the way in which states might respond to the excesses of market forces, that is, they have altered the shape that any Polanyian double movement might take. At the onset of the crisis in 2008, industrialized countries, led by the United States, did indeed respond with massive state intervention in the economy, with an enormous surge in public borrowing for deficit spending (including for both social protection and industrial support), historically high infusions of money into the banking and financial sectors, and with a political shift toward more regulation of the financial sector.

It would be a mistake to view the 2008 crisis as a result solely of developments in the financial sector. Our argument is that the structure of the global economy – and the business strategies that played a part in molding this structure – must be taken into account. An outsized focus on the financial sector, integral as that sector may be, makes the portrait of the crisis incomplete and risks limiting discussions of policy. The expansion of GVCs is one of the business strategies that has altered the structure of the global economy. As we have seen, the offshoring in GVCs by lead firms has increased economic insecurity in many industrialized nations. As for developing countries, there is considerable evidence of economic upgrading in GVCs, yet this has not usually been accompanied by upgrading in real wages and employment.

In this chapter we discuss the vertical disintegration of production and its role in the macroeconomic imbalances that contributed to the global recession. Our more general point is that the wave of externalization in the governance of global production has contributed to the marketization of economic activity that characterized the neoliberal period and the breakdown of embedded liberalism. Arm's-length GVC links were lauded by some as the global dimension of the increased efficiency of market-based transactions. They must also be understood as the expansion of market forces of the sort that Polanyi envisioned as potentially destabilizing. Our purpose in this chapter is to apply Polanyi's conception of political economy to the challenge of the new wave of globalization and the economic and social pressures it presents.

To this end, we first provide an analysis of how globalized production has realigned domestic interests in industrialized countries over questions of trade protection, exchange rate management, and macroeconomic imbalances. Then, drawing more broadly on our analysis of GVCs in capitalist development, we lay out a set of political implications that we believe are fundamental to the promotion of economic growth and security and fairer distribution of the gains from globalization. They are: (i) The encouragement of investment and discouragement of financialization. This would require altering incentives in finance and industry related to executive compensation, share buybacks, and corporate taxes. (ii) The establishment of social protections that are fully portable across jobs and available to the unemployed: health insurance, retirement income security, and traditional trade adjustment assistance. (iii) The adoption of trade regulations and corporate social responsibility (CSR) standards that would increase lead firms' accountability for labor and environmental conditions throughout the GVC, even when supplier relations are at arm's-length. (iv) The implementation of labor standards designed to increase the bargaining power of supplier firms and their workers. These too would be required even when supplier relations are at arm's length. (v) The expansion of domestic demand, especially in developing countries, and of the volume of South-South trade, to reduce reliance on GVCs.

We conclude this chapter with an appeal for a broadened conception of social welfare, and an expansion of economic analysis to account for the embedded nature of economic forces, and especially those of globalization. Beneath the apparent resurgence of markets in international trade is a reorganization of production and finance that requires a serious rethinking of how to manage the dynamics of global capitalism.

8.2 Trade and Exchange Rate Politics

We say surprisingly little in this chapter about the classic policy dichotomy regarding international trade: free trade versus protection. However, we do see a change in this debate occurring as a result of the new wave of globalization. While the goal of upgrading or of converting economic upgrading into social upgrading may very well require periods of selective protection and more generally of industrial policy, trade protection may at times have higher costs in the new wave of globalization. For one thing, when production occurs within a global network, there is a much greater reliance on imports (and thus on low tariffs on imported inputs), as the evidence of rising vertical specialization shows. Therefore, trade protection must be applied much more selectively than in the pre-GVC world, and it is the rate of effective protection that matters more than simply the tariff rate on final goods (Dadush 2012).

Second, in a world of globalized production, that is, with high levels of vertical specialization, bilateral trade balances are deceptive because they hide significant import content from third countries. Protectionist pressures based on countries' bilateral trade balances are thus misplaced. In China's Apple iPod exports, for example, China contributes just a tiny fraction of the value added, as shown in Chapter 2. Thus what appears in the trade statistics as a large Chinese bilateral surplus in iPods may in fact be a deficit, given that U.S. semiconductors are inputs to the assembled product (Xing and Detert 2010). That is, U.S. semiconductor shipments to China for the iPod valued more than the value added by China in iPod assembly. Therefore, if statistics reflected value added rather than gross value, the United States would in fact have a surplus in iPod trade with China. Using value added in trade rather than published trade statistics, the bilateral trade deficit of the United States vis-à-vis China in 2005 would be reduced from $218 billion to $101 billion and the deficit in 2008 would be 40 percent less (WTO-IDE JETRO 2011). The EU15-China deficit would be half if measured in value added terms (Koopman et al. 2010).

Trade liberalization is traditionally understood as expanding the scope of "competitive imports," which idles both domestic firms and their workers. The unutilized capital and labor must then be reabsorbed into other parts of the economy, in particular those sectors with a comparative advantage that are expanding. The gains from trade liberalization in this context are the result of the combined gains from specialization and from exchange at world prices (static efficiency gains). The welfare question, in this case, is about the impact on the return to capital and labor, or, in the contemporary literature, on the return to high-skill versus low-skill labor, as a result of some sectors shrinking and others growing as comparative advantage takes hold. Other labor market issues – such as the duration of job loss and the replacement wage for new jobs – do not immediately arise from trade theory, because unemployment is generally ruled out by assumption.

With the rise of GVCs and the associated vertical disintegration of production, the set of relevant labor market adjustment questions becomes broader. The gains from trade in tasks, as Grossman and Rossi-Hansberg (2006a, 2006b, 2008) have described offshoring in GVCs, are distributed differently than in standard models of international trade. The growth of trade in GVCs reflects corporate strategy and introduces a new terrain of conflict between management and labor. Task trade expands the amount of "competitive tasks," as distinct from traditional competitive imports. That is, imports now reduce firms' costs of production, raising profit margins, whereas some labor and capital within the firm are rendered obsolete. In this case, the static efficiency gains from trade liberalization accrue to profits and to those performing tasks not facing low-cost import competition. Losses are incurred most by those who perform tasks that are mobile or digitizable.

As we saw in Chapter 4, consumers gain from lower prices of goods and services, however there are also potential dynamic gains. Dynamic gains accrue because of the extra business spending (profit reinvestments) that the cost saving from offshoring spurs, not for traditional efficiency reasons. As we saw in Chapters 5 and 6, offshoring has indeed pushed up corporate profitability and the overall profit share of value added in the United States. Both services and materials offshoring were positively and significantly associated with lower sectoral labor shares between 1998 and 2006, implying higher sectoral profit shares.

We also saw in Chapter 6 that investment has been relatively insensitive to the rise in the profit share. As imports and the profit share rose, gross private fixed investment as a share of gross domestic income has recovered from its low levels in the early 1990s, but with the recent economic crisis has dropped to the lowest levels in forty years. Fixed investment of non-financial corporations as a share of gross profits has, with the exception of the period of the information technology (IT) boom, been below the levels of the 1970s. We also showed that offshoring was related to lower capital accumulation in manufacturing and services sectors in the United States between 1998 and 2006. Finally, we showed that the rise in offshoring has been associated with a financialization of non-financial corporations, specifically the purchase of share buybacks, dividend payments and even cash-based merger and acquisition activity.

If the expanded profits and profit share lead to the capture of dynamic gains, then employment, growth and innovation over the long-run should offset short-run losses. Our analysis indicates, however, that there has been an insufficient capture of the dynamic gains. The failure of the U.S. non-financial corporate sector to adequately capture dynamic gains occurred in an environment of relatively free trade, highly mobile capital and deregulated finance.

The decline in employment from offshoring has long-term consequences in terms of skills development and economic security. However, to reduce the scope of offshoring would also reduce the prospect for dynamic gains that come with profit reinvestment in growth and innovation. Reduced offshoring would also hurt supplier firms and their countries, especially developing countries, who are already competing for limited market share in input markets.[1] The goal should not be to reduce trade in intermediates, but to maximize dynamic gains from trade and to alter the asymmetries in the GVC so that economic security and social upgrading are not compromised in the expansion of global production.

The rise of task trade and its consequences for income distribution, and the nature of the gains from trade have created a new political economy of trade. Lead firms in vertically-disintegrated GVCs seek the removal of trade protection, whereby workers in those parts of the chain being offshored will have an interest in even greater protection than before. Traditionally in the United States, for example, management and organized labor in a given industry came to Washington as a team, lobbying together for trade protection. Today, free trade in tasks is more beneficial to profits than it is to wage income within an industry and even within a firm.

---

[1] We should note that Xing and Detert (2010) argue that Apple could perform all production of the iPhone, including assembly, in the United States and suffer only a minimal reduction in its profit margin.

As a result, management interests in an industry increasingly support trade liberalization, leaving labor unions alone in seeking protection or the blockage of free trade agreements with developing countries.

Mancur Olson's (1965) *The Logic of Collective Action* can help explain the shift in the political economy of trade as a result of the new wave of globalization. He writes, "Unless the number of individuals in a group is quite small . . . *rational, self-interested individuals will not act to achieve their common or group interests*" (Olson 1965, 2, emphasis in original). Olson's logic was typically seen as the reason that labor unions argue for trade protection, but consumers who benefit from the lower prices that free trade brings are too diffuse a group to organize on behalf of trade liberalization. Today, the calculus is reversed. Profits accrue to a relatively small part of the population – increasingly small, if the trends in U.S. income and wealth distribution are an indication, and the losses to labor income from the strong dollar are spread across the rest of the economy. According to Olson, "Where small groups with common interests are concerned, then, there is a systematic tendency for 'exploitation' of the great by the small!" (Olson 1965, 29). The new wave of globalization gives new meaning to these words from the 1960s.

U.S. government ambivalence on the issue of Chinese currency revaluation is also tied to this new political economy. The revaluation of the Renminbi would be detrimental to lead firm costs, despite its positive effects on particular labor tasks in these lead firms. This has produced a conflict among businesses regarding Renminbi revaluation. Those who offshore tasks to China favor a continued strong dollar, while business interests seeking to fend off traditional competitive imports are urging Renminbi revaluation. While a weaker U.S. dollar relative to the Renminbi would be justified by the structure of global imbalances, it is no longer in the interest of lead firms in GVCs, whose profits are driven as much by import performance as by export performance. Therefore, while it is popular for politicians and political campaigns to lambast China and to call publicly for Renminbi revaluation, there has not been a strong effort to accomplish this.

Exchange rate politics in the United States have thus shifted in the new wave of globalization. Although the Renminbi has appreciated by about 30 percent since 2000, this is much less than most economic studies show would be needed to reverse the trade imbalance. Europe, even amidst the current debt crisis in the Eurozone, is also undergoing a similar period of Renminbi undervaluation associated with a deficit with China and a rising profit share in many countries of Europe.

8.3 Profits and the Macroeconomic Imbalances[2]

If the new wave of globalization has affected the constellation of interests with respect to trade and exchange rate policy, then it is perhaps not surprising that it also affects the closely related issue of global payments imbalances. In the 2000s, the large imbalances in international payments that emerged are widely presumed to have contributed to the financial collapse and worldwide recession that began in 2008. Portes (2010) states that the macro imbalances were "the fundamental cause of the crisis" (Portes 2010, 40). (See also Portes 2009; Obstfeld and Rogoff 2009; Horn et al. 2009). Even now, with the immediate threat of financial collapse behind us, there are prominent voices claiming that the return of global imbalances puts the international financial system at great risk of a new collapse. According to Cline and Williamson (2009), "large external imbalances can only aggravate not moderate, fragility in the financial system" (cited in Suominen 2010, 88). IMF efforts to broker a United States-China agreement to reduce imbalances by targeted amounts over the next five years indicate how important such a rebalancing is perceived.

Our emphasis on GVCs puts lead firms' business strategies into the picture, implying that U.S. trade deficits are not simply the passive inverse of the capital account imbalance but are driven by autonomous microeconomic forces, including firm strategies. Lead firm governance of GVCs has resulted in a steady increase in the U.S. import share. We have seen that bilateral and sectoral trade balances may be quite different when measured in terms of value added rather than in terms of final goods and services trade values. Indirectly, these strategies have resulted in higher cost markups and firm profits and depressed labor demand and wages in the United States. This heightened inequality has contributed to the current account surplus, because stagnant real median wages over a long period in the United States created the need for American households to borrow heavily in order to maintain consumption standards.

Payments imbalances are typically understood as a reflection of imbalances in macroeconomic conditions, specifically between saving and investment. In one version of events, the current macro imbalances are the result of a "savings glut," notably in China, but also in other East Asian and developing countries (Bernanke 2005, 2007). In another version, the problem has been excessively loose U.S. monetary policy, resulting in extremely low interest rates and thus heightened borrowing and consumption

---

[2] This section draws extensively on Milberg and Schmitz (2011).

by American households (Taylor 2007), what Milberg and Schmitz (2011) refer to as the "money glut" explanation.

Following Milberg and Schmitz (2011), we propose an alternative microeconomic explanation that focuses on offshoring strategies of firms and the contribution of offshoring to, on the one hand, trade deficits, wage stagnation, and rising corporate profits and, on the other hand, to a rise in household borrowing and financial speculation. We call this the "profits glut" explanation because its fundamental feature is a rise in corporate profit rates (cost markups) and the profit share, the result of successful corporate strategies in the 2000s. The profits glut has contributed directly to deteriorating macroeconomic imbalances but was also a contributing cause of the crisis through the fall in median income and the subsequent rise in income at the top end. It has coincided with a shift in the role of the foreign sector in economic growth and in the politics of exchange rate management.

The hypothesis emphasizes corporate strategy in the 1990s and 2000s with its focus on mass customization, core competence, offshoring of production of parts and components, and a reduced commitment to long-term employment relations and secure worker pensions. The profits glut hypothesis can be simply put: Expanded offshoring by U.S. firms in China contributed directly to the trade deficit and to higher markups over cost, and indirectly to the U.S. imbalance through its contribution to wage stagnation in the United States through depressed demand for labor and a resulting increase in household borrowing. The linkages are depicted in Figure 8.1. To the extent that exports increase due to cheaper imported inputs, the negative effect of offshoring on the trade account would be offset.

Economists generally assert that the capital account determines current account movements, but the transmission channel from one to the other is a bit vague. Presumably capital inflows lead to exchange rate appreciation which in turn drives a current account deterioration. Firm-level considerations (which are likely to be behind the current account) are typically considered subsidiary to macroeconomic forces.

There are two types of transmission mechanisms from the macro to the micro in terms of global imbalances. One is through interest rates and exchange rates (Mundell-Fleming and portfolio-balance models) and the other through income (Thirlwall's model of balance of payments constrained growth). The problem with invoking the former is that exchange rates are notoriously unpredictable and thus any theory relying on a systematic relation between imbalances and exchange rates is likely to be empirically very weak. The problem with invoking the income-based model is that

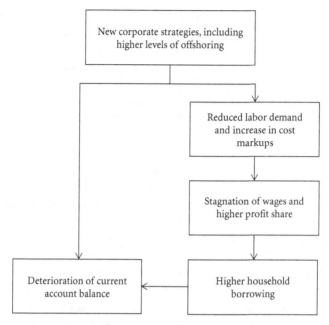

Figure 8.1. The "Profits Glut." *Source:* Own illustration. Based on Milberg and Schmitz (2011).

it considers the issue precisely in the opposite direction, which is to say that the imbalance leads to a particular constraint on the rate of growth, not the other way around.

Dorman (2007) and Blecker (1992, 2009) are among a group of economists who have questioned the reasoning that the capital account drives the current account, insisting instead that international competitiveness has autonomous and firm-level elements. Blecker (2009), for example, includes "the deterioration in U.S. competitiveness" among the various causes of the trade deficit, noting that, "it is difficult for the United States to engineer a reduction in its overall trade imbalance while the manufacturing sector has been restructured in ways that make it more dependent on imports" (Blecker 2009, 3).

By linking competitiveness to imports rather than exports, we take the argument a step further. Bernard et al. (2007) find that only a very small share of U.S. firms are involved in export, and a high percentage of the firms that export are also involved in importing. The standard notion that exporting is the source of profits (using a neoclassical Heckscher-Ohlin-Wood framework or an open economy Kaleckian model) may be based on a spurious correlation since imports too would be correlated with profits. Milberg and Schmitz (2011) analyze sectoral data on the relation between trade and profits, and they find a number of sectors with a very high correlation between the year-to-year change in the sector's profit share and its increased reliance on Chinese imports, including computer and electronics (0.81), miscellaneous manufactured commodities (0.71), fabricated metal products (0.71), and the machinery, except electrical (0.71) subsector.

A few recent studies of individual firms support this picture. A close analysis of Apple's 2005 30 GB fifth generation video iPod shows that out of the $299 retail price, the cost of inputs is $144.40. Apple's profit on the item is realized in its worldwide sales. Its ability to import the fully assembled item from China results in a much lower cost and thus higher markup than if the assembly were handled in the United States. Imports contribute to profitability especially in a monopoly or oligopoly product market because cost savings are not fully passed through to consumers. Note also that since China assembles the iPod using mostly imported components (from companies headquartered in Japan, the United States, Taiwan, and South Korea who themselves do some offshore production in China, Singapore, and Taiwan), the export and import data do not accurately capture the national identity of the problem in any specific case.[3]

A second example is Wal-Mart, which alone imported $27 billion in goods from China in 2006 and was responsible for 11 percent of the growth in the United States-China trade deficit between 2001 and 2006 (Scott 2007). Wal-Mart's profits in 2006 were $11.23 billion – a 78.4 percent increase in profits compared to 2001.[4] Wal-Mart undertook $62 billion in dividend payments and share buybacks in 2006, equivalent to 74 percent of its net income (Milberg 2008). Wal-Mart's reliance on low-cost imports and low-pay standards (such as health insurance benefits) for its domestic (U.S.) workforce has become one of the lightning rods for attacks on the new economy business model.

The profits glut implies that issues of firm competitiveness, and more generally corporate strategies, may directly be driving the current account imbalances, which in turn require capital imbalances for financing. We

---

[3] Linden et al. (2007). See Ma and Van Assche (2010) for an analysis of China's "process trade."
[4] From CNN Money.com: http://money.cnn.com/magazines/fortune/fortune500/2006/snapshots/1551.html.

have focused on corporate offshoring strategies, which have raised firm markups, depressed labor demand and wages, and contributed to a rising profit share in the United States. This contributes to the growing support for the view – recently offered in popular writings by Madrick and Papanikolaou (2010) and Reich (2010), for example – that the unsustainably high levels of household borrowing are the result of the increase in income inequality experienced in the United States and elsewhere. As Madrick and Papanikolaou (2010) point out, the real issue is not inequality *per se* but the long-term stagnation of real wages (see Figure 4.2). American households borrowed in order to maintain increases in consumption during a period when real wages were stagnant, whereas high-income households supported the speculative activity of investment banks that contributed to the immediate crisis in financial markets. In light of this view, promotion of an institutional framework of regulation, social protection and state support may be as vital to ensuring the future stability of global imbalances as any other macro-level adjustment.

8.4 Capturing the Gains from Globalization

The globalization of production has contributed to the macroeconomic imbalances, and altered the interplay of interests with respect to trade protection and exchange rate management. As capitalism has expanded globally and international capital mobility has increased – as reflected in the evidence on international portfolio capital flows, foreign direct investment (FDI), and foreign exchange transactions – national governments have less influence over economic change. But this influence remains considerable, and it is precisely at a time when economic security is weakened by global economic forces that the state is likely to play an enhanced role, as Polanyi envisioned. Greater liberalization is nonetheless one possible political response, and the austerity macroeconomics so popular in the United States and Europe at the moment are an indication of the strength of this policy direction. Support for this comes from both the business community and from economics.[5]

Our analysis – admittedly focused on the production side – indicates that a heightened disembedding of the market forces will not promote a socially sustainable growth path in either industrialized or developing economies. The policy discussion that follows includes some international policies and some national policies that, based on our analysis of the social and

[5] From the recent business books, see Kessler (2011). From economics, see Mann (2006).

economic consequences of globalized production, would be aimed at raising economic security, increasing the capture of the dynamic gains from trade, reducing obstacles to economic development, and increasing prospects for social improvement coming out of the process of industrial upgrading in GVCs.

8.4.1 Maximizing Dynamic Gains and Reducing Financialization

The question of how to increase the capture of dynamic gains from off-shoring is not a question strictly related to trade policy. As we identified in Chapter 6, an important offset to dynamic gains from trade is the financial activity of non-financial firms. Policy-seeking to raise economic growth and employment must venture into the areas of financial regulation, over-sight of executive compensation schemes and tax policy related to corporate income, capital gains and dividend income, and the treatment of corporate profits earned abroad.

Chapter 4 concludes with an overview of the dynamics of offshoring, where we identified a "substitution effect," a "productivity effect," a "scale effect," and a "markup effect" of offshoring on labor demand. Whereas the first three have been analyzed in the literature, the fourth effect emerges from the analysis of cost reduction and leaves open the possibility of pass-through to market prices, reinvestment, or increased shareholder returns. The latter we associate with financialization. In Chapter 5, we showed that labor market regulations – government protections including the laws around hiring and firing and active labor market programs – can significantly mitigate the economic insecurity created from offshoring. But even Danish "flexicurity" as a way of managing state-market relations in a globalized economy is unlikely to suffice over the longer-run to maintain high levels of economic security. For this, the macroeconomic effects of offshoring must be channeled away from finance and toward the domestic reinvestment of efficiency gains from offshoring.

In Chapter 5, we also looked more closely at the United States and the extent to which dynamic gains from offshoring have been realized. We estimated a model of the U.S. sectoral labor share, which is 1 minus the profit share, for the period from 1998 to 2006. Offshoring is positively and significantly related to the profit share. Gains from offshoring are real-ized when these profits are reinvested. In Chapter 6, however, we found that non-financial corporations generally used profits to raise shareholder returns, either directly with higher dividend payments, or indirectly with large amounts (sometimes exceeding profits) of share repurchases. Globalized production thus supports the financialization of the non-financial corporate sector rather than just spurring growth through productivity gains, which are described in many economic models.

This raises a number of very fundamental policy issues. The first is the need to reduce incentives to the financialization of non-financial corporations. Financial regulation can be a direct spur to the capture of greater dynamic gains from offshoring. One possibility would be to limit share buybacks by firms, especially when they are tied to executive compensation. When executive compensation is to a significant extent in the form of stock options, then the incentives of executives and shareholders coincide – just as the 1970s arguments for a "market for corporate control" urged (Jensen and Meckling 1976). But the shift may have thrown out the baby of long-term firm growth with the bathwater of the perceived excessive power of managerial capitalism. The explosive growth of share buybacks reflects a constellation of forces, where short-term increases in stock price are more important than long-term success, the latter typically requiring considerable innovative effort and long-term commitment to employees. This commitment to employees has often suffered, as reflected in our analysis of economic insecurity.

Financialization has come at the expense of productive investment, which certainly includes innovative effort – in fact much of the innovation that occurred in the 2000s was in the financial sector itself. Restricted stock units, in particular stocks which only vest after a certain amount of years, may discourage unsustainable and irrational behavior of executives that only focuses on short-term profit maximization. Nevertheless, it remains a curious view that the prime objective of the firm is to maximize shareholder value because shareholders typically do not have a long-term obligation to the company in the same way that employees and even customers do (Lazonick and O'Sullivan 2000; Lazonick 2009).

There is a very practical policy change that also would alter the current preference for share buybacks. This is to reduce the differential in the United States between the personal income tax rate (25 to 35 percent) and the capital gains and dividend income tax rates (15 percent). All other things equal, such a differential implies that managers *should* return value in the form of capital gains and thus share buybacks are completely reasonable from a shareholder perspective.

A second, but related, issue is the taxing of corporate profits on overseas operations. The deferral of taxes on unrepatriated profits of foreign subsidiaries of U.S. companies has been part of U.S. tax law since it was passed in the 1950s. U.S. corporations receive a tax credit for taxes paid to foreign countries on profits of subsidiaries. Companies are liable to pay taxes on profits earned abroad to the extent that the U.S. tax rate exceeds the rate charged in foreign countries. However, by law such taxes are deferred until the profits are repatriated to the parent company in the United States. Tax deferral gives an incentive to U.S. firms to hold profits abroad. It also gives firms a further incentive to shift foreign profits from high to low profits tax countries. Sullivan (2004) reports a dramatic shift in U.S. profits abroad from 1999 to 2002 from high tax to low tax locations, including Ireland, Bermuda, Luxembourg, and Switzerland. The traditional means to do this was through transfer pricing, whereby multinational corporations (MNCs) use input pricing among affiliates to raise profits in low tax jurisdictions and lower them elsewhere. The complex global web of arrangement for input production and assembly that characterizes many GVCs has provided a new channel for creating profits in low tax jurisdictions, which is the arrangement of production and shipping logistics that can considerably reduce the overall corporate tax liability.

Would the ending of deferral accomplish the stated goal of not rewarding U.S. companies that invest (and thus move jobs) abroad? As usual, estimates vary. But almost all see a positive effect on U.S. employment. Estimates of the employment impact of the deferral policy range from 200,000 jobs (Hufbauer, cited in Lynch, 2008) to 3 million jobs (Clausing 2004). The elimination of the deferral would also give companies an incentive to change their legal residence to another country, as discussed by Lynch (2008). This is a risk worth taking, as deferral is reducing the capture of dynamic gains from offshoring by U.S. corporations and should be phased out.

A popular proposal is for a "dividend repatriation tax holiday" that would provide a one-year reduction in tax rates on repatriated foreign profits from the 35 percent rate on domestic profits to zero or near zero. Such a tax holiday was adopted in 2004 (with a tax rate of 5.25 percent) and recent proposals call for reducing the moratorium rate to zero (Schink and Tyson 2009). Research shows convincingly that the holiday was ineffective in raising corporate investment and employment domestically, because firms were able to circumvent the conditions on the use of repatriated profits. Since firm revenues are fungible, firms benefiting from the tax holiday were able to expand executive compensation, dividends and especially share buybacks while using tax holiday funds for existing investment projects. Dharmapala et al. (2011) find that between 60 and 92 percent of the tax-free repatriated funds were used for share repurchases.

While the tax deferral should indeed be eliminated and a tax holiday avoided, there should also be adequate incentives in place for business to reinvest its profits rather than investing in financial assets and short-run share values through buybacks. The U.S. corporate profits tax rate of 35 percent is somewhat high by international standards, but the preponderance of loopholes makes the actual rate much lower. Lowering the rate to an international average while seriously closing loopholes and limiting share buybacks would be a strategy for increasing dynamic gains from foreign operations. Even more effective would be an agreement on a uniform international rate of tax on corporate profits, eliminating the possibility of tax havens at all.

The drastic decline in the rate of investment out of profits by non-financial corporations in the 2000s (see Figure 6.3, for example) reflected a much broader problem than the loss of dynamic gains from offshoring. That decade saw a breakdown in the relation between stock prices and investment, as has been predicted by Tobin's "q" theory and by evidence of rapid investment and strong innovative effort in the bull markets of the 1920s and the 1990s in the United States. Although all three decades experienced a financial bubble that eventually burst, only in the 2000s did investment fall as a share of profits during the boom period. And our empirical analysis showed that offshoring significantly lowered capital accumulation in the United States in the period from 1998 to 2006 while at the same time leading to higher financialization. The phenomenon of financialization in the 2000s thus represented a fundamental break from the historical pattern and may impose a drag on long-term growth in the industrialized world. Innovation became associated with finance and the expansion of the financial sector in the U.S. economy reached historic highs. In non-financial corporations, the emphasis on core competence – and in particular branding, marketing, and finance – and the drop in research and development spending out of internal funds have created strong concerns about the prospects for growth in decent-paying jobs in the future (see Shapiro and Milberg 2013).

By focusing our analysis on the labor share of income, we pointed to the issue of wage stagnation rather than simply wage inequality as at the root of the concern over the relation between globalization and social welfare. Only a combination of institutional change and macroeconomic stimulus are likely to reverse the long-run stagnation of wages. The likelihood of capturing dynamic gains from offshoring is increased when firm management has an incentive to invest rather than return profits immediately to shareholders. Moreover, public investment in infrastructure and education has often served to "crowd in" private investment, further enhancing the likelihood of dynamic gains.

8.4.2 Reducing the Cost of Job Loss and Promoting Innovation

There is already ample econometric evidence that offshoring has had an adverse impact on low-skill workers in industrialized countries, in terms of pay and employment, in both absolute and relative terms. Recent studies find a negative impact of offshoring on high-skill workers too (Geishecker 2008; Winkler 2009, 2013). In Chapter 5, we looked at the implications of offshoring for economic insecurity, comparing the United States to other industrialized countries. Over the past twenty-five years, the United States has experienced a dramatic shift in the burden of risk, from government to the households themselves. This has resulted from a combination of more volatile household income and an increase in health insurance costs, a greater reliance on private (as opposed to public) pensions and a continuation of policies of low levels of unemployment benefits. Hacker (2006) describes these political changes as "the great risk shift."

The new wave of globalization has raised worker insecurity in many industrialized countries. But vulnerability does not translate directly into economic insecurity. This depends on household efforts to reduce the risk of sudden loss and on national policies to absorb such risks. The decline in household saving driven by the massive expansion of household debt in many cases reflects the effort by households to buffer themselves from income shocks. Looking across Organisation of Economic Co-operation and Development (OECD) countries, we found that countries subject to the same degree of exposure due, say, to globalization, may experience very different levels of economic insecurity due to social support or employment protections provided by the state or even because of insurance obtained by households.

We identified five varieties of industrialized countries, characterized by national levels of "labor support" and "strictness of employment protection." On one extreme is the United States and other Anglo-Saxon economies with lax hiring and firing regulations, low unemployment benefits, and very limited spending on active labor market policies. On the other extreme is the Rhineland model, with relatively high levels of employment protection, large unemployment benefits, and significant spending on active labor market programs. Denmark (and a few other countries) seem to have found an effective combination of the two, comprising labor market flexibility with high replacement income programs for the unemployed and extensive active labor market programs.

We defined a fall in the labor share as an indicator of heightened economic insecurity. Our first econometric analysis focused on the effect of offshoring on the labor share in the United States. Holding all other variables constant, a 10 percent increase in services offshoring reduced the labor share by 0.8 percent between 1998 and 2006. A 10 percent increase in materials offshoring led to an average labor share decline of 1.8 percent. Our labor demand regressions also indicated a rise in economic insecurity. Thus, services and materials offshoring significantly reduced conditional and unconditional labor demand in the manufacturing and service sectors combined. In the manufacturing sectors, we also found a significantly negative effect of materials offshoring on conditional and unconditional labor demand and of services offshoring on unconditional labor demand. In the service sectors, services offshoring significantly lowered conditional labor demand. The results for the combined sector sample imply a drop in employment of approximately 3.5 million full-time equivalent jobs.

We then analyzed the importance of the role of the state in mediating the impact of globalization on economic security by assessing the impact of offshoring on the labor share of income across 15 OECD countries. We found that goods offshoring had a positive effect on the labor share in the period from 1991 to 1998 and no effect between 1999 and 2006. Our focus, however, has been on the mitigating role of labor market institutions on this general outcome. We found that for those countries providing more labor market support in the form of greater spending on active labor market policies and higher unemployment replacement benefits, offshoring had a larger positive effect in the more recent period.

If one goal of policy reform in advanced capitalism in the crisis that began in 2008 is the reduction of economic insecurity, then it will have to include not only the re-regulation of the financial sector, but also the expansion in many countries of social and labor market support that will allow globalization to continue while economic insecurity is maintained. Denmark has successfully raised economic security in that country despite vigorous globalization. U.S. labor market flexibility combined with relatively meager social protections in the context of rapid growth of imports from developing countries has contributed to an unprecedented rise in income inequality and economic insecurity.

The situation is unsustainable in the short-run as we have seen with the massive deleveraging of households, both with mortgage foreclosures and with a ratcheting down of consumer debt. It is also unsustainable in the long-run in terms of innovation, productivity growth, and economic expansion. Outside the confines of the model of comparative advantage, the provision of a solid and portable set of social protection does not reduce a nation's trade competitiveness and in fact may raise it as increased worker security leads to greater possibilities for innovation and rapid productivity growth.

We also showed that labor market institutions matter significantly in dampening – and in some cases reversing – the rise in economic insecurity associated with offshoring in industrialized countries. Minimizing economic insecurity from offshoring does not mean that all countries should emulate the institutional structure of Denmark. Our analysis does indicate, however, that to produce the economic security necessary for sustained innovation and growth in the new wave of globalization calls for a social safety net that is fully portable, that is, not tied to any particular job. This means universal health insurance, adequate pensions that are not tied just to earnings, and ample assistance for those forced out of work due to economic change including offshoring. The point would be to assure the compensation of losers, and yet to retain the flexibility to reignite innovation without provoking another bubble tied to inequality, excessive debt, and risk taking. A more comprehensive social safety net, delinked from employment or even employment status so as to reduce the insecurity we have seen to be associated with both the perception and the reality of globalization, will thus spread the benefits of globalization more fairly.

Such an institutional arrangement is not strictly a redistribution of income from owners to workers, but spreads the cost of raising economic security more broadly across society through the use of government. Innovation and flexibility should increase when business alone doesn't bear the brunt of the health and pension expenses. Moreover, workers are more willing to accept innovation and change in the workplace if a safety net is in place. These are the dynamic aspects of trade that should move the trade policy debate beyond the simplistic dichotomy between free trade and protection and take economics beyond the limitations of its potential Pareto criterion for welfare analysis.

The expansion of GVCs has fit into a new business model by allowing firms to focus on core competence and to reduce domestic investment demand even as profits rose. This new business model and a loose regulatory framework have contributed to rising income inequality and have supported financialization, which has furthered wealth inequality. At issue is the collapse of a set of institutions which are tied to globalization but which certainly are driven by forces broader than just the globalization of production or finance. This includes the decline of unions and labor protections generally, including minimum wages, the scaling back of the social safety net, and the rising cost of health care and education. These tendencies have been widely reported on in the press but are only with great difficulty integrated into traditional discussions of globalization and offshoring.

8.4.3 Reducing Asymmetries and Increasing Accountability for Social Standards in Global Value Chains

Chapter 3 provided an overview of the recent history of the theory of international trade, from the New International Economics to the economics of offshoring. This was the story of the rejection, and then revival, of the principle of comparative advantage among economists. We then presented some conceptual, historical, and ethical limitations of the theory of comparative advantage. In the chapter, we make the case for an institutionalist theory of international trade, where absolute advantage plays a role along with comparative advantage, and where international differences across a number of aspects of society – from innovation systems to labor market structures to ownership-management relations to the role of the state in social protection – can all make a difference for international trade patterns.

Chapter 4 built on the institutional framework and presented an alternative approach to offshoring by looking at the development of product and factor markets in major industries. We found that oligopoly margins are persistent across a variety of industries despite the fact that product price inflation has been minimal for over ten years. These constant – and in many cases rising – cost markups associated with the persistence of oligopoly are reflected in a rising profit share of national income. Effective development and management of GVCs has been an important channel for cost reduction. This is especially the case when there is intense competition in supplier industries. Evidence on industrial concentration globally shows that beginning in the mid-1980s there was a massive entry into medium- and low-technology manufacturing and services industries by developing countries. The pace of new entry slowed in the early 2000s, but there are no signs of exit, indicating that productive capacity remained in place and competition among suppliers remained intense.

What has emerged is an asymmetry of product markets internationally, with the persistence of lead firm power at the top and enormous competitive pressure among supplier firms. This creates two power imbalances, one in the product market and one in the labor market. When supplier firm margins are squeezed by the asymmetry of market structure in GVCs, these firms in turn are under enormous pressure to keep wages and labor standards low. We proposed that this asymmetry and the power imbalances it embodies is endogenous to lead firm value chain governance strategies. The endogenous asymmetry of market structure in GVCs is not only important for cost markups and profit shares in lead firm home countries, but also because it presents a series of obstacles to economic development in developing countries. The situation calls for intervention in two areas. One is to reduce obstacles to economic upgrading by supplier firms. The other is to raise the bargaining power of labor within lead and supplier firms so that economic upgrading is more likely to be associated with social upgrading.

The endogeneity hypothesis also has implications for the theory of the globalized firm. Whereas transactions cost economics sees the continued prominence of arm's-length transactions in international trade to be the result of more efficient markets, in the "strategic firm" approach we adopted it is understood as a result of the successful inducement of competition among supplier firms, especially in developing countries. Once operations cease to be rent-generating, there is no longer an incentive for firms to retain these operations internally. In this view, core competence is a synonym for the remaining rent-generating aspects of production. The difference between this view and the transactions cost approach may be one of emphasis, but it leaves open the possibility that shifts in the scope of the firm are not strictly efficient in the sense of Pareto.[6]

In Chapter 7, we defined "social upgrading" as the improvement in employment, real wages, labor, and environmental standards. If economic upgrading leads to social upgrading, then policy aimed at social upgrading can focus strictly on the former. In this case, policy should focus on barriers to economic upgrading, including intellectual property protections that limit supplier firm efforts at innovation and branding. We also showed that economic upgrading does not necessarily lead to social upgrading, both at the country and the GVC level. But we did not address the issue of causality between economic and social upgrading. One perspective

---

[6] Pitelis (2001) makes a similar point in his discussion of "market and non-market failures."

is that economic and social upgrading are endogenous to the process of economic growth. This view is held by those on both the right and the left of the political spectrum within the economics profession (see Flanagan 2005; Piore 2004; Reinert 2007). If economic upgrading results from economic growth, then macroeconomic policies that promote rapid growth should be the main policy goal. If economic upgrading does not occur as the outcome of economic growth, then a different sort of policy intervention is required, including sector-specific industrial policies that encourage innovation and productivity growth. Also, in this case, access to developed country markets is especially important, as the chance to upgrade in GVCs becomes a more important channel for development.

Our focus on economic upgrading as the objective of industrial policy has ignored one of the main conclusions of Chapter 7, which is that economic upgrading is a necessary but not sufficient condition for social upgrading that is likely to make any process of industrialization sustainable. In Chapter 7, we did not explicitly analyze any particular policies or institutions that would reduce the slippage from the cup of economic upgrading to the lip of social upgrading. One clear implication from the GVC perspective is the need to raise accountability for social standards in GVCs.

If social upgrading is not endogenous to the process of economic growth or even to the process of economic upgrading, then labor standards and regulations, the enforcement of labor bargaining rights, and the capacity to enforce them should be the policy priority. GVCs pose a political difficulty here. Most policy discussion of labor standards has been around CSR of MNCs. While the CSR movement in itself suffered from problems of coverage, coordination and compliance (UNCTAD 2011; Piore and Schrank 2008), the new wave of globalization poses additional problems because as GVCs have increasingly been organized around arm's-length supplier relations, lead firms can distance themselves from conditions in supplier firms. Foxconn's labor standards violations were until very recently disassociated from Apple's reputation as a firm, and even recent efforts to address labor standards violations at the Chinese supplier firm have focused more on the supplier than on the lead firm (Mayer 2012).

These theoretical positions do not lead to mutually exclusive policy conclusions. Especially if there are aspects of social upgrading that are income-driven and others that are not, as some have suggested, then it is likely that the promotion of social upgrading is helped by the simultaneous pursuit of more rapid economic growth and the implementation of regulations and the creation of institutions that directly address aspects of social upgrading that growth alone does not affect.

In the new wave of globalization, with GVCs so central to the expansion and distribution of the gains from trade, the policy focus in North-South trade negotiations should not just focus on free trade versus protection, but should allow for consideration of the place the lead firm and its governance strategies. In the realm of North-South trade, developed country protectionism will clearly not help firms and workers in the developing world. More to the point is that lead firm accountability for social standards and basic worker rights throughout the GVC would further distribute the gains from trade, both static and dynamic. In principle, there are a number of mechanisms for inducing greater accountability. One is to require it for participation in the global trading system, for example by including a labor standards clause in WTO agreements. Another is to regulate lead firms in GVCs so as to require accountability as part of lead firm home country policy. These top-down accountability schemes have had little political appeal, and national-level labor monitoring and non-governmental organization pressure have had more success on the ground. But these have not been implemented in any regular fashion and there is a strong case for a more ambitious and universal approach.

There is of course a structural problem at the most basic level here, rooted in the fact that lead firm entry into GVCs is so often premised on cost reduction, and especially on arm's-length relations aimed at lowering costs and redirecting the flow of rents in the direction of the lead firm. But there are some exceptions to the incentive compatibility problem and these seem to be of two sorts of companies: (i) Those concerned with the sustainability of their supply base (for example, Cadbury/Kraft investment in Ghanian schools and infrastructure as described by Barrientos 2010) and (ii) those concerned with negative publicity that hurts sales, public relations, or social responsibility reasons (for example, Nike or Apple's self- or semi-independent-monitoring following widespread public criticism for unacceptably low labor standards).

8.4.4 Industrial Policy in the Era of Vertically-Specialized Industrialization

To this point, our broad policy principles have focused more on how industrialized country policies or multilateral regulations might generate more equitable and sustainable outcomes. The issue of accountability by lead firms in GVCs will only be effective in the presence of legitimate, autonomous labor monitoring and regulation, but our focus was on how this may also require lead firm accountability and multilateral oversight. Here we turn more generally to the issue of industrialization and deindustrialization, and the question of the policies and economic structures that encourage dynamic gains from GVC expansion in supplier developing countries and in the industrialized countries as well.

With the shift from import substitution industrialization (ISI) to export-oriented growth beginning in the 1980s, economic development strategies at the level of the firm and the nation have increasingly focused on "indus-' trial upgrading" within existing production networks. This shift was the subject of our analysis in Chapter 7. ISI called for the development of vertically integrated infant industry through tariff protection, currency over-valuation and public investment, and ownership in monopolies in energy and basic industry appeals for inward FDI. Export-oriented industrialization (EOI) had two variants. The first was rooted in neoliberalism, and comprised both current account and capital account (including foreign exchange) liberalization, privatization, the end of ISI policy, the expansion of export processing zones, regional trade agreements, and bilateral investment treaties. The other variant of EOI is associated with the East Asian growth "miracle." The policies underpinning this "late industrialization" included export promotion along with import protection, strict regulation of inward FDI, subsidies to domestic industry along with production, and export targets.[7]

In vertically-specialized industrialization (VSI) production is typically for a portion of the GVC. Economic upgrading within GVCs has been highly successful in a number of well-known cases, most famously Chinese manufacturing and Indian IT and IT-enabled services. We identified evidence of it in many lesser-known cases, including Cambodian apparel and Kenyan horticulture.

Industrial upgrading can take a variety of forms (process, product, functional, and chain upgrading), but in the way we have defined it, it generally requires new capital, knowledge, and increased market access. In particular, it requires close coordination with (foreign) lead and other supplier firms to successfully compete in terms of product quality and specifications, and the scale and timing of input demands. China's success in VSI comes from its prominence in both buyer-led (such as Wal-Mart) and producer-led (such as Apple) GVCs, and a target for FDI both for efficiency-seeking and market-seeking, an unusual combination. China has combined low unit

---

[7] See Amsden (1989, 2001), Evans (1995), and Wade (1991).

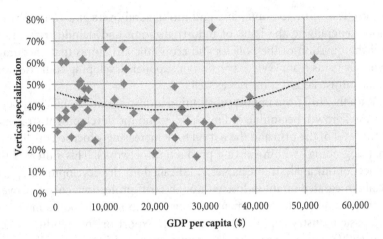

Figure 8.2. Vertical Specialization and Per Capita Income, Selected Developing Countries, 2005. *Source:* Own illustration. Data: OECD input-output dataset. Vertical specialization is for medium- and high-tech sectors.

costs, flexibility, and speed of response based on scale economies, modular production, undervaluation, low labor standards, massive infrastructure investment, industrial clusters, close relations with lead firms, aggressive pursuit of FDI, a willingness to seek raw materials abroad, and the great cooperation of neighboring countries in creating regional production networks.[8]

VSI then occurs as supplier firms upgrade, in particular by increasing the domestic functions in the production process. It would appear that as countries have reached higher levels of functioning in GVCs and higher levels of per capita income, they continue to grow based on a shedding of lower value added functions in the GVC, focusing on core competence and high value added aspects and outsourcing (domestically or internationally) the rest. A general depiction of the situation is Figure 8.2, which is a scatterplot for forty-two countries for the year 2005, where each point reflects the degree of vertical specialization in medium and high-tech industries in a country and its level of real per capita GDP. The figure shows that low-income countries seek to upgrade by reducing the overall degree of vertical specialization (raising domestic value added in exports) and then reach a point where rising incomes involves increasing vertical

---

[8] On different aspects of this long list of positive attributes, see Gereffi (2009), Appelbaum (2008), and Sturgeon (2002).

specialization while focusing on the highest value added components of the GVC.

GVCs are the structure within which upgrading occurs, but as we have seen, they present obstacles. The ability of lead firms to foster competition among suppliers allows lead firms to pressure suppliers to deliver at lowest possible cost and greatest flexibility in terms of delivery time, inventory management and even payment schedule. Competitive markets by definition do not bring positive economic profits over time. Thus, in addition to having to connect closely to, and bargain with, diverse sets of lead firms, supplier firms must compete for contracts with lead firms against supplier firms globally, and thus are under pressure to keep labor costs low. This is in stark contrast with the challenges of ISI, EOI and state-led "late industrialization".

In the era of VSI, successful exports may require initially very high levels of imports of intermediates, and firms must seek import liberalization for necessary intermediates, while promoting exports. Process upgrading alone may not bring the structural changes involving new capital and knowledge that broad-based industrialization requires. Functional upgrading requires the delicate balance of reducing imports of higher value added inputs while maintaining solid connections to lead firms. The challenges of VSI for developing countries are numerous and they raise a new role for the state in what has traditionally been called industrial policy (see Milberg, Jiang, and Gereffi 2013).

Industrialization is not just a concern for developing countries. Massive deindustrialization in the developed countries also signals the challenge of VSI for growth there. As we have seen, the growth in offshoring in many countries has raised the profit share, enabled financialization, and put downward pressure on the labor share. Most studies show that it has contributed to a skills-biased labor demand shift and thus to the rise in inequality in personal income distribution in these countries.

The focus on core competence has created an industrial structure with a low employment elasticity of innovation. Davis (2012) shows that the most innovative U.S. companies generate little employment in the United States. Total employment in six of the best-known innovative U.S. companies totaled just 291,392 in 2012 (see Table 8.1). This was less that the total employment of a single supermarket chain, Kroeger (338,000), and half the number of jobs lost during January 2009 of the U.S. recession (598,000). The long-term employment growth prospects in industrialized countries in the era of VSI are unclear. For the past three decades in the United States and other industrialized countries, productivity gains have not been shared

Table 8.1. *Employment in Selected Companies,*
United States, 2012

Company	Number of employees
Apple	60,400
Microsoft	90,000
Facebook	3,000
Cisco	71,825
Google	32,467
Amazon	33,700
All six	291,392

Source: Own illustration. Data: Davis (2012).

widely enough to generate economic security and sustainable economic growth.

There appear to be two models of industrial success in the period of the new wave of globalization. The one we have referred to most frequently in this book is the high-tech firm such as Apple which focuses on core competence and outsources the rest. Its success is found in very high value added per employee and low levels of employment. The other model is the firm that competes globally by operating globally. IBM is an example, as they have become profitable after making the transition from a manufacturing company to a services company and now compete on the same turf as the global providers of services (e.g. Wipro, Infosys). IBM's non-U.S. employment greatly exceeds its employment in the United States. In reducing U.S. employment, IBM has reduced its core of older workers, reduced its pension benefits, and moved to short-term contract-based employment in the United States.

Neither of these models solves the social problem of rising economic insecurity, and both are associated with a high profit share of income. They also point to the need for a new relation between firms and civil society, with mechanisms to redistribute profit income for social benefit, that is for greater economic security. In the new wave of globalization, if successful firms are not willing to undertake the needed social investment, the government must once again take a leading role.

8.4.5 Alternative Sources of Demand

Joseph Stiglitz (2009) has noted that the 2008 downturn was the first economic crisis in the era of globalization, in that the crisis was felt globally (rather than in just some regions) and spread in part because of the globalized nature of financial markets. His characterization also holds true for the production and trade sides of the economy. This has been the first economic crisis since the globalization of production – the expanded use of GVCs – became extensive and sophisticated.

Our analysis of the effects of the economic crisis on export-oriented developing countries in Chapter 2 confirms that the economic crisis that began in the United States in 2007, and quickly led to a large drop in demand for exports from developing countries, had a magnified effect on trade because of the prominence of GVC-based trade. Trade volumes rose much more rapidly than GDP for twenty-five years, and the reverse occurred in the recent recession. This reverse effect has been more pronounced and the upturn more delayed in the recent downturn.

Although international payments imbalances are large, they appear to be self-reinforcing, because capital inflows require higher profit rates that in turn require a relatively high reliance on cost- and risk-reducing offshore suppliers. The fact that more than 25 percent of U.S. imports from China are related party imports – that is, from firms with at least 5 percent ownership by U.S. MNCs – provides further reinforcement of the link. We have found, moreover, that the factors generating self-reinforcing imbalances have themselves led to rising income inequality in both the main deficit and surplus countries. In the United States, the profit share has increased even though real wages have risen much more slowly than productivity, and employment has not risen with economic growth in the proportion observed historically (Basu and Foley 2011).

Inequality has grown because much of the gains to higher-income managers and shareholders have been taxed at the lower rates on capital gains and dividends. Similar income distributional considerations are present in China. Low Chinese wages, lagging behind productivity growth, are an important driver of China's export surplus and thus of its foreign reserves accumulation. Chinese workers are effectively providing a subsidy to the Chinese government in the amount of the interest being earned on China's holdings of U.S. assets.

Another implication of the analysis is that countries need to find other, non-export sources of demand, or to diversify trade patterns to focus more on trade among developing countries. China's substantial stimulus packages in 2009 and 2012 are a prime example of expansionary fiscal policy as a boost to aggregate demand and China's growth has picked up following a large increase in unemployment from the initial shock to world trade. But China's success in domestic stimulus shows how difficult it can be to draw general

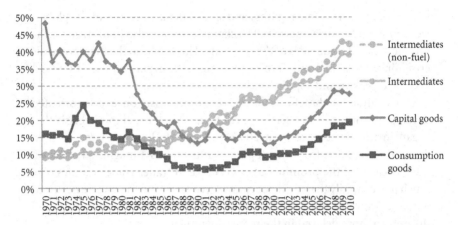

Figure 8.3. South-South Exports by Broad Economic Product Category (% of Total Exports), 1970–2010. *Source*: Own illustration. Data: United Nations Comtrade. Note: Figures are exports from LMICs to other LMICs by Broad Economic Categories.

conclusions about the possibilities for stimulus across the developing world. Capacity for stimulus depends to a great extent on the prior accumulation of foreign exchange reserves. China is exceptional in that it has accumulated substantial reserves over the past fifteen years. Most developing countries have very small reserve stocks.

The other prospect is to expand other sources of export demand. South-South trade is often cited as a potential source of growth in developing countries. This deep embedding in GVCs also appears in the structure of developing countries' imports. Figure 8.3 shows low- and middle-income countries' (LMICs) exports to other LMICs – that is, South-South trade – by Broad Economic Categories as a percentage of total exports within each category (see Appendix 2.1 for broad economic categories classification). During the past two decades, the export shares to other developing countries for capital goods, consumption goods, and intermediates have been growing steadily. This reflects the increased importance of South-South trade. By definition, high-income countries have absorbed a declining percentage of exports from developing countries.

Regarding the composition of South-South trade, around 40 percent of developing countries' exports of intermediates went to other developing countries in 2010. Capital and consumption goods are increasingly exported to developing countries as well, reaching shares of 28 percent and 19 percent in 2010, respectively. Yet the structure of world trade according to GVCs may create an obstacle in the short-run to South-South trade growth. Figure 8.3 shows that the greatest growth potential of developing countries' exports over the past decade has been in intermediates. This indicates that South-South trade is also molded to some extent by GVCs and the processing of intermediates to serve these chains. In this sense, the expansion of South-South trade still depends on the functioning of GVCs.

8.5 Capitalism's Explanation System

The severe economic downturn of 2008 brought renewed interest in the Keynesian view that an expansionary fiscal and monetary policy is necessary in times of economic slowdown. As we have argued throughout this chapter, the Keynesian response to the economic crisis of 2008, which was rapid and significant in some countries, required a relatively simple economic adjustment. The new era of globalization requires reforms that go beyond the expansion of demand to the promotion of innovation with sustainable growth and economic security. This is an area where Keynes cannot help us. Keynes was focused on the role of the state in generating aggregate demand when the level delivered by the private sector was inadequate. Deeply conscious of the inequity in the economic outcome in the advanced capitalism of his day, Keynes nonetheless explicitly resisted commenting on the deeper issues of the structure of capitalist production and the underlying power asymmetries they reflect. In the new wave of globalization, the important issues of economic security and social upgrading are not necessarily better advanced by either free trade or protectionism. The challenge that lies ahead is to rethink the social contract among governments, civil society, and the business sector to adapt to the changing world of international trade. This is a more difficult task than providing a Keynesian macroeconomic stimulus.

As Polanyi explains, markets function because they are embedded in social and political institutions that create trust and provide norms and limits. In the last twenty-five years, a shift in corporate strategy led to financialization and financial innovation rather than productivity growth, technological innovation and shared prosperity. Rising profits and profit share spurred speculation, which brought calamitous, system-wide risk. This has been accompanied by a steady erosion of the economic security of households. The rate of household savings fell, the labor share went down, the rate of poverty rose, and the mortgage foreclosure rate has remained at historic highs since the 2008 collapse.

Polanyi's point has an epistemological dimension, specifically, the recognition that the field of economics combines science, politics and ethics.

When economics is universally acknowledged as a truly *social* science, there will necessarily be greater modesty in the application of deductive models, and scaled-back expectations of the kind of knowledge these models can provide. Explicit attention to the embeddedness of markets would narrow the gap between academic and everyday discourse. Other disciplines in the social sciences have more successfully articulated the social costs of globalization. As we touched on in Chapter 1, the barely concealed condescension of economists towards the popular understanding of globalization is one of the things that isolates the field, and creates a rift between the pronouncements of economists and the lived reality of the public. Economists must produce a richer, embedded description, a better accounting for historical context and power asymmetries, within and outside of GVCs.

The crisis of 2008 resulted in widespread disappointment with the economics profession because it had failed to predict the great downturn and to propose policies to avoid it. This precipitated a discussion not only of faulty models and representations of risk, but of glaring lapses in professional ethics when it became clear that economic research was being carried out and published by people who had affiliations with financial firms, without revealing it in their published work. This striking lack of transparency surprised people inside and outside the profession, leading to calls for reform and the adoption of an economists' code of ethical conduct by the American Economic Association.[9] DeMartino (2011) roots this ethical crisis precisely in its failure to adequately represent downside risks, what he calls the profession's use of the "maxi-max principle," according to which only the upside benefits of a policy are quantified and discussed.

The economic treatment of offshoring suffers from a different sort of ethical problem. The standard interpretation of the theory of comparative advantage has led to decades of appeals for trade liberalization and only limited advocacy for a policy position that emerges just as organically as the free trade one: the need for compensation of losers by winners and the importance of dynamic gains relative to static efficiency gains. In particular, the potential dynamic gains from offshoring and the development of GVCs have not been realized, and the new wave of globalization has in many cases contributed to heightened economic insecurity in the industrialized countries and new obstacles to economic development in industrializing regions.

---

[9] The impact of the documentary film, "Inside Job," cannot be overstated. See Spiegler and Milberg (2013) for a critical overview of the current debate.

Trade models based solely on comparative advantage suffer also from conceptual and historical flaws. The theoretical consequence has been to remove capital and investment and thus firm profits and growth from the discussion, diminishing the importance of the distribution of income between profits and wages. The narrow focus on skilled and low-skill labor has also had theoretical and political consequences. The political consequence is that the analysis largely removes the state from the picture. Risk is seen as an increasingly private burden. Even the problem of skills-biased changes in labor demand would be solved, in this view, by individuals rationally and privately investing in their own capital.

It is important to consider the embeddedness of markets not just in the narrow sense of firm behavior as a consequence of shifts in corporate governance ideology, but in a broader sense that includes the governance and power relations that run through GVCs, their connection to finance and financial regulation, the role of the state, and of labor market structures. Our analysis of economic globalization represents an effort to bring knowledge from other disciplines into the economistic account. Global production is not the result of perfectly competitive market-based allocation of resources. Firms within GVCs have determined the international division of labor, with states, international law, and even household structures and gender relations in labor markets playing important roles.

While a few countries have been able to benefit from the new wave of globalization through industrial upgrading, such upgrading is not guaranteed, nor does it translate effortlessly into broad social improvements. Traditional economic theory predicts a very high correlation between industrial and social upgrading, but the evidence for developing countries over the past twenty years does not support such a conclusion at the national or GVC level. One of the reasons for this lack of correlation is the particular governance structure of GVCs. The presence of enormous competitive pressure on suppliers in a world of buyer power and excess capacity has made it extremely difficult for countries to improve their terms of trade. Suppliers have been forced to keep costs (especially labor costs) in check and to maintain markups over costs at a bare minimum.

***

Robert Heilbroner (1999) writes, "At its core, economics is an explanation system whose purpose is to enlighten us as to the workings, and therefore to the problems and prospects, of that complex social entity we call the economy" (Heilbroner 1999, 311). But what has the economics of offshoring been able to explain? By insisting on the general benefits of offshoring in the face of evidence to the contrary, economics has failed to connect to the popular experience of globalization of many firms, workers, industries, and countries. The explanation has thus been outsourced to non-economists: sociologists, geographers, industrial relations and management experts, journalists, and popular writers who describe and theorize global markets as they are interlinked with domestic and international institutions and, most importantly, the GVC and lead firm strategies that govern them. Our account has been informed by insights from these disciplines, as well as from some unorthodox circles in economics. We have drawn on the management and business history literature on corporate strategy, the GVC concept from economic sociology, geography and development studies, the classical theory of trade and investment, the Post Keynesian theory of oligopoly pricing, and feminist perspectives on trade and development.

The outsourcing of economics in the area of international trade and global production is just one example of the failure of economics in the recent crisis. The vast forces of globalization call for a more grounded, embedded approach to economics, which puts power and profits back into the center of the analysis, and which understands firms as evolving institutions that do not simply maximize short-term profits subject to given technology and factor prices. They also allocate resources in pursuit of growth and shareholder values, and actively seek to alter their cost structure through innovation, changes in labor relations, and offshoring. The expansion of GVCs has fundamentally altered the nature of work and the ability of workers to attain economic security. What is required now is an alternative analytical framework that does not exclude some of the basic institutions of capitalism and welcomes the insights from other disciplines. Once the field of economics broadens its scope it will be possible to imagine a different future for the global economy.

References

Abernathy, F. H., J. T. Dunlop, J. H. Hammond, and D. Weil. (1999). *A Stitch in Time: Lean Retailing and the Transformation of Manufacturing – Lessons from the Apparel and Textile and Apparel Industries.* Oxford: Oxford University Press.

Aggarwal, A. (2005). "Performance of Export Processing Zones: A Comparative Analysis of India, Sri Lanka and Bangladesh." Mimeo, Indian Council for Research on International Economic Relations, February.

Aggarwal, A. (2007). "Impact of Special Economic Zones on Employment, Poverty and Human Development." Working Paper No. 194, Indian Council for Research on International Economic Relations.

Akyuz, Y. and C. Gore. (1996). "The Investment-Profits Nexus in East Asian Industrialization." *World Development* 24(3): 461–70.

Alterman, W. (2010). "Producing an Input Price Index." Proceedings from a conference on Measurement Issues Arising from the Growth of Globalization," Upjohn Institute and National Academy of Public Administration, August.

Amendola, G., G. Dosi, and E. Papagni. (1993). "The Dynamics of International Competitiveness." *Weltwirtschaftliches Archiv* 129(3): 451–71.

Amighini, A. (2006). "Upgrading in International Trade: Methods and Evidence from Selected Sectors." In *Upgrading to Compete: Global Value Chains, Clusters, and SMEs in Latin America*, edited by C. Pietrobelli and R. Rabelloti, 221–51. Washington, DC: Inter-American Development Bank.

Amiti, M. and S.-J. Wei. (2005). "Fear of Service Outsourcing: Is it Justified?" *Economic Policy* 20(4): 305–47.

Amiti, M. and S.-J. Wei. (2006). "Service Offshoring, Productivity and Employment: Evidence from the US." CEPR Discussion Paper, No. 5475, February.

Amiti, M. and S.-J. Wei. (2009). "Service Offshoring and Productivity: Evidence from the US." *World Economy* 32(2): 203–20.

Amiti, M. and D. E. Weinstein. (2009). "Exports and Financial Shocks." Mimeo, Federal Reserve Bank of New York and Columbia University, September.

Amsden, A. H. (1989). *Asia's Next Giant: South Korea and Late Industrialization.* New York: Oxford University Press.

Amsden, A. H. (2001). *The Rise of the Rest.* Oxford: Oxford University Press.

Anderson, R. and C. Gascon. (2007). "The Perils of Globalization: Offshoring and Economic Security of the American Worker." Working Paper 2007–004A, Federal Reserve Bank of St. Louis.

Andersson, T., C. Haslam, E. Lee, and N. Tsitsianis. (2007). "Financialized Accounts: A Stakeholder Account of Cash Distribution in the S&P 500 (1990–2005)." *Accounting Forum* 31(3): 217–32.

Andersson, T., C. Haslam, E. Lee, and N. Tsitsianis. (2008). "Financialization Directing Strategy." *Accounting Forum* 32(4): 261–75.

Anderton, R. and P. Brenton. (1999). "Outsourcing and Low-Skilled Workers in the UK." *Bulletin of Economic Research* 51(4): 267–85.

Anderton, R., P. Brenton, and E. Oscarsson. (2002). "What's Trade Got to Do with It? Relative Demand for Skills." *Review of World Economics* 138(4): 629–51.

Andrews, E. (2004). "Democrats Criticize Bush Over Job Exports." *New York Times* February 11, 2004.

Anker, R. (1997). "Theories of Occupational Segregation by Sex." *International Labour Review* 136(3): 315–39.

Antràs, P. (2003). "Firms, Contracts, and Trade Structure." *Quarterly Journal of Economics* 118(4): 1375–418.

Antràs, P. (2005). "Property Rights and the International Organization of Production." *American Economic Review Papers and Proceedings* 95(2): 25–32.

Appelbaum, R. (2008). "Big Suppliers in East Asia: A Growing Counterweight to the Power of Giant Retailers?" Mimeo, Department of Sociology, University of California at Santa Barbara.

Arestis, P. (2005). "Financial Liberalization and the Relationship between Finance and Growth." University of Cambridge, Centre for Economic and Public Policy (CEPP) Working Paper, No. 05/05.

Arestis, P. and W. Milberg. (1993–1994). "Degree of Monopoly, Pricing and Flexible Exchange Rates." *Journal of Post Keynesian Economics* 16(2): 167–88.

Armas, E. and M. Sadni-Jallab. (2002). "A Review of the Role and Impact of Export Processing Zones in World Trade: The Case of Mexico." Working Paper 02–07, Centre National de la Recherche Scientifique, Paris.

Arndt, S. (1997). "Globalization and the Open Economy." *North American Journal of Economics and Finance* 8(1): 71–99.

Arndt, S. (1999). "Globalization and Economic Development." *The Journal of International Trade and Economic Development* 8(3): 309–18.

Arndt, S. (2001). "Offshore Sourcing and Production Sharing in Preference Areas." In *Fragmentation: New Production Patterns in the World Economy*, edited by S. Arndt and H. Kierzkowski, 76–87. New York: Oxford University Press.

Arndt, S. and H. Kierzkowski. (eds.) (2001). *Fragmentation: New Production Patterns in the World Economy*. New York: Oxford University Press.

Autor, D. (2010). "Polarization of Job Opportunities in the U.S. Labor Market: Implications for Employment and Earnings." The Center for American Progress and The Hamilton Project/Brookings Institution, April.

Badgett, M. V. and N. Folbre. (1999). "Assigning Care: Gender Norms and Economic Outcomes." *International Labour Review* 138(3): 311–27.

Badhuri, A. (2011). "Financialization in the Light of Keynesian Theory." *PSL Quarterly Review* 64(256): 7–21.

Bagwell, K. (1989). "The Economic Analysis of Advertising." In *The Handbook of Industrial Organization*, edited by M. Armstrong and R. Porter, Vol. 3., 1701–1844. Amsterdam: North-Holland Press.

Bair, J. and G. Gereffi. (2001). "Local Clusters in Global Chains: The Causes and Consequences in Export Dynamism in Torreon's Blue Jeans Industry." *World Development* 29(11): 1885–903.

Baissac, C. (2003). "Maximizing the Developmental Impact of EPZs: A Comparative Perspective in the African Context of Needed Accelerated Growth." Mimeo, presented at EPZ symposium, Johannesburg, South Africa.

Baldone, S., F. Stogati, and L. Taljonie. (2007). "On Some Effects of International Fragmentation of Production on Comparative Advantages, Trade Flows and the Income of Countries." *World Economy* 30(11): 1726–69.

Baldwin, R. (1992). "Are Economists' Traditional Trade Policy Views Still Valid?" *Journal of Economic Literature* 30(2): 804–29.

Baldwin, R. (2006). "Globalisation: the Great Unbundling(s)". Paper for the Finnish Prime Minister's Office, Economic Council of Finland, September.

Baldwin, R. (2009). "The Great Trade Collapse: What Caused It and What Does It Mean?" In *The Great Trade Collapse: Causes, Consequences and Prospects*, edited by R. Baldwin, 1–14. Centre for Economic Policy Research, The Graduate Institute, Geneva.

Baldwin, R. (2012). "Trade and Industrialisation after Globalisation's Second Unbundling: How Building and Joining a Supply Chain are Different and Why it Matters." Forthcoming in *Globalization in an Age of Crisis: Multilateral Economic Cooperation in the Twenty-First Century*, edited by R. Feenstra and A. Taylor. Cambridge, MA: National Bureau of Economic Research.

Baldwin, R. and F. Robert-Nicoud. (2007). "Offshoring: General Equilibrium Effects on Wages, Production and Trade." NBER Working Paper, No. 12991, National Bureau of Economic Research, Cambridge, MA.

Barbosa-Filho, N. H., C. Rada, L. Taylor, and L. Zamparelli. (2005). "US Macro Imbalances: Trends, Cycles and Policy Implications." Policy Note, Schwartz Center for Economic Policy Analysis, New School for Social Research, December.

Barboza, D. and C. Duhigg. (2012). "Pressure, Chinese and Foreign, Drives Changes at Foxconn." *New York Times*, February 19, 2012.

Bardhan, A. and D. Jaffee. (2004). "On Intra-Firm Trade and Multinationals: Foreign Outsourcing and Offshoring in Manufacturing." Mimeo, Haas School of Business, University of California, Berkeley.

Bardhan, A., D. Jaffee, and C. Kroll. (eds.) (2013). *The Oxford Handbook of Offshoring and Global Employment*. Oxford University Press: New York.

Bardhan, P. (2010). *Awakening Giants, Feet of Clay: Assessing the Economic Rise of China and India*. Princeton: Princeton University Press.

Bardhan, P., D. Mookherjee, and M. Tsumagari. (2010). "Middlemen, Margins and Globalization." Working Paper, Department of Economics, University of California, Berkeley, version of July 9.

Bas, M. and J. Carluccio. (2009). "Wage Bargaining and the Boundaries of the Multinational Firm." CEP Discussion Paper 963, Center for Economic Performance, December.

Basu, D. and D. K. Foley. (2011). "Dynamics of Output and Employment in the US Economy." Department of Economics Working Paper No. 2011-02, University of Massachusetts at Amherst.

Bates, T. W., K. M. Kahle, and R. M. Stulz. (2006). "Why Do U.S. Firms Hold So Much More Cash than They Used to?" NBER Working Paper No. 12534, National Bureau of Economic Research, Cambridge, MA.

Becker, G. (1957). *The Economics of Discrimination.* Chicago: University of Chicago Press.

Becker, S., K. Ekholm, and M. Muendler. (2009). "Offshoring and the Onshore Composition of Tasks and Skills." CEPR Discussion Paper, No. 7391, August.

Belloc, M. (2004). "Do Labor Market Institutions Affect International Comparative Advantage? An Empirical Investigation." Department of Economics, University of Siena, Series 444.

Bentolila, S. and G. Saint-Paul. (2003). "Explaining Movements in the Labor Share." *Contributions to Macroeconomics* 3(1): Article 9.

Berg, J. (2005). *Miracle for Whom? Chilean Workers Under Free Trade.* London: Routledge.

Berg, J. and D. Kucera. (eds.) (2007). *In Defence of Labor Market Institutions: Cultivating Justice in the Developing World.* London: Palgrave Macmillan.

Bernanke, B. (2005). "The Global Saving Glut and the U.S. Current Account Deficit." Speech Delivered for the Sandridge Lecture at the Virginia Association of Economists, Richmond, March 10.

Bernanke, B. (2007). "Global Imbalances: Recent Developments and Prospects." Bundesbank Lecture, Berlin, September 11.

Bernard, A., B. Jensen, S. Redding, and P. Schott. (2007). "Firms in International Trade." *Journal of Economic Perspectives* 21(3): 105–30.

Bernhardt, T. and W. Milberg. (2011). "Economic and Social Upgrading in Global Value Chains: Analysis fo Horticulture, Apparel, Tourism and Mobile Telephones." Working Paper No. 6, Capturing the Gains, Brooks World Poverty Institute, University of Manchester, U.K.

Bernhardt, T. and W. Milberg. (2013). "Does Industrial Upgrading Generate Employment and Wage Gains?" In *The Oxford Handbook of Offshoring and Global Employment,* edited by A. Bardhan, D. Jaffee, and C. Kroll, Chapter 20. New York: Oxford University Press.

Bhagwati, J., A. Panagariya, and T. N. Srinivasan. (2004). "The Muddles over Outsourcing." *Journal of Economic Perspectives* 18(4): 93–114.

Bivens, L. (2005). "Truth and Consequences of Offshoring." EPI Briefing Paper #155, Washington, DC: Economic Policy Institute.

Black, S. and B. Brainerd. (2004). "Improving Equality? The Impact of Globalization on Gender Discrimination." *Industrial and Labor Relations Review* 57(4): 540–59.

Blecker, R. (1989). "International Competition, Income Distribution and Economic Growth." *Cambridge Journal of Economics* 13(3): 395–412.

Blecker, R. (1992). *Beyond the Twin Deficits.* Armonk, NY: M.E. Sharpe.

Blecker, R. (1999). "Kaleckian Macro Models for Open Economies." In *Foundations of International Economics: Post Keynesian Perspectives,* edited by J. Deprez and J. T. Harvey 116–49. London: Routledge.

Blecker, R. (2009). "The Trade Deficit Trap: How It Got So Big, Why It Persists and What To Do About It." EPI Working Paper, No. 284, Washington, DC: Economic Policy Institute.

Blecker, R. (2012). "Stolper-Samuelson Revisited: Trade and Distribution with Oligopolistic Profits." *Metroeconomica* 63(3): 569–98.

Blecker, T. and G. Friedrich. (2010). *Mass Customization: Challenges and Solutions, International Series in Operations Research & Management Science*. New York: Springer.

Blinder, A. (2005). "Fear of Offshoring." CEPS Working Paper No. 119. Center for Economic Policy Studies, Princeton University.

Blinder, A. (2006). "Offshoring: The Next Industrial Revolution?" *Foreign Affairs* 85(2): 113–28.

Blinder, A. (2007a). "Offshoring: Big Deal, or Business as Usual?" CEPS Working Paper No. 149, Center for Economic Policy Studies, Princeton University.

Blinder, A. (2007b). "Free Trade's Great, but Offshoring Rattles Me." *The Washington Post*, May 6, 2007.

Blinder, A. (2009). "How Many U.S. Jobs Might Be Offshorable?" *World Economics* 10(2): 41–78.

Block, F. (2001). "Introduction" to Karl Polanyi, *The Great Transformation: The Political and Economic Origins of Our Time*. Boston, MA: Beacon Press.

Block, F. and P. Evans. (2005). "The State and the Economy." In *Handbook of Economic Sociology* edited by N. J. Smelser and R. Swedberg, 505–26. Princeton: Princeton University Press.

Boeri, T. (2002). "Making Social Europe(s) Compete." Mimeo, University of Bocconi and Fondazione Rodolfo Debenedetti.

Bowen, H., E. Leamer, and L. Sveikauskas. (1987). "Multicountry, Multi-Factor Tests of the Factor Abundance Theory." *American Economic Review* 77(5): 791–809.

Boyer, R. (2000). "Is a Finance-Led Growth Regime a Viable Alternative to Fordism?: A Preliminary Analysis?" *Economy and Society* 29(1): 111–45.

Brailovsky, V., J. Eatwell, and J. Ros. (1982). "Cumulative Causation in Industrial Development." Mimeo, Cambridge: Cambridge University Press.

Brainard, S. L. and D. A. Riker. (1997). "Are U.S. Multinationals Exporting U.S. Jobs?" NBER Working Paper No. 5958, Cambridge, MA: National Bureau of Economic Research.

Brewer, A. (1985). "Trade with Fixed Real Wages and Mobile Capital." *Journal of International Economics* 18(1–2): 177–86.

Bronfenbrenner, K. and S. Luce. (2004). "The Changing Nature of Corporate Global Restructuring: The Impact of Production Shifts on Jobs in the US, China, and Around the Globe." Prepared for the US-China Economic and Security Review Commission.

Brummund, P. (2011). "Variation in Monopsonistic Behavior Across Establishments: Evidence from the Indonesian Labor Market." Job market paper, Cornell University.

Buchele, R. and J. Christiansen. (1992). "Industrial Relations and Productivity Growth: A Comparative Perspective." *International Contributions to Labour Studies* 2: 77–97.

Burke, J., J. Epstein, and M. Choi. (2004). "Rising Foreign Outsourcing and Employment Losses in U.S. Manufacturing, 1987–2002." Working Paper, Political Economy Research Institute, University of Massachusetts-Amherst.

Busse, M. and C. Spielman. (2006). "Gender Inequality and Trade." *Review of International Economics* 14(3): 362–79.

Calmfors, L. (1993). "Centralisation of Wage Bargaining and Macroeconomic Performance – A Survey." *OECD Economic Studies* No. 21: 161–91.

Calmfors, L. and J. Driffill. (1988). "Centralization of Wage Bargaining." *Economic Policy* 3(1): 14–61.

Campa, J. and L. Goldberg. (1997). "The Evolving External Orientation of Manufacturing Industries: Evidence from Four Countries." NBER Working Paper 5919, National Bureau of Economic Research, Cambridge, MA.

Cassidy, J. (2005). "The Customer is King." *The New Yorker*, February 14 and 21, 2005.

Caves, R. (1982). *Multinational Enterprise and Economic Analysis*. Cambridge: Cambridge University Press.

Ceglowski, J. and S. Golub. (2005). "Just How Low are China's Labor Costs?" Mimeo, Bryn Mawr College Department of Economics.

Chandler, A. (1962). *Strategy and Structure: Chapters in the History of American Enterprise*. Cambridge, MA: MIT Press.

Chang, H.-J. (2002). *Kicking Away the Ladder: Development Strategy in Historical Perspective*. New York and London: Anthem Press.

Chang, H.-J. (2007). *Bad Samaritans – Rich Nations, Poor Policies, and the Threat to the Developing World*. London: Random House.

Chen, H., M. Kondratowicz, and K. Yi. (2005). "Vertical Specialization and Three Facts About U.S. International Trade." *North American Journal of Economics and Finance* 16(1): 35–59.

Chen, S. and M. Ravaillon. (2008). "The Developing World Is Poorer Than We Thought But No Less Successful In The Fight Against Poverty." Policy Research Working Paper 4073, World Bank, Washington, DC.

Choi, M. (2001). "Threat Effect of Foreign Direct Investment on Labor Union Wage Premium." PERI Working Paper 27, University of Massachusetts.

Christopoulou, R. and P. Vermeulen. (2008). "Markups in the Euro Area and the US over the Period 1981–2004." ECB Working Papers, No. 856, European Central Bank.

Clarence-Smith, W. and S. Topik. (2003). *The Global Coffee Economy in Africa, Asia, and Latin America, 1500–1989*. Cambridge: Cambridge University Press.

Clasen, J. (2007). "Flexicurity – A New Buzzword in EU Labour Market Policy." Mimeo. University of Edinburgh School of Social and Political Studies, presented at Scottish Policy Innovation Forum, Edinburgh.

Clausing, K. (2004). "The American Jobs Creation Act of 2004: Creating Jobs for Accountants and Lawyers." Urban Institute/Brookings Institution Tax Policy Center. *Tax Policy Issues and Options*, Brief No. 8.

Cline, W. and J. Williamson. (2009). "Equilibrium Exchange Rates." VoxEU, June 18, 2009.

Cling, J. and G. Letilly. (2001). "Export Processing Zones: A Threatened Instrument for Global Economy Insertion?" Working Document, Developpement et Insertion National (DIAL).

Coase, R. (1937). "The Nature of the Firm." *Economica* 4(16): 386–405.

Conelly, M. (2012). "Poll Finds Consumers Confusion on Where Apple Devices are Made." *New York Times*, January 25, 2012.

Cowell, A. (2002). "War Inflates Cocoa Prices But Leaves Africans Poor." *New York Times*, October 31, 2002.

Cowling, K. and R. Sugden. (1987). *Transnational Monopoly Capitalism*. Brighton: Wheatsheaf.

Cowling, K. and R. Sugden. (1989). "Exchange Rate Adjustment and Oligopoly Pricing Behaviour." *Cambridge Journal of Economics* 13(3): 373–93.

Cowling, K., F. and G. Vernon. (2000). "Declining Concentration in UK Manufacturing? A Problem of Measurement." *International Review of Applied Economics* 14(1): 45–54.

Crinò, R. (2009). "Offshoring, Multinationals and Labour Market: A Review of the Empirical Literature." *Journal of Economic Surveys* 23(2): 197–249.

Crinò, R. (2010). "Service Offshoring and White-Collar Employment." *Review of Economic Studies* 77(2): 595–632.

Crinò, R. (2012). "Service Offshoring and the Skill Composition of Labour Demand." *Oxford Bulletin of Economics and Statistics* 74(1): 20–57.

Crotty, J. (2005). "The Neoliberal Paradox: The Impact of Destructive Product Market Competition and 'Modern' Financial Markets on Nonfinancial Corporation Performance in the Neoliberal Era." In *Financialization and the World Economy*, edited by G. Epstein, 77–110. Cheltenham: Edward Elgar Publishers.

Dadush, U. (2012). "Broader Implications of the Growing Trade in Intermediates." World Economic Forum.

Davidson, C., L. Martin, and S. Matusz. (1999). "Trade and Search Generated Unemployment." *Journal of International Economics* 48(2): 271–99.

Davis, G. (2009). *Managed by the Market: How Finance Reshaped America.* New York: Oxford University Press.

Davis, G. (2012). "Corporate Innovation Will Not Save Us in a Shareholder Value Economy." Presentation at The New School, updated in 2012.

De Marchi, N. (1976). "Anomaly and the Development of Economics: The Case of the Leontief Paradox." In *Method and Appraisal in Economics*, edited by S. Latsis, 109–28. New York: Cambridge University Press.

Deardorff, A. (1979). "Weak Links in the Chain of Comparative Advantage." *Journal of International Economics* 9(2): 197–209.

Deardorff, A. (1994). "Exploring the Limits of Comparative Advantage." *Review of World Economics (Weltwirtschaftliches Archiv)* 130(1): 1–19.

Deardorff, A. (2001a). "Fragmentation in Simple Trade Models." *North American Journal of Economics and Finance* 12(2): 121–37.

Deardorff, A. (2001b). "Fragmentation Across Cones." In *Fragmentation: New Production Patterns in the World Economy*, edited by S. Arndt and H. Kierzkowski, 35–51. New York: Oxford University Press.

DeMartino, G. (2011). *The Economists' Oath: On the Need for and Content of Professional Economic Ethics.* New York: Oxford University Press.

Dew-Becker, I. and R. Gordon. (2005). "Where Did Productivity Growth Go? Inflation Dynamics and the Distribution of Income." *Brookings Papers on Economic Activity* 36 (2): 67–127.

Dharmapala, D., C. F. Foley, and K. Forbes. (2011). "Watch What I Do, Not What I Say: The Unintended Consequences of the Homeland Investment Act." *Journal of Finance* 66(3): 753–87.

Dixit, A. and J. Stiglitz. (1976). "Monopolistic Competition and Optimum Product Diversity." *American Economic Review* 67(3): 297–308.

Dobbs, L. (2004). *Exporting America: Why Corporate Greed is Shipping American Jobs Overseas.* New York: Warner Business Books.

Dolan, C. and J. Humphrey. (2000). "Governance and Trade in Fresh Vegetables: The Impact of UK Supermarkets on the African Horticulture Industry." *Journal of Development Studies* 37(2): 147–76.

Dollar, D., W. Baumol, and E. Wolff. (1988). "The Factor Price Equalization Model and Industry Labor Productivity: An Empirical Test Across Countries." In *Empirical Methods for International Trade*, edited by R. Feenstra, 23–47. Cambridge, MA: MIT Press.

Dooley, M. and P. Garber. (2009). "Global Imbalances and the Crisis: A Solution in Search of a Problem." VoxEU, March 23, 2009.

Dorman, P. (2007). "Low Savings or a High Trade Deficit? Which Tail is Wagging Which?" *Challenge Magazine* 50(4): 49–64.

Dosi, G., K. Pavitt, and L. Soete. (1990). *Technology and International Competitiveness*. New York: NYU Press.

Dossani, R. and M. Kenney. (2003). "Went for Cost, Stayed for Quality: Moving the Back Office to India." Mimeo, University of California-Davis.

Duhigg, C. and K. Bradsher. (2012). "How the U.S. Lost Out on iPhone Work." *New York Times*, January 21, 2012.

Dumenil, G. and D. Levy. (2005). "Costs and Benefits of Neoliberalism: A Class Analysis." In *Financialization and the World Economy*, edited by G. Epstein, 17–45. Cheltenham: Edward Elgar Publishers.

Dunning, J. H. (2000). "The Eclectic Paradigm as an Envelope for Economic and Business Theories of MNE Activity." *International Business Review* 9(2): 163–90.

Eatwell, J. and L. Taylor. (2002). *International Capital Markets: Systems in Transitions*. Oxford: Oxford University Press.

Egger, H. and P. Egger. (2005). "Labor Market Effects of Outsourcing Under Industrial Interdependence." *International Review of Economics and Finance* 14(3): 349–63.

Eichengreen, B. and K. O'Rourke. (2009). "A Tale of Two Depressions." VoxEU, March 8, 2010.

Eichner, A. (1976). *The Megacorp and Oligopoly*. Cambridge: Cambridge University Press.

Ekholm, K. and K. Hakkala. (2006). "The Effect of Offshoring on Labour Demand: Evidence from Sweden." CEPR Discussion Paper, No. 5648, London: Centre for Economic Policy Research.

Ellis, L. and K. Smith. (2007). "The Global Upward Trend in the Profit Share." BIS Working Paper No. 231, Bank for International Settlements.

Elmslie, B. (2004). "Adam Smith and Noneconomic Objectives." *Review of International Economics* 12(4): 689–92.

Elson, D. (2007). "International Trade and Gender Equality: Women as Achievers of Competitive Advantage and as Sources of Competitive Advantage." Paper prepared for *International Symposium on Gender at the Heart of Globalization*, Paris.

Engman, M., O. Onodera, and E. Pinali. (2007). "Export Processing Zones: Past and Future Role in Trade and Development." OECD Trade Committee, May, Organisation for Economic Co-operation and Development, Paris.

Epstein, G. and A. Jayadev. (2005). "The Rise of Rentier Incomes in OECD Countries: Financialization, Central Bank Policy and Labor Solidarity." In *Financialization and the World Economy*, edited by G. Epstein, 46–72. Cheltenham and Northampton: Edward Elgar.

Escaith, H. and F. Gonguet. (2009). "Supply Chains and Financial Shocks: Real Transmission Channels in Globalised Production Networks." VoxEU, June 16, 2009.

Ethier, W. (1984). "Higher Dimensional Issues in Trade Theory." In *Handbook of International Economics*, edited by R. Jones and P. Kenen, 131–84. Amsterdam: North Holland.

Evans, P. (1995). *Embedded Autonomy: States and Industrial Transformation*. Princeton: Princeton University Press.

Fafchamps, M. and R. Vargas Hill. (2008). "Price Transmission and Trader Entry in Domestic Commodity Markets." *Economic Development and Cultural Change* (56)4: 729–66.

Fagerberg, J. (1996). "Technology and Competitiveness." *Oxford Review of Economic Policy* 12(3): 39–51.

Falk, M. and B. Koebel. (2002). "Outsourcing, Imports and Labour Demand." *Scandinavian Journal of Economics* 104(4): 567–86.

Farrell, V. and D. Agrawal. (2005). "Who Wins in Offshoring?" *The McKinsey Quarterly*. Member edition: 1–4.

Feenstra, R. (1998). "Integration of Trade and Disintegration of Production in the Global Economy." *Journal of Economic Perspectives* 12(4): 31–50.

Feenstra, R. and G. Hanson. (1996). "Globalization, Outsourcing and Wage Inequality." *American Economic Review* 86(2): 240–45.

Feenstra, R. and G. Hanson. (1999). "The Impact of Outsourcing and High-Technology Capital on Wages: Estimates for the United States, 1979–1990." *The Quarterly Journal of Economics* 114(3): 907–40.

Feenstra, R. and G. Hanson. (2001). "Global Production Sharing and Rising Inequality: A Survey of Trade and Wages." NBER Working Paper 8372, National Bureau of Economic Research, Cambridge, MA.

Feenstra, R. and G. Hanson. (2003). "Global Production Sharing and Rising Inequality: A Survey of Trade and Wages." In *Handbook of International Trade: Volume I*, edited by E. K. Choi and J. Harrigan, 146–87. Oxford: Blackwell Publishing.

Feenstra, R. and G. Hanson. (2004). "Intermediaries in Entrepot Trade: Hong Kong Re-Exports of Chinese Goods." *Journal of Economics & Management Strategy* 13(1): 3–35.

Feenstra, R., W. Hai, W. Woo, and S. Yao. (1998). "The US-China Bilateral Trade Balance: Its Size and Determinants." NBER Working Paper No. 6598, National Bureau of Economic Research, Cambridge, MA.

Ferrantino, M. and A. Larsen (2009). "Transmission of the Global Recession Through U.S. Trade." In *The Great Trade Collapse: Causes, Consequences and Prospects*, edited by R. Baldwin, 173–82. Centre for Economic Policy Research for VoxEU, The Graduate Institute, Geneva.

Findlay, R. and R. Jones. (2000). "Factor Bias and Technical Progress." *Economics Letters* 68(3): 303–08.

Findlay, R. and R. Jones. (2001). "Input Trade and the Location of Production." *American Economic Review* 91(2): 29–33.

Fitter, R. and R. Kaplinsky. (2001). "Who Gains from Product Rents as the Coffee Market Becomes More Differentiated? A Value-chain Analysis." *IDS Bulletin* 32(3): 69–82.

Flanagan, R. J. (2005). *Globalization and Labor Conditions: Working Conditions and Worker Rights in a Global Economy*. New York: Oxford University Press.

Foss, N. J. (1997). "Equilibrium vs Evolution in the Resource-Based Perspective: The Conflicting Legacies of Demsetz and Penrose." DRUID Working Paper, No. 97–10, October.

Foss, N. J. (1998). "Edith Penrose and the Penrosians Or, Why There Is Still So Much to Learn from The Theory of the Growth of the Firm." Department of Industrial Economics and Strategy, Copenhagen K, Denmark, Revised, January.

Frankel, J. and D. Romer. (1999). "Does Trade Cause Growth?" *American Economic Review* 89(3): 379–99.

Freeman, R. (1995). "Are Your Wages Set in Beijing?" *The Journal of Economic Perspectives* 9(3): 15–32.

Freeman, R. (2007). "The Challenge of the Growing Globalization of Labor Markets to Economic and Social Policy." In *Global Capitalism Unbound: Winners and Losers from Offshore Outsourcing*, edited by E. Paus, 23–40. London: Palgrave Macmillan.

Freund, C. (2009). "The Trade Response to Global Downturns: Historical Evidence." Policy Research Working Paper 5015, World Bank, Washington, DC.

Frey, B., W. Pommerehne, F. Schneider, and G. Gilbert. (1984). "Consensus and Dissension among Economists: An Empirical Inquiry." *American Economic Review* 74(5): 986–94.

Friedman, T. (2005). *The World is Flat: A Brief History of the Twenty-First Century*. New York: Farrar, Straus and Giroux.

Gallagher, K. and L. Zarsky. (2007). *The Enclave Economy: Foreign Investment and Sustainable Development in Mexico's Silicon Valley*. Cambridge: MIT Press.

Gazier, B. (2006). "Flexicurity and Social Dialogue, European Ways." Seminar on Flexicurity, Brussels.

Geishecker, I. (2006). "Does Outsourcing to Central and Eastern Europe Really Threaten Manual Workers' Jobs in Germany?" *World Economy* 29(5): 559–83.

Geishecker, I. (2008). "The Impact of International Outsourcing on Individual Employment Security: A Micro-Level Analysis." *Labour Economics* 15(3): 291–314.

Gereffi, G. (1994). "The Organization of Buyer-Driven Global Commodity Chains: How U.S. Retailers Shape Overseas Production Networks." In *Commodity Chains and Global Capitalism*, edited by G. Gereffi and M. Korzeniewicz, 95–122. Westport, CT: Greenwood Press.

Gereffi, G. (1999). "International Trade and Industrial Upgrading in the Apparel Commodity Chain." *Journal of International Economics* 48(1): 37–70.

Gereffi, G. (2002). "Outsourcing and Changing Patterns of International Competition in the Apparel Commodity Chain." Paper presented at the conference on "Responding to Globalization: Societies, Groups, and Individuals," Boulder, Colorado, April 4–7.

Gereffi, G. (2006). "The New Offshoring of Jobs and Global Development." ILO Social Policy Lectures, International Labour Office, Geneva.

Gereffi, G. (2009). "Development Models and Industrial Upgrading in China and Mexico." *European Sociological Review* 25(1): 37–51.

Gereffi, G. and D. L. Wyman. (eds.) (1990). *Manufacturing Miracles: Paths of Industrialisation in Latin America and East Asia*. Princeton: Princeton University Press.

Gereffi, G., J. Humphrey, and T. Sturgeon. (2005). "The Governance of Global Value Chains." *Review of International Political Economy* 12(1): 78–104.

Gereffi, G., J. Humphrey, R. Kaplinsky, and T. Sturgeon. (2001). "Introduction: Globalisation, Value Chains and Development." *IDS Bulletin* 32(3): 1–8.

Gereffi, G., V. Wadhwa, B. A. Rissing, and R. Ong (2008). "Getting the Numbers Right: International Engineering Education in the United States, China, and India." *Journal of Engineering Education* 97(1): 13–25.

German Marshall Fund. (2007). Perspectives on Trade and Poverty Reduction: A Survey of Public Opinion. Key Findings Report.

Gerschenkron A. (1962). *Economic Backwardness in Historical Perspective.* Cambridge, MA: Harvard University Press.

Ghosh, J. (2001). "Globalisation, Export-Oriented Employment for Women and Social Policy: A Case Study of India." UNRISD Project on Globalization, Export-Oriented Employment for Women and Social Policy.

Gibbon, P. (2002). "At the Cutting Edge?: Financialisation and UK Clothing Retailers' Global Sourcing Patterns and Practices." *Competition and Change* 6(3): 289–308.

Gibbon, P. and S. Ponte. (2005). *Trading Down: Africa, Value Chains and the Global Economy.* Philadelphia: Temple University Press.

Gimet, C., B. Guilhon, and N. Roux. (2011). "Fragmentation and Immiserizing Specialization: The Case of the Textile and Clothing Sector." Mimeo, University of Lyon.

Glen, J., K. Lee, and A. Singh (2002). "Corporate Profitability and the Dynamics of Competition in Emerging Markets: A Time Series Analysis." Working Paper No. 248, ESRC Centre for Business Research, University of Cambridge.

Glyn, A. (2006). *Capitalism Unleashed: Finance Globalization and Welfare.* Oxford: Clarendon Press.

Gomory, R. (2009). "Manufacturing and the Limits of Comparative Advantage." *The Huffington Post,* July 8, 2009.

Gordon, D. M. (1996). *Fat and Mean: the Corporate Squeeze of Working Americans and the Myth of Managerial Downsizing.* New York: The Free Press.

Gordon, R. and I. Dew-Becker. (2006). "Unresolved Issues in the Rise of American Inequality." Mimeo, Department of Economics, Northwestern University.

Görg, H. and E. Strobl. (2002). "Multinational Companies and Indigenous Development: An Empirical Analysis." *European Economic Review* 46(7): 1305–22.

Görg, H. and A. Hanley. (2004). "Does Outsourcing Increase Profitability?" *The Economic and Social Review* 35(3): 267–88.

Görzig, B. and A. Stephan. (2002). "Outsourcing and Firm-Level Performance." Discussion Paper No. 309, DIW, Berlin.

Gosselin, P. (2008). *High Wire: The Precarious Financial Lives of American Families.* New York: Basic Books.

Graham, F. (1948). *Theory of International Values.* Princeton: Princeton University Press.

Green, J. and T. Weisskopf (1990). "The Worker Discipline Effect: A Disaggregative Analysis." *Review of Economics and Statistics* 72(2): 241–49.

Grossman, G. (1986). "Strategic Export Promotion: A Critique." In *Strategic Trade Policy and the New International Economics,* edited by P. Krugman, 37–68. Cambridge, MA: MIT Press.

Grossman, G. and E. Helpman. (2002). "Integration versus Outsourcing in Industry Equilibrium." *Quarterly Journal of Economics* 117(1): 85–120.

Grossman, G. and E. Helpman. (2005). "Outsourcing in a Global Economy." *Review of Economic Studies* 72(1): 135–59.

Grossman, G. and E. Rossi-Hansberg. (2006a). "The Rise of Offshoring: It's Not Wine for Cloth Anymore." In *The New Economic Geography: Effects and Policy Implications*, 59–102. Jackson Hole Symposium, Federal Reserve Bank of Kansas City.

Grossman, G. and E. Rossi-Hansberg. (2006b). "Trading Tasks: A Simple Theory of Offshoring." NBER Working No. 12721, National Bureau of Economic Research.

Grossman, G. and E. Rossi-Hansberg. (2008). "Trading Tasks: A Simple Theory of Offshoring." *American Economic Review* 98(5): 1978–97.

Guscina, A. (2006). "Effects of Globalization on Labor's Share in National Income." IMF Working Paper 06/294, Washington DC: International Monetary Fund.

Hacker, J. (2006). *The Great Risk Shift*. New York: Oxford University Press.

Hamermesh, D. (1993). *Labor Demand*. Princeton: Princeton University Press.

Hamilton, G. (2006). "Remaking the Global Economy: U.S. Retailers and Asian Manufacturers." Presentation before the U.S.-China Economic and Security Review Commission, Hearing on "China and the Future of Globalization," New York, May 19–20.

Hamilton, G. and R. Feenstra. (2006). *Emergent Economies, Divergent Paths: Economic Organization and International Trade in South Korea and Taiwan*. New York: Cambridge University Press.

Hanson, G., Mataloni, R. and M. Slaughter. (2001). "Expansion Strategies of U.S. Multinational Firms." NBER Working Paper No. 8433, National Bureau of Economic Research, Cambridge, MA.

Hansson, P. (2000). "Relative Demand for Skills in Swedish Manufacturing: Technology or Trade?" *Review of International Economics* 8(3): 533–55.

Hansson, P. (2005). "Skill Upgrading and Production Transfer Within Swedish Multinationals." *Scandinavian Journal of Economics* 107(4): 673–92.

Harcourt, G. C. and P. Kenyon. (1976). "Pricing and the Investment Decision." *Kyklos* 29(3): 449–77.

Harrison, A. (2002). "Has Globalization Eroded Labor's Share? Some Cross-Country Evidence." Mimeo, Department of Agricultural and Resource Economics, University of California, Berkeley.

Harrison, A. and M. McMillan. (2006). "Dispelling Some Myths about Offshoring." Mimeo, University of California, Berkeley.

Harrison, A. and Rodríguez-Clare. (2009). "Trade, Foreign Investmen and Industrial Policy for Developing Countries." Working Paper 15261, Cambridge, MA: National Bureau of Economic Research.

Hausmann, R., J. Hwang, and D. Rodrik (2006). "What You Export Matters." Mimeo, Harvard University Kennedy School of Government.

Hawtrey, R. G. (1913). *Good and Bad Trade*. Longmans: London.

Head, K. and J. Ries. (2002), "Offshore Production and Skill Upgrading by Japanese Manufacturing Firms." *Journal of International Economics* 58(1): 81–105.

Heilbroner, R. (1999). *The Worldly Philosophers: The Lives, Times and Ideas of the Great Economic Thinkers*. Seventh edition. New York: Touchstone.

Heilbroner, R. and W. Milberg. (1996). *The Crisis of Vision in Modern Economic Thought*. New York: Cambridge University Press.

Hein, E. and E. Stockhammer. (2009). "A Post-Keynesian Macroeconomic Policy Mix as an Alternative to the New Consensus Approach." In *Unemployment: Past and Present*, 104–130, edited by P. Arestis and J. McCombie, 104–30. Basingstoke: Palgrave Macmillan.

Heintz, J. (2006). "Low-Wage Manufacturing and Global Commodity Chains: A Model in the Unequal Exchange Tradition." *Cambridge Journal of Economics* 30(4): 507–20.

Helg, R. and L. Tajoli. (2005). "Patterns of International Fragmentation of Production and the Relative Demand for Labor." *North American Journal of Economics and Finance* 16(2): 233–54.

Helpman, E. and P. Krugman. (1989). *Trade Policy and Market Structure*. Cambridge, MA: MIT Press.

Heron, T. (2004). "Export Processing Zones and Policy Competition for Foreign Direct Investment: The Caribbean 'Offshore' Development Model." In *Global Encounters: International Political Economy, Development and Globalization*, edited by G. Harrison, 213–228. London: Palgrave Macmillan.

Hijzen, A., H. Görg, and R. Hine. (2005). "International Outsourcing and the Skill Structure of Labour Demand in the United Kingdom." *Economic Journal* 115(506): 860–78.

Holmstrom, B. and J. Roberts. (1998). "The Boundaries of the Firm Revisited." *Journal of Economic Perspectives* 12(4): 73–94.

Hopkins, T. and I. Wallerstein. (1977). "Patterns of Development of the Modern World-System." *Review (Fernand Braudel Center)* 1(2): 111–45.

Horn, G., H. Joebges, and R. Zwiener. (2009). "From the Financial Crisis to the World Economic Crisis (II)." *IMK Report No. 40* (English Version), Düsseldorf: Macroeconomic Policy Institute (IMK).

Houseman, S., S. Kurz, C. Lengermann, and B. Mandel. (2010). "Offshoring and the State of Amerian Manufacturing." Upjohn Institute Working Paper, No. 10–166.

Howell, D. and A. Okatenko. (2010). "Beyond Unemployment: A Comparison of French and U.S. Labor Market Performance With New Indicators of Employment Adequacy." *International Review of Applied Economics* 24(3): 319–31.

Howell, D. (ed.) (2005). *Fighting Unemployment: The Limits of Free Market Orthodoxy*. Oxford: Oxford University Press.

Hsieh, C. and K. Woo. (2005). "The Impact of Outsourcing to China on Hong Kong's Labor Market." *American Economic Review* 95(5): 1673–87.

Hume (1985[1777]). "Of the Balance of Trade." In *Essays Moral, Political and Literary*, edited by E. F. Miller, Essay 5, Part II, Vol. 1. Indianapolis, IN: Liberty Fund.

Hummels, D., D. Rapaport, and K. Yi. (1998). "Vertical Specialization and the Changing Nature of World Trade." *Economic Policy Review* 4(2): 79–99.

Hummels, D., J. Ishii, and K. Yi. (2001). "The Nature and Growth of Vertical Specialization in Trade." *Journal of International Economics* 54(1): 75–96.

Humphrey, J. (2004). "Upgrading in Global Value Chains." Working Paper No. 28, Policy Integration Department, International Labour Office, Geneva.

Humphrey, J. and H. Schmitz. (2002). "How Does Insertion in Global Value Chains Affect Upgrading in Industrial Clusters?" *Regional Studies* 36(9): 1017–27.

Hung, H. (2008). "Rise of China and the Global Overaccumulation Crisis." *Review of International Political Economy* 15(2): 149–79.

Hurst, R., M. Buttle, and J. Sandars. (2009). "The Impact of the Global Economic Slowdown on Value Chain Labour Markets in Asia." Background paper for conference, Impact of the Global Economic Slowdown on Poverty and Sustainable Development in Asia and the Pacific, September 28–30, Hanoi, Vietnam.

Hymer, S. (1972). "The Multinational Corporation and the Law of Uneven Development." In *Economics and World Order*, edited by J. N. Bhagwati, 113–40. London: Macmillan.

Hymer, S. (1976). *The International Operations of National Firms: A Study of Direct Foreign Investment.* Cambridge, MA: MIT Press.

ICC. (2009). "Rethinking Trade Finance in 2009: An ICC Global Survey." Document 470–1120, March, International Chamber of Commerce, Paris, France.

ILO. (2002). *International Labour Organization, Employment and Social Policy in Respect of Export Processing Zones (EPZs)*, GB.285/ESP/5. Geneva: International Labour Office.

ILO. (2003). *Report of the Committee on Employment and Social Policy.* GB.286/15, Geneva: International Labour Office.

ILO. (2004). *Breaking Through the Glass Ceiling.* Geneva: International Labour Office.

ILO. (2005). *Promoting Fair Globalization in Textiles and Clothing in a Post-MFA Environment.* Geneva: International Labour Office.

ILO-WTO (2007). *Trade and Employment.* Edited by M. Jansen and E. Lee. Geneva: International Labour Office and World Trade Organization.

ILO. (2009). *Global Employment Trends for Women.* Geneva: International Labour Office, March.

IMF. (2005). *World Economic Survey.* Washington, DC: International Monetary Fund.

IMF. (2007). "The Globalization of Labour." In *World Economic Outlook*, Chapter 5. Washington, D.C.: International Monetary Fund.

Irwin, D. (1996). *Against the Tide: An Intellectual History of Free Trade.* Princeton: Princeton University Press.

Irwin, D. (2005). *Free Trade Under Fire.* Second edition. Princeton: Princeton University Press.

Jenkins, M. (2005). "Economic and Social Effects of Export Processing Zones in Costa Rica." Working Paper No. 97, Geneva: International Labour Office.

Jenkins, M., G. Esquivel, and F. Larrain. (1998). "Export Processing Zones in Central America." Development Discussion Paper No. 646, Harvard Institute for International Development, Harvard University.

Jensen, B. (2011). *Global Trade in Services: Fear, Facts, and Offshoring.* Washington, D.C.: Peterson Institute for International Economics.

Jensen, M. and W. Meckling. (1976). "Theory of the Firm: Managerial Behavior, Agency Costs and Ownership Structure." *Journal of Financial Economics* 3(4): 305–60.

Jiang, X. and W. Milberg. (2012). "Vertical Specialization and Industrial Upgrading: A Preliminary Note." Working Paper 2012/10, Capturing the Gains Project, Brooks World Poverty Institute, University of Manchester.

Joekes, S. (1999). "A Gender-Analytical Perspective on Trade and Sustainable Development." In *Trade, Gender and Sustainable Development.* Geneva: United Nations Conference on Trade and Development.

Jomo, K. S. (2009). "Export-oriented Industrialisation, Female Employment and Gender Wage Equity in East Asia." *Economic and Political Weekly* 45(1): 41–9.

Jones, R. (1961). "The Structure of Simple General Equilibrium Models." *Journal of Political Economy* 73(6): 557–72.

Jones, R. (1980). "Comparative and Absolute Advantage." *Schweizerische Zeitschrift fiir Volkswirtschaft und Statistik* 116(3): 235–60.

Jones, R. (2000). *Globalization and the Theory of Input Trade.* Cambridge: MIT Press.

Jones, R. and H. Kierzkowski. (2001). "A Framework for Fragmentation." In *Fragmentation: New Production Patterns in the World Economy*, edited by S. Arndt and H. Kierzkowski, 108–43. New York: Oxford University Press.

Jones, R. and S. Marjit. (1992). "International Trade and Endogenous Production Structures." In *Economic Theory and International Trade: Essays in Memoriam J. Trout Rader*, edited by W. Neuefrind and R. Riezman, 173–96. Berlin: Springer.

Jones, R., H. Kierzkowski, and G. Leonard. (2002). "Fragmentation and Intra-Industry Trade." In *Frontiers of Research in Intra Industry Trade*, edited by P. J. Lloyd and H. Lee, 67–86. London: Macmillan.

Kaldor, N. (1954). "The Relation of Economic Growth and Cyclical Fluctuations." *Economic Journal* 64(253): 53–71.

Kalecki, M. (1991[1954]). "Theory of Economic Dynamics." Reprinted in *Collected Works of Michael Kalecki*, Vol. II, edited by J. Osiatynski. Oxford: Clarendon.

Kalecki, M. (1971). *Selected Essays on the Dynamics of the Capitalist Economy.* Cambridge: Cambridge University Press.

Kalmbach, P., R. Franke, K. Knottenbauer, and H. Krämer. (2005). *Die Interdependenz von Industrie und Dienstleistungen, Zur Dynamik eines komplexen Beziehungsgeflechts.* Berlin: Edition Sigma.

Kaplinsky, R. (2005). *Globalization, Poverty and Inequality.* London: Polity Press.

Kaplinsky, R. and J. Readman. (2004). "Globalisation and Upgrading: What Can (and Cannot) be Learnt from International Trade Statistics in the Wood Furniture Sector?" Mimeo, Centre for Research in Innovation and Management.

Kapner, S. (2009). "The Unstoppable Fung Brothers." *CNN Money*, December 8, 2009.

Kessler, A. (2011). *Eat People: And Other Unapologetic Rules for Game-Changing Entrepreneurs.* London: Penguin Group.

Keynes, J. M. (1964[1936]). *The General Theory of Employment Interest and Money.* New York: Harcourt.

Kierkegaard, J. (2007). "Offshoring, Outsourcing, and Production Relocation – Labor-Market Effects in the OECD Countries and Developing Asia." Peterson Institute Working Paper 07-2, Peterson Institute for International Economics, Washington, DC.

Kimmit, R. and M. Slaughter. (2010). "The Foreign Investment Solution for American Jobs." *The Wall Street Journal*, 27 July, 2010.

Kimura, F. (2002). "Subcontracting and the Performance of Small and Medium Firms in Japan." *Small Business Economics* 18(1–3): 163–75.

Kletzer, L. (2001). *Job Loss from Imports: Measuring the Costs.* Washington, DC: Peterson Institute for International Economics.

Kohler, W. (2004). "International Outsourcing and Factor Prices with Multistage Production." *Economic Journal* 114(3): C166-C185.

Kongar, E. (2007). "Importing Equality or Exporting Jobs? Gender Wage and Employment Differentials in US Manufacturing." In *The Feminist Economics of Trade*, edited by I. van Staveren, D. Elson, C. Grown, and N. Cagatay, 215–36. New York: Routledge.

Koopman, R., W. Powers, Z. Wang, and S.-J. Wei. (2010). "Give Credit Where Credit is Due: Tracing Value Added in Global Production Chains." NBER Working Paper Series, No. 16426. National Bureau of Economic Research, Cambridge, MA.

Kozul-Wright, R. and P. Rayment. (2008). *The Resistible Rise of Market Fundamentalism: Rethinking Development Policy in an Unbalanced World.* New York: Zed Books, 2008.

Krämer, H., H. Kurz, and H.-M. Trautwein. (eds.) (2012). *Macroeconomics and the History of Economic Thought: Festschrift in Honour of Harald Hagemann.* Routledge: London.

Krugman, P. (1979). "Increasing Returns, Monopolistic Competition, and International Trade" *Journal of International Economics* 9(4): 469–79.

Krugman, P. (1983). "New Theories of Trade among Industrial Countries." *American Economic Review* 73(2): 343–47.

Krugman, P. (1991). "Myths and Realities of U.S. Competitiveness." *Science* 254(5033): 811–15.

Krugman, P. (1993). "What Do Undergrads Need to Know About Trade?" *American Economic Review* 83(2): 23–6.

Krugman, P. (1994). "Competitiveness: A Dangerous Obsession." *Foreign Affairs,* 73(2): 28–44.

Krugman, P. (1995). "Growing World Trade: Causes and Consequences." *Brookings Papers on Economic Activity* 1995(1): 327–77.

Krugman, P. (2008). "Trade and Wages, Reconsidered." *Brookings Papers on Economic Activity* 39(1): 103–54.

Kucera, D. (2001). "The Effects of Core Worker Rights on Labour Costs and Foreign Direct Investment: Evaluating the 'Conventional Wisdom.'" IILS Working Paper No. 130, International Labour Office, Geneva.

Kucera, D. and R. Sarna. (2004). "How do Trade Union Rights Affect Trade Competitiveness?" Working Paper No. 39, ILO Policy Integration Department, Statistical Development and Analysis Group International Labour Office, Geneva.

Kujis, L. (2005). "Investment and Saving in China." World Bank Policy Research Working Paper No. 3633, The World Bank Office, Beijing.

Kusago, T. and Z. Tzannatos (1998). "Export Processing Zones: A Review in Need of an Update." SP Discussion Paper No. 9802, The World Bank, Washington, DC.

Kuttner, R. (2008). "The Copenhagen Consensus: Reading Adam Smith in Denmark." *Foreign Affairs* 87(2): 78–94.

Lamy, P. (2011). "'Made in China' Tells us Little About Global Trade." *The Financial Times,* January 24, 2011.

Langlois, R. N. 2003. "The Vanishing Hand: The Changing Dynamics of Industrial Capitalism." *Industrial and Corporate Change* 12(2): 351–85.

Larsen, P. T. (2007). "Facts and Figures: Numbers Behind the M&A Boom." *The Financial Times,* May 30, 2007.

Lazonick (1991). *Business Organization and the Myth of the Market Economy.* Cambridge: Cambridge University Press.

Lazonick (2007). "Globalization of the ICT Labor Force." In *The Oxford Handbook of Information and Communication Technologies,* edited by R. Mansell, C. Avgerou, D. Quah, and R. Silverstone, 75–99. New York: Oxford University Press.

Lazonick, W. (2008). "The Quest for Shareholder Value: Stock Repurchases in the US Economy." *Louvain Economic Review* 74(4): 479–540.

Lazonick, W. (2009). *Sustainable Prosperity in the New Economy?: Business Organization and High-Tech Employment in the U.S.* Kalamazoo: The Upjohn Institute.

Lazonick, W. and M. O'Sullivan. (2000). "Maximizing Shareholder Value: A New Ideology for Corporate Governance." *Economy and Society* 29(1): 13–35.

Lee, J. (1995). "Comparative Advantage in Manufacturing as a Determinant of Industrialization: the Korean Case." *World Development* 23(7): 1195–214.

Levy, D. (2005). "Offshoring in the New Global Political Economy." *Journal of Management Studies* 42(2): 685–93.

Lin, J. and H. Chang. (2009) "Should Industrial Policy in Developing Countries Conform to Comparative Advantage or Defy it? A Debate Between Justin Lin and Ha-Joon Chang." *Development Policy Review* 27(5): 483–502.

Linden, G., K. Kraemer, and J. Dedrick. (2007). "Who Captures Value in a Global Innovation System? The Case of Apple's iPod." *UC Irvine: Personal Computing Industry Center.*

Linden, G., K. Kraemer, and J. Dedrick. (2011). "Who Captures Value in the Apple iPad?" Mimeo, March.

Locke, R., F. Qin, and A. Brause. (2007). "Does Monitoring Improve Labor Standards? Lessons from Nike." *Industrial and Labor Relations Review* 61(1): 3–31.

Locke, R., T. Kochan, M. Romis, and F. Qin. (2007). "Beyond Corporate Codes of Conduct: Work Organization and Labour Standards at Nike's Suppliers." *International Labour Review* 146(1–2): 21–40.

Lorentowicz, A., D. Marin, and A. Raubold. (2005). "Is Human Capital Losing From Outsourcing? Evidence for Austria and Poland." Discussion Paper 5344, Centre for Economic Policy Research, London.

Lucas, R. (1990). "Review of '*Trade Policy and Market Structure*', by E. Helpman and P. Krugman." *Journal of Political Economy* 98(3): 664–7.

Lynch, D. (2008). "Does Tax Code Send U.S. Jobs Offshore?" *USA Today*, March 20, 2008.

Lynn, B. (2005). *The End of the Line: The Rise and Coming Fall of the Global Corporation.* New York: Doubleday.

Ma, A. and A. Van Assche. (2010). "The Role of Trade Costs in Global Production Networks: Evidence from China's Processing Trade Regime." World Bank Working Paper No. 4959, The World Bank, Washington, DC.

Madani, D. (1999). "Review of the Role and Impact of Export Processing Zones." Policy Research Working Paper, Series No. 2238, The World Bank, Washington, DC.

Madrick, J. and N. Papanikolaou. (2010). "The Stagnation of Male Wages in the US." *International Review of Applied Economics* 24(3): 309–18.

Mahoney, M., W. Milberg, M. Schneider, and R. von Arnim. (2007). "Dynamic Gains from U.S. Services Offshoring: A Critical View." In *Global Capitalism Unbound: Winners and Losers from Offshore Outsourcing*, edited by E. Paus, 77–95. London: Palgrave Macmillan.

Mandel, M. (2008). "Multinationals: Are They Good for America?" *Business Week*, March 10, 2008.

Maneschi, A. (1983). "Dynamic Aspects of Ricardo's International Trade Theory." *Oxford Economic Papers* 35(1): 67–80.

Maneschi, A. (1992). "Ricardo's International Trade Theory: Beyond the Comparative Cost Example." *Cambridge Journal of Economics* 16(4): 421–37.

Maneschi, A. (1998). *Comparative Advantage in International Trade: A Historical Perspective.* Cheltenham: Edward Elgar.

Mankiw, N. G. and P. Swagel. (2005). "The Politics and Economics of Offshore Outsourcing." AEI Working Paper No. 122, American Enterprise Institute for Public Policy Research.

Mann, C. (2003). "Globalization of IT Services and White Collar Jobs: The Next Wave of Productivity Growth." International Economics Policy Briefs, Number PB03–11, Peterson for International Economics, Washington, DC.

Mann, C. (2006). *Accelerating the Globalization of America: The Role of Information Technology.* Washington, DC: Institute for International Economics.

Manning, A. (2005). *Monopsony in Motion.* Princeton: Princeton University Press.

Markusen, J. (2005). "Modeling the Offshoring of White-Collar Services: From Comparative Advantage to the New Theories of Trade and FDI." In *Brookings Trade Forum: Offshoring White-Collar Work,* edited by L. Brainard and S. M. Collins, 1–23. Washington, DC: Brookings Institution Press.

Markusen, J. and G. MacDonald. (1985). "A Rehabilitation of Absolute Advantage." *Journal of Political Economy* 93(2): 277–97.

Marris, R. (1964). *The Economic Theory of Managerial Capitalsm.* London: Macmillan.

Marx, K. (1991[1894]). *Capital: A Critique of Political Economy, Volume Three.* Translated by David Fernbach, London: Penguin Books.

Mas-Colell, A., M. Whinston, and J. Green. (1995). *Microeconomic Theory.* New York: Oxford University Press.

Mayer, F. (2012). "Beyond the Business Case: What the Apple-Foxconn Case Demonstrates About the Interaction Among Corporate Self-Governance, Civil Society, and the Re-Emerging State." Mimeo, Duke University, April.

Mayer, J. (2002). "The Fallacy of Composition: A Review of the Literature." *World Economy* 25(6): 875–94.

Mayer, J., A. Butkevicius, and A. Kadri. (2002). "Dynamic Products in World Exports." UNCTAD Discussion Paper No. 159, United Nations Conference on Trade and Development, Geneva.

McKinsey Global Institute. (2003). "Offshoring: Is it a Win-Win Game?" San Francisco, August.

McMillan, M., K. Horn, and D. Rodrik. (2003). "When Economic Reform Goes Wrong: Cashews in Mozambique." *Brookings Trade Forum 2003.*

Mehra, R. and S. Gammage. (1999). "Trends, Counter-trends and Gaps in Women's Employment." *World Development* 27(3): 533–50.

Melitz, M. (2003). "The Impact of Trade on Intra-Industry Reallocations and Aggregate Industry Productivity." *Econometrica* 71(6): 1695–725.

Meng, B., N. Yamano, and C. Webb. (2011). "Application of Factor Decomposition Techniques to Vertical Specialization Measurements." *IDE Discussion Paper No. 276.*

Milberg, W. (1994a). "Is Absolute Advantage Passe? Towards a Post Keynesian/Marxian Theory of International Trade." In *Competition, Technology and Money: Classical and Post-Keynesian Perspectives,* edited by M. Glick, 153–69. Cheltenham: Edward Elgar.

Milberg, W. (1994b). "Technology Gap." In *The Elgar Companion to Radical Political Economy,* edited by P. Arestis and M. Sawyer, 415–19. Aldershot, UK: Edward Elgar.

Milberg, W. (1999). "Foreign Direct Investment and Development: Balancing Costs and Benefits." In *International Monetary and Financial Issues for the 1990s* 11, 99–116. Geneva: United Nations, UNCTAD.

Milberg, W. (2004a). "After the "New Economics" – Pragmatist Turn?" In *Dewey, Pragmatism and Economic Methodology*, edited by E. Khalil, 357–77. London: Routledge.

Milberg, W. (2004b). "The Changing Structure of International Trade Linked to Global Production Systems: What Are the Policy Implications?" *International Labour Review* 143(1–2): 45–90.

Milberg, W. (2007). "Export Processing Zones, Industrial Upgrading and Economic Development." Background paper for ILO Governing Board, International Labour Office, Geneva.

Milberg, W. (2008). "Shifting Sources and Uses of Profits: Sustaining US Financialization with Global Value Chains." *Economy and Society* 37(3): 420–51.

Milberg, W. (2009a). "Pricing and Profits Under Globalized Competition: A Post Keynesian Perspective on U.S. Economic Hegemony." In *Money and Macrodynamics: Alfred Eichner and Post-Keynesian Economics*, edited by M. Lavoie, L. Rochon and M. Seccareccia, 116–138. Armonk: M.E. Sharpe.

Milberg, W. (2009b). "The New Social Science Imperialism and the Problem of Knowledge in Contemporary Economics." In *Economic Persuasions*, edited by S. Gudeman, 43–61. Oxford: Berghan.

Milberg, W. and E. Houston. (2005). "The High-Road and the Low-Road to International Competitiveness: Extending the Neo-Schumpeterian Model Beyond Technology." *International Review of Applied Economics* 19(2): 137–62.

Milberg, W., X. Jiang, and G. Gereffi. (2013). "Industrial Policy in the Era of Vertically-Specialized Industrialization." Mimeo, prepared for ILO-UNCTAD conference on industrial policy.

Milberg, W. and L. Schmitz. (2011). "The Business of Macroimbalances: Comparing Gluts in Savings, Money and Profits." In *Income Distribution and Economic Growth: Essays in Honour of Malcolm Sawyer*, edited by P. Arestis, 72–98. London: Palgrave Macmillan.

Milberg, W. and D. Winkler. (2010a). "Trade, Crisis, and Recovery: Restructuring Global Value Chains." In *Global Value Chains in a Postcrisis World, A Development Perspective*, edited by O. Cattaneo, G. Gereffi and C. Staritz, 23–72. Washington, DC: The World Bank.

Milberg, W. and D. Winkler. (2010b). "Economic Insecurity in the New Wave of Globalization: Offshoring and the Labor Share Under Varieties of Capitalism." *International Review of Applied Economics* 24(3): 285–308.

Milberg, W. and D. Winkler. (2010c). "Financialization and the Dynamics of Offshoring." *Cambridge Journal of Economics* 34(2): 275–93.

Milberg, W. and D. Winkler. (2011a). "Offshoring and Economic Insecurity: Worker Perceptions and Labor Market Realities." In *Making Globalization Socially Sustainable: A Joint ILO-WTO Volume*, edited by M. Jensen and M. Bacchetta, 47–198. Geneva: International Labour Office and World Trade Organization.

Milberg, W. and D. Winkler. (2011b). "Economic and Social Upgrading in Global Value Chains: Problems of Theory and Measurement." *International Labour Review* 150(3–4): 341–65.

Milkman, R. (1987). *Gender at Work: The Dynamics of Job Segregation by Sex During World War II*. Urbana and Chicago: Illini Books.

Mill, J. S. (1968[1848]). *Principles of Political Economy, with Some of Their Applications from Social Philosophy. Collected Works of John Stuart Mill,* Volume Three. London: Routledge & Kegan Paul.

Minondo, A. and G. Rubert. (2006). "The Effect of Outsourcing on the Demand for Skills in the Spanish Manufacturing Industry." *Applied Economics Letters* 13(9): 599–604.

Mirodout, S., R. Lanz, and A. Ragoussis. (2009). "Trade in Intermediate Goods and Services." OECD Trade Policy Working Paper No. 93, Organisation for Economic Co-operation and Development, Paris.

Mirowski, P. (1989). "The Probabilistic Counter-Revolution, or How Stochastic Concepts Came to Neoclassical Economic Theory." *Oxford Economic Papers* 41(1): 217–35.

Mirowski, P. and S. Sklivas. (1991). "Why Economists Don't Replicate (Although They do Reproduce)." *Review of Political Economy* 3(2): 146–63.

Mitra-Kahn, B. H. and T. Mitra-Kahn. (2007). "Gender Wage Gaps and Growth: What Goes Up Must Come Down." Unpublished manuscript.

Montgomerie, J. (2007). "From Financialization to Finance-Led Capitalism: Exploring the Frontiers of Global Finance." Paper presented at conference of International Studies Association, Chicago, March.

Mora, J. and W. Powers. (2009). "Did Trade Credit Problems Deepen the Great Trade Collapse?" In *The Great Trade Collapse: Causes, Consequences and Prospects,* edited by R. Baldwin, 115–25. Centre for Economic Policy Research for VoxEU, The Graduate Institute, Geneva.

Mortimer, M. (2002). "When Does Apparel Become a Peril? On the Nature of Industrialization in the Caribbean Basin." In *Free Trade and Uneven Development,* edited by G. Gereffi, D. Spener, and J. Bair, 287–307. Philadelphia: Temple University Press.

Mundell, R. (1957). "International Trade and Factor Mobility." *American Economic Review* 47(3): 321–35.

Nastepaad, R. and S. Storm. (2006/2007). "OECD Demand Regimes (1960–2000)." *Journal of Post Keynesian Economics* 29(2): 213–48.

Nathan, D. and S. Sarkar. (2011). "A Note on Profits, Rents, and Wages in Global Production Networks." *Economic and Political Weekly* XLVI(36): 53–7.

Nolan, P. (2008). "Contradictions of Capitalist Globalization." In *Issues in Economic Development and Globalization: Essays in Honour of Ajit Singh,* edited by P. Arestis and J. Eatwell, 115–74. Basingstoke: Palgrave Macmillan.

Nolan, P., D. Sutherland, and J. Zhang. (2002). "The Challenge of the Global Business Revolution." *Contributions to Political Economy* 21(1): 91–110.

Obstfeld, M. and K. Rogoff. (2009). "Global Imbalances and the Financial Crisis." Federal Reserve Bank of San Francisco Conference, 18–20 October.

OECD. (2005). *Employment Outlook.* Paris: Organisation for Economic Co-operation and Development.

OECD. (2007a). *Economic Outlook.* Paris: Organisation for Economic Co-operation and Development.

OECD. (2007b). *Offshoring and Employment: Trends and Impact.* Paris: Organisation for Economic Co-operation and Development.

OECD. (2013). "Trade in Value-Added: Concepts, Methodologies and Challenges." Joint OECD-WTO Note, Paris: Organisation for Economic Co-operation and Development.

Olson, M. (1965). *The Logic of Collective Action.* New Haven: Yale University Press.

Onaran, Ö., E. Stockhammer, and L. Grafl. (2011). "Financialisation, Income Distribution and Aggregate Demand in the USA." *Cambridge Journal of Economics* 35(4): 637–61.

Orhangazi, O. (2008). "Financialization and Capital Accumulation in the Nonfinancial Corporate Sector: A Theoretical and Empirical Investigation on the US Economy, 1973–2004." *Cambridge Journal of Economics* 32(6): 863–86.

Palma, G. (2003). "Trade Liberalization in Mexico: Its Impact on Growth, Employment and Wages." ILO Employment Paper 2003/55, International Labour Office, Geneva.

Paloheimo, H. (1990). "Between Liberalism and Corporatism: the Effect of Trade Unions and Governments on Economic Performance in Eighteen OECD Countries." In *Labour Relations and Economic Performance*, edited by R. Brunetta and C. Dell'Aringa, 325–352. New York: New York University Press.

Palpacuer, F. (2005). "Globalisation, Firme-Réseau et Responsabilité Sociale: Vers de Nouvelles Formes de Régulation?" *La Responsabilité Sociale de l'Entreprise: Mélanges en l'Honneur du Professeur Roland Pérez*, edited by F. Le Roy and M. Marchesnay, 233–42. Paris: Management et Société.

Palpacuer, F., P. Gibbon, and L. Thomsen. (2005). "New Challenges for Developing Country Suppliers in Global Clothing Chains: A Comparative European Perspective." *World Development* 33(3): 409–43.

Penrose, E. (1959). *Theory of the Growth of the Firm*. New York: Oxford University Press.

Picot, A. (1982). "In der Organisationstheorie – Stand der Diskussion und Aussagewert." *Die Betriebswirtschaft* 42(2): 267–84.

Picot, A. (1991). "Ein neuer Ansatz zur Gestaltung der Leistungstiefe." *Zeitschrift für betriebswirtschaftliche Forschung* 43(4): 336–57.

Pieper, U. (2000). "Deindustrialization and the Social and Economic Sustainability Nexus in Developing Countries: Cross-Country Evidence on Productivity and Employment." *Journal of Development Studies* 36(4): 66–99.

Pietrobelli, C. and R. Rabellotti. (2006). "Clusters and Value Chains in Latin America: In Search of an Integrated Approach." In *Upgrading to Compete: Global Value Chains, SMEs and Clusters in Latin America*, edited by C. Pietrobelli and R. Rabellotti, 1–40. Cambridge, MA: Harvard University Press.

Pine, B. J. (1993). *Mass Customization*. Boston: Harvard Business School Press.

Piore, M. (1998). "Trade and the Social Structure of Economic Activity." In *Imports, Exports, and the American Worker*, edited by S. M. Collins, 257–86. Washington, DC: Brookings Institutions Press.

Piore, M. (2004). "Rethinking International Labor Standards." In *Labor and the Globalization of Production: Causes and Consequences of Industrial Upgrading*, edited by W. Milberg, 249–65, Houndmills: Palgrave Macmillan.

Piore, M. and A. Schrank. (2008). "Toward Managed Flexibility: The Revival of Labour Inspection in the Latin World." *International Labour Review* 147(1): 1–23.

Piore, M. and C. Sabel. (1984). *The Second Industrial Divide*. New York: Basic Books.

Pitelis, C. (1991). "Market Failure and the Existence of the State: A Restatement and Critique." *International Review of Applied Economics* 5(3): 325–40.

Pitelis, C. (2001). "Industrial Strategy." In *International Encyclopedia of Business and Management*, second revised edition, edited by M. Warner, 2026–44. London: Routledge/ITBP.

Polanyi, K. (2001[1944]). *The Great Transformation: The Economic and Political Origins of Our Time.* Boston: Beacon Press.

Polaski, S. (2008). "Trade and Labor Standards." Concept Note Prepared for DFID grant: "Capturing the Gains: Economic and Social Upgrading in Global Production Networks," presented at University of Manchester, December.

Porter, M. (1998). *Competitive Strategies: Techniques for Analyzing Industries and Competitors.* New York: Free Press.

Posner, M. V. (1961). "International Trade and Technological Change." *Oxford Economic Papers* 13(3): 323–41.

Posner, M. V. and S. Steer. (1979). "Price Competition and the Performance of Manufacturing Industry." In *Deindustrialisation*, edited by F. Blackaby, 141–65. London: Heinemann.

Powell, W. (1990). "Neither Market nor Hierarchy: Network Forms of Organization." *Research in Organizational Behavior* 12: 295–336.

Prahalad, C. K. and G. Hamel. (1990). "The Core Competence of the Corporation." *Harvard Business Review* 68(3): 79–91.

Prebisch, R. (1949). *Economic Survey of Latin America 1948.* New York, United Nations.

Purvis, D. (1972). "Technology, Trade and Factor Mobility." *Economic Journal* 82(327): 991–99.

Razmi, A. and R. Blecker. (2008). "Developing Country Exports of Manufactures: Moving Up the Ladder to Escape the Fallacy of Composition?" *Journal of Development Studies* 44(1): 21–48.

Reich, R. (2008). *Supercapitalism: The Transformation of Business, Democracy, and Everyday Life.* New York: Knopf.

Reich, R. (2010). *Aftershock: The Next Economy and America's Future.* New York: Alfred A. Knopf.

Reinert, E. (2007). *How the Rich Countries Got Rich . . . and Why Poor Countries Remain Poor.* New York: Carroll and Graf.

Ricardo, D. (1981[1817]). *On The Principles of Political Economy and Taxation, Vol. 1 of The Works and Correspondences of David Ricardo*, edited by P. Sraffa. Cambridge: Cambridge University Press.

Roberts, M. J. and J. Tybout. (1996). "A Preview of the Country Studies" In *Industrial Evolution in Developing Countries: Micro Patterns of Turnover, Productivity and Market Structure*, edited by M. J. Roberts and J. Tybout, 188–99. New York: Oxford University Press.

Robertson, R., R. Dehejia, and D. Brown. (2011). "Working Conditions and Factory Survival: Evidence from Better Factories Cambodia." ILO Better Work Discussion Paper No. 4.

Robinson, J. (1973). "The Need for a Reconsideration of the Theory of International Trade." In *International Trade and Money, the Geneva Essays*, edited by M. Connolly and R. Swoboda, 15–25. Toronto: University of Toronto Press.

Rodríguez-Clare, A. (2007). "Offshoring in a Ricardian World." NBER Working Paper, No. 13203, National Bureau of Economic Research, Cambridge, MA.

Rodrik, D., A. Subramanian, and F. Trebbi. (2002). "Institutions Rule: The Primacy of Institutions Over Geography and Integration in Economic Development." NBER Working Paper No. 9305, National Bureau of Economic Research, Cambridge, MA.

Rosenberg, N. (1982). *Inside the Black Box: Technology and Economics*. Cambridge University Press.

Rubery, J. (1988). *Women and Recession*. London: Routledge and Kegan Paul Ltd.

Rubery, J., A. Simonazzi, and K. Ward. (2009). "Exploring International Migration and Outsourcing through an Institutional Lens." In *Globalisation, Labour Markets and International Adjustment, Essays in Honour of Palle S Andersen*, edited by D. Mihaljek, BIS Papers No. 50.

Ruccio, D. and J. Amariglio. (2003). *Postmodern Moments in Modern Economics*. Princeton: Princeton University Press.

Ruggie, J. (1982). "International Regimes, Transactions and Chainge: Embedded Liberalism in the Postwar Economic Order." *International Organization* 36(2): 379–415.

Ruggie, J. (1998). "Globalization and the Embedded Liberalism Compormise: The End of an Era?" In *Internationale Wirtschaft, nationale Demokratie: Herausforderungen für die Demokratietheorie*, edited by W. Streek. Frankfurt/Main, New York: Campus Verlag.

Ruggie, J. (2003). "Taking Embedded Liberalism Global: The Corporate Connection." In *Taming Globalization: Frontiers of Governance*, edited by D. Held and M. Koenig-Archibugi, 93–129. Cambridge: Polity Press.

Sala-i-Martin, X. (1997). "I Just Ran Two Million Regressions." *American Economic Review* 87(2): 178–83.

Salvatore, D. (2007). *International Economics*. Ninth edition. Hoboken: John Wiley & Sons.

Samuelson, P. (1948). "International Trade and the Equalisation of Factor Prices." *The Economic Journal* 58(230): 163–84.

Samuelson, P. (1969). "The Way of an Economist." In *International Economic Relations: Proceedings of the Third Congress of the International Economic Association*, edited by P. Samuelson, 1–11. London: Macmillan.

Samuelson, P. (2004). "Where Ricardo and Mill Rebut and Confirm Arguments of Mainstream Economists Supporting Globalization." *Journal of Economic Perspectives* (18)3: 135–46.

Samuelson, P. (2005). "Response from Paul A. Samuelson." *Journal of Economic Perspectives* 19(3): 242–4.

Sanchez-Ancochea, D. (2006). "Development Trajectories and New Comparative Advantages: Costa Rica and the Dominican Republic under Globalization." *World Development* 34(6): 996–1015.

Sanchez, J. (2003). "Lou's Blues: Lou Dobbs and the New Mercantilism." *Reason*, October 30, 2003.

Scheve, K. and M. Slaughter. (2003). "Economic Insecurity and the Globalization of Production." Mimeo, Yale University.

Schink, G. and L. Tyson. (2009). "A Temporary Reduction in Taxes on Repatriated Profits for the Purpose of Economic Stimulus and Investment in National Priorities: An Economic Assessment." LECG, January 30.

Schmitz, H. (1999). "Global Competition and Local Cooperation: Success and Failure in the Sinos Valley, Brazil." *World Development* 27(9): 1627–50.

Schrank, A. (2001). "Export Processing Zones: Free Market Islands or Bridges to Structural Transformation." *Development Policy Review* 19(2): 223–42.

Schumpeter, J. (1994[1954]). *History of Economic Analysis*. Oxford University Press.

340

References

Schumpeter, J. (1942). *Capitalism, Socialism, and Democracy*. Third edition. New York: Harper & Row.

Scott, R. (2009). "Invest in America: Essential Policies Needed to Secure U.S. Jobs and Broadly Shred Prosperity in the Auto Industry." EPI Briefing Paper, Economic Policy Institute, Washington, DC, April 8.

Scott, R. (2007). "The Wal-Mart Effect: Its Chinese Imports Have Displaced Nearly 200,000 U.S. Jobs." Issue Brief No. 235, Economic Policy Institute, Washington, DC.

Scott, R. (2009). "Invest in America: Essential Policies Needed to Secure U.S. Jobs and Broadly Shared Prosperity in the Auto Industry." EPI Briefing Paper 233, Economic Policy Institute, Washington, DC.

Seguino, S. (1997). "Export-Led Growth and the Persistence of Gender Inequality in the Newly Industrialized Countries." In *Economic Dimensions of Gender Inequality*, edited by J. Rives and M. Yousifi 11–34. Westport, CT: Praeger Publishers.

Seguino, S. (2000). "Accounting for Gender in Asian Economic Growth." *Feminist Economics* 6(3): 27–58.

Senses, M. Z. (2010). "The effects of Offshoring on the Elasticity of Labor Demand." *Journal of International Economics*. 81(1): 89–98.

Serfati, C. (2008). "Financial Dimensions of Transnational Corporations, Global Value Chain and Technological Innovation." *Journal of Innovation Economics* 2(2): 35–61.

Shapiro, N. and W. Milberg. (2013). "Implications of the Recent Crisis for Firm Innovation." Mimeo, New School for Social Research, Department of Economics.

Shapiro, N. and T. Mott. (1995). "Firm-Determined Prices: The Post-Keynesian Conception." In *Post-Keynesian Economic Theory*, edited by P. Wells, 35–48. Boston: Kluwer Academic Publishers.

Shapiro, N. and M. Sawyer. (2003). "Post Keynesian Price Theory." *Journal of Post Keynesian Economics* 25(3): 355–66.

Silverberg, G., G. Dosi, and L. Orsenigo. (1988). "Innovation, Diversity and Diffusion: a Self- Organization Model." *The Economic Journal* 98(393): 1032–54.

Singa Boyenge, J. (2007). "ILO Database on Export Processing Zones (Revised)." Working Paper 251, Sectoral Activities Programme, International Labour Office, Geneva.

Singer, H. W. (1950). "The Distribution of Gains between Investing and Borrowing Countries." *American Economic Review* 40(2): 473–85.

Slater, M. (1980). "The Managerial Limitation to the Growth of Firms." *The Economic Journal* 90(359): 520–8.

Slaughter, M. (2000). "Production Transfer Within Multinational Enterprises and American Wages." *Journal of International Economics* 50(2): 449–72.

Slaughter, M. (2001). "International Trade and Labor-Demand Elasticities." *Journal of International Economics* 54(1): 27–56.

Spence, M. and S. Hlatshwayo. (2011). "The Evolving Structure of the American Economy and the Employment Challenge." Council on Foreign Relations, Maurice R. Greenberg Center for Geoeconomic Studies, March.

Spiegler, P. and W. Milberg. (2013). "*Methodenstreit* 2013? Historical Perspective on the Contemporary Debate Over How to Reform Economics." Mimeo, New School for Social Research, Department of Economics.

Standing, G. (1989). "Global Feminization through Flexible Labor." *World Development* 17(7): 1077–95.

Standing, G. (1999). "Global Feminization Through Flexible Labor: A Theme Revisited." *World Development* 27(3): 583–602.

Staritz, C. (2010). *Competing in the Post-Quota and Post-Crisis World: Global Buyers and the Clothing Sector in Low-Income Countries.* Washington, DC: The World Bank.

Stiglitz, J. (2009). "5 Lessons from the Crisis We May Need to Learn All Over Again." *The Huffington Post*, March 18, 2009.

Stiglitz, J. and A. Charlton. (2010). *Fair Trade for All: How Trade Can Promote Development.* Oxford University Press: New York.

Stockhammer, E. (2004). "Financialisation and the Slowdown of Accumulation." *Cambridge Journal of Economics* 28(5): 719–41.

Stockhammer, E. and O. Onaran. (2012) "Wage-Led Growth: Theory, Evidence, Policy." Working Paper No. 300, Political Economy Research Institute, University of Massachusetts Amherst.

Strange, R. and J. Newton. (2006). "Stephen Hymer and the Externalization of Production." *International Business Review* 15(2): 180–93.

Strauss-Kahn, V. (2004). "The Role of Globalization in the Within-Industry Shift Away from Unskilled Workers in France." In *Challenges to Globalization: Analyzing the Economics*, edited by R. Baldwin and L. A. Winters, 209–31. Chicago: University of Chicago Press.

Sturgeon, T. and O. Memedovic. (2011). "Mapping Global Value Chains: Intermediate Goods Trade and Structural Change in the World Economy." Development Policy and Strategic Research Branch Working Paper 05/2010, United Nations Industrial Development Organization, Vienna.

Sturgeon, T. (2001). "How Do We Define Value Chains and Production Networks?" *IDS Bulletin* 32(3): 9–18.

Sturgeon, T. (2002). "Modular Production Networks: A New American Model of Industrial Organization." *Industrial and Corporate Change* 11(3): 451–96.

Sturgeon, T. and J. Van Biesebroeck. (2010). "Effects of the Crisis on the Automotive Industry in Developing Countries: A Global Value Chain Perspective." In *Global Value Chains in a Postcrisis World, A Development Perspective*, edited by O. Cattaneo, G. Gereffi, and C. Staritz, 209–44. Washington, DC: The World Bank.

Sullivan, M. A. (2004). "Data Show Dramatic Shift Of Profits to Tax Havens." *Tax Notes* 104(12): 1190–200.

Suominen, K. (2010). "This Time Will Be Different? Addressing the Unsound Post-Crisis Drivers of Global Imbalances." In *Rebalancing the Global Economy: A Primer for Policymaking*, edited by S. Claessens, S. Evenett, and B. Hoekman, 87–95. London: Centre for Economic Policy Research and VoxEU.

Sweezy, P. (1939). "Demand Under Conditions of Oligopoly." *Journal of Political Economy* 47(4): 568–73.

Taylor, J. (2007). "Housing and Monetary Policy." *Housing, Housing Finance and Monetary Policy* Symposium, sponsored by the Federal Reserve Bank of Kansas City, Jackson Hole, Wyoming, August 30 and September 1.

Taylor, L. (2004). *Reconstructing Macroeconomics: Structuralist Proposals and Critiques of the Mainstream.* Cambridge, MA: Harvard University Press.

Tejani, S. and W. Milberg. (2010). "Industrial Upgrading, Deindustrialization and the Defeminization of Manufacturing Employment." SCEPA Working Paper No. 2010–1, Schwartz Center for Economic Policy Analysis, New School for Social Research.

Temin, F. and P. Levy. (2007). "Inequality and Institutions in 20th Century America." MIT Department of Economics Working Paper No. 07–17, MIT Department of Economics.

Thirlwall, A. (1979). "The Balance of Payments Constraint as an Explanation of International Growth Rate Differences." *Banca Nazionale del Lavoro Quarterly Review* 32(128): 45–53.

Thurow, L. (2004). "Do Only Economic Illiterates Argue that Trade Can Destroy Jobs?" *Social Research* 71(2): 265–78.

Thweatt, W. (1976). "James Mill and the Early Development of Comparative Advantage." *History of Political Economy* 8(2): 207–34.

Tobin, J. (1969). "A General Equilibrium Approach to Monetary Theory." *Journal of Money, Credit, and Banking* 1(1):15–29.

Tybout, J. (2000). "Manufacturing Firms in Developing Countries: How Well Do They Do, and Why?" *Journal of Economic Literature* 38(1): 11–44.

UNCTAD. (2010). *World Investment Report*. Geneva: United Nations Conference on Trade and Development.

UNCTAD. (2011). *World Investment Report*. Geneva: United Nations Conference on Trade and Development.

UNIDO. (2002). *Industrial Development Report 2002/2003*. Vienna: United Nations Industrial Development Organization.

United Nations. (1999). *Employment and Displacement Effects of Globalization, The 1999 World Survey on the Role of Women in Development: Globalization, Gender and Work.* New York: United Nations.

Van Biesebrock, J. (2011). "Wages Equal Productivity. Fact or Fiction? Evidence from Sub-Saharan Africa." *World Development* 39(8): 1333–46.

Van Treek, T. (2008). "Reconsidering the Investment-Profit Nexus in Finance-Led Economies: An ARDL-Based Approach." *Metroeconomica* 59(3): 371–404.

Varian, H. (1992). *Microeconomic Analysis*. Third edition. New York: Viva Books.

Venables, A. (1999). "Fragmentation and Multinational Production." *European Economic Review* 43(4–6): 935–45.

Wade, R. (1991). *Governing the Market*. New York: Cambridge University Press.

Wagner, J. (2007). "Exports and Productivity: A Survey of the Evidence from Firm-Level Data." *World Economy* 30(1): 60–82.

Wallerstein, I. (2011[1974]). *The Modern World-System, I: Capitalist Agriculture and the Origins of the European World-Economy in the Sixteenth Century*. Revised with new prologue. San Francisco: University of California Press.

Warsh, D. (2006). *Knowledge and the Wealth of Nations: A Story of Economic Discovery*. New York: W.W. Norton.

Watson, M. (2007). "Whither Financialisation? The Contradictory Microfoundations of Finance-Led Growth Regimes." Presented at annual meeting of International Studies Association, Chicago, March.

Weisskopf, T. E. (1987). "The Effect of Unemployment on Labour Productivity: An International Comparative Analysis." *International Review of Applied Economics* 1(2): 127–51.

Wernerfelt, B. (1984). "A Resource-Based View of the Firm." *Strategic Management Journal* 5(2): 171–80.

Williams, R. (1991). "Competition, Discrimination, and Differential Wage Rates: On the Continued Relevance of Marxian Theory to the Analysis of Earnings and Employment Inequality." In *Economic and Social Analyses of Discrimination*, edited by R. R. Cornwall and P. V. Wunnava, 65–92. New York: Praeger Publishers.

Williamson, O. (1975). *Markets and Hierarchies: Analysis and Antitrust Implications: A Study in the Economics of Internal Organization*. New York: Free Press.

Williamson, O. (1985). *The Economic Institutions of Capitalism: Firms, Markets, Relational Contracting*. New York: The Free Press.

Williamson, O. (1996). "Transaktionskostenökonomik." In *Ökonomische Theorie der Institutionen*, Vol. 3, second edition, edited by H. Dietl, C. Erlei, M. Erlei, and M. Leschke. Hamburg: LIT Verlag.

Williamson, O. (2002). "The Theory of the Firm as Governance Structure: From Choice to Contract." *Journal of Economic Perspectives* 16(3): 171–95.

Willmore, L. (1995). "Export Processing Zones in the Dominican Republic: A Comment on Kaplinsky." *World Development* 23(3): 529–35.

Winkler, D. (2009). *Services Offshoring and its Impact on the Labor Market – Theoretical Insights, Empirical Evidence, and Economic Policy Recommendations for Germany*. Heidelberg: Physica-Verlag.

Winkler, D. (2010). "Services Offshoring and Its Impact on Productivity and Employment: Evidence from Germany, 1995–2006." *World Economy* 33(12): 1672–701.

Winkler, D. (2013). "Services Offshoring and the Relative Demand for White-Collar Workers in German Manufacturing." In *The Oxford Handbook of Offshoring and Global Employment*, edited by A. Bardhan, D. Jaffee, and C. Kroll, Chapter 4. New York: Oxford University Press.

Winkler, D. and W. Milberg. (2012a). "Bias in the 'Proportionality Assumption' Used in the Measurement of Offshoring." *World Economics* 13(4): 39–59.

Winkler, D. and W. Milberg. (2012b). "Classical and Neoclassical Theories of Offshore Outsourcing." In *Macroeconomics and the History of Economic Thought: Festschrift in Honour of Harald Hagemann*, edited by H. Krämer, H. Kurz, and H.-M. Trautwein, 400–414. Routledge: London.

Wolff, E. (2003). "What's Behind the Rise in Profitability in the US in the 1980s and 1990s in the US?" *Cambridge Journal of Economics* 27(4): 479–99.

Wood, A. (1975). *A Theory of Profits*. Cambridge: Cambridge University Press.

Wood, A. (2001). "Give Heckscher and Ohlin a Chance!" *Review of World Economics (Weltwirtschaftliches Archiv)* 130(1): 20–49.

Wood, A. (1994). *North-South Trade, Employment and Inequality: Changing Fortune in a Skill-Driven World*. Oxford: Clarendon Press.

Wood, A. (1995). "How Trade Hurt Unskilled Workers." *Journal of Economic Perspectives* 9(3): 57–80.

Wood, A. and J. Mayer. (2011). "Has China De-Industrialised Other Developing Countries?" *Review of World Economics (Weltwirtschaftliches Archiv)* 147(2): 325–50.

WTO and IDE-JETRO. (2011). *Trade Patterns and Global Value Chains in East Asia: From Trade in Goods to Trade in Tasks*. Jointly published by WTO and IDE-JETRO, Geneva: World Trade Organization.

Xing, Y. and N. Detert. (2010). "How iPhone Widens the US Trade Deficits with PRC." GRIPS Discussion Paper 10–21, National Graduate Institute for Policy Studies, Tokyo.

Yan, B. (2006). "Demand for Skills in Canada: The Role of Foreign Outsourcing." *Canadian Journal of Economics* 39(1): 53–67.

Yeats, A. J. (2001). "Just How Big Is Global Production Sharing?" In *Fragmentation: New Production Patterns in the World Economy*, edited by S. Arndt and H. Kierzkowski, 108–43. New York: Oxford University Press.

Yi, K. (2003). "Can Vertical Specialization Explain the Growth of World Trade?" *Journal of Political Economy* 111(1): 52–102.

Ziegler, C. (2007). *Favored Flowers: Culture and Economy in a Global System.* Duke University Press Books.

Zysman, J. (1983). *Governments, Markets and Growth: Finance and the Politics of Industrial Change.* Ithaca: Cornell University Press.

Index

Printed in the United States
By Bookmasters